Clausewitz and America

This book demonstrates how Carl von Clausewitz's thought influenced American strategic thinking between the Vietnam War and the current conflict in Iraq.

Clausewitz's thought played a part in the process of military reform and the transition in US policy that took place after the Vietnam War. By the time of the 1991 Gulf War, American policymakers demonstrated that they understood the Clausewitzian notion of utilising military force to fulfil a clear political objective. The US armed forces bridged the operational and strategic levels during that conflict in accordance with Clausewitz's conviction that war plans should be tailored to fulfil a political objective. With the end of the Cold War, and an increasing predilection for technological solutions, American policymakers and the military moved away from Clausewitz. It was only the events of 11 September 2001 that reminded Americans of his intrinsic value. However, while many aspects of the "War on Terror" and the conflict in Iraq can be accommodated within the Clausewitzian paradigm, the lack of a clear policy for countering insurgency in Iraq suggests that the US may have returned full circle to the flawed strategic approach evident in Vietnam.

The book will be of great interest to students of strategy, military history, international security and US politics.

Stuart Kinross holds a Ph.D. in International Relations from the University of Aberdeen.

Strategy and history
Series Editors: Colin Gray and Williamson Murray
ISSN: 1473-6403

This new series will focus on the theory and practice of strategy. Following Clausewitz, strategy has been understood to mean the use made of force, and the threat of the use of force, for the ends of policy. This series is as interested in ideas as in historical cases of grand strategy and military strategy in action. All historical periods, near and past, and even future, are of interest. In addition to original monographs, the series will from time to time publish edited reprints of neglected classics as well as collections of essays.

Clausewitz and America

Strategic thought and practice from
Vietnam to Iraq

Stuart Kinross

Routledge
Taylor & Francis Group

LONDON AND NEW YORK

First published 2008
by Routledge
2 Park Square, Milton Park, Abingdon, Oxon, OX14 4RN

Simultaneously published in the USA and Canada
by Routledge
270 Madison Ave, New York NY 10016

Routledge is an imprint of the Taylor & Francis Group, an informa business

Transferred to Digital Printing 2009

© 2008 Stuart Kinross

Typeset in Times by Wearset Ltd, Boldon, Tyne and Wear

British Library Cataloguing in Publication Data
A catalogue record for this book is available from the British Library

Library of Congress Cataloging in Publication Data
A catalog record for this book has been requested

ISBN10: 0-415-38023-5 (hbk)
ISBN10: 0-415-56963-X (pbk)
ISBN10: 0-203-08912-X (ebk)

ISBN13: 978-0-415-38023-2 (hbk)
ISBN13: 978-0-415-56963-7 (pbk)
ISBN13: 978-0-203-08912-5 (ebk)

Contents

Acknowledgements

This work began life in late 1996 as a Ph.D. thesis for the University of Aberdeen, which examined the influence of Clausewitz on American strategic thought from Vietnam to the Gulf War of 1990–91. Ten years later, it has been completed after an expansion of its remit to include the tumultuous events of the past few years.

The completion of this work would not have been possible without the help of a number of people. My researches were greatly aided by two visits I made to the United States in 1999 and 2000. On the first of those trips I visited the US Army Command and General Staff College at Fort Leavenworth, Kansas, and the US Army War College at Carlisle Barracks, Pennsylvania. On the second trip I returned to Carlisle.

Colonel James Holcomb, then of the Department of National Security Studies at the Army War College, arranged the Carlisle visits while that to Leavenworth was arranged by Professor Robert Berlin of the Command and General Staff College's faculty. Professors Roger Spiller and Robert Epstein of the Command and General Staff College kindly took the time to discuss issues related to this work with me. I also enjoyed stimulating discussions with Lieutenant-Colonel Antulio Echevarria and Drs Stephen Blank, Steven Metz and Earl Tilford of the Strategic Studies Institute, US Army War College. Colonel Echevarria was also kind enough to comment on a draft of my thesis, while I would also like to express my thanks to the anonymous reviewers who also read it.

I also had fruitful discussions with a number of military and academic delegates at several conferences, particularly the conference on "Clausewitz and the 21st Century" at the University of Oxford in March 2005. I am also grateful to Brigadier-General (retd.) Huba Wass de Czege, Professor Peter Paret, Colonel Paul Herbert and Dr Christopher Bassford for corresponding their thoughts with me by e-mail.

The excellent staff at a number of libraries deserve my gratitude. Those at the Combined Arms Library, Leavenworth, were very helpful in easing my way around their archives. The staff at the library of the US Army Military History Institute, Carlisle, particularly David Keough and Louise Arnold Friend, provided invaluable help in arranging for me to look at the Institute's archives. I am also grateful to the staff of the British Library, Kings College, and the Ministry of Defence Library, all in London, who were kind enough to provide assistance to me during the many hours I spent trawling their archives.

Finally, but by no means last, I wish to thank my supervisor at Aberdeen University, Jim Wyllie, for his advice and encouragement; my editor at Routledge, Andrew Humphrys, for his understanding and patience; and my family for their support during what has been a long haul.

Stuart Kinross
London

Introduction

This work is a study in strategic thought. Its objective is to demonstrate how the analyses and arguments of Carl von Clausewitz (1780–1831) have been adapted to the development of American strategic thinking since the Vietnam War. It examines the making of strategy and the conduct of operations during the period concerned, and sets this against the background of Clausewitz's theory of war and traditional US strategic thought. Though written almost a century ago, Clausewitz's impact on strategic thought was well summarised by General Jacob Meckel of the Imperial German Army: "Everyone who nowadays either makes or teaches war in a modern sense, bases himself upon Clausewitz, even if he is not conscious of it."[1]

Clausewitz's "influence"

One of the problems in examining the contemporary and historical influence of a writer who died in the early nineteenth century is the temptation to relate everything, past and present, to his way of thinking. For example, many historians have attempted to discuss the North's strategy in the American Civil War through a Clausewitzian prism. Jay Luvaas has highlighted the absurdity of such a course through parody. He invented a letter from Ulysses S. Grant that purported to show that the Union general's strategy had been strongly influenced by a staff officer of German origin who had quoted *On War* to Grant at great length. Luvaas argued that it is extremely difficult to discover the way in which intellectual concepts are transmitted, especially those that, like Clausewitz's, are basic common sense and are therefore open to constant recycling.[2]

In addressing the influence of Clausewitz, one needs to be very careful about exactly what one means by that word. Michael Howard, rightly regarded as one of the world's foremost military historians, wrote an essay introducing the version of *On War* that he published together with Peter Paret. The essay was entitled "The Influence of Clausewitz". However, Howard did not explain what he meant by influence. Christopher Bassford, who prefers to write of Clausewitz's "reception", has written: "*Influence* is rather hard to define. One can be influenced by a book without agreeing with it, without reading it, or without even being aware of its existence."[3]

In an essay written in 1959, Bernard Brodie argued that Clausewitz's contemporary and rival, Antoine-Henri Jomini, has exercised the greater influence of the two. Brodie did so on the basis that Jomini lived to witness the changes in warfare wrought by the Industrial Revolution, whereas Clausewitz did not, and that he wrote in French, a far more accessible language than Clausewitz's native German. Perhaps more pertinent, in the context of this work, is Daniel Moran's observation that Jomini's interpretation of Napoleon's achievements ignored their revolutionary roots and began a school of military theory that was politically and socially naive. It is a tradition that the American military has generally embraced: "Schooled to prefer formulaic answers, checklists, and school solutions, the American military is decidedly Jominian, not Clausewitzian."[4]

Clausewitz's ideas themselves owed much to the efforts of others, particularly his mentor, Gerhard von Scharnhorst. Paret has summed up the dilemma facing the writer who tries to trace a Clausewitzian influence in the thoughts and actions of later generations of soldiers and statesmen:

> The influence of a theorist whose intentions in his major work are not prescriptive is perhaps especially difficult to determine. It is not surprising that the search for Clausewitz's influence, which began in the second half of the 19th century, has been confused and inconclusive. That one or two sentences from *On War* have entered common usage, or that some of its arguments have been misinterpreted to support the military fashions of the day, scarcely proves that the ideas have had a genuine impact. On the contrary, if we examine the conduct of war since Clausewitz wrote, [it has] repeatedly demonstrated the relevance of Clausewitz's theories, but nothing has proved more elusive to discover than an application of "lessons" learned from *On War*.[5]

Problems of interpretation

Another difficulty in interpreting the thoughts and actions of contemporaries in a Clausewitzian light is that Clausewitz, for all his wonderful use of language, is very difficult to read, especially if one does not take the time to reflect on what it is he is trying to say. Brigadier-General (retd.) Huba Wass de Czege has explained the need for such careful reflection when studying Clausewitz:

> There is no doubt that Clausewitz stands head and shoulders above all others, ancient or modern ... But you have to be very careful here because many people who are not soldiers who read him do not understand what he is saying. They take things literally, or read from the less developed chapters and so on. I have to say that I didn't really understand Clausewitz much until I had taught him to bright, inquisitive and skeptical majors at least twice.[6]

One other point that must be borne in mind in any study of Clausewitz is that not only was *On War* unfinished but there are also problems in translating the work, many of which have led to serious misinterpretations. The Howard and Paret translation did not necessarily always translate the same term in a similar way if they felt the context did not warrant it. The late Brigadier Richard Simpkin, British Army, himself a professional translator, has written:

> To anybody who writes, the original [*On War*] bears all the marks of a draft. There are the blurrings and lapses of syntax, the *non sequiturs*, the occasional incorrect or inconsistent use of a word. What is more, there are all the signs of the emotional top-hamper one has to "write out" of one's head to clear the way for reason, and subsequently to discard or completely rewrite. Another familiar sign is the way the quality and clarity of his [Clausewitz's] language trails off as he tackles a different idea. Some passage where these factors compound each other could mean anything – or nothing; they can only be interpreted from their context.[7]

Of course, many writers have taken the view that Clausewitz could "mean anything". A recent article in *Parameters*, the journal of the US Army War College, is a case in point. It betrayed a complete misunderstanding of Clausewitz's method: "Some works are so broad in scope, so inclusive, even of contradictions internal to themselves, that they can be used to justify almost anything."[8]

Clausewitz's definitions of theory and doctrine are important pointers for this work. His conception of theory was rooted in historical experience. Theory is to be used as "a guide to anyone who wants to learn about war from books; it will light his way, ease his progress, train his judgment, and help him to avoid pitfalls ... [Theory] is meant to educate the mind of the future commander, or, more accurately, to guide him in his self-education, not to accompany him to the battlefield..."[9]

Thus theory is not dogma. As Clausewitz also wrote, theory "should be study, not doctrine". Doctrine derives from an understanding both of theory and of the lessons to be disseminated from actual experience. Clausewitz, who did not give an exact definition of doctrine, was careful not to suggest the existence of a rigid set of principles that would render war susceptible to scientific analysis in keeping with the thinking inspired by the Enlightenment. Such a course would contradict his belief in war's universal nature, its eternal spirit:

> If the theorist's studies automatically result in principles and rules, and if truth spontaneously crystallizes into these forms, theory will not resist this natural tendency of the mind...[10]

However, Clausewitz inserted an important caveat:

> Even these principles and rules are intended to provide a thinking man with a frame of reference for the movements he has been trained to carry out, rather than to serve as a guide which at the moment of action lays down precisely the path he must take.[11]

Strategic context

Although the second chapter of this work will discuss the relationship between American strategic thought and Clausewitz, it was the revolution in warfare that the invention of the atomic bomb wrought that greatly concentrated American minds on the work of the long-deceased Prussian. The community of civilian strategic thinkers that mushroomed during the 1950s and 1960s found Clausewitz's thinking to be of relevance to the new environment of Cold War international relations.[12] Such thinking was eventually to penetrate the armed forces themselves in the aftermath of the confidence-sapping events of the Vietnam War that had, to an extent, rendered much of the post-1945 making of American strategic thought irrelevant. There is no paradox in this statement. Just as Clausewitz said that all wars are unique, those of his disciples who attempted to apply his thinking to the zero-sum scenario of the Cold War were unable to adjust to the different environment of the Vietnam War. The military, too, had failed to change their mindset from one of superpower confrontation to fighting a conflict at a lower level of intensity. Remarkably, we are seeing history repeating itself today in Iraq.

The "back to basics" movement that emerged in the military after Vietnam was a timely antidote to the traditional anti-intellectualism of the American (and, if we are seeking Anglo-Saxon comparisons, the British) military. It is a tradition that has been pithily summed up by former chief of the Joint Chiefs of Staff, General David Jones, who said "we've never sired a Clausewitz. In our system Clausewitz would probably make full colonel, retire at 20 years, and go to work for a think tank".[13]

The post-Vietnam reformers recognised the need to learn the lessons of the previous decades, and *On War* was adopted as a source for the reformulation of American strategic and operational thinking. Its introduction as a major text for military teaching in each of the services' war colleges played a role in the revival in American military power that found its affirmation in the Gulf War. But, at the same time, one must question the extent to which Clausewitzian thought was an influence at the operational level in relation to the technological changes simultaneously taking place in the 1980s as the United States sought Cold War ascendancy.

The US Army defines operational art as the use of military forces to achieve strategic objectives through the planning and conduct of battles and campaigns.[14] In his analysis of the conceptual basis of AirLand Battle, Shimon Naveh has argued that operational art has developed during the twentieth century from an emphasis on what he describes as the Clausewitzian model of the "battle of annihilation" to a more advanced paradigm of operational manoeuvre. Naveh contends that during the Gulf War, the Iraqis were proponents of the former, while the Americans practised the latter:

> The recent Gulf Conflict witnessed a vigorous encounter between two military cultures: the first [American] based its professional ethos and strategic

credo on system logic, which exemplified the complexities of the post-modern reality; the second [Iraqi] derived its rationale from the dynamics of the industrial era. It was a confrontation between a military system which had undergone a conceptual transformation accomplished through the application of the innovative paradigm of operational manoeuvre, and a system locked in the archaic conventions of the 19th century Clausewitzian paradigm.[15]

Given that Clausewitz's mature thought did *not* exclusively advocate annihilation, Naveh's argument is fundamentally flawed. It is not the case that the move away from Active Defense to AirLand Battle, or from tactical destruction to operational manoeuvre, signalled a rejection of Clausewitzian thought. Moreover, there is no appreciation of the Clausewitzian impact upon American grand strategy, notably the Weinberger Doctrine of 1984. As S. J. Lepper has argued, "Clausewitz's theories on military strategy and war have become so ingrained in American military thought that almost every US engagement fought or planned today relies heavily on his concepts."[16]

It is a hazard of the theorist's business that his thinking is subject to the measure of relevance. Clausewitz's thought has been declared redundant by many commentators throughout the period since his death, and yet it has endured and continues to flourish long after many of his critics have been forgotten. If anything, the problem may be that he has been overemphasised and consequently misunderstood by his advocates. Bassford cites a valid criticism of the school of post-Vietnam American military thinkers that will be examined in this study. They are accused of the "prostitution of Clausewitz since 1981, particularly in FM 100–5 and its degenerate offspring".[17]

Clausewitz is over-emphasised at the expense of neglecting his own teaching, which recognised the eclectic nature of strategic thought. Recent events, including the terrorist attacks of 11 September 2001 and the conflict in Iraq, have only served to demonstrate this truth. Just prior to the American-led invasion of Iraq, Lani Kass, who teaches at the National War College, spoke in Clausewitzian terms of the enduring characteristics of war: its violence, its passion, and its enmity. These elements were present during combat operations and during the ensuing insurgency, as can be discerned from the following graphic description of the circumstances surrounding the battle for Fallujah in November 2004:

> In the torture houses the stink of death clung to the walls, and bodies lay rotting in curdled black blood, the heads of the mutilated victims thrown back in agony. You could imagine their last screams echoing out the windows as neighbors looked the other way. Fallujah looked like a tornado had roared down the streets with Force 10 winds occasionally stopping to hammer a building into a heap of bricks before battering the rest of the block. Perhaps 2,000 buildings were demolished and 10,000 others smashed up. The Marines swept through like a hurricane, never pausing to let the insurgents get their feet under them. It was the only way to root out the jihadists.[18]

Contrary to the doom-mongering of some military commentators that traditional strategic thinking is incompatible with the contemporary strategic environment, this study illustrates the former's continuing relevance. Theories such as Fourth Generation Warfare cannot claim precedence over traditional strategy, which can best be studied through the works of the great military theorists among whom Clausewitz is *primus inter pares*. Nevertheless, Hew Strachan is right to caution that strategy is today in danger of being a catch-all term: "The word 'strategy' has acquired a universality which has robbed it of meaning, and left it only with banalities."[19]

The core considerations underpinning this analysis will be those concerned with strategy (as traditionally understood) and operations. The latter has been especially emphasised in recent years, and is more than just a bridge between strategy and tactics. It is a notion that has altered the appreciation of such concepts as mobility, firepower, command, intelligence and logistics. The need to understand the operational level of war during the 1980s led to a revival of interest among the American military in military history and, by extension, in Clausewitz. By separating the "historical" Clausewitz from the strategically significant Clausewitz of today, the major similarity between Clausewitz's philosophy as he developed it and that of his modern-day acolytes rests on the basic assumption that war is an instrument of politics serving the state's interest.[20]

1 Clausewitz's theory of war

The development of Clausewitz's thought

Clausewitz's world-view was shaped, first, by the upheaval of the French Revolutionary and Napoleonic Wars; and, second, by the intellectual climate of his times during which the Enlightenment was giving way to the age of Romanticism. The wars with the French taught Clausewitz that the military institution of a state, and the manner in which it is deployed, is a reflection of that state's political, economic, and social conditions; the thinking of the German Counter-Enlightenment persuaded him that no single set of rules existed that could systematically master the art of war. Clausewitz's practical experiences and his learning coalesced in his historicist outlook, which was embodied in his rejection of absolute standards, in his emphasis on the relevance of the "spirit of the age" to all historical epochs, and, in his desire to properly encapsulate the nature of war in his work.[1]

The complex and seemingly contradictory nature of Clausewitz's thought, which was influenced by many of the elements of the Enlightenment and of the Romantic Movement, can best be understood if one acknowledges the milieu within which he lived.[2] In this respect, Clausewitz's intellectual debt to Gerhard von Scharnhorst (1755–1813) cannot be overestimated. Between 1801 and 1804, Clausewitz attended the Institute for Young Officers in Berlin where he heard Scharnhorst's lectures, which were intended to address "war as it actually is" in contradistinction to the attempts by Enlightenment thinkers to describe "war as it should be".[3]

As one of the major military *Aufklärers*,[4] not only did Scharnhorst support the theoretical underpinnings of the Enlightenment but he simultaneously opposed some of its most radical interpretations. Scharnhorst perceived theory to be intimately linked with reality. In this respect he was influenced by Montesquieu's enquiry into the conception of laws. Montesquieu epitomised a distinctive break with the central thought processes of the Enlightenment in that he did not "believe that ideal solutions could ever be realised" in response to moral and metaphysical problems, "only approximations to them".[5]

Scharnhorst, therefore, criticised the systems and principles propounded by such military thinkers as Heinrich von Bülow (1757–1807) and Antoine-Henri

Jomini (1779–1869). The notion of an erroneous conflict between theory and reality was one that Clausewitz took from Scharnhorst. In the former's own words: "[Scharnhorst's] influence will continue to oppose artificial and learned theorizing by encouraging a certain naturalness of thought, which defeats empty phraseology and brings the false conflict between theory and practice to an end."[6]

As Peter Paret notes, previous thinkers had wished to constrain the element of chance in war whereas Scharnhorst saw it as something to be accepted and bequeathed this lesson to Clausewitz:

> Rather than emphasise that sound theory could eliminate accident, which obviously was sometimes the case, it might be pedagogically more productive, he [Scharnhorst] thought, and far more realistic, to stress the ability of theory to help men deal with surprise, to help them exploit the unforeseen. From there it was only a short step, which Clausewitz was soon to take, to recognise the fortuitous not as a negative but as a positive force, an indispensable part of reality.[7]

Clausewitz would develop this approach further. In his view, the phenomenon of war was not susceptible to prescriptive theorising. Rather, theory should be based on a combination of experience and an understanding of reality, particularly natural constraints. He would confront these constraints in war by developing the concept of friction – encompassing the imponderables of war, for example uncertainty, accidents, weather, and technical difficulties, which can accumulate to potentially overwhelm the commander – and that of genius, which accommodates friction through the use of intellectual and emotional energy. Friction "is the only concept that more or less corresponds to the factors that distinguish real war from war on paper".[8]

Friction also ensures that war is not susceptible to pure scientific analysis, something that was lost on Clausewitz's Enlightenment predecessors:

> Clausewitz's concept of friction is important because it marks a turning point in professional military thinking. By attempting to define what was up until that point an undefined abstraction, he was the first to deal head on with the uncertainties of war and the first to try to understand and gain some control over them.[9]

Clausewitz derived the concept of friction from physics. He adapted the centre of gravity from the same discipline. In physics, the centre of gravity is where the mass is most heavily concentrated. In war, however, there can be more than one centre of gravity. Although he identified several centres of gravity, both moral and physical, Clausewitz almost always came back to what he considered to be the most important of these, the enemy's army, the eradication of which was the key to victory:

> [O]ne must keep the dominant characteristics of both belligerents in mind.

Out of these characteristics a certain center of gravity develops, the hub of all power and movement, on which everything depends. That is the point against which all our energies should be directed.[10]

Joseph Strange and Richard Iron have taken issue with the translation of this passage in the Howard and Paret version of *On War*. They argue that it overlooks the *adversarial* nature of centres of gravity. The term "dominant characteristics", in their view, gives the impression that centres of gravity exist in their own right whereas they must be taken in the context of the balance between the contestants.[11] Antulio Echevarria has written that Clausewitz thought the centre of gravity should only be sought in wars where the intention is to overthrow the enemy completely. In more limited conflicts, centres of gravity must compete with more restricted political objectives. Certainly, Clausewitz discussed the centre of gravity in the context of a chapter devoted to a war that was aimed at achieving the enemy's total defeat. Moreover, the centre of gravity is not applicable to any particular level of war, though its nullification would have a strategic effect. As Echevarria says, the centre of gravity "is defined by the entire system (or structure) of the enemy, not by a level of war".[12]

It is little wonder that Colin Gray has argued that the centre of gravity is so susceptible to being misunderstood that the strategic planner could "be likened to a medieval alchemist seeking earnestly but hopelessly for the base material that can be transmuted into gold".[13]

Clausewitz lived during a period of remarkable transformation. In his youth, he served in an army that was wholly beholden to the personal whim of Prussia's autocratic ruler. He witnessed the crushing defeat of the Prussian Army by Napoleon in 1806, was briefly a prisoner-of-war in France, and contributed to the Prussian revival that culminated in the Wars of Liberation between 1813 and 1815, although for much of the latter period he served in the army of Tsarist Russia. After 1815, Clausewitz was forced to take a back seat as he sought to maintain his influence within a very reactionary polity in post-liberation Prussia. "He was born into one period, lived through another very different one, and died during a third which in some ways attempted to restore the spirit of the first but differed from it profoundly in others."[14]

Clausewitz's reflections on the experiences of these times allowed him to draw the lessons that were to inform his writing of *On War* from 1819. During the next eight years he completed the first six books, together with drafts of Books VII and VIII. After 1823, he also wrote a number of military history works on the campaigns of the Napoleonic Wars. Consequently, in 1827, Clausewitz decided to undertake a significant revision of *On War* because of his realisation, based on historical evidence, that no two wars are exactly the same, and his conviction that the phenomenon of war is political in nature. These two cornerstones of his thought are reflected in his note of 10 July 1827 in which he outlined his plans for completing *On War*, particularly the need to revise the first six books thoroughly. Clausewitz's world-view, particularly his historicist interpretation of history, provides the intellectual context for this thinking.[15]

If one does not appreciate this background, then there appears to be a significant dichotomy between the note of July 1827 and Chapter 1 of Book I of *On War*, which was written later and is generally taken to be the most complete part of the whole work. In it, Clausewitz describes war as "an act of force" to which there is no logical limit. As each side compels its opponent to follow suit, war can lead, "in theory, to extremes". War is, by its very nature, intense. However, as soon as one considers "real" war, as opposed to the abstract, "absolute" variant of war, "it becomes a matter of judgement what degree of effort should be made". In other words, just as the absolute definition of war would permit a rise to extremes because of "a clash of forces freely operating and obedient to no law but their own", so "real" war has the opposite impact as "[a]nything omitted out of weakness by one side becomes a real, *objective* reason for the other to reduce its efforts, and the tendency toward extremes is ... reduced".[16]

Because it would be impossible to practice "war in the abstract" – absolute war – Clausewitz concentrated on examining "real" war. This was because "were it a complete, untrammeled, absolute manifestation of violence (as the pure concept would require), war would of its own independent will usurp the place of policy the moment policy had brought it into being".[17]

Clausewitz goes on to emphasise the degree to which real wars range in intensity from those of extermination to simple armed observation rather than distinguishing between two particular "kinds" of war. He describes war as being "more than a true chameleon" – a brilliant metaphorical peg on which to hang his belief that war can assume a multitude of forms.[18] The aforementioned dichotomy can be thus be reconciled in that Clausewitz perceived all conflicts to reflect the spirit of their particular age because, as history illustrates, the intensity of warfare at any given time is a manifestation of the political environment during the period in question.[19]

While Clausewitz now gave an equal status to a variety of war aims and operational objectives, he still regarded the *clash of forces* as the dominant means for attaining the war's purpose. However, in contrast to the generally held perception that Clausewitz saw the physical destruction of the enemy's army as the key to victory, moral factors were of more significance to him: "The decision rests chiefly on the state of morale ... This becomes the means of achieving the margin of profit in the destruction of the enemy's physical forces which is the real purpose of the engagement."[20]

Clausewitz alludes not only to the morale of the enemy's army. In recognition of the wider strategic situation, he pays equal attention to the need to break the will of the enemy people:

> The effect of all this [i.e., defeat in battle] outside the army – on the people and on the government – is a sudden collapse of the most anxious expectations, and a complete crushing of self-confidence. This leaves a vacuum that is filled by a corrosively expanding fear which completes the paralysis. It is as if the electric charge of the main battle had sparked a shock to the whole nervous system of one of the contestants.[21]

It is in this context that one should be aware of Clausewitz's conception of a "paradoxical [*wünderlichte*] trinity", which is always at work in real war. Its three components are "primordial violence, hatred, and enmity", "the play of chance and probability", and war's subordination as an instrument of policy. The first element involves the people, the second the commander and his forces, and the third "is the business of government alone". These factors encompass the whole gamut of conflict from its preparation to the peace that arises afterwards. They also illustrate that, although the battle may still be the centrepiece of his thinking, Clausewitz examines war in its wider social, political and economic context.[22]

In Book VIII of *On War*, "War Plans", Clausewitz asserts that the character and objectives of military operations reflect the scale and nature of the political aims for which the war is being fought. "War cannot be divorced from political life [otherwise] we are left with something pointless and devoid of sense."[23]

However, Clausewitz ends the book by discussing a plan of war designed to lead to the destruction of the enemy's armed forces and not one designed to achieve less ambitious objectives. Even at this late stage in his thinking he may have felt that the sheer variety of possibilities in conflicts of a lower intensity were too complex to articulate on paper. While the commander could rely on certain principles with which to conduct a major campaign, prudence and common sense were more applicable to conducting a campaign of lesser intensity.[24]

Unfortunately, of course, Clausewitz died before he could complete *On War*, which has ensured that the nature of the fundamental reappraisal of his work has been overlooked by many of his later readers, leading to what Azar Gat has called an "endemic misinterpretation" of Clausewitz's ideas.[25] These commentators have failed to appreciate the extent to which Clausewitz's work incorporated dialectical thinking through the use of theses and antitheses, notably that of absolute war and real war, which has been distorted somewhat by later theories of total war and limited war.[26]

Recent studies by Gat and Echevarria suggest that Clausewitz's undated note or *Nachricht*, which accompanies the note of July 1827 in the introduction to *On War*, and which it has been assumed was written in 1830, provides vital evidence when trying to establish the parameters of his thought. Gat has convincingly argued that the undated note was in fact written prior to the note of 1827 and that consequently Clausewitz felt *On War* to be more complete than is normally assumed. Indeed, Books VI–VIII, which represent the most mature parts of the work together with the first chapter of Book I, deal almost exclusively with the conduct of operations. It was this aspect of warfare that Clausewitz believed represented "the true subject of theory, not yet discovered by the early military thinkers of the Enlightenment".[27]

Echevarria has examined the last paragraph of the undated note in which Clausewitz identifies a number of self-evident "propositions" that he believed could be used as a basis for constructing a scientific theory of war or, as Echevarria suggests, an operational level theory for the conduct of war:

[A] whole range of propositions can be demonstrated without difficulty: that defense is the stronger form of fighting with the negative purpose, attack the weaker form with the positive purpose; that major successes help bring about minor ones, so that strategic results can be traced back to certain turning-points; that a demonstration is a weaker use of force than a real attack, and that it must therefore be clearly justified; that victory consists not only in the occupation of the battlefield, but in the destruction of the enemy's physical and psychic forces, which is usually not attained until the enemy is pursued after a victorious battle; that success is always greatest at the point where the victory was gained, and that consequently changing from one line of operations, one direction, to another can at best be regarded as a necessary evil; that a turning movement can only be justified by general superiority or by having better lines of communication or retreat than the enemy's; that flank-positions are governed by the same consideration; that every attack loses impetus as it progresses.[28]

That Clausewitz, who poured scorn on attempts to develop a set of rigid principles for strategy makers, should develop such a list does not necessarily suggest any inherent contradiction in his thought. On the contrary, he realised that the strategic level of war, where the fate of nations is decided, is not readily amenable to definitive theorising. However, if one goes down to the campaign level, which Clausewitz recognised in his statement "that major successes help bring about minor ones", the more there is that is susceptible to such analysis:

[F]or Clausewitz, the dialectical logic of action and reaction, which no ideological preconception prevented him from following to its necessary conclusion, provided the assurance that his pronounced pragmatic outlook craved: violence on the tactical and operational level, and therefore violence on all levels could be analyzed and mastered intellectually.[29]

That Clausewitz already had an inkling that another level of war was coming into existence can be seen in his later writings, which reflect the fact that the Napoleonic Wars had ushered in the concept then known as "grand tactics" because of the numbers and distances involved. Richard Swain has written that *On War* shows an understanding of the operational level of war in its commentary on the defence:

Chapter 8 [of Book VI] addresses the defense of a theater of war which, in contrast to the defense of a position (a tactical matter) or the defense of a country (influenced by political circumstances), is more clearly illustrative of the phenomenon of the defense itself.[30]

In fact, one can go beyond the sentiments expressed in this quote and, indeed, beyond a speculative analysis of how Clausewitz would have revised *On War*, to show that he most certainly understood the operational level of war as we understand it today. Some contemporary commentators tend automatically to assume that Clausewitz did not discuss the operational level of war because he refers only to strategy and tactics in *On War*.[31] That this assumption is incorrect can be seen by examining the detail of his writings. Clausewitz's notion of strategy – "the use of engagements for the object of the war" – equates to our understanding of the operational level. It makes sense to treat Clausewitz's level of strategy, where he writes of the campaign, as being the same as the operational level. However, he also writes of the influence of heads of state, cabinets, and policy. These matters belong firmly within the purview of strategy. The following quote from *On War*, which incidentally comes from an unrevised part of the work, brilliantly explains the operational level:

> If we do not learn to regard a war, and the separate campaigns of which it is composed, as a chain of linked engagements each leading to the next, but instead succumb to the idea that the capture of certain geographical points or the seizure of undefended provinces are *of value in themselves*, we are liable to regard them as windfall profits. In so doing, and in ignoring the fact that they are links in a continuous chain of events, we also ignore the possibility that their possession may later lead to definite disadvantages.[32]

Herbert Rosinski favourably contrasted the sophistication of Clausewitz's writings with those of later German theorists. He argued that Clausewitz had taken the concepts of the classical German military school, founded by Scharnhorst, to their ultimate expression:

> Philosophy ... gave him [Clausewitz] a unique insight into "War as a Whole", the fact that over and above all individual aspects and elements of its conduct, war constituted a process with its own peculiar issues and problems ... It is the core of his achievement, the most characteristic, as well as the most original part of his great treatise, the one in which he has most to give us today, partly because these issues have never been discussed with anything like the same comprehensiveness and appreciation, even after he had opened the way to them, partly because of their predominant importance.[33]

Clausewitz therefore redefined theory in the context of a new intellectual paradigm, removing it from its formulaic connotations as seen by most Enlightenment thinkers, and instead giving it a broader meaning of a "framework for study" that was in line with a more Romantic outlook. For Clausewitz, theory was required as a tool for explanation and not prediction. "[H]e did not merely search for universal principles, but sought to strike a tri-namic balance between them, historical change, and the force of circumstances."[34]

Clausewitz's influence on American strategic thought, which is the subject of this work, will be examined in due course but, first, it is important to examine the effect his thinking had on approaches to warfare in Imperial Germany and the Soviet Union. Although each was distinct, both benefited from drawing on the legacy left by Clausewitz and both would provide some inspiration for thinkers in the United States.

Clausewitz's influence in Imperial Germany

The embryonic Industrial Revolution had some impact during the Napoleonic Wars, given Great Britain's role in the effort to defeat the French. However, Clausewitz was able to overlook this fact without compromising the value of his work. When he did allude to technology in *On War*, he did so to illustrate the fact that, at that time, there was little difference in weapons, training, and equipment between the "best and the worst" of armies. However, the beginnings of the Industrial Revolution on the European continent after Clausewitz's premature death from cholera almost coincided with the posthumous publication of *On War* (1832). As the military historian, Hans Delbrück, remarked:

> With the appearance of Clausewitz's works after his death in 1831, the Napoleonic period of the history of the art of war comes to a close … It leads into the new period [which] is defined in its content by the new technology, not only of weapons but also of transportation and all the resources of life, from the railroads and telegraph to the foodstuffs which increased in such unlimited proportions in the course of the 19th century.[35]

Napoleon had fought in a way that the inter-war Soviet theorist, Georgiy Isserson, interpreted as the "strategy of a single point" whereby an enemy could be compelled to give battle, the loss of which could lead to his political collapse. While Clausewitz himself wrote that in battle "all action is compressed into *a single point* in space and time", the advances made possible by the Industrial Revolution allowed for the dispersion of forces across the battlespace thanks to technological advances such as the steam engine, the railroad, and the telegraph. The constraints of geography, time, and space were being modified by technological innovation. Moreover, armies became "algorithmically complex" – the number of stages required to fulfil the objective of defeating the enemy had increased considerably. Wars no longer consisted of a few battles. The campaigns of the American Civil and Franco-Prussian wars would demonstrate the manner in which the conduct of warfare had changed since the Napoleonic Wars.[36]

James Schneider has argued that Clausewitz was eclipsed by the emergence of a more extensive battlefield. Writing prior to the Industrial Revolution, Clausewitz perceived a clear distinction between armies and territory, with the former being an objective in any strategy to end a war. This emphasis changed from the mid-nineteenth century when it increasingly came to be recognised that the occupation of the enemy's territory was as significant as the Clausewitzian notion of destroying his armies. Industrialised, protracted war required armies to ensure that the territory on which their factors of production existed was held.

Clausewitz, according to this interpretation, could write about defeating the enemy army *or* occupying his territory, but not necessarily both. "If the treatise of Clausewitz is to shed light upon the near shore of operational art [as opposed to the far shore of the Industrial Revolution], greater care must be exercised in its use."[37]

It is a pertinent question as to whether Clausewitz would have revised his work in the light of these advances had he lived longer. When one considers the evidence from the *Nachricht* and its description of the foundations of a theory of war, and the fact that the railroad, for example, was introduced to Germany in the 1830s – by the end of which decade, Clausewitz would have been only 59 – the answer to this question is almost certainly yes.

The mid-nineteenth-century Prussian Army was at the forefront of efforts to exploit the potential of the Industrial Revolution to transform the conduct of war. The telegraph and the railroad were the precursors of modern integrative technology.[38] The railroad, in particular, offered great military opportunities with its ability to compress the constraints of time and space. An army could be moved six times faster than was the case during the Napoleonic Wars. A nation that developed a good rail network would therefore gain a tremendous advantage in times of war. In exploiting the greatly increased speed of mobilisation, the art of war would leave the Napoleonic strategy of the single point behind in favour of accommodating extended lines of deployment. In the aftermath of the Franco-Prussian War of 1870–71, an anonymous article in the Prussian military periodical, *Militär Wochenblatt* (*Military Weekly*) emphasised the continuing relevance of Clausewitz's work:

> Clausewitz is rightly regarded in the German Army as the principal military-scientific authority, since he rejected all theories which had tried to ... prescribe [war] and its nature in a scientific way ... The tremendous successes of the wars of 1866 and 1870–71 support this way of viewing things, according to which strict discipline, good weapons, expedient elementary-tactics, good marching orders, railways, practical supply measures and the telegraph decide everything in war.[39]

The individual most responsible for reconciling reality, as represented by the technological and doctrinal advances wrought by the Industrial Revolution, with theory, as advocated by Clausewitz, was Helmuth von Moltke (1800–91), chief of the Prussian, and later German, Great General Staff from 1857. Intellectually, Moltke was a product of the German Movement though, given the passage of time since it was at its peak, he inevitably had "an appreciative enjoyment of its fruits [rather] than ... active participation in it".[40]

One of Moltke's subordinates, Colonel Sigismund von Schlichting, drew on Clausewitz's work to inform his understanding of the quantitative and qualitative changes in warfare that had occurred as a result of the Industrial Revolution. Daniel Hughes has described Schlichting's concepts, based on those of Clausewitz and Moltke, as being a key component of modern thinking about the operational level of war. However, he does recognise that, for Schlichting, "operational" was a kind of activity, in the sense of movement, that was a part of both strategy and tactics rather than existing on a separate level. Schlichting's main concern was with the way in which industrialised warfare had outpaced developments in tactics, a consequence of which was seen during the Franco-Prussian War when high casualty rates were the norm.[41]

In his *Tactical and Strategic Principles of the Present Day* (1897), Schlichting argued that the description of the battle portrayed by Clausewitz in *On War* could no longer hold. In particular, the way in which a battle began had changed because of the numbers of men and the types of weapons involved. It was no longer a case of organising, in Clausewitz's words, "the army in huge masses next to and behind each other" but rather the battle developing directly from the process of movement rather than concentration. Modern firepower meant that "the whole antiquated Clausewitzian picture of battle [could] be thrown overboard".[42]

Schlichting did, however, acknowledge that Clausewitz's interpretation of war as being a contest between two separate wills remained valid. He described Clausewitz as a "teacher and trailblazer" and believed *On War* to be a "military bible". However, Schlichting was conscious of the need to reconcile the advances in technology with tactics: "Where Clausewitz had defined strategy as the art of battles for the purpose of the war, Schlichting emphasised the importance of using operational (*operativ*) maneuver to achieve the purposes of war."[43]

In such circumstances, it was vital that the commander's intent should be clearly understood by subordinates who would have to maintain a clear understanding of this despite a chaotic situation on the battlefield. Schlichting, like Moltke, therefore favoured a decentralised approach to command and control known as *Auftragstaktik* or task-oriented orders. The origins of *Auftragstaktik* have been traced back to the American Revolutionary War, from where Hessian soldiers took the concept home to Germany. It subsequently found its way into Prussian doctrine via Scharnhorst after 1806, and Paret hints at Clausewitz's awareness of the concept in 1813:

> A plan for guerrilla operations in Silesia he [Clausewitz] drafted during this period provides a good example of the operational concepts of the reformed [Prussian] general staff in its combination of setting specific objectives and allowing the commander considerable latitude in his manner of achieving them.[44]

Schlichting ensured that *Auftragstaktik* was codified in the German Army's Infantry Regulations of 1888. These regulations acknowledged the growing effects of firepower on communications and movement by specifying "the narrow line that both superiors and subordinates must walk if initiative from below was not to lead to chaos, or supervision from above to paralysis".[45]

Clausewitz's distinction between absolute war and real war was distorted by Delbrück in his *History of the Art of War*, published between 1900 and 1920,[46] into a twin approach to strategy revolving around annihilation (*Niederwer-fungsstrategie*) and exhaustion (*Ermattungsstrategie*). Exhaustion, which Del-brück viewed as a bipolar concept consisting of battle and manoeuvre, was contrasted with annihilation, which focused solely on the battle. However, the term "exhaustion" is interchangeable with "attrition", which can be intepreted as being concerned with destroying the enemy's mass through a battle of destruction therefore giving it Delbrück's definition of annihilation.[47]

Delbrück's misunderstanding of Clausewitz arises from his misreading of the Note of July 1827, which he erroneously interpreted as Clausewitz's articulation of the strategic "truth" that there are "two different basic forms of strategy". Delbrück himself wrote that his use of the term *Ermattungsstrategie* in juxtaposition to Clausewitz's expression, *Niederwerfungsstrategie*, "has the weakness of coming close to the misconception of a pure maneuver strategy".[48]

Clausewitz, as we have seen, described the way in which real war is a manifestation of the political conditions prevailing at the time. Therefore, in this respect, Delbrück held the upper hand over his critics in that he considered limited wars to be as valid as those of an "unlimited" nature. However, the German military of the time were right to criticise Delbrück for arguing that Clausewitz had articulated different types of strategy as well as different types of war. In their view, regardless of the type of war being waged, the strategy remained the same: to destroy the ability of the enemy to resist, usually through the overwhelming defeat of his armed forces. Moreover, Delbrück's dual-poled concept of strategy drew a false distinction between battle and manoeuvre, which are in fact complementary and not contradictory methods of waging war.

The supposed fixation of the Kaiser's Army with the ideal of annihilation was epitomised by Alfred von Schlieffen, the chief of the Great General Staff from 1891 to 1905. Schlieffen used Clausewitz as an authority to propound such thinking, and wrote in the introduction to the fifth edition of *On War* (1905): "[T]he permanent merit of the work *On War* lies, in addition to its high ethical and psychological value, in its emphatic accentuation of the annihilation idea."[49]

Despite his common association with the annihilation ideal, Schlieffen's main concern arose from the need to avoid a protracted war through an approach that could yield decisive strategic results. In contrast to both Moltke and Clausewitz, Schlieffen viewed friction as something that might be overcome by using a method of command that would drive the tempo of operations rather than placing an overreliance on subordinates to fulfil the overall plan as they saw fit.[50] This represented a change in Schlieffen's thinking as he had supported the Infantry Regulations of 1888, which had formally recognised *Auftragstaktik*. One must understand the context in which Schlieffen came to a change of heart. Since 1871, war had become even more difficult to wage as the discrepancy between firepower and mobility widened, and a prolonged conflict might impose unacceptable social and economic burdens upon the state. It was, therefore, imperative that a decisive result should be achieved as quickly as possible. Furthermore, the militaries of Europe had become increasingly homogenised as the discrepancies between command systems, organisations, and even numerical strengths that had favoured Prussia-Germany in 1866 and 1870–71 had largely been eroded.

Where Clausewitz was a philosopher, Schlieffen was a "field manual"-type thinker. Clausewitz viewed war as a phenomenon that was subject to limited human control. Schlieffen sought to "do" rather than speculate – and this was perhaps understandable given the circumstances of his times. Nevertheless, Schlieffen and his disciples followed the rest of the so-called "Epigoni" in citing Clausewitz as an influence, albeit through adapting his thought to fit contemporary circumstances. The most damning indictment of Schlieffen is that he ignored Clausewitz's axiom regarding the primacy of policy with the result that he formulated his plans for war in isolation from political authority. For Schlieffen, the essence of strategy was the "Cannae principle", or the envelopment of the enemy's flanks. In fact, if he had studied that ancient battle more carefully, he would have recognised that a stunning tactical victory did not yield a decisive strategic result for the Carthaginians. It is, therefore, difficult to disagree with Holger Herwig's opinion that Schlieffen "jettisoned intellectual honesty to prove his theory".[51]

The Soviet influence

Clausewitz has always exerted some influence on the Russian military, both Tsarist and Soviet. He served with the Russian Army as a colonel between 1812 and 1813, and his work influenced the Imperial Russian Army officer, Nikolai Mikhnevich, chief of the general staff during the First World War. It also contributed to the thinking of Alexander Svechin (1878–1938), a pre-war Tsarist officer, who wrote a treatise on Clausewitz and later served as a professor in the Soviet General Staff Academy. As late as 1991, the Soviet officer I. V. Tsybulskiy wrote that "the ideas of Clausewitz largely have not lost their importance even today, and so in our view they demand careful study".[52]

In 1927, Svechin described Clausewitz's contribution to military thought as being tantamount to the "Copernican revolution" in science when compared to the impact of eighteenth-century thinkers such as Bülow. Svechin was a Clausewitzian in the sense that he viewed war as a social phenomenon and consequently distrusted those who took a more technocratic approach to the subject. Despite this, Svechin had recognised the impact of industrialisation on the conduct of warfare as a result of his analysis of the Russo-Japanese War of 1904–05 and, together with other Russian officers of the time, perceived the emergence of another level between strategy and tactics, war and battle. Svechin acknowledged a debt to Schlichting in formulating his strategic appraisals, and the German's influence is also evident in the writings of Mikhnevich.[53]

During the First World War, the linear form of operation was the preferred approach to warfare, particularly on the Western Front where mass firepower convinced soldiers of the need to concentrate on attrition.[54] By contrast, Red commanders in the Russian Civil War recognised the potential for manoeuvre that their large numbers of cavalry and the size of the theatre presented. The low ratio between force and space that dictated strategy during the Russian Civil War rendered the linear form of operation superfluous. By forming corps and armies of cavalry, and by thinking of the battlefield in terms of having a rear as well as a front, deep penetrations could be made to achieve strategic gains.

Major David Mock has shown that Clausewitz had at least a rudimentary understanding of the notion of deep operations. Where Clausewitz writes of the effect of a force applied against the enemy's rear or flanks, he appreciates that the threat is greater than that if the force is applied against the enemy's front in the manner of a linear battle. However, Clausewitz also realises that the risk involved is equally as great:

> Clausewitz perceived the purpose and objectives of deep operations. He knew the potential benefits of a deep operation versus a frontal operation and he appreciated the risks associated with sending a force into the enemy rear. Recognising which objectives are worth the risks and when to take those risks is a difficult condition to establish.[55]

After the Civil War had ended, Soviet officers studied the works of Clausewitz, Moltke, and Schlichting, among others, at the General Staff Academy. Drawing on Delbrück's work, Svechin identified two possible strategic postures – annihilation (*sokrushenie*) and attrition (*izmor*) – that would serve the state in any future war. Svechin thought that the First World War had confirmed Clausewitz's belief that the defence is the stronger form of war. He was puzzled that soldiers on both sides who had a knowledge of Clausewitz had failed to recognise this principle when conducting operations. Svechin was convinced that utilising the defensive would allow the defender to reap "where it sows ... since an offensive is often stopped by false reconnaissance data, false fears, and inertness".[56]

Moreover, Svechin placed political and economic objectives ahead of the enemy's armed forces in terms of importance and, in 1923–24, he coined the term "operational art" to illustrate its place in a new, threefold definition of war. Svechin defined operational art as the "totality of maneuvers and battles in a given sector of the theater of military activities, directed at achieving the overall, final goal in a given period of a campaign".[57]

Svechin's analysis of the defensive was rare among the Soviet officer corps. Mikhail Tukhachevskii (1894–1937) epitomised the opposite view. He believed that the primary purpose of military theory was not to rationalise the past – although he did study warfare as it had evolved since Napoleonic times – but rather to look boldly into the future and to revise conceptual thinking to accommodate the way in which warfare had changed. As early as 1926, he foresaw the potential of the operational level to meet the challenges posed by modern warfare:

> Modern operations involve the concentration of forces necessary to deliver a strike, and the infliction of continued and uninterrupted blows of these

forces against the enemy throughout an extremely deep area. The nature of
modern weapons and modern battle is such that it is impossible to destroy
the enemy's manpower by one blow in a one-day battle. Battle in modern
operations stretches out into a series of battles not only along the front but
also in depth ... In that regard, modern tactics of a theatre of military operations are tremendously more complex than those of Napoleon.[58]

Basically, the extended frontages involved in modern war made it impossible to
destroy the enemy army in a single blow. Rather, an iterative process of conducting successive blows in the depth of the enemy's position through operational shock was required to neutralise him and achieve the strategic aim. This
aim was defined by Tukhachevskii as being the outcome of Clausewitz's subordination of the military action to the political objective, an idea confirmed by
Lenin. Clausewitz himself used language that is strongly similar to that of
Tukhachevskii when he discussed the strategic context within which war is conducted:

[T]he main lines of every major strategic plan are *largely political in
nature*, and their political character increases the more the plan encompasses the entire war and the entire state. The plan for the war results
directly from the political conditions of the two belligerent states, as well as
from their relations to other powers ... the political element even extends to
the separate components of a campaign; rarely will it be without influence
on such major episodes of warfare as a battle, etc. According to this point of
view, there can be no question of a *purely military* evaluation of a great
strategic issue, nor of a purely military scheme to solve it.[59]

The Soviets were also aware that Clausewitz's notion of a fascinating trinity was
impacting upon the advent of the operational level, given that, as states increasingly relied on their people to make war, the connection between the front and
the rear became more apparent. The decision on the battlefield was shifting to
the rear as nations were forced to build up an industrial base relying on the input
of scientists, innovators, and workers as much as the armed forces themselves.
Tukhachevskii advocated a "complete militarization" of the Soviet economy so
as to prepare for the demands of mechanised warfare. He further advocated the
total destruction of the enemy through the deployment of a mass, mechanised
combined-arms force and, as such, diverged from Svechin who had identified
attrition as being as valid as annihilation. Indeed, Tukhachevskii used his foreword to the Russian translation of Delbrück's *History of the Art of War* to deni-
grate the belief that attrition could be a suitable strategy for the Soviet Union to
pursue. Tukhachevskii accused Svechin of renouncing the offensive and also of
a "willingness to accept capitalism's military superiority".[60]

The 1936 Field Service Regulations emphasised the linkage between the use
of tactics and the achievement of strategic objectives. In this sense the Soviets
relied on the explicit dissemination of their strategic conceptions, in contrast to

the Germans who placed more reliance on the implicit ability of their officer corps to execute operations. Although Tukhachevskii wrote much on the question of command and control, and demonstrated an understanding of the *Auftragstaktik* concept, he did not "suggest what should happen at the interface where the result of initiatives flowing upwards and orders flowing downwards meet".[61]

Consequently, the innate Russian respect for authority ensured that a top-down approach to command and control tended to be the norm in the Red Army. Nevertheless, as the Australian colonel J. D. Kelly points out, there is no disguising the common conceptual origins of the Soviet and German approaches to conducting warfare in the industrial age.[62] The raw Soviet commanders who began the Second World War gradually adapted to the demands of modern warfare. Backed by a society geared to produce the weapons required to conduct deep, mobile operations, in the later stages of the war the Soviets achieved the types of objectives foreseen by the inter-war theorists. Dr Stephen Blank is convinced that the inter-war Soviet military had the "most creative theorising in Europe bar none".[63]

After the Second World War, the Soviet Army was convinced that war, whether it was nuclear or not, would be dominated by manoeuvre. It developed a "land-air" battle concept that embraced the three-dimensional, deep structure of the modern battlefield. Manoeuvre at the tactical level would neutralise the enemy's forward defences while Operational Manoeuvre Groups fought the battle in depth. By the mid-1970s, the advances in conventional weapons to a level where their destructive power was almost equivalent to that of tactical nuclear weapons had made deep operations on the part of a single echelon of an all-arms force possible. As Soviet marshal Nikolai Ogarkov commented: "[The] modern combined-arms battle is fought throughout the whole depth of the enemy battle formation, both on the forward edge of contact and in the depth, on the ground and in the air."[64]

Conclusion

The context provided by the times in which Clausewitz lived has been lost on many of his readers, and they have tended to see in selective elements of his work the confirmation of their own prejudices and concerns. As Heuser comments, many of Clausewitz's readers have looked for a telling quote when in fact he "mainly supplies philosophical reflections on the nature of war that are difficult to translate into simple, memorable prescriptions for action".[65]

Clausewitz's most original contribution to strategic thought is his analysis of the nature of war through formulating the mutually exclusive concepts of absolute war and real war. The former has no bounds, while the latter is constrained by political circumstance. This constraint ensures that real wars vary by degree. Clausewitz was also the first thinker to begin to understand the existence of another level of war beside strategy and tactics. The closest Clausewitz came to today's threefold definition of strategy, operations and tactics was when he referred to the "concepts characteristic of time – war, campaign and battle" – as being "parallel to those of space – country, theater of operations and position".[66]

While Clausewitz recognised that technology acted as a stimulus to the development of warfare, he could not foresee the impact of the Industrial Revolution in war, a precursor to the technological changes that have continued to revolutionise the conduct of war ever since. Nevertheless, the development of strategic thought in Imperial Germany and the Soviet Union was built on his conceptual foundations – though there were adaptations and misinterpretations of his ideas – most notably Delbrück's bipolar notion of strategy. However, these experiences comply with Richard Simpkin's observation that strategic thought cuts across national and cultural boundaries, with the absorption of knowledge and experience from different nations.[67]

2 The development of American strategic thought and practice

An American way of war?

A body of literature has built up in the past few decades debating whether there is a distinct "American way of war" that explains the way in which Americans think about, and conduct, warfare. The starting point in the debate was the publication of Russell Weigley's *The American Way of War* in 1973. Weigley's thesis was that, from the American Civil War onwards, Americans conducted war in a way that sought to achieve their objectives through destroying the enemy's armed forces on the battlefield through the use of overwhelming force. It was an approach dominated by deeds, not words: "[T]he evolution of American strategy before the 1950s has to be traced less in writings about strategy than in the application of strategic thought in war. It has to be a history of ideas expressed in action."[1]

Weigley's work was severely undermined by his attempt to base it on what was a misreading of Clausewitz's note of July 1827. As with so many others before and since, Weigley misinterpreted Clausewitz's discussion of absolute war and assumed that he was referring to any war where the aim was to overthrow the enemy. Therefore, he interpreted conflicts such as the Indian Wars, the American Civil War, and the Second World War in this context. On the other hand, he viewed the Revolutionary War as being one that did not fit Clausewitz's theory when in fact it did, because Clausewitz was describing a phenomenon – war – that is conducted at various levels of intensity.[2]

Both Bruce Linn and Antulio Echevarria have pointed to Weigley's use of Hans Delbrück's dual concept of strategy as being culpable for the flaws in his work. Indeed, in responding to Linn's critique, Weigley admitted as much: "I have regretted characterizing the two main strategic categories in American (and other) military history as a strategy of annihilation and a strategy of attrition. It would have been better to designate the latter as a strategy of erosion."[3]

More recently, Echevarria and Max Boot have produced analyses on the American way of war. Echevarria's timely monograph, given the ongoing conflicts in Afghanistan and Iraq, described a concept that has not developed beyond being a "way of battle". To become something more concrete, Echevarria argued that military triumphs must be converted into strategic successes. He cited contemporary events as evidence that this has still not registered with the American military and policymakers, given the emphasis on destroying enemy forces ahead of securing the support of indigenous populations.[4]

Boot's *Savage Wars of Peace* was based on the thesis that there has, in fact, been an American way of "more than one war". The large number of "small wars" in which the United States has traditionally been involved has outweighed its contribution to more intense conflicts. Writing prior to the ongoing insurgency in Iraq, Boot also described a *new* American Way of War arising out of the conflict in Afghanistan:

> [T]he US military has adopted a new style of warfare that eschews the bloody slogging matches of old. It seeks a quick victory with minimal casualties on both sides. Its hallmarks are speed, maneuver, flexibility, and surprise. It is heavily reliant upon precision firepower, special forces, and psychological operations. And it strives to integrate naval, air, and land power into a seamless whole.[5]

The debate about the American way of war illustrates the difficult task that the student of strategic theory faces in unravelling the threads that make up American strategic thought. In the words of Colin Gray:

> It is difficult to comprehend why *the* pre-eminent guardian state of the West, with its wealth of competence in analytical techniques, makes and irregularly unmakes decisions on matters of peace, war, and survival in an undisciplined and deeply astrategic manner.[6]

The task is further complicated by the realisation that an understanding of Clausewitz's philosophy of war has become more firmly embedded within the US military than was traditionally the case. It is interesting to relate that this has occurred in a nation which, at least prior to 1941, had very little experience as a player in the international system with which Clausewitz was so familiar. Historically, the main influence on the American military was exercised by Jomini. His obsession with reducing the complexities of war to a few simple principles, as if it were a branch of mathematics, rested easily with a nation that is comfortable with adopting an engineering approach to solve problems. General Donn Starry has written that American military thought is based on "three fundamental influences: Napoleon, the industrial revolution and modern technology".[7]

There are, however, a number of wider themes that illustrate the way in which American strategic thinking has been shaped in the past two centuries: moral influences, the factor of space, the nation's size, the American constitution, and civil–military relations.

The morality of going to war constitutes a fundamental difference between American strategic thought and the Clausewitzian paradigm. Clausewitz did not believe that morality impinged upon the theory or practice of war given that war is a social act, and the decision to resort to force lies beyond war itself. Furthermore, morality would jeopardise the factors of morale, loyalty, and the psychology of the military, all of which Clausewitz deemed to be vital to any successful warfighting capability. The impact of the Enlightenment upon Clausewitz's thought can be seen in his belief that war is inevitable given that the nature of the relationship between states is rational, although amoral. This is the antithesis of the traditional American view that war is an aberration. On many of the occasions when it has gone to war, the United States has espoused "ethical" reasons for its war making, most recently in Kosovo, Afghanistan and Iraq. Yet early American strategic thought and practice was not entirely devoid of *raison d'état* considerations. During the Revolutionary War, for example, an alliance was concluded with France that was crucial to the outcome of the conflict. John Jay's *Federalist No. 3* used language that would have earned Clausewitz's praise: "Among the many objects to which a wise and free people find it necessary to direct their attention, that of providing for their safety seems to be the first."[8]

Comparing the virtues of *realpolitik* to the drawbacks of altruism as frequently espoused by American policymakers, particularly since President Woodrow Wilson, Henry Kissinger has highlighted the problems that the latter presents: "To foreign leaders imbued with less elevated maxims, America's claim to altruism evokes a certain aura of unpredictability; whereas the national interest can be calculated, altruism depends on the definition of the practitioner."[9]

Moreover, the conviction of Americans that their liberal, democratic institutions are the highest form of government known to man ensures that altruism is coloured by a form of arrogance that tends towards either ignorance of, or disdain for, other cultures. Such an approach has been cited as being responsible for the struggles to defeat insurgency in Vietnam and Iraq.[10]

The waters are further muddied when one examines the relationship between international law, a concept that any altruist would firmly support, and American military doctrine. The Hague Conventions (1899 and 1907) and Geneva Conventions (1864, 1906 and 1929) explicitly stipulated that the amount of force used by a belligerent should be reasonable, and should not be disproportionate to its objective. However, a direct line can be traced through American history from Sherman's march through Georgia in 1864 to the strategic bombing campaigns of the Second World War to the Cold War plans, which advocated the wholesale destruction of the USSR, to the air campaigns against North Vietnam and later Iraq and Serbia, all of which attempted to maximise the firepower at America's disposal to achieve swift and decisive victory. Clausewitz advocated the maximum use of force, but only if it was properly exercised. One can only agree with the irony of S. J. Lepper's observation that "Clausewitz's theories remain relevant today because the law of war – a concept he viewed sceptically – remains one of war's key limits".[11]

The element of space has been a determining factor in US strategy. One of the legacies of occupying a vast part of the North American subcontinent where distance is transparent is that space has ensured that the US military has generally been a master of the art of logistics. Although this has not always been complemented by operational brilliance or strategic dexterity, the ability to organise its supply services has invariably proved a stimulant to improved performance by the military in the field. A commensurate reliance on technology remains one of the most distinctive features of US strategy making. Weigley has written of the American propensity "to seek refuge in technology from hard problems of the American character and [after 1945] by the complexity of nuclear-age technology".[12]

America's "Manifest Destiny" has been fulfilled through the creation of a nation of remarkable size and strength. Its abundance of resources, coupled with its invention of mass production technique, influenced its ability to wage war. This was crucial in the Second World War when it was able to fight two massive wars in Europe and Asia, out-produce all other nations combined, develop the atomic bomb and also the means to deliver it: the incredibly expensive B-29. This wealth and ingenuity is still as apparent today, with its consequences for relations with the rest of the world, as it was in 1945. It is symptomatic of a scientific approach to war, rather than one that recognises war as an art. Another legacy of the "moving frontier" is that the United States is primarily a continentalist rather than a maritime power. This is despite its position as the globe's strongest naval power, which relies heavily on access to the sea lanes of the world, and also despite the precepts of Alfred Thayer Mahan, America's most prominent military theorist. This stance inadvertently reflects the tone of *On War* in that Clausewitz concentrated almost exclusively on land warfare. Decisive battle rather than maritime blockade is a common thread in both Clausewitzian and American strategic thought. As General George C. Marshall famously remarked, a democracy cannot be expected to fight a seven years' war.[13]

The liberalism of the Founding Fathers ensured that the US military is exclusively answerable to neither the Executive nor the Legislature. Therefore, the role of domestic opinion is as important in shaping and determining the role of the military as is the role of government. As James Madison emphasised in *The Federalist* in January 1788, the Constitution emphasises "that the ultimate authority, wherever the derivative may be found, resides in the people alone".[14]

This factor was actually built into the Army's force structure. Its central core consisted of a small, standing force that was supported by what would become the National Guard and the Army Reserve, and, ultimately, by universal conscription. This army could only be deployed if the people consented to such a course of action via their elected representatives in Congress. It was only after the Second World War that this link between army and people began to weaken as the United States was forced to maintain a large, professional military presence in peacetime to counter the Soviet threat to the nation's security. As reserve forces simultaneously decreased in importance, the effect was to create an army that was more responsive to the Executive than to the people. The disturbance of this equilibrium allowed successive presidents to commit the armed forces to Korea and Vietnam without first asking Congress to declare war, actions that were reminiscent of those of an *ancien régime* monarch. However, given the

Vietnam experience, Congress clipped the Executive's wings by passing the War Powers Act in 1973. This limits the time a president can commit US forces to hostilities overseas without Congressional consent to a maximum of 90 days. Whereas Colin Powell holds that the US armed forces are still a "people's army", one is more inclined to agree with Hew Strachan who argues that contemporary Western militaries are representatives of their political leaderships rather than their peoples.[15]

Since 1945, the United States has been an active participant in international relations. The effect has been that, as the only superpower to have existed throughout the whole post-war period, America's policy choices have been the major factor behind the shifting balance of the international security environment. Military power, even more so than the making and breaking of alliances through diplomacy, has been at its heart. Unfortunately, the dichotomy that has arisen between diplomacy and strategy during this process has also had a pernicious effect, as Kissinger points out: "In American thinking foreign-policy and strategy were compartmentalized into successive phases of national policy. In the ideal American universe, diplomats stayed out of strategy, and military personnel completed their task by the time diplomacy started."[16]

This distinction is a legacy of the impact of Moltke's thinking on late nineteenth-century military reformers such as Emory Upton. Indeed, Robert Cassidy has traced the emphasis on offensive operations and attrition in US strategic thought to Upton and his fellow reformers, who drew on a way of war that was most suited to campaigning on the European continent. The Moltkean influence on US civil–military relations was made clear in American military doctrine in 1936 with the publication of the US Army Command and General Staff College's manual, *The Principles of Strategy for An Independent Corps or Army in a Theatre of Operations*. It stated that "politics and strategy are radically and fundamentally things apart. Strategy begins where politics ends. All that soldiers ask is that once the policy is settled, strategy and command shall be regarded as being in a sphere apart from politics."[17]

According to Christopher Bassford, it was a view that reflected that School's orthodoxy more than anything else. One would be hard pushed to imagine a better example of unClausewitzian thinking than this. It was axiomatic in Clausewitz's mind that military planning should not be divorced from the political aims of the war. Likewise, political ends had to accommodate military means. "[One] does not imply that the political aim is a tyrant. It must adapt itself to its chosen means, a process which can radically change it ... Policy is the guiding intelligence and war only the instrument, not vice versa."[18]

However, Clausewitz's own experience illustrated the extent to which this distinction could be ambiguous. As one of the most radical members of Scharnhorst's post-Jena military reform circle, Clausewitz was frequently opposed to the political aims of his sovereign, the Prussian king. Indeed, the reform movement's concerns went beyond questions of military reform to challenging the nature of Prussian foreign policy and even the very social structure of the state itself. It was against this background that Clausewitz left for Russia in 1812 to fight the French, contrary to government policy, which was concerned with pursuing closer relations with Napoleon. As Azar Gat has commented, this position blurred the institutional link between the civil authority and the military:

> This irony has escaped those who today have raised to prominence Clausewitz's conception of the relationship between political leadership and military command. They have had in mind the controversies between Bismarck and Moltke (during which the latter cited Clausewitz), and Truman and MacArthur, where a rejection of the particular positions held by the military command was happily in union with our contemporary political outlook that postulates the supremacy of the political leadership.[19]

The ramifications of the stark distinction between civil and military authorities is still being felt today, perhaps more so than ever. John Nagl has illustrated its dire effects for policy in operations that are of a nature that can be categorised as low-intensity conflict: "[T]he American way of war is marked by a belief that the nation is at war or at peace; the binary nature of war leaves no space for political-military interface."[20]

The notion that the military should be carefully controlled by the civil authority is, of course, very liberal in the traditional sense of that word. It was recognised by the Founding Fathers, but its virtue has been somewhat offset by the way in which this hinders preparations for war. As George C. Marshall, the then Army chief-of-staff, said in a speech in 1923, "we continue to follow a regular cycle in the doing and undoing of measures for the National Defense ... from the earliest days of this country, [the military] was materially increased in strength and drastically reduced with somewhat monotonous regularity".[21]

Citing such examples of unpreparedness as the ordeal of Valley Forge in the winter of 1777–78 during the Revolutionary War, the early days of the Civil War, and the material impoverishment of the American Expeditionary Force in the autumn of 1917, Marshall may have had a feeling of *deja vu* during the early days of US involvement in the Second World War, given events at Pearl Harbor, Bataan and Corregidor, and the Kasserine Pass. Even during the Korean War, the first American units to go into action were defeated by their far-better equipped North Korean opponents. Clausewitz, too, advocated preparation.

> The aggressor is always peace-loving (as Bonaparte always claimed to be); he would prefer to take our country unopposed. To prevent his doing so one must be willing to make war and be prepared for it ... Thus decrees the art of war.[22]

Given the drawbacks and contradictions in American strategic culture discussed above, the ability of the United States to focus on its strengths at the expense of these has allowed it to carve out a dominant role in world affairs since 1945. Indeed, it is remarkable that, given the impatience which is inherent in the American character, the United States managed to steer the Western alliance to victory in the Cold War after 40 years of gradually wearing down the communist world. This was despite setbacks such as Vietnam, the doubts expressed by some wayward allies, notably the French, as to American trustworthiness, and the constant risk of annihilation, which the Americans ran if their intentions were misperceived by the Kremlin. A similar demonstration of patience may be required to execute today's "long war" against terrorism successfully.

From revolutionary war to civil war

The manner in which the American colonists endured an eight-year war and simultaneously consolidated their social order through creating a new system of government is praiseworthy. Contrary to the opinion of some commentators, however, the American Revolutionary War is not a model comparable to the French Revolution.[23] The latter was highly centralised and involved the overthrow of a social system, not the creation of a new nation. The Clausewitzian aspects of the American Revolutionary War are obvious: the importance of moral factors; the interplay of the three elements of the fascinating trinity; and the maintenance of aim on Washington's part whereby he realised that the main enemy centre of gravity, other than its armed forces, was the British polity and its patience in waging a long war. As long as Washington could preserve his army, he would eventually erode the British will to fight. Washington's conduct in adversity and his political nous would earn him the praise of no less an authority than Moltke.[24]

Although Washington tended to eschew guerrilla methods, certain of his acolytes, notably Nathaniel Greene in the South, did not, and their hit-and-run tactics in a sympathetic countryside ensured that British regular forces expended a lot of effort in trying to counter this ploy. Indeed, these tactics foreshadowed those of the Maoist "Wars of National Liberation" of the twentieth century. Just as the United States would discover in Vietnam, the British were gradually exhausted of men and material as they fought what became an unwinnable war. The performance of the Continental Army, meanwhile, improved over time almost to the extent where it reached the qualitative level of its adversary. Washington's first inspector-general, Friedrich Wilhelm von Steuben, wrote the first doctrinal text in American history, his so-called Blue Book, *Regulations for the Order and Discipline of the Troops of the United States*, and also introduced the staff concepts of Frederick the Great into the Army. However, these did not develop into a full-blown military staff system until the reforms initiated by Secretary of War Elihu Root in the early twentieth century. This was despite the intervention of the American Civil War, and also despite the reforms of Root's distant predecessor, John C. Calhoun (secretary between 1819 and 1821), which improved the general staff created in the War of 1812 against Britain through establishing the role of commanding general. But Washington "bequeathed to the American Army a legacy of tactical excellence from its beginning".[25]

Washington's "Sentiments on a Peace Establishment" (1783) suggested constructing a three-tiered military establishment: a land force consisting of a small regular army, a regular reserve and a common militia. To support this, he proposed the building of arsenals, factories, laboratories and military academies. It was Thomas Jefferson who approved the creation of the US Military Academy at West Point in 1802, although Washington had earlier established artillery and engineering schools there in 1794. The early Republic's foreign policy was based around maintaining political freedom, securing economic strength, and making temporary alliances with foreign powers if the situation required it. In manipulating the balance of power, the Americans heeded Washington's warning given in his "Farewell Address" of 1796 against being party to "entangling alliances", and also Secretary of State John Quincy Adams's speech of 1821, which warned against going abroad in search of "monsters to slay". The Monroe Doctrine (1823) reinforced American isolationism from European affairs, and confirmed that while the United States portrayed its own policy in the Western Hemisphere as what would later be called "Manifest Destiny", it was in fact acting similarly to the Europeans elsewhere.

Washington's sound geopolitical advice was turned into a virtue. Neutrality became a moral axiom on the grounds that Europe's problems had arisen from cynical means of statesmanship. In a theme taken up by some strategists in recent years, that democracies do not make war on each other, the New World was portrayed as being the arena where the promotion of democratic institutions would render the ways of the *ancien régime* anachronistic. Clausewitz, on the other hand, may have seen democracy as a harbinger of war, given the greater influence of the people. These notions have certainly coloured US foreign policy in recent times, given the conviction that democracy can somehow be transplanted to lands where it has no tradition.[26]

The War of 1812 demonstrated the vulnerability of the eastern American seaboard to naval power. Consequently, the United States would adopt what Linn has called a policy of "deterrence and repulse". Weigley termed the national approach to strategy after 1815 as "Jominian rather than Clausewitzian", though it could easily be likened to Clausewitz's allusion to "armed observation".[27]

The deficiencies of amateur officers highlighted by the War of 1812 ensured that West Point was to become a centre of excellence for officer education. It reflected a European influence in that it was a response to the Enlightenment ideal of military education, which had seen similar institutions being established across Europe in the late eighteenth century. Dennis Hart Mahan was the Professor of Military and Civil Engineering and of the Science of War at West Point from 1832 to 1871. He was, more than anyone, responsible for introducing the systematic study of the conduct of war to the Academy. Among his pupils can be numbered many of the generals of the American Civil War. Basically, Mahan was a conduit for the ideas of Napoleon. Such was the latter's appeal that the experiences of Washington were more or less ignored in the curriculum. It can be argued that the destructive marches of Sherman were in some way influenced by Mahan's didactic framework. Mahan argued in his lectures that "carrying the war into the heart of the assailant's country ... is the surest way of making him share its burdens and foiling his plans".[28]

Much of Mahan's teachings and published work was strongly influenced by Jomini, whose works were translated more extensively in America than elsewhere. Mahan's *Advanced Guard, Outpost and Detached Service of Troops, with the Essential Principles of Strategy and Ground Tactics*, was, as its convoluted title suggests, a Jominian cookbook. However, it was to serve as the main doctrinal text for officers on both sides in the Civil War. In 1862, Sherman wrote "should any officer ... be ignorant of his tactics, regulations or even the principles of the art of war (Mahan and Jomini), it would be a lasting disgrace".[29]

Despite this, there is some evidence to suggest that Clausewitz's ideas were not totally lost on American soldiers prior to the Civil War. As Bassford has pointed out, Jomini's famous *Summary of the Art of War* had been revised so as to take many of Clausewitz's precepts into account. Indeed, this realisation has countered a growing perception among many strategic theorists that Jomini had failed to grasp the essential nature of Napoleonic strategy when in fact Clausewitz himself acknowledged that Jomini saw "the engagement [as] the only effective means in war".[30]

Much of President Polk's conduct during the Mexican War (1846–48) was Clausewitzian: ensuring initial support; attempting to defeat the enemy by the cheapest means – blockade; and capturing an important centre of gravity, the enemy's capital city. On the other hand, General Winfield Scott's expeditionary campaign of 1846–47, which resulted in the capture of Mexico City, was marked by caution and a refusal to seek battle with the main body of the Mexican Army. Weigley has therefore described Scott's conduct as reminiscent of a pre-Napoleonic commander's though Clausewitz's mature theory of war would have accommodated this approach. Polk's subsequent failure to end the war quickly almost led to the fatal loss of domestic support. His conduct was highly criticised by Ulysses S. Grant whose constitutional piety led him, like Washington, to believe that America should not incur the stain of aggression. He called the conflict a "political war, and [that] the administration conducting it desired to make political capital out of it".[31]

Although all war is driven by politics in its broadest sense, Clausewitz would not have approved of conducting a war purely from the need to make some abstract political point when it was clear that it was becoming more costly in blood and treasure than the original objective warranted: "The original means of strategy is victory ... its ends, in the final analysis, are those objects which will lead directly to peace."[32]

At the outset of the Civil War, President Abraham Lincoln's objective was to combine limited force aimed at occupying the enemy's capital, Richmond, with a conciliatory policy towards the South. However, the Emancipation Proclamation issued in 1863 ensured that the North's aim became unlimited, threatening the South's very existence. The initial belief in a short conflict had been dissipated by experience, and it meant that the North could now mobilise its huge industrial capacity against its agriculturally dominated opponent. The advent of the railroad also nullified the South's use of interior lines.

Lincoln was no man of war. He was forced to teach himself the rudiments by borrowing the military works of the Congressional library, and reading them in his spare time. It was his political intuition, combined with common sense, that made him a good strategist. He began to appreciate the need to mobilise the North's superior resources and to maintain an eye on the whole picture without being distracted by sideshows such as capturing Richmond. To that end, he foresaw the need to pursue a strategy of simultaneous advance against the South. His general-in-chief after June 1862, Henry Halleck, had been one of D. H. Mahan's best pupils at West Point, and had written a Jominian treatise on the conduct of operations in 1846. A man who shunned responsibility, Halleck's background meant that he was unable to appreciate the problems of campaign-ing in the huge expanses of North America. He was restricted to thinking in terms of geometry, believing that an army's "base of operations" should also form the base of a right-angled corridor within which all manoeuvre would occur. His response to Lincoln's advocacy of simultaneous advance was scathing: "To operate on exterior lines against an enemy occupying a central position will fail, as it has always failed, in ninety-nine cases out of a hundred. It is condemned by every military authority I have ever read."[33]

Halleck was to be replaced in early 1864 by Grant who, as commander of the Federal armies in the West, had almost resigned owing to Halleck's intransi-gence over strategy. Grant was aware that when campaigning in a vast, rich but sparsely populated land, an army needed no permanent "base of operations". All that was required was for it to be supplied by river and railroad to the rear, and to live on the land through which it marched. This approach yielded dividends during the vital Vicksburg campaign of May–July 1863, which nullified the Confederate strategy of holding the choke point of communications. Further-more, the peak of his campaigning, the victory at Chattanooga in November 1863, enabled him to sever the Chattanooga–Atlanta link, the key to all opera-tions in that vast theatre. Grant quickly made veterans out of the amateur army he had inherited in 1862, instilling it with his philosophy of war. "Find out where your enemy is. Get at him as soon as you can. Strike at him as hard as you can and as soon as you can, and keep moving on."[34]

Once Grant became the Federal commander-in-chief, his concern was with achieving total victory. To do so, he was not overly concerned with defeating the enemy in a set-piece battle but instead concentrated on ending the Confeder-acy's ability to continue waging the war by destroying its logistical base as part of a two-pronged thrust, or the method of simultaneous advance advocated by Lincoln. The 1864 campaign in Virginia was intended to defeat General Robert Lee's army by severing its lines of communication. However, Lee was too clever to fall for this, and instead a grim war of attrition was fought out in the knowledge that casualties would be more easily borne by the North. It was else-where that the Confederacy was finally brought to its knees, with a simultaneous advance from Chattanooga in the west. Sherman's "March to the Sea" was designed to devastate the Confederate heartland, deprive the enemy of resources, and bring the war home to its people. The destruction of Atlanta and the subsequent march to the Atlantic coast was followed by a turn north to attack Lee's rear. It was designed with the Clausewitzian aim of breaking the enemy's will. In the event, however, the enemy armies still had to be defeated so as to allow the campaign to succeed, and the war to be won. While Weigley is right to say that Grant "became the most influential figure in the shaping of American strategic thought for the next hundred years, not always with fortunate results", it is not true that he "was always a Jominian rather than a Clausewitzian strategist" just because he preferred to avoid battle if that was at all possible.[35]

Donn Starry's summation of the war is nearer the mark: "In the perception of the need to destroy the enemy means for supporting war, as well as the means for waging war, Grant and Sherman were perhaps more Clausewitzian than they were disciples of Jomini."[36]

The evolution of American strategic thought, 1865–1918

The brutality and indecisiveness of many of the Civil War's battles may have left a lasting impression on those who participated in them, but the conflict itself made little impact upon the organisation of the US military. Most politicians, safe in the knowledge that foreign invasion was unlikely, found it impossible to justify paying for a larger military establishment. Consequently, the Army remained relatively immune to any attempts to develop a systematic analysis of modern warfare, or even to absorbing the lessons of the Civil War, which were to prove so relevant to the conduct of the First World War. As has already been remarked, no General Staff worthy of the name existed. The army did not produce its first proper tactical manuals until the Leavenworth series was published in 1891. In short, by the time it was involved in operations during the Spanish–American War of 1898, the US Army was unprepared for anything other than a "small war". Even that conflict stretched the Army's ability to cope with an expansion of its staff structure.

The most influential officer in the late-nineteenth-century US Army was Emory Upton, owing to his advocacy of as little civilian influence on military affairs as possible. While this thinking bore a Jominian imprimateur, Upton was an enthusiastic admirer of the Prusso-German military system that had matured under Moltke and, consequently, was also familiar with Clausewitz whose *On War* had been translated into English in 1873. Upton genuinely believed that any defects in the military were the result of excessive civilian control. His way of thinking would ensure that the American military would tend to eschew wider strategic thinking in favour of focusing on narrow tactical and doctrinal concerns epitomised by the principles of war. Cassidy has concluded that Upton contributed to "the following contradiction: the US Army has embraced Clausewitz as the quintessential oracle of war, but it has also tended to distance itself from Clausewitz's overarching theme – the linkage of the military instrument to political purposes".[37]

It is a cliché to speak of the Indian Wars as being wars of annihilation. This is partly because of Sherman's well-known remarks about "annihilating" the Sioux people. However, those campaigns are really a part of America's long tradition of small wars and mainly involved skirmishes and patrols rather than punitive war fighting.[38]

The late-nineteenth-century US Navy enjoyed a period of innovation in strategic thought, thanks mainly to Alfred Thayer Mahan, the son of D. H. Mahan. The Naval War College was established at Newport, Rhode Island in 1884. Despite *On War* being the very first book on the college's recommended reading list by 1894, Mahan drew heavily on Jomini, although he did occasionally refer to Clausewitzian themes. In a recognisably Clausewitzian passage of a speech to the Naval War College class of 1892, he said: "all the world knows gentlemen, that we are building a new navy ... Well, when we get our navy what are we going to do with it?"[39]

Like Mahan, President Theodore Roosevelt believed that America's strength ensured that it must have a role in international relations as he could not conceive of a global balance of power that was bereft of American influence. While he believed in American exceptionalism, Roosevelt was a hard-nosed realist who advocated the national interest. As was the case with Clausewitz, he could not conceive of the notion of a utopian foreign-policy:

> I regard the [Woodrow] Wilson–[William J.] Bryan attitude of trusting to fantastic peace treaties, to impossible promises, to all kinds of scraps of paper without any backing in efficient force, as abhorrent. It is inherently better for a nation and for the world to have the Frederick the Great and Bismarck tradition as regards foreign-policy than to have the Bryan or Bryan–Wilson attitude as a permanent national attitude.[40]

Roosevelt's approach to international relations could not have been more different to that of his next-but-one successor Woodrow Wilson. It was Wilson who translated the ideals of American exceptionalism into foreign policy, and the resulting altruism has never since been absent. Wilson despised such notions of power politics as the balance of power and spheres of influence. While Roosevelt had a greater understanding of the way in which international politics worked, Wilson had a keener appreciation of domestic politics and grasped the reality that the bulk of American opinion saw their nation as being unique and untainted by the aberrations of European-style diplomacy. Remarkably, whereas Roosevelt's approach failed to convince the American people of the need to enter the First World War, Wilson managed to convert the people from favouring neutrality to supporting intervention. Unfortunately, his high ideals were to do lasting damage to the peoples of Europe as a result of the Treaty of Versailles. To cite Henry Kissinger, "[Roosevelt] was the warrior-statesman; Wilson was the prophet-priest. Statesmen, even warriors, focus on the world in which they live; to prophets, the 'real' world is the one they want to bring into being."[41]

Wilson's approach also had a pernicious effect upon the capability of the US military to play a major role in a large continental war 3,000 miles from home. There was a heated debate after 1914 between those who saw an urgent need to reform the armed forces and those who wished to limit military power, given its implied danger to constitutional government. On the whole, the American military believed that superior numbers and resources, rather than manoeuvre and surprise, would prevail just as Grant had shown in Virginia in 1864–65. Robert M. Johnson's work, *Clausewitz to Date* (1917), attempted to apply Clausewitz's ideas to American military minds, albeit with little success. Johnson's concept of a small, but highly professional army was no answer to the problems posed by the mass, industrialised warfare being waged on the Western Front.

America's unpreparedness hindered its ability to aid the Allied powers during 1917. The commander-in-chief of the American Expeditionary Force, General John Pershing, was right to hold back his troops until they had been trained to the extent where they could operate independently of their allies. America's desire to discover the quickest route to victory was illustrated by its Air Service's plans, albeit embryonic, for long-range bombardment during the final months of the war. Pershing saw the Air Force as being no more than an auxiliary to the general effort, supplying aerial artillery. However, this operational myopia obscured some of the strategic promise held by a shrewd use of air power. Edgar Gorrell, an American air officer on Pershing's staff, drew on British thinking in his belief that air power could have a detrimental effect upon the morale of the enemy's population through the targeting of industrial centres. He used a very interesting metaphor, reminiscent of some of those in *On War* (there is no evidence to suggest that Gorrell read Clausewitz), to describe the context in which the military operated in the era of "total" war:

> An army may be compared to a drill. The point of the drill must be strong and must stand up and bear the brunt of the much hard work with which it comes into contact; but unless the shank of the drill is strong and continually reinforcing the point, the drill will break. So with the nation in a War of these days – the army is like the point of the drill and must bear the brunt of constant conflict with foreign obstacles; but unless the nation – which represents the shank of the drill – constantly stands behind and supplies the necessary aid to the point, the drill will break and the nation will fail.[42]

Had the war lasted another year, theory may have been converted into practice by the capacity of American production. To some extent, the link between bombing and morale was overemphasised, and this continued to distract air-power enthusiasts throughout the twentieth century.

Isolationism and American strategic thought

American strategic thought during the inter-war period maintained the pre-war pattern of intellectual void, even within the Navy. The Marine Corps was a notable exception. As early as 1920, its chief, Major-General John Lejeune, embraced the concept of amphibious warfare, formulated by Major Pete Ellis, thereby radically altering the Corps' role from providing infantry to acting as the US Navy's spearhead through the seizure of distant bases for naval operations. By 1933 a Fleet Marine Force had been created, and the following year a manual entitled *Tentative Landing Operations Manual* became a source of official doctrine. A series of Fleet Landing Exercises (FLEXes) was to provide the laboratory in which this doctrine could be improved. According to Lieutenant-Colonel H. T. Hayden, this manual "was perhaps the most important contribution to military science made by the US Marine Corps until their current attempts to adopt a culture of maneuver warfare".[43]

The Army continued to neglect strategy, probably because any projection of American power overseas was dependent upon the Navy. Even the experiences of 1917–18 were neglected, given the expectation that the United States would not intervene in European affairs a second time. Pershing declared in 1919 that the primary function of the army was to defend the continental United States, an operational requirement that required a mobile capability. Ironically, "since tank doctrine had evolved in a static warfare situation, tanks were viewed as siege weapons. Pershing endorsed the view that tanks had no role to play in continental defense."[44]

Pershing's opinion was fundamental in persuading Congress to disband the Tank Corps as an independent entity under the terms of the National Defense Act of 1920, and to allot it to the infantry. Furthermore, the almost pacific attitude prevalent in society at large ensured that army officers, cocooned in their own little world, found it difficult to innovate despite increasing mechanisation in the 1920s and 1930s. The experience of Dwight D. Eisenhower was typical. Even although he belonged to the small coterie of senior Tank Corps officers, his commander refused to let him put his other duties before his role as the successful Tank School football team coach! Yet, together with Patton, Eisenhower published prescient articles in the *Infantry Journal* as early as 1920, which suggested combining manoeuvre with artillery support by advocating that well-designed tanks could manoeuvre in mass and either outflank the enemy or else penetrate his line and cause it to collapse while the infantry played a holding role in support. Such revolutionary thinking was discouraged by their superiors in Washington. As a result, by 1933 the chief-of-staff, General Douglas MacArthur, noted that the few tanks possessed by the Army were "completely useless for employment against any modern unit on the battlefield".[45]

Patton himself made the interesting observation that "between the Prussian concept of professionalism and the needs of the American democratic society" there existed "a linkage: conditioning young men for courage and sacrifice, drilling them in the knowledge of their calling, [and] motivating them to perform with dedication".[46]

The vehicle for achieving this lay not only at West Point but also in the institutions of the Army Command and General Staff College established by Sherman at Leavenworth in 1881, and the elite US Army War College located at

Fort McNair, Washington, DC, until 1951 when it moved to its present location at Carlisle Barracks, Pennsylvania. In 1931–32, the War College, which existed to prepare its students for future higher command and staff duties, defined its mission as:

> (1) to train officers for the conduct of field operations of the Army and higher echelons; (2) to instruct officers in the War Department General Staff duties; (3) to train officers for joint operations of the Army and Navy; (4) to instruct officers in the strategy, tactics and logistics of large operations in past wars with specific reference to the [first] world war.[47]

There is little evidence to suggest that Clausewitz's work was being disseminated to any significant extent within the American military education system during this period. Many of his ideas were discovered by the Navy second hand, either through the work of such notable disciples as the Briton, Sir Julian Corbett, or else through an appreciation of the relationship between war and policy as articulated by Mahan. However, the Naval War College did not revert to its role as a centre of intellectual study after the First World War, and *On War* was not much in evidence. Nevertheless, one can make a stronger case for a Clausewitzian influence within the Navy than within the Army, particularly where the political nature of war is concerned.[48]

Clausewitz's lack of influence undoubtedly had something to do both with the absence of a satisfactory translation of *On War* into English and with the general hostility to his views in much of the military literature being produced in English during the inter-war period. It was only in 1943 that the first complete edition of *On War*, a translation by J. J. Matthijs Jolles, was published in the United States. (Clausewitz's essay on the *Principles of War* was translated and edited by H. W. Gatzke in 1942.) Coincidentally, a superb essay on Clausewitz by the German émigré Hans Rothfels was published as part of the collection *Makers of Modern Strategy* during the same year. This helped to raise the American understanding of Clausewitz to a new level.[49]

Some aspects of Clausewitz's approach regarding military history and doctrine did make their way onto the curriculum of the Army's schools, albeit indirectly, in some cases. In 1922, Colonel W. K. Naylor drew upon Delbrück's misreading of Clausewitz in a lecture:

> The great generals of history were not per se proponents of the strategy of attrition or annihilation, did not belong to one or the other school of thought, but acted, if they were real generals, according to circumstances. They always endeavored to encompass the annihilation of the enemy, if their available forces sufficed thereof.[50]

Clausewitz's name also appeared with more frequency in certain Army publications such as the *Infantry Journal* during the 1930s. However, *On War* was not used as a textbook at either Fort McNair or Leavenworth. Eisenhower was a pupil at the Army War College in 1938, and his group's report, "War and Its Principles, Methods and Doctrines" was heavily influenced by Clausewitz. However, it is hard to discern the extent to which this reflected Eisenhower's own views. William Pickett has argued, with a touch of hyperbole, that "[a]ny explanation of Eisenhower's remarkable rise to world prominence is incomplete without consideration of what he learned from Clausewitz".[51]

Nevertheless, the report by Eisenhower's group tended to gloss over the political aspect of war and, as such, it was no different to the treatment of Clausewitz elsewhere within the US Army. There is, for example, a tantalising glimpse of Clausewitz's influence in a purely military context in the Army's *Field Service Regulations* (FSR) of 1923: "The ultimate objective of all military operations is the destruction of the enemy's armed forces by battle. Decisive defeat in battle breaks the enemy's will to war and forces him to sue for peace."[52]

While Weigley has dismissed a penchant for quoting Clausewitz in the inter-war period as a "vogue", a contrary view has recently been propounded by Michael Matheny regarding thinking about the operational level of war. He argues that key Clausewitzian concepts, notably the centre of gravity and the culminating point, were becoming familiar terms at the service schools and in doctrine. The *Field Service Regulations* of 1925 signalled an increasing Clausewitzian influence that culminated in *The Principles of Strategy* produced at Fort Leavenworth in 1936.[53]

The *Field Service Regulations*, forerunner of FM 3–0: *Operations*, had first appeared in 1905, and were part of a trend that attempted to incorporate "principles of war" into US military doctrine.[54] First World War experience had placed great emphasis upon maintaining the enemy's armed forces as a major objective, while the lessons of the Civil War illustrated the role of economic power in modern war. As has already been noted, Clausewitz himself was not particularly comfortable with the notion of condensing centuries of experience into a few simple maxims. Such rigidity could never deal with the unforeseen in war's friction. Their major drawback lies in a failure to realise that political considerations permeate war even at its operational level. However, the US Army's FM 3–0 of 2001 continued to justify the principles of war as having "stood the tests of analysis, experimentation, and practice".[55]

The development of Air Force doctrine after 1918 was also stunted by public apathy and institutional obfuscation. Airpower theorists were concerned not only with the industrial-economic aspects of war but also with minimising casualties, both of air crew and the enemy's civilian population, although the desire to damage morale was emphasised. As Billy Mitchell wrote in 1925: "The influence of air power on the ability of one nation to impress its will on another in armed conflict will be decisive."[56]

Events later rendered this analysis as over-optimistic. The possibility of attacking actual population centres was left open to interpretation by the Air Corps Tactical School. As Tami Davis Biddle has written, "the relationship between capacity to fight and will to fight – the oft-cited dyad of strategic bombing theory – has never been entirely clear in American air doctrine".[57]

The Clausewitzian relationship between war and politics became more apparent as the international situation worsened in the late 1930s. The deteriorating political situation in the Far East, where the United States was prevented from exercising real power projection through the constraints of the Washington Naval Treaty, concentrated American minds. Planning assumptions made at the Naval War College, as well as the aforementioned series of FLEXes executed by the Marine Corps, were concerned with the need to provide this capability through carrier aviation and amphibious warfare. "From a mere transit itinerary, the Navy produced a doctrine of progressive transoceanic operations [to support those] civilians who defined the national interest as defence of the Philippines and the Open Door in China."[58]

As the United States approached the Second World War, a debate continued within the Army between those who favoured the old cavalry-style tactics of the Midwest, which had been based on manoeuvre, and those who advocated the use of massive force in the tradition of Grant. The dilemma facing General George Marshall lay in combining both strands through enlarging the Army and making it capable of successfully challenging the mobility of the German Army that mechanisation had made possible. In the event, the Americans were able to adapt to the revolution in technology and doctrine that occurred during the inter-war period with a mass and mobility provided by American democracy and industrial strength.

Global war, 1941–45

The Second World War highlighted the extent to which ambiguities exist in American strategy in that it tended to be either flexible or rigid. For example, the military was forced to improvise at short notice, planning campaigns such as the attack at Guadalcanal in August 1942 and the invasion of North Africa later that year with very little margin for error. On the other hand, they refused to yield to the proposed British "maritime" strategy of exploiting Allied success in North Africa and attacking the "soft underbelly" of the Axis in the Mediterranean. Instead, from almost the moment that they entered the war against Germany, the Americans were intent on avoiding what one Pentagon planner called "scatterization" of resources by securing victory through a cross-Channel invasion of France, a direct, "continental" approach.[59] The victory in the Pacific, however, depended upon a combination of combined-arms operations as well as the Mahanian concept of winning large, set-piece naval battles. Battles such as Midway laid the foundation for the amphibious campaigns in that theatre, and the latter affirmed the foresight of the Marine Corps during the inter-war period.

While American planning was greatly eased by superb intelligence and its dissemination by operational analysts, victory was made possible by a combination of mass (men and materiel) and the direct assault. The Second World War turned out to be as significant in the long-term development of American strategic thought as the Civil War had been. Indeed, as Weigley remarks, Grant's influence could be detected in "Overlord", and Sherman's in the strategic bombing of Germany and Japan.[60]

The American system of strategy making was dependent to a large extent upon the keen interest President Roosevelt took in the day-to-day conduct of the war, a process aided by the creation of the Joint Chiefs-of-Staff (JCS) in 1942 to oversee strategy, and the president's neglect of Congress. The JCS reported directly to Roosevelt. He was aided by the complete acquiescence of the military, which took civilian supremacy in strategic matters for granted even where this affected operational considerations. Battles were treated as ends in themselves rather than as means to a political end. Roosevelt's conduct of strategy was sound in its concentration on the main goal; namely, the total defeat of Germany and Japan. On the other hand, his personality also hindered strategy in that he allowed his idealism to encroach upon the policymaking process. This tied the Western Allies' hands at the conferences with Stalin, particularly at Yalta, for unlike in the First World War the Americans were very much the senior partner in the Allied coalition. Roosevelt was fortunate in that he had a very competent chief military adviser in Marshall, who has rightly been described as the "organiser of victory". The historian Thomas Parrish has described their relationship as "the most triumphantly effective political-military team in American history – a team whose achievements rested on candor and hard won mutual respect".[61]

In his analysis of American strategic bombing during the Second World War, Bernard Brodie criticised the air campaigns against Germany and Japan despite recognising a certain operational efficacy in them. Strategically, however, he was far from convinced, believing that force had been employed out of all proportion to the objective being sought. One can criticise the bombing campaigns as being indiscriminate, despite the dedication of planners to military targeting. On the other hand, it can be argued that the desire of the Allies to save their own soldiers' lives, through hastening the end of the war via airpower, justified the campaigns. This argument applies especially to the atomic bombing of Japan.

The Americans were not completely unClausewitzian in their approach. They realised that the decisive centre of gravity lay in north-west Europe, and that as few resources as possible should be diverted from there. It was only there that the Wehrmacht could be decisively defeated, and the overriding political aim of the war – Germany's defeat – hastened. While a peripheral approach may have suited British tradition, American experience suggested the opposite, and culminated in the Normandy campaign. William Pickett is convinced that Clausewitzian principles were evident in Eisenhower's strategy from D-Day onwards, given the surprise attack on Normandy, the subsequent pursuit as Allied strength increased, and the major battles in the Ruhr Valley that he interpreted as being synonymous with Clausewitz's "plan of a war designed to lead to the total defeat of the enemy".[62]

It has been argued that Eisenhower was, as J. F. C. Fuller has stated, "a non-Clausewitzian soldier". This assertion is based on the decision, taken in the face of Churchill's protests, not to take Berlin, Prague and Vienna in the spring of 1945. However, Clausewitz is a red herring in this case because, as we have seen, the Americans left the responsibility for strategic decision-making in the hands of the political authority. The plans of the JCS were very much driven by narrow military considerations: "Such psychological and political advantages as would result from the possible capture of Berlin ahead of the Russians should not override the imperative military consideration, which in our opinion is the destruction and dismemberment of the German armed forces."[63]

Cold War, 1945–75

In November 1945, Bernard Brodie responded to the challenge of the nuclear age by predicting that deterrence would now be the dominant strategic concept. This prediction swiftly became reality when, after the rapid demobilisation of its conventional forces, America's policy moved to threatening to utilise its atomic monopoly (which consisted of a handful of weapons in the late 1940s) in retaliation for any attack upon its interests. Clausewitz had written that strategy could have (and indeed frequently had) the negative object of making clear to the opponent "the improbability of victory ... [and] its unacceptable cost".[64]

Weigley, drawing on his adaptation of Clausewitz's definition of strategy, has noted that the advent of deterrence was a turning point in American strategic thought:

> To shift the American definition of strategy from *the use of combats for the object of wars* to the use of military force for the deterrence of war, albeit while still serving the national interest in an active manner, amounted to a revolution in the history of American military policy.[65]

Deterrence complemented America's sudden elevation to a major role in peacetime international relations. The exceptionalist nature of the American outlook ensured that the American polity would concentrate on portraying their relationship with the USSR in Manichaean terms, rather than as being open to manipulation in the manner to which traditional players of balance-of-power politics would have been accustomed. The tone of the key document of American foreign policy at this time, NSC-68 (April 1950), was consistent with this strand of thinking in that it implied that the United States could "persuade" the Soviet Union to mend its ways fundamentally in the face of America's determination to preserve its essential values. Containment of the Soviet menace through collective defence would cause the communist world to implode over the long term, just as George Kennan had predicted it would in 1946–47. The document also stressed the need for the United States to continue exercising the advantage its nuclear monopoly gave it for as long as possible.[66]

Realism did fortuitously combine with altruism in that the generosity of the Marshall Plan allowed the war-weary European economies the breathing space they needed to recover. As early as November 1948, NSC-20/4 recognised the need to maintain the balance of power on the Eurasian land mass by preventing an increase in Soviet power and influence. In order to appease American public opinion, which feared a permanent European commitment, Secretary of State

Dean Acheson sold the NATO Treaty of 1949 to Congress as a temporary solution to the Soviet military presence in Eastern Europe. However, American strategy had now become decidedly Eurocentric. President Truman's response to the trials and tribulations of 1947 to 1950, beginning with his announcement of the Truman Doctrine in 1947, has rightly been described as "an exercise in strategy that would almost certainly have won Clausewitz's approbation".[67]

The North Korean communists could not possibly have known that the assumptions made in NSC-68 ensured that the Americans would not acquiesce in their absorption of South Korea as they had over the communist victory in China in 1949, a victory that secured a far greater prize. Although the geopolitical aspects of the Korean conflict were extremely important, Truman based his intervention on principle rather than interest, declaring that the rule of force had to bow to the rule of law. While this appeased the American people, it was far more difficult to translate into sound strategy. The American military's thinking was dominated by a general war scenario, whereby Soviet aggression would be defeated in the same way as German aggression had been in the Second World War. However, the need to pursue a more limited approach in South Korea ensured that the Americans were placed in strategic limbo.

The United Nations Security Council passed a resolution to restore the *status quo ante*, which would require driving the North Koreans back to the 38th Parallel. However, the Americans did not regard this as being sufficient punishment to deter future aggression. Somehow they had to threaten to escalate the conflict to a point where the communists would submit to their will, something that required a very careful assessment of the risk involved. In the event, MacArthur's landing at Inchon in July 1950 was sufficient to realise enough momentum to roll the North Koreans back across the 38th Parallel. This momentum persuaded Truman suddenly to make "reunification" his aim in October 1950, ensuring that the war escalated to a point where the Chinese intervened, and the Americans found that they had overstepped the mark between prudence and recklessness. Despite MacArthur's desire to go for broke, Truman again changed objectives to "halting aggression" in the absence of a negotiated settlement. This led to a stalemate based on an American attempt to persuade the communists to abandon their efforts.

MacArthur's desire to have a showdown with the communists in Korea contradicted Truman's overriding goal of maintaining America's ability to contain Soviet aggression in Europe. In the end, Truman had no choice but to sack MacArthur in April 1951. Major Charles McFetridge has used this example to illustrate the dangers of allowing a situation where a theatre commander is allowed to pursue strategy without due regard to its political consequences. "It is perhaps ironic that one of the greatest leaders in US history [MacArthur] failed to honor one of Clausewitz's basic tenets. Truman may have never read *On War*, but he certainly understood its message."[68]

The use of "nuclear diplomacy" enabled America to escape the Korean morass. Escalation dominance is a concept that arises from deterrence that requires its practitioner to be prepared to fight across the whole spectrum of conflict from a low-intensity situation to all-out nuclear war. Clausewitz understood this, even in the pre-nuclear age. "War is an act of force and there is no logical limit to the application of that force. Each side, therefore, compels its opponent to follow suit; a reciprocal action is started, which must lead, in theory, to extremes."[69]

The incoming Eisenhower Administration was faced with the problem of the Korean stalemate in early 1953, and there is evidence to suggest that the threat, or implied threat, of nuclear strikes cajoled the Chinese and North Koreans into signing the Armistice agreement of July 1953. The JCS recommended that atomic bombs should be dropped in May 1953, a suggestion that led Secretary of State John Foster Dulles to issue a message implying that this might happen. This stood in stark contrast to Truman's approach to negotiating with the communists. The American offensive of spring 1951, which liberated Seoul once more, had been halted when the communists parleyed for negotiations. This was a manifestation through Truman of America's strategic approach being dictated by their general belief that peace is normal and goodwill is reciprocal.[70]

That Eisenhower had the will to threaten escalation to nuclear war is explained by the climate in which he operated. At that time nuclear weapons were viewed by many American policymakers as being fit for use. NSC-30 of 1948 had already given the military the freedom to plan for general nuclear war, an approach that did not discriminate between civilian and military targets. However, nuclear use in Korea would have been limited to striking communist sanctuaries in the North and in China, effectively making it a rational instrument of policy and reflecting the words of the Army's 1954 field manual, FM 100–5, that nuclear weapons represented "additional firepower of large magnitude". Nevertheless, it is difficult to disagree with Bret Cillessen's conclusion that "what *did not* happen in [Korea] was even more important in determining the course of the atomic age than what did happen at Hiroshima".[71]

Eisenhower's strategy was forged by his belief that the budgetary costs imposed by an over-reliance on conventional forces should be avoided by relying on nuclear forces. This was a consequence of the fact that for the first time in its history the United States could no longer rely on mobilising mass to overwhelm the enemy, given the Soviets' insurmountable conventional superiority. Starry has written that this placed "our whole concept, of mass conscript armies and mass industrial means to support battles of military and national annihilation ... at risk".[72]

The ramifications of this were to be felt in the 1970s and 1980s when the concepts of Active Defense and AirLand Battle were formulated to try and solve the dilemma of overcoming Soviet conventional superiority without resorting to nuclear weapons. In the meantime, the Americans tried to utilise their nuclear superiority over the Soviets. Tactically, the atomic weapon was seen by the Army as usable on the battlefield. In 1957, the Army Command and General Staff College changed its instruction from an emphasis on the conventional battlefield to the nuclear, a course that was not reversed until the mid-1960s with the introduction of the Reorganisation Objectives Army Division (ROAD). As

Major Robert Doughty puts it: "The Army probably has never experienced a more radical change during peacetime in its thought, doctrine, and organization."[73]

The "New Look", which emphasised "massive retaliation", ensured that under Eisenhower the administration's strategy was underpinned almost wholly by a reliance on the nuclear weapon. The policy's most passionate advocate was Dulles. In January 1954, he announced that in future the US would deter aggression against the Free World by depending "primarily upon a great capacity to retaliate, instantly, by means and at places of our own choosing".[74]

However, as many of the policy's critics argued at the time, massive retaliation was fundamentally flawed in that it implied a choice between either all-out war or compromise. Military men such as Army chief-of-staff, General Matthew Ridgway, and his successor, General Maxwell Taylor, attacked what they called the "great fallacy". Their concerns were highlighted by the unravelling of American policy over Indo-China in 1954–55. Concerns about the capabilities of the indigenous communist forces and the limitations of airpower prevented the Americans from activating plans to send forces to aid the beleaguered French at Dien Bien Phu as much as any concerns about Chinese intervention.[75]

Eisenhower concurred with the Army's synopsis of the situation in Indo-China. It is probable that both he and Dulles realised that massive retaliation was unsustainable over the long run, given that the Soviets would close the nuclear gap. Therefore, it is possible that they were attempting to extract as much leverage from it as possible. It was almost certainly never envisaged that a limited conflict should immediately be escalated into a general war, particularly somewhere such as the Far East where America's interests were secondary to its European concerns. Unfortunately, the military's intelligent summary of the situation in 1954 and 1955 was not repeated ten years later, the result of an increasing reassertion of the traditional military concern with military matters without regard to wider policy implications.

There is some evidence to suggest that Eisenhower's reading of *On War* as a soldier affected some of his thinking as president. Whether this was because of the change in the nature of warfare and grand strategy heralded by the atomic bomb one cannot say. John Lewis Gaddis, the distinguished American historian of the Cold War, has detected some indirect Clausewitzian influences upon Eisenhower's presidency, especially concerning the "New Look". Basing his analysis on Clausewitz's discussion in Book I, Chapter 2 of *On War*, "Ends and Means in War", Gaddis interpreted the way in which Eisenhower adjusted means to ends and vice versa. His reliance on nuclear superiority to deter Soviet aggression was made possible by economising on defence expenditure, thereby husbanding America's greatest asset, its economic strength:

> To maintain weapons irrelevant to the threat at hand – and Eisenhower put excess missile capacity in this category ... was to expend limited resources carelessly, with the result that the nation in the end would be unable to afford what really was necessary.[76]

Dulles's massive retaliation speech acted as a stimulant for American civilian strategists to examine the administration's policy, and to analyse its contradictions. Their analyses tended to be more political than military in nature, and this partly explains their interest in Clausewitz. However, their penchant for quantitative analysis arose from their belief that they could calculate the "correct" answers to the questions posed by war and peace. Thus, while these analysts were respectful of Clausewitz, their writings betrayed a faith in a more Jominian tradition. Herman Kahn, whose *On Thermonuclear War* has a Clausewitzian-sounding title, conceived his ideas in a rather surrealistic mode. His thinking rested upon maintaining the will (as important as the capacity) to visit complete annihilation on those residing in the enemy homeland. We can only speculate as to whether or not Clausewitz ever envisaged there being no distinction between military and civilian targets. In a similar vein, these theorists no longer distinguished between diplomacy and war-making, something that Clausewitz would have counselled against.[77]

More rational strategic theorists, including Kissinger, Brodie and Robert Osgood, arrived at a consensus over the need to limit war.[78] Using the elements of "Clausewitz *that they wanted to find* in *On War*", theorists found the recognition that war can be waged at all levels of intensity to be useful in developing a framework to deal with an unprecedented strategic situation.[79] Given the impossibility of fighting an all-out war, it was advocated that reliance should no longer be placed on nuclear weapons, given the inbuilt dangers of escalation. Unfortunately, partly because of the problem in reconciling the need to limit war with the need to maintain a necessary degree of resolve, the Vietnam War was to prove that the United States had failed to address this conundrum properly.

The advent of Intercontinental Ballistic Missiles (ICBMs) and the entry of West Germany into NATO signalled the end not only of massive retaliation but also of any notions that the American military had of using tactical nuclear weapons to drive back a Soviet advance into West Germany. Instead, a new concept, that of flexible response, began to find favour with American strategic theorists. This incorporated a policy of forward defence, whereby the inner-German border would be defended rather than sacrificing space for time. If the almost exclusive use of conventional forces proved futile, then NATO would be forced to pursue a policy of gradual escalation to nuclear use.

The originator of the term "flexible response" was Maxwell Taylor whose interpretation of it in his 1955 paper, "A National Military Program", was different to that outlined above. He believed that the West should use all the means at its disposal – diplomatic, economic, political and military – to contain communism around the globe. The military aspect entailed the use of conventional weapons and the avoidance of all-out war, if at all possible. As Taylor put it in 1960:

[I]t is just as necessary to deter or win quickly a limited war as to deter general war. Otherwise, the limited war which we cannot win quickly may result in our piecemeal attrition or involvement in an expanding conflict which may grow into the general war we all want to avoid.[80]

When John F. Kennedy became president in 1961, he absorbed Taylor's ideas with enthusiasm and made him chairman of the JCS in October 1962. It was to be a fatal decision. Taylor's ideas reinforced the change in American strategy that had resulted in Korea. The United States no longer had the belief that it could fight and win a limited war in Asia, regardless of Chinese intervention. Rather, it approached the question from the standpoint of conducting a damage-limitation exercise whereby communist influence would be contained within its present bounds. The shortcomings of flexible response were compounded by Secretary of Defense Robert S. McNamara's approach to strategy making. He brought with him the techniques that had served him so well as president of Ford Motors. While his concept of a Planning, Programming and Budgetary System (PPBS) was sound in the sense of preparing logistically for war, it was disastrous when applied to its actual conduct. Economists and accountants were incapable of answering questions of military strategy, which is based more on intangibles, instinct and friction than it is on rationalistic systems analysis. Thus, while improved capabilities of strategic lift and analyses of different weapon systems ensured that America had the means at hand to wage war, there was no reciprocal improvement in America's ability to succeed in achieving its strategic ends. Indeed, the new mentality had the opposite effect.

During the month before Kennedy came to power (December 1960), the Joint Strategic Target Planning Staff (JSTPS), directed by the commander of the Strategic Air Command (SAC), completed its investigation of what would constitute a minimum adequate deterrence and retaliatory capability for the United States. Its conclusion resulted in the Single Integrated Operational Plan-62 (SIOP-62) to enter force in July 1961. It was designed as both a retaliatory and a pre-emptive option. It also provided proof that the United States had the potential to obliterate the military capability and the population of vast tracts of the Sino-Soviet bloc within a matter of hours:

> SIOP-62 incorporated operational choices that aimed to reduce the friction of war, coordinate and protect bomber forces, and integrate bomber and missile forces at the cusp of two eras in warfare. It was an American Schlieffen Plan, an ultimate strategy for war winning under all circumstances of war initiation, with an even less tenable basis in political and military realities than the German plan, infamous for its inflexibility, executed in 1914.[81]

Although, in March 1961, Kennedy stated that the United States would not "strike first", he sent no such instructions to the Pentagon. One should also note Lawrence Freedman's assertion that Kennedy did not act in accordance with the rationale behind flexible response during the Cuban Missile Crisis when he denied the Soviets a counterforce option by dispersing US military aircraft to civilian airfields and threatened a "full retaliatory strike". This contradiction can be explained by the threat that a Soviet nuclear presence in Cuba posed to the US homeland. Interestingly, the one other area of tension during the early 1960s, Berlin, was the only part of NATO that could not be defended by conventional means.[82]

McNamara had little faith in a first strike counter-force, preferring instead the concept of "assured destruction" through a secure second-strike capability, a concept better known as Mutual Assured Destruction (MAD). He was concerned with finite deterrence, which would ensure that the nuclear threshold was not passed, and he consequently failed to give much thought to what would happen if it was. SIOP-62 convinced McNamara of the difficulties in revising existing war plans, although he did investigate the possibilities of a "no cities" counter-force approach whereby "only" 20 to 25 per cent of the population in large cities would be destroyed. In other words, he was forced to accept the existing state of affairs. The guidance issued with SIOP-5 in 1974–75 emphasised the need to target urban-industrial areas first. SIOP-5, drawn up by Secretary of Defense James Schlesinger, concentrated on limited nuclear options. The SIOPs are interesting in a Clausewitzian context in that he did not believe in military planning *per se*. Planning resulted from the political aims of the war, and in this respect one cannot but agree with Rosenberg that the SIOPs resembled the Schlieffen Plan in that military planning was the "tyrant" that Clausewitz denied the political aim was.[83]

The main threat to MAD came from anti-ballistic missiles (ABMs), and both the United States and the Soviet Union started to develop the necessary technology for these in the late 1960s. Once again in history, the offensive–defensive paradigm was being resurrected. President Nixon supported the ABM programme, including multiple independently targeted re-entry vehicles (MIRVs), as a bargaining chip in the Strategic Arms Limitation Treaty (SALT) talks with the Soviet Union, while the latter had already abandoned efforts to deploy first-generation ABMs by exploring the possibility of constructing more advanced systems to counter American advances in this field. Arms control also became a vehicle to allow each side to draw back from the dangers imposed by relying on MAD.

The balance of terror that existed led some to question Clausewitz's relevance. In 1974, Senator William Fulbright declared that "there is no longer any validity in the Clausewitzian doctrine of war as a 'carrying out of policy by other means'. Nuclear weapons have rendered it totally obsolete because the instrument of policy is now fully disproportionate to the end in view."[84]

Yet only the previous year, the Americans responded to the Arab–Israeli conflict by raising the alert status of their strategic forces to deter the Soviets from directly aiding Egypt, a utilisation of the political value of nuclear weapons in a truly Clausewitzian manner. It was a case of nuclear diplomacy that left something to chance. Freedman has best summed up American nuclear strategy in the Cold War era as "one of those areas where a policy has worked far better in practice than an assessment of ... theory might lead one to expect".[85]

Conclusion

Robert Kagan has recently described the way in which American and European approaches to strategy have diverged during the two centuries since the United States came into existence:

When the US was weak, it practised the strategies of indirection, the strategies of weakness; now that the US is powerful, it behaves as powerful nations do. When the European great powers were strong, they believed in strength and martial glory. Now, they see the world through the eyes of weaker powers.[86]

During the first century of the republic's existence, US foreign-policy reflected the weakness of the nation's position in international relations. With the exception of the Civil War, American experience in war tended to be restricted to limited conflicts, particularly "small wars" in its sphere of influence in the Western Hemisphere. With its entry into the First World War, American strategy was confronted for the first time with the problems of conducting large-scale warfare in the European theatre. Latterly, and in particular since 1945, American power has enabled the nation to pursue an assertive foreign policy, not only in defending its own national interests but also in defending those of the West in general.

This historical experience also shows that the American way of war has more often than not been focused on narrow operational concerns at the expense of wider strategic objectives. This is partly as a result of a Jominian tradition and a consequent focus on achieving tactical excellence. Although the dissemination of Clausewitz among the US military has increased over time, an understanding of his articulation of war as being a continuation of policy has been overlooked because of the stark division between the responsibilities of US military and civilian policymakers. A more integrated approach to strategy making therefore remains elusive to this day.

3 The legacy of Vietnam

Counter-insurgency theory

The debate surrounding the Vietnam debacle has, not surprisingly, been rather intense. It is important to avoid believing that it is polarised between one side and another. Rather, differences of opinion tend to be of degree rather than substance. On the one hand, John Shy and Thomas Collier have argued that American strategic theory as applied to the war was:

> [S]hallow, lacking either the fusion of mysticism and rationalism of *guerre revolutionnaire*, or the phlegmatic pragmatism of British civil-military co-ordination. It was almost a purely military approach, like the Normandy landings or the liberation of Luzon in 1944, targeted on an enemy presumed to be the mirror image of American combat units, the peasants waiting passively for the blessings attendant on American liberation.[1]

Colonel Harry G. Summers, on the other hand, has argued that the Americans completely ignored the roots of strategy. His seminal *On Strategy*, notable for its use of Clausewitzian concepts, first appeared as a monograph at the Strategic Studies Institute at the Army War College in 1981, and remained at the top of the Army chief-of-staff's reading list until 2004. Summers believed that the United States could have succeeded in Vietnam if only it had had a clear idea of its objective before deciding to intervene. The Americans committed the cardinal sin of failing to see how they could use military means to achieve a political end. They thus failed to address the question posed by Robert Osgood in the late 1950s: "[The] problem is this: How can the US utilise its military power as a rational and effective instrument of national policy?"[2]

Andrew Krepinevich, in *The Army and Vietnam* (1986), has interpreted the war as being primarily a Southern-based insurgency that the Americans should have countered through emphasising intelligence, policing, and night operations. Such an approach would have dispensed with the need for attrition, given the requirement to nullify the enemy's infrastructure rather than his physical forces. Summers, however, argues that the Viet Cong's effort was dependent upon the North's ability to wage conventional warfare and to supply the insurgents via

Laos and Cambodia. He emphasises that the United States should have concentrated on conventional warfare, an argument supported by Colonel Rod Paschall:

> [P]acification [was not] an alternative to the "big unit war". There *was* no alternative. To ignore the Viet Cong 9th Division in '64 and '65 was to risk certain defeat in detail of ARVN [the Army of South Vietnam]. The "big unit war" was not an American idea ... [It] was purely Vietnamese and was well underway prior to the introduction of US combat troops.[3]

Jeffrey Record argues that the theses of Krepinevich and Summers have merit – up to a point. Krepinevich is right about the insurgent nature of the conflict – until the Tet Offensive of 1968 – while Summers is correct post-Tet. Where both men fall down is in their assumption that the Military Assistance Command Vietnam (MACV) could have concentrated on one or other of counterinsurgency (CI) and conventional warfare. Rather, it was the communists who had the necessary flexibility to use both methods successfully. General William E. DePuy, who served as operations officer between 1964 and 1966 to the theatre commander, General William Westmoreland, tends to reflect Record's view:

> [P]eople back in the US still thought of war in terms of lines, and concluded that if the enemy could get into Saigon, then we were losing ... Eventually, however, historians will write about the Vietnam War and say, "The kind of things we were doing in Vietnam before Tet were right for that kind of war. But it would have taken a very long time."
>
> The other way to have won the war was General LeMay's concept – "Bomb North Vietnam back into the stone age." In retrospect, his solution was more American than the sophisticated CI efforts which couldn't finish the job within the tolerance of the American people and their political leaders.[4]

Captain Matthew Collins, USMC, and Conrad Crane have both taken issue with Summers, arguing that despite its professed drawing on the writings of Clausewitz, *On Strategy* was more Jominian in its approach, particularly through being structured on the principles of war. Collins has concluded that "Summers introduced Clausewitz to back into a Jominian argument".[5] Crane accuses Summers of oversimplifying the strategy of the Vietnamese communists to support his argument that the Americans should have pursued a more conventional approach, something that has since contributed to an aversion to low-intensity conflict among the military with unfortunate consequences. Crane also comments that H. R. McMaster's *Dereliction of Duty*, with its critique of the military's failure to challenge the civilian leadership, had superseded Summers as an influential tract on the Vietnam War among American officers by the end of the 1990s.[6]

Finally, at this point, it is worth citing Lieutenant-Colonel William Staudenmaier's criticism of those who argue that the United States could take some comfort from its "victory" at the tactical level during the conflict. "To talk of a military victory and political defeat [in Vietnam] is not only a contradiction in Clausewitzian terms, but it is also a failure to grasp the whole point of the painful experience."[7]

In 1954, the Eisenhower Administration had decided that America should not intervene directly in Indo-China on France's behalf against the Viet Minh. However, this decision was never translated into policy, and the Americans inexorably slid further into involvement in the region. The slow nature of this process inevitably led to half measures, providing an unfortunate precedent for the Vietnam War itself. As the survival of South Vietnam remained low among American strategic priorities until the early 1960s, those American advisers who were sent to the theatre tended to be of low calibre, recruited from the ranks of the military and civilian bureaucracies. This affected their influence to pursue a coherent policy. Even as the situation deteriorated further under President Kennedy, the Americans did not deviate from this approach, which was further exacerbated by a policy decision that had its origins in the 1961 Geneva conference on Laos. Trusting that the Soviets would respect Laotian neutrality, Kennedy approved only internal support for South Vietnam. This meant that CI was given strategic precedence by the Americans and that the North Vietnamese could use Laos as the fulcrum of their logistical system to supply the insurgency in the South. Furthermore, America's fear of becoming involved in a land war in Asia because of the possibility of Chinese intervention ensured that it was in "an untenable strategic position where the enemy's territory was inviolable while the territory of our ally was open to attack".[8]

While Eisenhower had viewed the Vietnam conflict in conventional terms, as being between North and South Vietnam, Kennedy interpreted Viet Cong attacks in the South as being an insurgency, which could be met by encouraging the South to engage in "nation-building" with American aid. However, while this may have worked in post-war Europe, it was futile to believe that it could work among the nations of South-East Asia, which were far too immature for such a process, not to mention impervious to importing Western values.

Kennedy was also hampered by his belief that nuclear parity now existed between the superpowers, therefore making general war an impossibility. He believed that the communists had arrived at the same conclusion by adopting their doctrine of "wars of national liberation". It was also assumed that the administration's conventional build-up within the context of flexible response would prevent the communists from waging conventional war as they had in Korea. Therefore, the only means left to the communists was guerrilla warfare, resistance to which would now be the litmus test of the policy of containment. In 1961, Kennedy declared that "the basic problems facing the world today are not susceptible to a military solution".[9]

The military had found itself in a quandary after the Korean War. The 1954 *Field Service Regulations* (FSR) introduced "wars of limited objective", and declared "victory alone as an aim in war cannot be justified, since in itself victory does not always assure the realisation of national objectives".[10] While this apparent paradox is correct in the context of countering insurgency, it did not provide a solution to negate what was essentially a conventional effort by North Vietnam. The 1962 FSR compounded the problem by erasing the line between war and peace by stating that there was no distinction between cold war and limited war. This, as Summers contends, led the Americans into not declaring war over Vietnam at the outset, thereby failing to elicit the support of the American people.

Doctrinal shortcomings were compounded by the administration's policies. Its emphasis on CI was so all-embracing that Kennedy was able to make it plain that the future promotion of high-ranking officers would depend upon their expertise in this area. A number of officer courses were introduced on CI, and Kennedy even went as far as to insist on the creation of "guerrilla warfare libraries". General Maxwell Taylor was given the task of handling the CI initiative through a Special Interdepartmental Group (CI). Publications such as *ARMY* were encouraged to spread the CI gospel and, in the end, it became an accepted part of *conventional* army doctrine thereby ossifying strategic theory for the next decade.[11] Journal articles tended to focus on micro-policy in that they concentrated on a particular branch's role in CI or else attempted to show how minor alterations to conventional doctrine would allow for successful operations against guerrillas. Traditional methods of closing with and destroying the enemy remained the focal point of tactical doctrine and foreshadowed search-and-destroy tactics in Vietnam.

The ambiguous development of doctrine in the early 1960s occurred because, in truth, the army distrusted any notion of special forces, particularly where close co-operation with the CIA was concerned, even though some success was achieved in counterguerrilla operations in 1962 and 1963. Once the specialist Green Berets came under the control of MACV, it was quickly given a conventional mission in support of the Army. Indeed, the proportion of special to regular forces was never to rise above 10 per cent throughout the time of the American involvement in Vietnam.[12]

The Army's main concern at this time was with eliminating the Pentomic division structure of the massive retaliation era by creating Reorganisation Objectives Army Division (ROAD) units designed for general war in Europe in line with flexible response. These were "a common division base for all division types, combined with brigades as tactical headquarters commanding flexible mixes of maneuver battalion types".[13] They would remain standard, with changes, for 20 years. Furthermore, in 1962 a committee formed by Defense Secretary Robert S. McNamara, and chaired by Lieutenant-General Hamilton Howze, proposed that the Army should deploy several air-assault divisions equipped with helicopters. However, despite the increase in helicopter operations in Vietnam during this period, the 11th Air Assault Division focused almost exclusively on increasing mobility and supplementing the Air Force's tactical air support operations in a conventional war in Europe.

When all of this was coupled with the McNamara school's notion that the advanced nostrums of social science could be successfully applied to military strategy, the effects were pernicious. Douglas Blaufarb, a former CIA analyst, remarked that:

> there was a period in the 1960s when military intellectuals were advancing the notion that the US Army was the arm of government best equipped to carry out in the field the entire range of activities associated with nation building.[14]

It can therefore be seen that the stereotype of the "mass firepower" doctrine as being responsible for the American defeat in Vietnam is too simplistic. The Americans fell between the two stools of overwhelming force and the subtlety required in low-intensity conflict.

In February 1963, Army chief-of-staff, General Earl Wheeler, submitted a report to Maxwell Taylor – and briefed Kennedy – on the need to expand raids and sabotage missions against North Vietnam. However, it failed to give a clear guide as to who should take responsibility for this. The Joint Chiefs-of-Staff (JCS) directed Pacific Command to produce a plan (OPLAN 34A), which President Johnson subsequently approved in January 1964; but the military failed to show any enthusiasm for it. Indeed, its originators saw it as a supporting command to MACV. This ensured that the organisation's chief was of subordinate rank.

America's intelligence effort in Vietnam was hampered from the beginning. In 1962, acting on Taylor's suggestion, MACV attempted to establish a Joint Evaluation Centre in Saigon to be manned by military, CIA, and Embassy intelligence staff. However, this was abandoned because of the jurisdictional difficulties involved. Therefore, the Americans failed to grasp the nature of the conflict in the South and implemented a response through CI that was inappropriate. The lack of intelligence co-ordination was illustrated when Kennedy received contradictory reports at an NSC meeting of 6 September 1963. General Victor Krulak, a CI expert, reported that the South Vietnamese president, Diem, required more American support. On the other hand, Joseph Mendenhall of the State Department reported that the South Vietnamese people hated Diem and that his presence was an obstacle to victory in the battle for "hearts and minds". Not surprisingly, Kennedy enquired if both had been to the same country.[15]

People's war

Clausewitz was the first strategic theorist to study the phenomenon of people's war seriously. Not only did he argue that "any nation that uses it [people's war] intelligently will, as a rule, gain some superiority over those who disdain its use", Clausewitz also recognised that the support of at least some sections of the regular army was essential to success.[16] This came to pass in the case of the National Liberation Front (NLF) or Viet Cong whose campaign was aided by the People's Army of North Vietnam (PAVN). The NLF named its paramilitary forces "Dan Quan" ("civilian soldiers"), which indicated that the United States was not fighting a guerrilla insurgency but rather the whole Vietnamese nation. This had the added advantage of placing the onus of indiscriminate warfare, which is always a danger in CI operations, on the Americans.

Linked to the need to draw a distinction between regulars and irregulars, the Americans faced another problem in that they needed to be prepared to fight over a long period of time if necessary. The longer a conflict continues, the less likely it is that the CI effort can be maintained at the same rate, given that the insurgents are likely to be more committed to their cause. While superior fire-power works well in a purely conventional war, where guerrilla action is involved control of territory is less important than safeguarding the security of the population. The use of technology capable of bypassing large swathes of enemy territory leaves behind a vacuum willingly filled by lightly armed guerril-las behind the lines. Thus geography – which has always been central to stra-tegic thought – is not a firm guide, given that guerrillas can ignore it.

Ironically, the Vietnamese, despite their "Eastern" notions of deception and diversion, showed more awareness than the Americans of Clausewitz's thought, even if they absorbed this second hand from the Chinese communists. Townsend says:

> While nearly repetitive of Clausewitz in areas of philosophy and strategy, Mao's and [Vo Nguyen] Giap's works go on to lay down specific tactical guidelines and give solutions to particular problems. Giap explains that he has developed a natural extension of Marxist-Leninist military doctrine for use in Vietnam. If one assumes that Clausewitz's theories of warfare are correct, the final outcome in Vietnam was not surprising.[17]

On the other hand, the Vietnamese strategy of encirclement from within and without contrasted sharply with Western theories of encirclement made famous by Alfred von Schlieffen. Taking Maoism as the doctrinal basis for his party's code of warfare, Truong Chinh, the Vietnamese Communist Party Secretary, outlined the Vietnamese version of people's war in a tract called *The Resistance Will Win* (1947). It included a variation on the third and final stage of Mao's people's war, the General Offensive/General Uprising, where the people's revo-lutionary zeal is unleashed with sudden attacks on the cities. On the other hand, the Vietnamese realised that the first Indo-China War had not been won in the cities. Rather, it ended when the people and government of France had been per-suaded by events at Dien Bien Phu that they could not win. The Vietnamese interpreted this as a "decisive victory" that had resulted as much from psycho-logical and diplomatic success as it had from a military triumph. The Americans completely ignored the findings of the French inquiry into their defeat in Indo-China in the mid-1950s, a report made available to them by the French govern-ment in 1964.[18]

The dual notions of the "General Uprising" and the "Decisive Victory" became the centrepieces of Vietnamese communist military theory. Although their definition would not be instantly recognised in the West, they do carry some Clausewitzian resonance because the armed struggle took place in tandem with a political struggle. The Vietnamese communists decided to follow a protracted people's war against the South, a decision confirmed by their observation of the American military advisers with the ARVN. The Americans were generally disappointed with the lack of aggression shown by the South Vietnamese, an attitude that betrayed American impatience and that contrasted with the Northerner's willingness to sacrifice himself to his cause. Thus while the North hoped to avoid an American escalation, it covertly escalated the war in the South under the cover of the "neutralist" NLF. If the Americans were to intervene, the North Vietnamese were determined to increase the role of their guerrilla proxies in the South so as to dissipate American firepower.

The North Vietnamese were not monolithic in that they debated the merits of these two approaches. This debate was further complicated by the Sino-Soviet split. The Soviets wanted to see a negotiated settlement take place, while the Chinese advocated a protracted conflict strategy. While the Vietnamese hoped to avoid a confrontation with American combat forces, the Americans themselves failed to exploit the rifts in the centres of gravity of the enemy's political leadership and the enemy's allies.

The build-up, 1964–66

The Americans were put at an immediate disadvantage when the administration did not ask Congress to declare war on the North Vietnamese after the incident in which it was believed that two US destroyers were attacked by North Vietnamese patrol boats in the Gulf of Tonkin in August 1964. Instead, a resolution was passed by Congress that basically gave Johnson a green light to retaliate for this action.[19] In the end, it turned out to be an open-ended commitment leading to a conflict lasting almost a decade. In mitigation of Johnson, it should be said that his actions were similar to those of Roosevelt as he moved the United States toward involvement in the Second World War. Moreover, it was impossible to foresee the extent to which American involvement would grow, given the belief that air power and the limited use of US troops would force the North Vietnamese to halt their campaign. However, this surrendering of Congressional power isolated the American people – who were generally enthusiastic about American involvement at the time – from having any say in the conduct of the American commitment.[20]

By the time that it became obvious that the American build-up was irreversible, Johnson decided not to go back to Congress to request a declaration of war. Operationally, this would have allowed for a call-up of the reserves, which would have enabled the military to adopt a more sensible approach to dealing with North Vietnamese aggression rather than attempting to fight a "brush-fire war" against the insurgency in the South. The Americans swallowed communist propaganda about a "people's war" and this compounded their problem by making it more difficult for the counter-insurgent to clarify, for its own people, the identity of the enemy. As the Clausewitzian trinity implied, committing the military without the people's support was foolhardy. "Steeped in the legalistic concept that wars are between states, the American people became confused by its government's failure to declare war on North Vietnam and thereby identify the *state* with which the US was at war..."[21]

Without the commitment of the American people, it was difficult to see how the American military could successfully execute a prolonged campaign in Vietnam. This was exacerbated by a lack of purpose. Within the administration there were disputes as to the extent to which the Americans should commit themselves. Acting Secretary of State William Bundy, acting on behalf of the JCS, believed that 40,000 troops had a chance of "*arresting* things",[22] a policy that would have done nothing to solve the long-term Vietnamese problem and, indeed, would have undermined the faith of America's allies elsewhere in its ability to come to their aid. It showed no appreciation of the determination of the North Vietnamese to triumph, and no knowledge of the lessons of the prolonged campaign that drove out the French.

Victory, on the other hand, would require 205,000 troops according to McNamara and the JCS, particularly if Hanoi and Peking were active in supporting the NLF. Not only does this illustrate McNamara's tendency to overanalyse matters by "playing for percentages", but it also failed to see the problem as being anything beyond that of an insurgency within South Vietnam. The Americans had to decide whether their objective was victory through a total commitment or the abandonment of South Vietnam to defend itself. The latter course would have sent the wrong signal, not only to the Europeans but also to those other American allies, such as South Korea and Israel, who felt threatened by potential aggression. Unfortunately, the Americans did not pursue the former course either. Instead, a process of gradual escalation took place that, at its peak in 1968, sucked in 500,000 men.

> Each limited commitment involved the danger of being interpreted as inhibition rather than resolve, thereby encouraging the adversary to continue his climb along the ladder of escalation; time enough to settle, he might reason, when and if the risk in fact became intolerable.[23]

The Americans made a tactical error by colluding in the overthrow of President Diem, a course of action that undermined the legitimacy of the South Vietnamese state. This was apparent when the populace failed to rally behind the competing generals who made up the junta that replaced him. It was compounded by an absence from American strategy of a Clausewitzian understanding of the relationship between war and politics. Too much responsibility was left in the lap of Westmoreland, who was held in low regard by his superiors. At the higher level of strategy making, McNamara and the JCS failed to provide any overall guidelines. The belief that the enemy could be worn down and blasted into submission by the deployment of superior technology was revealed to be devoid of all logic. Other problems arose from Kennedy's restructuring of the NSC, which became a fragmented body with policy decisions being left to the discretion of the president and a small team of advisers who failed to take a long-term view. Moreover, the military command structure was inappropriate. MACV was responsible to the commander-in-chief Pacific Command (CINCPAC) in Honolulu, 5,000 miles away, not to the JCS in Washington. Westmoreland later recognised the folly of this set-up:

> The White House seldom dealt directly with me but through the JCS ... What many failed to realise was that not I but [Admiral U. S. Grant Sharp, CINCPAC] was the theater commander in the sense that General Eisenhower, for example, was the theater commander in the Second World War. My responsibilities and prerogatives were basically confined within the borders of South Vietnam.[24]

As Summers says, the Americans failed to distinguish between what Clausewitz called "preparation for war" and "war proper".[25] Washington's dead hand stifled the effort at the front. Strict rules of engagement were enforced upon the air offensive, for example, so as to avoid attacking surface-to-air missile (SAM) sites under construction – and even enemy airfields – in case Soviet and Chinese advisers were killed. As far as the naval war was concerned, it hardly deserves such an appellation. The US Navy was forbidden by its government to blockade North Vietnam until 1972. Instead, it had to focus on conducting so-called "brown water" operations along the coastal and inland waters of South Vietnam, a role for which its Mahanian roots left it unprepared.

Major Charles D. McFetridge has noted that even individual bombing targets and minor tactical matters were discussed at presidential level during the conflict. He cites Clausewitz as proof that such interference is unwarranted at the tactical level: "Policy, of course, will not extend its influence to operational details. Political considerations do not determine the posting of guards or the employment of patrols."[26]

But MACV itself was not without blame. Westmoreland drew up elaborate rules regarding tactical air strikes, artillery, and ground fire that were issued to newly arrived troops and updated every six months. Furthermore, there was a lack of consistency between CIA and MACV intelligence assessments. These disputes hindered American thinking about the numbers of men required to tackle the situation, and also as to whether or not Laos and Cambodia were significant in keeping the revolution alive through the supply lines emanating from there.

When American combat units were despatched to Vietnam in 1965, Westmoreland immediately assigned them to the CI effort that had already been going on for several years under American auspices. Yet, he still possessed a conventional mindset that somehow managed to apply the notion of quantitative analysis to the conflict. The Army force planners in Washington and Saigon reckoned on obtaining a 3:1 advantage in manoeuvre battalions to achieve success in conventional war. MACV, with 44 battalions, found itself with a 3.2:1 advantage. By determining force requirements by the measure of battalions, however, the Americans omitted 100,000 NLF irregulars from the equation. They also ignored the fact that in an insurgency, an advantage of 10–15:1, not 3:1, is required.[27]

Westmoreland positioned the units least well organised for defensive operations – the 1st and 3rd US Marine Divisions – along the demilitarised zone (DMZ) opposite the North Vietnamese. Even though they stabilised the situation through gathering intelligence that severely diminished the NLF's freedom to operate, the US Army and Marines, with their Combined Action Platoons, continued to undertake "search-and-destroy" operations as part of the CI campaign. This owed much to the communists' ability to dictate events. The Ia Drang Valley campaign at the end of 1965 had seen two PAVN divisions being defeated by the 1st Cavalry Division (Airborne). Learning their lesson, the communists resorted to guerrilla operations, knowing that the US Army could not be the centre of gravity of their effort. This in turn forced Westmoreland to adopt an attrition strategy, the object of which was to bleed the enemy white, an object that tailored neatly with search and destroy. These operations ignored the fact that the enemy were able to hide among the indigenous population. Westmoreland's strategy also allowed the communists to turn their attention to a different centre of gravity, the alliance between the United States and South Vietnam, echoing Clausewitz's words concerning "the community of interest [between allies] and in popular uprisings between the personalities of the leaders and public opinion".[28]

Tactical successes were enjoyed by the Americans, but these made no impact on the overall strategic situation. The South Vietnamese themselves were reduced by CI to a passive defensive, thus playing into the North's hands by allowing them to continue to infiltrate the South. Sir Robert Thompson, the architect of Britain's successful CI strategy in Malaya, wrote in 1970 that the United States should have taken a supporting role in the South's CI effort. He also castigated US doctrine and, by implication, its misuse of Clausewitz:

> With regard to military strategy, Americans seem to have been influenced only by the *very worst* of Clausewitz's doctrine and by the Prussian example of Moltke, so that the sole aim of most American orthodox military commanders has always been the destruction of the enemy's main forces on the battlefield.[29]

The Americans organised the ARVN along familiar lines so that it could ape them in their emphasis on attrition. Moreover, the attempt to oppose the insurgency in the South by engaging in "nation-building" was doomed to long-term failure. McNamara, rapidly losing touch with reality, was quoted as saying in 1965 that "the greatest contribution Vietnam is making – right or wrong is beside the point – is that it is developing an ability in the US to fight a limited war, to go to war without arising the public ire".[30]

The most perceptive observers of American failings at this early stage were their enemy. While General Thanh, the leader of the revolutionaries in the

South, acknowledged the problems that American intervention posed for his side, he was confident in the knowledge that the Americans were

> tall but stupid ... why is it that in [the South] throughout the last dry season, although the Americans had nearly six divisions and a very strong air force, they could not annihilate one company of the liberation armed forces; and why is it, on the contrary, that tens of US battalions were completely annihilated by the liberation armed forces? How could that be?
>
> If one merely counted the number of men and weapons of a US division, one would not be able to evaluate its combat capability correctly, unless one made such an evaluation for parade purposes. Fighting is a different thing.[31]

Thanh's evidence contradicts Summers and concurs with the testimony of General Bernard Trainor, USMC:

> Those who actually fought at the squad, platoon, and company level know [Summers's explanation in *On Strategy*] is largely myth. Far too often, VC and regulars of the NVA savaged American units in battle before withdrawing and leaving Americans in command of a battlefield strewn with their own dead.[32]

At the time of the successes in the Ia Drang Valley (November 1965), the United States could have taken the strategic offensive, given the enemy's discomfiture. Unfortunately, American strategy called for containment of the insurgency, and any invasion of the North was ruled out because of the fear of Chinese intervention. The fears of a repeat of Korea paralysed American strategy making in Vietnam, while the obsession with countering the guerrillas in the South meant that the Americans failed to even take the tactical offensive to isolate the battlefield and destroy the PAVN units infiltrating the area from the North. In April 1967, Westmoreland asked for at least a limited reserve call-up so as to undertake a drive across the DMZ into Laos and Cambodia. Johnson refused. By January 1968, when MACV planned to construct a "strong point obstacle system" in the border areas in preparation for Operation York, an invasion of North Vietnam and Laos, the initiative had passed to the communists to the extent that the Americans were forced to abandon it in the face of the Tet offensive.

Stalemate, 1966–67

Although American military advisers had been operating with the South Vietnamese military for several years, Westmoreland showed little interest in reforming his ally's military organisation. While MACV concentrated on search-and-destroy operations, it actively discouraged any role that the Army might be able to play in the winning of "hearts and minds" in the countryside, a prerequisite of Clausewitz's remedy to counter "people's war". Large tracts of the countryside were cleared so as to deny the communists the support of the population. The locals were then placed in the hands of a civilian government that had no facilities or resources to resettle them. Free-fire zones were created to allow American artillery and aircraft to destroy the deserted landscape. This tactic was a manifestation of the delusion that massive firepower would deliver victory. Reliance on the helicopter may have increased mobility, but it did not solve the problem of overcoming the "invisible" enemy. The solution lay as much in the political and social realms as the military. Any initiatives towards this end, such as a campaign by marine commanders to undertake a small-unit, civil-action operation to protect the population in their region, were severely restricted.[33]

As Major-General John Kiszely, British Army, remarks, Westmoreland resembled the Imperial German general, Falkenhayn, at Verdun in 1916, in his belief in pounding the enemy until he no longer existed. This was a *modus operandi* that had been exorcised from European strategic thought after the First World War. "We'll just go on bleeding them until Hanoi wakes up to the fact that they have bled their country to the point of natural disaster for generations."[34]

Operation *Rolling Thunder* (March 1965–November 1968) was an independent air campaign to interdict the movement of the North Vietnamese into the South; but it was flawed in that it was one-dimensional:

> Those who see battlefield success as a matter of enemy dead [admittedly, some of them are interpreters of Clausewitz] tend to view Rolling Thunder as moderately successful. But ... it was [actually] a total failure – the more so because it wasted resources (ammunition, time, and national will) without achieving an operational pay-off.[35]

Rolling Thunder also highlighted the discrepancies between CIA and Defense Intelligence Agency (DIA) assessments of the war. The DIA's contention that 657 bridges had been destroyed in the five years that air campaigns had been waged in Vietnam was based on pilot claims. The CIA used more reliable means of assessment and came up with the number of 216. By contrast, the later operation known as "Linebacker I" (March–October 1972) was more effective in that the air offensive was combined with ground manoeuvre. It succeeded in slowing down a rapid North Vietnamese offensive, and gave the South Vietnamese military time to organise an effective defence.[36]

From 1965 to the end of 1967, the communists were able to revert to guerrilla operations while refusing to engage in any risky conventional warfare, although this approach was not eschewed altogether. As Lieutenant-General Nguyen Van Vinh remarked to Southern leaders in April 1966:

> We will not do what Algeria has done (long people's war), and we will not do what Korea did in using armed troops to liberate the South Koreans (large conventional unit tactics). We will not do what the Soviet Union did

in the war against Germany (combine the use of conventional units with an overwhelming partisan or people's war).[37]

By 1967, the guerrillas in the South had resorted to using large units to deliver sudden attacks before disappearing. The inevitable massive response was then met by guerrilla action, which harassed the Americans and kept them off balance. However, on the whole, the communists had realised post-Ia Drang Valley that to mass was to invite destruction. Guerrilla tactics, on the other hand, allowed them to pursue protracted war and hence to demoralise American opinion. Krepinevich notes that battalion-sized attacks by the NLF and PAVN decreased from 9.7 in the last quarter of 1965 to 1.3 a year later.[38] Meanwhile, the number of small-unit attacks increased by 150 per cent during the same period. Even more revealingly, MACV noted that the communists were instigating 88 per cent of all actions. Despite this, Westmoreland plunged into yet more large-scale operations such as Operation "Junction City", an attack into War Zone C's communist sanctuary during February 1967, where he noted that it was the first occasion on which he employed all of the different types of combat forces at his disposal, including large armoured and mechanised units, and even paratroopers.

The creation of CORDS (Civil Operations and Revolutionary Development Support) in May 1967 to advise the South Vietnamese military, police, and civil service was the largest attempt to date by the Americans to make some semblance of progress towards countering the insurgency. Although it had some short-term successes, the Vietnamese themselves had become so used to allowing the Americans to take the initiative in everything that, when the time came for them to exert some control, they could not.

The quantitative analyses beloved of the leadership in Washington were having a pernicious effect in two ways. On the front line, the absurdity of using body counts is illustrated by an incident involving the 1st Infantry Division that has been recounted by James Kitfield:

> While he was surveying the horrifying scene, a senior officer came up and told [Major Jack] Galvin to add 45 dead VC to his count. When asked from where, the man distractedly indicated an area that Galvin had already counted.[39]

Second, at home, there had been a loss of enthusiasm among the American people by late 1967. The Clausewitzian centre of gravity, public opinion, was being brilliantly exploited by the communists. A secret cable from Admiral Sharp, CINCPAC, to General Wheeler, chief of the JCS, in August 1967 demonstrated American nervousness about this:

> I am ... most concerned with the general attitude of the public regarding the progress of the war ... In my opinion, we have trapped ourselves because of our obsession to quantify everything. If you can't put a number on it, it isn't worth talking about.[40]

The Vietnamese communists continued to fight, willing to acknowledge American feelers for negotiations until such time as they could negotiate and fight simultaneously. This would be when stalemate was achieved. In the meantime, extending the people's war in the South would maintain Chinese support. It was obvious that this would not extend to intervention. The North Vietnamese would have to rely on themselves. Realising that the Americans wanted to maintain a democratic government in South Vietnam, although not at any price, Ho Chi Minh decided to implement a strategy on two fronts. By calling for a legitimate Southern "coalition" government, which would be an eclectic mix of Vietnamese, the communists would have a useful bargaining chip in negotiations. At the same time, a successful offensive in South Vietnam would pave the way for the General Uprising. The General Offensive would be launched against the cities of the South as a prelude to a popular uprising. The American military, confident in its ability to win the war having consistently outclassed its opponent in open engagements, expressed incredulity at the evidence that suggested this might happen.

Tet and its aftermath, 1968–69

The Tet Offensive would have been ineffective if the Americans had not responded to the North Vietnamese probes hinting at negotiation in late 1967. This diplomatic offensive was combined with military operations that involved a combination of large-scale conventional operations in the countryside to draw the Americans away from the cities, and then fighting in the less-well-defended urban areas so as to prepare the people for the General Uprising. The communist offensive at Con Thien in October 1967 was brutally repulsed by American ground and air power. However, this was not followed by an invasion of the North – even although Westmoreland advocated one – and the North Vietnamese Politburo interpreted their tactical defeat as a signal of America's lack of resolve. They could safely continue to prepare for Tet without fear of an American invasion of the North.

The Americans completely failed to grasp the significance of the communist preparations for Tet despite possessing what turned out to be accurate intelligence assessments of the situation. The NLF and PAVN were preparing to assault the ARVN and South Vietnam's civil structure in a mass, countrywide offensive simultaneous to a political call to the nationalistic zeal of the South Vietnamese people. The end result was intended to convince the Americans that the cost of continuing the war was outweighed by the benefits of withdrawal through leaving behind a Southern "coalition" government in their stead. Tet would allow the North Vietnamese to enter negotiations holding the upper hand. A captured document of June 1967 confirms this:

> If peace talks materialise, our attacks will be targeted against the US and GVN (Saigon) governments. Our efforts will then be devoted to the isolation of the US and acquiring the sympathy of countries of the world. It is

imperative that we hit the enemy harder before engaging in any negotiations.[41]

Furthermore, the prospect of American retaliation through intensified bombing of the North would mobilise international support in the communists' favour, given their successful ability to portray the conflict as a purely Southern affair. As Ford has correctly noted, the final Tet plan was formulated by the North with respect to its own security. Giap, the plan's mythological architect, was in fact actually opposed to it, believing that it would fail, taking massive casualties in the process. However, as defence minister, he oversaw the logistical preparations for it.[42]

The Americans were further weakened on the eve of Tet by their decision to abide by the Tet holiday ceasefire, a choice that meant their acquiescing to a 50 per cent reduction in the strength of the ARVN owing to leave. Despite Westmoreland's protestations to the contrary, the administration refused to cancel the ceasefire. Although the MACV supremo did not believe that the NLF was capable of launching a mass attack on South Vietnam's cities, he was concerned by the North Vietnamese preparations for an offensive in the region of the Northern I Corps around Khe Sanh. There were 6,000 US Marines deployed there in one of Westmoreland's fortified border base camps, part of his "strong point obstacle system".

When the storm fell on Khe Sanh on 21 January 1968, Westmoreland's response was to utilise all of the firepower at his disposal. In this respect, Hanoi's deception worked. On the other hand, by massing their regular troops in the region, including the first use of armour by the communists in the South, they were unable to reinforce the so-called "first wave" attack on the cities. Nevertheless, the administration, with visions of another Dien Bien Phu, were deeply concerned about Westmoreland's ability to hold Khe Sanh. However, the comparison was false. Unlike General Navarre's French forces, the Americans at Khe Sanh were constantly resupplied by transport aircraft and helicopters. Whereas the hilly terrain at Dien Bien Phu had favoured the Vietnamese, who were attacking an isolated outpost, Khe Sanh was situated on a plateau, with all the high ground nearby occupied by American troops. It would have been impossible for the communists to have repeated their success of 1954 against an enemy that had now reached the peak of its military power during the conflict.

Operation "Niagara", the American counter-offensive against the communist attack, lasted two months. Whereas 16 kilotons of explosives fell on Hiroshima, American aircraft, notably B-52s, pounded the communists with 108 kilotons in defence of the marines at Khe Sanh. Up to 65,000 American troops were redirected to defend the position, and accurate computer-guided bombs were rained on the PAVN forces from within the marine firebase. Robert Citino has remarked: "[w]hatever they thought they may have been doing at Khe Sanh, the soldiers of the NVA were actually going to school in the 'American way of war'".[43]

However, Khe Sanh did divert American attention from Saigon and South

Vietnam's other cities, which were attacked on the night of 29–30 January. Tactically, this surprise was to be the North's only success. At Khe Sanh, a large part of the PAVN had been destroyed, and the guerrillas further south were left without the anticipated help from North Vietnamese regulars when it came to attempting to achieve the main objective of capturing Hue and Danung, the crest of the "second wave" of the Tet plan. Thus, the General Uprising did not occur, a fact that the communist Vietnamese have since admitted. Indeed, the combined American–South Vietnamese pacification programmes were to resume with a vengeance shortly afterwards.

The real significance of Tet, however, could be found by reading *On War*:

> Not every war need be fought until one side collapses. When the motives and tensions of war are slight we can imagine that the very faintest prospect of defeat might be enough to cause one side to yield. If from the very start the other side feels that this is probable, it will obviously concentrate on bringing about *this probability* rather than take the long way round and totally defeat the enemy.[44]

Despite the fact that the American military regained control, the administration was too demoralised to go for decisive victory in the face of a North Vietnamese military bereft of its guerrilla shield. It is simplistic to suggest that the Americans could have done so, as it would have involved extending the war into the rest of Indo-China. In this respect, attrition warfare through the use of overwhelming force might have succeeded, albeit at a horrendous cost. The Americans would still not have been spared the anguish and national soul-searching of the post-Vietnam period. Johnson himself wilted under combined Congressional and media pressure (public opinion was still in favour of continuing the bombing). On 31 March 1968, he announced a unilateral partial halt to the bombing north of the 20th Parallel and indicated that America's forces in Vietnam would no longer be reinforced, and he repeated his assertion that "our objective in South Vietnam has never been the annihilation of the enemy".[45]

This was no doubt the reason why Johnson went public with his decision to call a bombing halt as soon as the communists came to the negotiating table. He also announced that he would not stand for re-election. Meanwhile, McNamara had been replaced by Clark Clifford, and Johnson had removed Westmoreland, making him the Army chief-of-staff and replacing him with General Creighton Abrams. While the army advised Clifford to continue with his predecessor's policy, Johnson pulled the rug from under the military's feet. Refusing the JCS's request for an extra 200,000 troops, Johnson set in motion the process that led to withdrawal. Revealingly, for every infantryman and artilleryman in the field between seven and nine were required to maintain him. Thus, although the United States had 500,000 men at the peak of its commitment, only about 80,000 could actually operate on the front line. By contrast, the communists deployed three combat troops for every support soldier (although they could draw on the services of a million civilian "porters" to supply them).[46] Therefore, while the United States was a master of industrial war through technology and logistics, it was unable to overcome the defects that came with this. MACV was now forced to emphasise "Vietnamisation", with the South Vietnamese being given the aid and training to defend themselves. This policy was reinforced under Richard Nixon, Johnson's successor.[47]

Vietnamisation was an integral part of the "Nixon Doctrine", which drove Nixon and Kissinger's move towards *détente* with the communist world. The Nixon Doctrine encompassed an approach that relied upon America's allies taking a greater burden of the share for their own defence. The "Twin Pillars" strategy of bolstering Iran and Saudi Arabia was implemented in 1971, with the Shah of Iran being "a showpiece for the Nixon Doctrine".[48] Unfortunately, his later overthrow revealed the futility of trying to shore up far-flung allies in the face of US military weakness outside its core sphere of influence compared to the Soviet Union. While Kissinger applied the principles of *realpolitik* to his statecraft, it lacked the backing of sufficient military force to give it impetus. The drawdown in American conventional forces in response to the Vietnam experience therefore gave the Nixon Doctrine a hollow ring.

The North Vietnamese accepted Johnson's offer for peace talks on condition that they began immediately, and also that the bombing should be halted. Johnson had already ordered numerous pauses in the bombing in the belief that he could persuade the communists to negotiate. Clausewitz would have been highly critical: "If the enemy is to be coerced you must put him in a situation that is even more unpleasant than the sacrifice you call on him to make."[49]

The communists' parleying illustrated the extent to which they had been jolted by the failure of Tet. However, their political nous remained intact. Tet had been costly, but they remained in control. In the period prior to the beginning of the peace talks in May 1968, what was left of the NLF was ordered to continue its campaign in the South. Unlike the Americans, who, realising that they could not win, decided to withdraw, for the communists it was a case of "victory or death": compromise would be as much an admission of the latter as outright defeat.

Nixon had hardly had an opportunity to settle into office when the communists launched the so-called mini-Tet offensive in early 1969, killing 4,000 Americans inside four months. Nixon was convinced that unilateral withdrawal would be a geostrategic disaster for the US. He therefore decided to pursue a combined political–military approach. Gaining Congressional endorsement to continue the war, the administration ordered the military to concentrate on defending the urban areas in the South, while attempting to interdict the Ho Chi Minh Trail in Laos, bombing the sanctuaries in Cambodia and mining the harbours of North Vietnam. The river-based forces in the Mekong Delta area of the South stepped up their campaign against the lines of communication from Cambodia. Their role in preventing a repeat of Tet has led Harold Henderson to remark that "riverine forces proved again the importance of strength and mobility and demonstrated the significance of the type of combined operations that [Sir Julian] Corbett had advocated over a half-century earlier".[50]

Air power and drawdown, 1970–73

The American military in Vietnam was given the leeway to experiment with novel tactics and weapons, particularly helicopter gunships and precision-guided munitions (PGMs). The defeat of the 12-division strong North Vietnamese attack across the DMZ in March 1972, the Eastertide Offensive, pointed towards the future.[51] The severe losses inflicted on the North Vietnamese heavy armour by a Huey UHI helicopter and TOW anti-tank missile combination foreshadowed the Gulf War of 1991. Tactical mobility through the exploitation of the battlespace in a three-dimensional environment, as opposed to a linear one, was developed by the Americans to a point hitherto unrealised in practice. Novel air refuelling techniques were also developed. However, within the wider context of strategic ineptitude, the Americans failed to turn tactical improvisation to their advantage.

The air campaigns against the communists were waged in steadily increasing increments in the hope that, as the stakes were raised, the enemy would eventually capitulate once it could no longer absorb the punishment – but escalation dominance was futile when waged against an enemy willing to go to any lengths to succeed. Furthermore, North Vietnam had a primitive infrastructure, the destruction of which did not adversely affect its resolve to continue the war. The bombing tended to be inaccurate, at least prior to the advent of the PGM. The historical evidence provided by the Second World War that, up to a point, indiscriminate bombing actually strengthens, rather than undermines, the morale of those bombed was ignored. Thus stalemate ensued, reinforcing the North Vietnamese in their conviction that they could win, and heightening American frustration at being unable to bring the resistance to an end. At home, the perceived imbalance between means (the air campaign) and ends (the protection of South Vietnam) increased domestic opposition to the war.

Controversy surrounded the decision to attack the sanctuaries in Cambodia and Laos in 1970, and this became part of the debate surrounding the war. It is a decision that may have weighed on Congress's mind when it later gradually withdrew support for Nixon's Vietnam policy. However, one should examine the context in which Nixon's decision was taken. American forces were gradually being run down in the face of an undiminished enemy who continued to rely on logistical bases throughout the Indo-China region, and was now upping the ante in the South with renewed attacks. Nixon's first priority as commander-in-chief lay with his combat forces still engaged in Vietnam. Therefore, the bombing of Cambodia and Laos was right in the circumstances. Indeed, as has already been noted, similar action should have taken place a decade earlier as the Americans became more involved in the region. At the operational level, the Americans have always recognised the importance of logistics. In this case, operational considerations dovetailed with strategic ones, and Nixon had the will to ensure that this was so. In a memorandum to Kissinger in May 1972, Nixon said: "we have the power to destroy [North Vietnamese] warmaking capacity. The only question is whether we have the *will* to use that power. What distinguishes me from Johnson is that I have the *will* in spades."[52]

Between May and October 1972, American aerial bombing pounded Hanoi to such an extent that the North Vietnamese parleyed for negotiations in return for a halt to the bombing. However, as soon as the bombing ended, the North Vietnamese reverted to type, stalling the talks that they interpreted as proof of a lack of willpower on the part of the Americans.

The air campaign was resumed in December 1972, and thanks to the use of large numbers of B-52s for the first time, it had the effect of finally bringing the communists to the negotiating table. While conventional bombing had at last proved to be effective, the Americans had previously discussed escalation to nuclear weapons. As early as 1954, nuclear use was considered as an aid to the French at Dien Bien Phu, while in 1967 MACV organised a nuclear planning group that was soon disbanded after considering the possible use of nuclear weapons to break the PAVN siege of Khe Sanh. In April 1975, just as Hanoi was on the verge of falling, Summers, who was there negotiating terms for the withdrawal of the US Embassy, told a PAVN officer: " 'You know, we had the means to destroy North Vietnam with nuclear weapons at any time of our choosing.'

" 'We knew that', he replied. 'We also knew you'd never do it.' "[53]

In the end, despite the assertions of Nixon and Kissinger that the Paris Peace Accords of January 1973 had reinforced the South's position, the peace agreement actually undermined this situation. Remarkably, the North Vietnamese were able to maintain forces in the South while Congress's refusal in June 1973 to fund any further military activities in South-East Asia signalled America's final extrication from the conflict. Against the background of the Watergate crisis and the subsequent souring of Presidential–Congressional relations, all of the efforts to shore up the South Vietnamese position in the previous four years went for nothing and, uniquely among America's allies, South Vietnam was abandoned to its fate. The North Vietnamese, with no intention of honouring the agreement, renewed their infiltration of the South, finally launching a conventional attack in December 1974, and by April 1975 their numerical and material supremacy had told as Congress steadfastly refused to allow a resumption of the bombing campaign.[54]

Why did the United States fail?

While writing a guide to the Paret/Howard edition of *On War*, Bernard Brodie highlighted the problem that confronted the US in Vietnam with a quote from that work:

> To discover how much of our resources must be mobilised for war, we must first examine our own political aim and that of the enemy. We must gauge the strength and situation of the opposing state. We must gauge the character and abilities of its government and people and do the same in regard to our own. Finally, we must evaluate the political sympathies of other states and the effect the war may have on them.[55]

While Clausewitz went on to say that a rapid and proper appraisal of these factors and their possible consequences required the "intuition of a genius", it is clear that no such analysis was undertaken in the United States during the 1960s. What this illustrates is that, given the infatuation with quantitative analysis during the McNamara years, a scientific approach to war is incompatible with treating war as an art as all successful strategists in history have. Again Clausewitz provides the perfect summation:

> No one starts a war – or rather, no one in his senses ought to do so – without first being clear in his mind what he intends to achieve by that war and how he intends to conduct it. The former is its political purpose; the latter its operational objective.[56]

Clausewitz's most fundamental contribution to strategic thought is his analysis of the relationship between war and politics. Vietnam demonstrated that although one can be winning militarily, it is at the political level that wars are won and lost. This is certainly the case where strategic objectives are ambiguous or, worse, unknown. Whereas the policy of gradual escalation ensured that the Americans chose not to have a fixed centre of gravity to aim at, the communists were able to focus on public opinion, both within South Vietnam and the United States. They understood the importance of moral factors, as did Clausewitz who warned that ignoring them in the belief that war could be "[reduced] to a few mathematical formulas" would be fatal.[57] As P. L. Townsend has pointed out:

> [Clausewitz's] objection would not have been that the military efforts were fettered by politicians and the mighty potential of the US military was never turned loose ... but that the military effort was not well enough coordinated with the political side. The fact that the attack on the moral force of the NVA/VC was so poorly executed is a responsibility that the military must share with their political brethren.[58]

Of course, one cannot ignore other factors. American strategy was self-defeating: it had no comprehension of the North Vietnamese mentality, and its attempts to compromise with the communists, whereby the military stalemate would induce an American-funded reconstruction programme in the region, evoked only contempt in Hanoi where the communists were prepared to sit and wait. Strategically, the aim of the war, if one existed, was the preservation of South Vietnam, which ruled out any campaign by ground forces to advance into North Vietnam and defeat the enemy's armed forces in traditional Clausewitzian fashion. As ARVN colonel Hoang Ngoc Lung later remarked: "The Americans had designed a purely defensive strategy for Vietnam. It was a strategy that was based on the attrition of the enemy through a prolonged defense and made no allowance for decisive offensive action."[59]

In 1968, the CINCPAC, Admiral Sharp, was explicit in his belief that the objective of the US military in South Vietnam was defensive; that is, to provide a secure environment for its people by supporting the legitimate government. However, this "nation building" could only be achieved by the South Vietnamese themselves, and if the American military was unable to take the strategic offensive then it was pointless its being there. The US Army's principles of war, as endorsed in FM 100–5 of 1962 and 1968, overlooked the moral aspects of war, and failed to home in on the impact of psychologically reducing the enemy's will to continue. "This was especially paradoxical since this was ostensibly what we were trying to do in Vietnam, having been denied the objective of destruction of the enemy's armed forces."[60]

Much of Summers's *On Strategy* is focused on his analysis of the Vietnam War in the context of such principles of war as the objective, the offensive, mass, manoeuvre, economy of force and simplicity, all of which he believes the Americans failed to apply. While Summers has been criticised for "whitewashing" the military's role in Vietnam, and placing the fault firmly with the civilian leadership, there is a lot of validity in his analysis of the conflict, both at the strategic and operational level. This is heightened by the Clausewitzian perspective he brings to the subject. One must also bear in mind that the emotional impact of Vietnam on those who fought there was such that they were understandably bitter about the experience:

> As military professionals, it was our job to judge the true nature of the Vietnam War, communicate those facts to our civilian decision-makers, and to recommend appropriate strategies. As Clausewitz said, that was the first strategic question and the most comprehensive. It is indicative of our strategic failure in Vietnam that almost a decade after our involvement the true nature of the Vietnam War is still in question.[61]

Vietnam was to teach America that there are limits to the benefits that an altruistic framework for instituting policy can achieve. Rather, one must justify one's involvement in terms of the national interest, as Kissinger later made clear:

> Precisely because America was reluctant to accept lessons so contrary to its historical experience, it also found cutting its losses extraordinarily difficult. Thus the pain associated with both these frustrations was the result of its best not its worst qualities. America's rejection of national interest as the basis of foreign-policy had cast the country adrift on a sea of undifferentiated moralism.[62]

Part of the Americans' problem lay in their inability to realise that South Vietnamese society was not ripe for democratisation, given its alien culture and completely different historical experience. The drawbacks of American exceptionalism were most obvious in this respect. Once it was realised that democracy could not easily be transplanted in South Vietnam, the American polity became disillusioned. A Eurocentric approach would not work. Despite his recent *mea culpa* concerning the conflict, McNamara is still inclined to pour some of the blame on the South Vietnamese; but this is unfair.[63]

The United States did not adopt a strategy commensurate with its objectives because these were never made clear other than via the abstract notions of traditional American foreign policy or "Wilsonianism". Even the "domino theory", that if South Vietnam fell, the rest of South-East Asia would follow, was something of a chimera. After all, the United States had been selective in applying this dictum in the past, failing to do so in China but doing so in Korea. If one distinguishes operations from tactics, where the Americans at least showed some imagination, then the Vietnam War is a classic case of the lack of a grasp of policy at the strategic level being mirrored at the operational level – that emphasised superior firepower, whether dealing with conventional or with guerrilla forces – precisely because the United States was unsure as to exactly the kind of conflict in which it was engaged.

One of the underlying themes of these opening chapters has been the criticism for the theories propagated by the civilian strategists who held sway in the United States during the 1960s, particularly those that influenced the technocrats under McNamara. These men were capable of providing means in abundance – numbers of weapons, men, etc. – without realising that the ends required a more subtle approach to strategy. This was especially true of the flawed application of the theory of escalation dominance, which began with limited support to South Vietnam through Kennedy's policy of CI and ended with massive air raids against the North. While one cannot absolve the military – there had been little original strategic thought in that quarter post-1945 – Kissinger has written well of the impact that the systems analysts had upon them:

> Throughout the 1960s the military were torn between the commitment to civilian supremacy inculcated through generations of service and their premonition of disaster, between trying to make the new system work and rebelling against it. They were demoralised by the order to procure weapons in which they did not believe and by the necessity of fighting a war whose purpose proved increasingly elusive.[64]

American strategy was also undermined by the disorganisation of the chain of command. Westmoreland was only responsible for the South Vietnamese theatre; he had no authority over the air campaign against the Ho Chi Minh Trail and North Vietnam. Nor did he exert any control over naval operations outside South Vietnam's territorial waters. These were the responsibility of CINCPAC, based 5,000 miles away in Honolulu. Westmoreland's plea for a "South-East Asia Command" to co-ordinate these diverse responsibilities fell on deaf ears. The existence of the South Vietnamese military further complicated command problems. Summers has noted that during the entire American involvement in Indo-China from the 1950s, 22 different official justifications for America's role were issued, while some 70 per cent of American generals who fought in the war were unsure of its objectives, a damning indictment of the American strategic malaise. It also ensured that overwhelming public support for the war was never secured. It was a lesson that the American military drew from the conflict. As Robert Cassidy notes, many officers, among them Lieutenant-Colonel Colin Powell, were determined "never again to prosecute a war without the degree of public support more characteristic of a world war than a small war".[65]

The main drawback in Vietnam was that the United States did not focus on any particular enemy centre of gravity, with the possible inappropriate exception of his armed forces, in sharp contrast to North Vietnamese strategic dexterity. Indeed, the United States also had to juggle with wider geopolitical responsibilities:

> While to at least some in Honolulu the question of where to mass and where to use economy of force revolved around China, in Washington it revolved around America's world-wide interests. The Department of Defense was more concerned with "preparation for war" rather than "war proper" as seen in its concern not only with Vietnam, but also with NATO strategy, nuclear strategy and major defense programs.[66]

America's micro-management of the war was a technocratic exercise in folly. Measurements of effectiveness, arising out of PPBS, and including body counts, battlefield cost effectiveness, 12-month tours, and statistical indices of air strikes, were all products of a structure that did indeed concern itself more with "preparation for war" than "war proper" in Clausewitzian parlance. While the end was willed, the means were not considered. PPBS may have been effective when managing the Cold War deterrent, but it was counter-productive during "hot war". In the final analysis, Vietnam cost 50,000 American lives and between $150 and $175 billion, while just about every non-nuclear device of military hardware was used. But bereft of any clear strategic context these statistics, rather than being measures of effectiveness, are an epitaph to the waste imposed by the bankruptcy of strategy. Summers quotes a passage from *On War* to critique PPBS:

> They aim at fixed values; but in war everything is uncertain, and calculations have to be made with variable quantities.
>
> They direct the inquiry exclusively toward physical quantities, whereas all military action is intertwined with psychological forces and effects.
>
> They consider only the unilateral action, whereas war consists of a continuous interaction of opposites.[67]

The JCS system failed in Vietnam partly because Johnson placed operational restrictions on when and where the military could fight, thus sending them down a route where they fought attrition warfare that inevitably led to stalemate. The emphasis on the roles of the theatre commanders – roles that were themselves unclear – eliminated the JCS from the strategy-making process. The chief-of-staff of the JCS rarely saw Johnson in private during the critical years of 1965 to 1968, while the other members – the heads of the Services – hardly met him in private at all. Clearly, the civilian policymakers at the Department of Defense were far more influential. To be fair, Johnson was never kept fully in the picture by the military in the field, while the JCS did not take the responsibility to inform the president that they disagreed with certain of his policy objectives. In the final analysis, however, McGregor Knox is correct to write that "McNamara and his civilian analysts confused bean-counting with strategic judgement, and infected their military-bureaucratic antagonists with their own shallow rationalism."[68]

To compound the problems of strategy making, Congress tended to be impotent, meekly following the Executive's lead during the Johnson Administration. McNamara has written that, in retrospect, a War Cabinet along the lines of Churchill's in the Second World War should have been put in place. These factors make it simplistic to blame, as many commentators do, media pressure and domestic dissent.[69]

The Americans also failed to achieve any unity in their intelligence effort in Vietnam. This proved to be just as detrimental to the war effort as the lack of a clear chain of command. It was particularly important in that the Americans were fighting in a distant country with an alien environment and culture, against an enemy that used the tools of conventional warfare and LIC interchangeably. Intelligence jurisdiction was never resolved between the competing claims of the CIA and MACV. The tragedy was that most of the intelligence gathered by the Americans in Vietnam was valuable. The problem lay in dissemination. Thus, the Americans were unable to look beyond "the adoption of a ghetto form of warfare only to be paralleled by the ghetto mind displayed by the vast bulk of American personnel faced with the richness and alienness of experience in Vietnam".[70]

Summers has criticised Johnson for conducting the war in the style of an eighteenth-century monarch who viewed the enemy as an instrument of government, rather than as an instrument of the people in what he terms the "trinitarian" sense.[71] This allowed the president to control the war effort to such an extent that he could begin and halt the aerial bombing almost at will. It enabled him to pursue his illusion that he could negotiate with the communists on equal terms. Kissinger has written of the naivete of such an approach, while Clausewitz echoed this in a passage in *On War*:

> Every pause between one success and the next gives the enemy new opportunities. One success has little influence on the next, and often none at all. The influence may well be adverse, for the enemy either recovers and rouses himself to greater resistance or obtains help from somewhere else.[72]

While it is true that North Vietnamese conventional forces, and not the Viet Cong guerrillas, were decisive in the final analysis – particularly after the American withdrawal – the United States cannot escape the fact that it did not have a coherent CI strategy in place. The bitter irony is that the North Vietnamese eventually defeated South Vietnam by utilising the very type of forces that the US military was best equipped to tackle. Unfortunately, the Americans had a naive belief in the "people's war" rhetoric of the communists. Even as late as 1973, Westmoreland commented:

> An understanding of the American ground strategy in Vietnam begins with an understanding of the nature of the war the enemy waged, for that always affects the nature of the riposte. The communists in Vietnam waged a classic revolutionary war.[73]

In contrast to the Americans, the North Vietnamese communists displayed a unity of purpose that enabled them to make up the gap in material superiority that the US enjoyed. Although it was a developing nation, the lack of internal dissent in North Vietnam ensured that the harmonious civil--military relations that resulted were important in enabling it to use technology. The PAVN's Soviet-supplied, integrated air defence system was responsible for shooting down 2,000 US aircraft between 1965 and 1972. The PAVN also developed techniques that nullified the effect of American electronic countermeasures. Indeed, PAVN pilots were of such quality that the Americans later absorbed the lessons from the air war, with the US Navy and Air Force instigating the "Top Gun" programme for their fighter pilots. Finally, the clear distinction in the communists' mind between politics and war, whereby the military accepted a subordinate role, albeit important, to the polity, is very apparent. Lack of internal resistance also made it very difficult for the United States to launch any covert operation to sow the seeds of dissent within North Vietnam, and to weaken it from the inside.

The Vietnam War occurred simultaneously to a great upheaval in American society. The underlying current of the 1960s intellectual movement was that history was irrelevant – which was actually only a continuum of "New World" thinking – and, as Summers notes, many speakers at Leavenworth and Carlisle during this period warned the army about the consequences of the so-called "post-industrial" social order. The hedonism associated with the 1960s (drug abuse, sexual promiscuity), together with radical politics, found its way into the ranks of those who fought in Vietnam. The result was that the traditional virtues of military discipline were called into question by those who needed to heed them so as to ensure that the United States would prevail. Yet the myth that public opinion turned against Vietnam should be scotched. It did so to an extent, but the overwhelming majority always abhorred the thought of capitulation. This mood was encapsulated when the candidates urging such a course during the 1972 elections were crushed at the polls. Unfortunately, many politicians – notably those in Johnson's administration – lost their nerve. The real public anger was directed at the way in which American military power was being ineffectively deployed. As General Fred Weyand commented: the Vietnam War reaffirmed "the peculiar relationship between the American Army and the American people".[74]

In the final analysis, the US military overlooked the classic roots of strategy. It was diverted by an obsession with the quick fix, a peculiarly American approach, which also happened to contradict the incrementalist approach of the political authorities. In the end, all this ensured was a conflict that lasted for over seven years, culminating in stalemate and a peace agreement that paved the way for the communisation of Indo-China. In 1990, a student at Leavenworth, Major Michael Brady, examined the influences that shaped the opinions of his generation of officers regarding Vietnam. While the Army's senior leaders at this time had drawn lessons from Vietnam based on their own experiences, the overwhelming majority of Brady's contemporaries had not even read anything on Vietnam. Their impressions of the conflict were anecdotal, mainly from movies. Of those that had read something, Summers was the most common source. However, when Brady presented a list of propositions comparing Summers's work with Krepinevich's, the vast majority were inclined to agree with the latter's thesis that the US failed to understand guerrilla warfare.[75]

The need for the American military to rediscover the "classic roots of strategy" after the war was summed up by Summers in the conclusion to his account of American strategy in Vietnam: "The quintessential 'strategic lesson learned' from the Vietnam War is that we must once again become masters of the profession of arms."[76]

Conclusion

Clausewitz's relevance to Vietnam has really arisen in the post hoc sense in that he was used by Summers to shed light on the American defeat. Unfortunately, Summers's work was weakened by using a Jominian approach based on the principles of war. Moreover, despite some shrewd uses of *On War*'s aphorisms, Summers misinterpreted Clausewitz. He distorted the fascinating trinity by discussing the influences of people, army and government, thereby allowing later critics of Clausewitz to attack what they saw as his state-centric approach. Summers also took concepts such as friction out of context by referring to it in the context of domestic politics, "an egregious example of quotation ... the Prussian never intended".[77]

A major lesson of Vietnam is that tactical successes do not necessarily yield favourable strategic decisions. Objectives to destroy the enemy physically distorted Clausewitzian thought in that he also emphasised the need for psychological effects. Most importantly, the Americans had no proper conception of Clausewitz's centre of gravity, unlike the communists who exploited the American Achilles' heel of public opinion. Clausewitz's perceptive writings on people's war, which to some extent influenced their opponents, were also overlooked by the Americans.

Incrementalism and the Cold War theory of escalation dominance were impotent in the face of the Viet Cong, which was supported by North Vietnamese regulars. The United States learned that if force was to be committed at all, it had to be utilised in support of a clear and unambiguous strategic objective. Ultimately, therefore, the main lesson to be drawn from Vietnam revolves around Clausewitz's analysis of the relationship between war and policy.

4 The renaissance of American strategic thought

"Back to basics"

The traumatic effect of the Vietnam War upon the American military and upon society at large mirrored the impact of the First World War upon the democracies of Western Europe. Fortunately for the Americans, an intellectual effort began to absorb the lessons of Vietnam and therefore to prevent the slide into demoralisation and pacifism that had afflicted inter-war France, for example. The comparisons with 1914–18 do not end there. The US officer corps was emaciated by the conflict. One officer who was commissioned in 1966 later recalled that half of his colleagues on the basic officer's course died during the Tet offensive. Of those who survived, two-thirds were victims of a post-war purge. "Any history of the Army after the Vietnam War that does not address the social and cultural stresses experienced by those who stayed on will be incomplete."[1]

That the American armed forces did not slide into permanent decline owed much to the revival in strategic thought that originated during Admiral Stansfield Turner's tenure as president of the Naval War College after 1972. This renaissance signalled a move away from notions polarised in unconventional war and nuclear war, and instead heralded a return to more traditional thinking. Turner believed that officers were being taught in an environment that did not allow them to expand their minds. He overhauled the College's curriculum by placing an emphasis on rigorous instruction based on historical examples. Authors such as Thucydides and Clausewitz would provide students with valuable practical and theoretical lessons. Turner also criticised the

> increased reliance on civilians and on 'think tanks' to do our thinking for us [the military]. We must be able to produce military men who are a match for the best of the civilian strategists or we will abdicate control of our profession.[2]

Not surprisingly, the move away from strategic myopia would take some time to penetrate the military, particularly the Army. An excellent translation of *On War*, edited by Michael Howard and Peter Paret, was published in 1976. While the Naval War College adopted this edition during that very year, and the

Air War College had done so by 1978, it was not until 1981 that it became a primary textbook for officers at the Army War College. At the US Military Academy, West Point, students also read this edition of *On War* and, in so doing, became aware of the political objectives of war. In the case of the Air Force, "David MacIsaac got Clausewitz put back in the curriculum at the Air War College following a stint teaching at the Naval War College when Stansfield Turner was the President."[3]

The Howard and Paret translation has become the definitive edition of *On War* in the American military's schools. Paret was an expert on the period during which Clausewitz lived, while Howard was determined that the work should be available in comprehensible English. Bernard Brodie was also involved in the project. His concern was that Clausewitz should be available to the public and also be put into the hands of soldiers.[4]

The Vietnam War had convinced some officers of the importance of the Clausewitzian relationship between war and policy. Articles began to appear in the *Naval War College Review* and the Army's *Military Review* that explicitly referred to Clausewitz as a theorist who provided the didactic framework that the American military needed in its process of rigorous self-examination. In 1976, for example, a scholarly essay by the late Herbert Rosinski appeared in the former publication. It illustrated the way in which German military thought had declined from the zenith it reached with "the profundities (and obscurities) of Clausewitz".[5]

Simultaneous to Turner's tenure at the Naval War College, General Creighton Abrams took office as Army chief-of-staff in 1972. He was well aware of the inadequacies of the material with which he had to work, and set to tailor it to the strategic changes presented by the Nixon Doctrine's emphasis on avoiding another regional conflict like Vietnam. Abrams inherited a situation demanding that the Army be reduced from the peak of 1.5 million men it had reached in 1968 to a projected level of half that figure by 1975. However, of the 13 active divisions under his command only four were classified as being combat ready. Despite this, Abrams was intent on increasing the establishment from 13 to 16 divisions.

In the spring of 1973, Abrams founded a strategic studies think-tank, the Astarita Group (named after its chief, Colonel Edward Astarita), which examined the future role of the US military. The group concluded that the United States was in a strong position given its close links with the two other economic powerhouses of the world, Western Europe and Japan. The primary role of American military power was to bolster this strength. It was important that given the abandonment of South Vietnam, the United States should reassure its main allies of its commitment through maintaining its military presence in these regions. Such a conclusion tailored well with the *realpolitik* of the Nixon Doctrine, but the group's recommendations were only made public in 1981.

Another significant development at this time was the establishment of the Army Training and Doctrine Command (TRADOC) at Fort Monroe, Virginia, under the command of vice chief-of-staff, General William DePuy. TRADOC was designed to oversee the Army's training and education programme and was later mirrored by similar initiatives in the Air Force (the Centre for Aerospace Doctrine, Research and Evaluation), and in the Navy (the Naval Doctrine Command).

DePuy, who had been Westmoreland's deputy in Vietnam, was to establish a position in the vanguard of reform in the wake of Abrams's incapacitation through illness. DePuy's approach to reforming the Army's way of preparing for war centred around training rather than doctrine. It is an irony that the early days of going "back to basics" in the Army began in this way. Doctrine entails knowledge; without knowledge, one is left without a compass with which to construct a body of thought. As Clausewitz pointed out, the journey from knowledge to ability is a long one. However, DePuy had to justify TRADOC's existence and, in so doing, he needed to ensure that his way of thinking would become the blueprint for Army doctrine. "The necessity to defend [TRADOC's] budget drove Depuy [*sic*] to codify as army doctrine the concepts that underlay TRADOC's analyses."[6]

DePuy believed that the next conflict in which America would be involved would not be a general war in central Europe but rather a limited, albeit intense, conflict, possibly in the Middle East. In such a conflict there would be no time to mobilise and then transport forces from the continental United States. Rather, small but well-equipped American forces would be expected to fight and win quickly. To do so, their training would have to be of an order of magnitude that would enable them to match any enemy they faced.

Rather than dwelling on the Vietnam experience, an important body of lessons was drawn from the Arab–Israeli War of 1973. This conflict had featured the largest armoured battle since the Second World War, providing a graphic illustration of both the intensity and destructive power of modern warfare. Important tactical lessons from the conflict – clever use of terrain, the use of suppressive fire, camouflage, and the emphasis on the combined-arms battle – were absorbed by DePuy. Roger Spiller has argued that the 1973 war provided the Americans with a reference point uncontaminated by the Vietnamese experience. Years later, DePuy recalled it as "a marvelous excuse or springboard ... for reviewing and updating our own doctrine".[7]

Shortly after the conclusion of the Yom Kippur War, a US Army study team under Brigadier-General Morris Brady investigated its significance. Their findings convinced DePuy that the US Army was ill-prepared for modern war. This was especially so given that the Egyptians had employed Soviet-style combined-arms tactics with some success and had deployed Soviet-model tanks that were capable of performing under conditions of nuclear and chemical warfare. Precise, long-range fire inflicted large losses on Israeli armour lacking infantry support. This illustrated the extent to which the Soviets had modernised their forces and doctrine while the Americans had been distracted by Vietnam. DePuy drew the lesson that sheer weight of firepower would prevail on the battlefield. "To DePuy [weapon characteristics and effects] were inextricably associated with the need to train to a new and higher standard of combat performance."[8]

In May 1974, Secretary of Defense James Schlesinger emphasised the need for reform in the Army during a visit to its Command and General Staff College at Fort Leavenworth:

> The army has a great opportunity for regeneration after some of the disappointments of the Vietnam War. Other armies have had periods of ferment after similar disappointments. This opportunity to reform and to improve the institution in which they work is denied to institutions after glorious victories.[9]

One of the elements in the reform process would be to replace the Vietnam-era FM 100–5: *Operations* of 1968 with an updated field manual. This task, which might have been expected to be Fort Leavenworth's, became TRADOC's responsibility. Thus, one of the most important issues facing the US Army in the aftermath of the most traumatic war in its history was shifted from a school devoted to teaching and research to one concerned mainly with training. DePuy chose General Donn Starry, then posted at the Armor School, as his principal assistant in the writing of FM 100–5. Starry shared DePuy's beliefs about the potential for modern armoured operations as illustrated by the Arab–Israeli conflict. James Kitfield has written that Starry "experienced an epiphany" when he visited the Golan Heights after the war.[10]

Where Starry and DePuy differed in their interpretations of the Arab–Israeli War was that Starry saw the potential for manoeuvre operations while DePuy was more interested in repulsing a breakthrough head-on. Starry's staff conducted a historical analysis of campaigns going back to the time of Alexander the Great that illustrated the potential for a smaller army to defeat a larger one. Starry later recognised the Arab–Israeli War as heralding the end of an era in the American approach to war:

> [It] spelled ... an urgent need to rethink mass conscript armies, nations in arms, mass industrial mobilisation, and battles of military and national annihilation as relevant concepts for the use of military force as an instrument of national policy in our time.[11]

DePuy's analysis of the Arab–Israeli War led him to view the central European theatre from a technical perspective, ensuring that the new field manual was designed to concentrate on the tactical level without a proper interface with the wider strategic objectives for which such a war would be fought. TRADOC's debate over the writing of the manual concerned itself with the way in which company-sized units and armoured battalion-sized combat teams would operate in the theatre of war. Field trials conducted at Fort Hood in 1975 were based on the tactical concepts derived from the 1973 war. Although the results of these exercises raised doubts about the feasibility of such attrition-oriented tactics (better known as Active Defense) to counter the Soviets in central Europe, it was believed that tactical excellence devoted to winning the first battle would overcome the problem of strategic inferiority in the European theatre. DePuy compounded this problem by failing to take on board some of the useful tactical lessons from Vietnam, notably the use of airmobile units. As for the main lesson of Vietnam, the ignoring of the Clausewitzian relationship between war and policy, it was conspicuous by its absence in these deliberations.

The role of the Federal German Army was highly significant in influencing the new field manual. The West Germans were intent on waging a war of attrition as dictated by their geopolitical situation and as codified in their 1973 Army Regulations. DePuy established close relations with the West German High Command, giving him the opportunity to supplant the influential hold that the Army's main formation in Europe, the 7th Army, had over operational concepts in that theatre, and to replace it with TRADOC's design. Nevertheless, DePuy still had to have the 7th Army onside, and a doctrine that could be applied primarily to NATO Europe was his way of doing this. DePuy was impressed by the West Germans, noting the reorganisation of their mechanised infantry. West Germany's influence on NATO's defensive linear strategy, whereby land could not be easily traded for space, played into DePuy's hands. Any operational plan that conceived of a cross-border offensive was politically unacceptable to the West Germans. DePuy was convinced that his tactical concepts were compatible with the West German desire to operate as closely to the border as possible. He therefore summed up the notion of Active Defense as being "at best ... a formula for a stalemate or for deterrence".[12]

Despite the criticism that can be levelled at DePuy, his role was important in kick-starting the reform process in the US Army. He devoted a great deal of time to thinking seriously about the army's institutional role, and dispelled many of the cobwebs that had threatened to ossify its thinking, paving the way for later innovations. His "draft concept plan" of 1974 articulated his thoughts on modern warfare: the inherent superiority of the defence in modern war; the need to prepare to fight against superior numbers and firepower; the hegemony of the tank on the battlefield; and the notion that America must have the best-trained and best-led army in the world to overcome the Soviets' quantitative and qualitative superiority in men and materiel respectively.

While Clausewitz had also stressed the superiority of the defence, he did so in the context of preparing for a situation that would allow the defender to go over to the offensive having nullified the enemy attack. Most of the advantages that Clausewitz attributed to the defence were strategic rather than tactical – the defender usually enjoys short lines of communication; the attacker must extend his and will inevitably lose strength while advancing. Thus, while the defender has to await the initial blow, he can choose the time and place of his counterblow.[13] Ultimately, the defence and the offence cannot be categorised into stronger and weaker forms of war. This is determined not only by the available technology, but also by the conditions that prompt their usage: the state or leader that undertakes a pre-emptive offensive, for example.

In an article for the *Naval War College Review* in 1977, James King, director of strategic research at the Naval War College, showed how DePuy could have

maximised Allied contributions to NATO's defence by studying Clausewitz and
relating this to his operational problem:

> In [chapter 6 of Book VI], Clausewitz considers, among other things, the
> contribution that allies may make to the defensive side in war. The para-
> graphs he devotes to this topic are of especial interest because they repre-
> sent, almost uniquely in *On War* and ... rarely elsewhere in his writings, a
> venture on Clausewitz's part into the theory of international relations.[14]

FM 100–5, 1976: an imperfect solution

DePuy's main priority was to tailor the conceptual thinking behind the manual
to the strategic reality facing the Americans and NATO in central Europe. He
explained his rationale for this in an interview in 1987:

> [As] a commander-in-chief ... your job then is to develop an operations
> plan which responds to the political imperatives from the top and fits the
> tactical resources you have at the bottom. You try to find middle ground ...
> to do something useful militarily that isn't in conflict with the political
> objective or is not excessive to resources that you have ... AirLand Battle,
> in its laboratory sense, if you will, like going back and studying Clausewitz
> ... is absolutely essential ... but when you finally come face to face with the
> political realities of the actual mission you do a lot of tailoring.[15]

While this line of thought should always provide the foundation on which doctrine is made, DePuy's reading of the political reality was based on a misunderstanding of the strategy of flexible response. Although this concept was
defensive in nature, given the strategic need to prevent a Warsaw Pact attack on
NATO, it did not necessarily extend to the tactics to be deployed when defending the inner-German border. Nonetheless, DePuy applied a penchant for the
tactical defence to the manual as he believed that this would offer the best
opportunity to overcome the problem of numerical inferiority vis-à-vis the
Soviets. In so doing, he failed to account for the fact that the Soviets possessed a
sophisticated offensive capability that could easily overcome any NATO attempt
to impose a stalemate conventionally. That this was an erroneous approach to
take is illustrated by the words of the manual itself.

> The defender has every advantage but one – he does not have the *initiative*.
> To gain the initiative he must attack ... Counter attacks should be con-
> ducted only when the gains to be achieved are worth the risks involved in
> surrendering the innate advantages of the defense.[16]

When Clausewitz wrote that the defence was superior to the offence, he did
so in the knowledge that the aim – victory, whether in its own right or as a step
towards a compromise peace – had still to be achieved. Defence is "a means to

win a victory that enables one to take the offensive after superiority has been gained; that is, to proceed to take the active object of the war".[17]

DePuy's solid grip on the making of army doctrine ensured that dissenting voices were pushed to the periphery when it came to drafting the manual. Forces Command, which accounted for the majority of the US Army's infantry and airborne capability, rightly objected to the ignoring of the lessons that heliborne operations in Vietnam could yield. The Infantry School was alarmed by the lack of reference to the potential of mechanised infantry – despite DePuy's examination of the West Germans' employment of this arm. Surprisingly, chemical and nuclear warfare, as well as urban warfare, were paid only lip service in the manual's early drafts, no doubt partly because of the need to avoid dissent from the West Germans. To his credit, DePuy did his best to accommodate the objectors into the discussions concerning the final draft, the writing of which he shared with Starry and General Paul Gorman. However, "none of these objections challenged DePuy's fundamental tactical philosophies".[18]

Early in 1976, the manual was launched internally within the Army under its tactical *nom de guerre*, "Active Defense". (It was officially published on 1 July 1976.) DePuy reported on his findings to General Fred Weyand, who had replaced Abrams as chief-of-staff. DePuy alluded to the assistance he had received from the Israelis and Germans, as well as from the US Air Force, although he acknowledged that differences with these authorities remained. Links with Tactical Air Command had begun in 1973 in order to develop closer co-operation in terms of concepts and tactics. In retrospect, one can safely say that there is a certain hubris in DePuy's summing up of the manual: "The impact of [FM100–5] will be a thousand fold. It will be more significant than anyone imagines. [It] will be *the* Army way and it will show up for decades."[19]

The significance of the new manual lay not so much in what was in it, but rather in what was absent from it. The emphasis it placed on winning the first battle eschewed the need to consider winning the *ultimate* battle. The need to "fight outnumbered" and without a deep rear in which to retreat, ensured that the manual overlooked manoeuvre in favour of firepower. Active Defense was based on the erroneous belief that by concentrating force, NATO would make the Soviets do likewise, therefore making them vulnerable to counter-fire. However, such a notion would rely heavily on gaining the initiative at the outset, a challenge that was surely beyond such a defensively oriented doctrine. It was more likely that the Soviets would seize the initiative and use their subsequent room for manoeuvre to outflank and envelop the narrowly concentrated NATO forces. At this point, NATO's lack of an operational reserve would come into play. Nuclear escalation would be the only choice left open to the Alliance if it wanted to continue fighting. The myopic fixation on the tactical battle, rather than the overall campaign, was epitomised by the manual's adoption of a dysfunctional approach to command and control: "In the division of responsibilities on the battlefield, generals commanding corps and divisions *concentrate the force*. Colonels and lieutenant-colonels of brigades and battalions *control and direct the battle*. Captains and their companies, troops and batteries *fight the battle*."[20]

There is very little, if any, direct Clausewitzian influence on FM 100–5, 1976. Colonel Paul Herbert has alluded to a folder he was shown by one of DePuy's aides, which contained extracts from Clausewitz, Jomini, and Liddell Hart on the defence. These notes were, in fact, assembled after the manual had been written and were to be used as preparation for a conference with the Germans. Peter Paret, who together with Michael Howard published his influential translation of *On War* at around this time, also fails to detect any significant impact of Clausewitz upon the manual:

> I don't recall any associates of DePuy being in touch with us while we were translating *On War*. Officers from Leavenworth and Carlisle did contact me during this period, but I don't believe there was any significant transmission of ideas.[21]

DePuy's expectation that the manual would be the authoritative guide to solving the problems posed by modern warfare to the US Army was to be disappointed. Nevertheless, the very fact that the manual had been published, opened the way for a much-needed debate in the US Army about its role on the modern battlefield. DePuy deserves credit for initiating this discussion.

William Lind's critique

A movement to reform the US military extended beyond the armed services to the academic and political worlds. This trend culminated in 1981 with the formation of a bipartisan Congressional Military Reform Caucus. William Lind, a civilian reformer and a legislative aide to Senator Gary Hart, was one of the most staunch opponents of the Active Defense concept. Colonel John Studt, USMC, has acknowledged that Lind and his fellow civilian reformers were in the vanguard of change: "[T]he entire movement for military reform is driven largely by civilian intellectuals, not military officers ... [T]his is not surprising. [The military] have never institutionalised a system that encourages innovative ideas or criticism from subordinates."[22]

Lind's thoughts on FM 100–5, 1976, were crystallised into an article for *Military Review*, published in March 1977,[23] although he had made his views known to TRADOC as soon as the manual was published. Lind's was the first of eighty essays dealing with the doctrinal debate to be published by *Military Review* alone up to 1981. He would later write in the same journal that Active Defense's formulation "in an almost total historical vacuum" owed much to a misunderstanding of German tactical *and* operational concepts, and also to a misreading of America's performance in the Second World War, which suggested to DePuy *et al.* that American junior officers often lacked initiative.[24]

Lind believed that the authors of FM 100–5 were caught in the trap of seeing war as a purely physical process when in fact their Soviet opponents were aware of its psychological essence:

In their search for a way to fight outnumbered and win, the authors of 100–5 did not adequately consider that it was through a concept of war as dislocation rather than destruction that outnumbered forces achieved most of their victories.[25]

Lind compared the inadequacies of the 1976 manual with those of its 1968 predecessor, thereby emphasising the way in which attrition had remained the focus of the Army's attention. He also pinpointed the manual's lack of appreciation for tailoring the military resources at America's disposal to its strategic aims, thereby highlighting the Clausewitzian relationship between war and policy. Although he lacked the professional expertise to advocate a completely new doctrine, Lind succeeded in building on John Boyd's theory of the OODA loop to show that an approach based on operational art was required. Boyd, a retired US Air Force colonel, had derived his observation-orientation-decision-action (OODA) cycle from an analysis of the air war in Korea. There, American pilots had made up for the inferiority in speed of their aircraft by exploiting better hydraulics and cockpit design to allow them to observe rapidly the tactical situation and to orient from one tactical situation to the next in quicker time than their opponents. Boyd applied his theory in the mid-1970s to ground manoeuvre with the intention of achieving operational shock. Basically, if one can complete the Boyd Cycle faster than one's adversary, then one has a crucial advantage. This approach highlights the importance of movement on the battlefield. In Robert Leonhard's words:

> The commander who desires to increase the effectiveness of his "applied will" – his force – can concentrate upon his unit's ability to accelerate, since he can do little to increase his mass. By improving his staff's ability to cycle through Boyd's [OODA] loop, the commander adds to his acceleration and multiplies his force ... The Boyd cycle is a component not of momentum, but of force: the applied will of the commander.[26]

The Boyd Cycle was to be fully developed by Lind in his *Maneuver Warfare Handbook* (1985), which was written expressly with the Marine Corps in mind. Lind's thinking revolved around three major concepts borrowed from German experience: *Auftragstaktik*, which has been discussed previously, *Schwerpunkt*, and *Lücken und Flächentaktik*. *Schwerpunkt* in this context does not refer to the decisive point with its connotations of a fixed geographical location; rather, it means the focus of effort.[27] This concept reflects the substance of Boyd's paradigm, which was concerned with dislocating the rival's operational system. *Lücken und Flächentaktik* refers to the concept of "surfaces and gaps", a means of describing the opponent's strong points, which are to be avoided, and his weak points, which are to be exploited by placing one's *Schwerpunkt* opposite the "gap". As Colonel Mike Wyly pointed out in his autumn 1981 lectures to the Marine Corps Amphibious Warfare School, Clausewitz had written about pitting strength against weakness when he discussed defensive positions in *On War*:

The attack cannot prevail against them. It has no means at its disposal to counteract their advantage. In practise, not all defensive positions are like this. If the attacker sees that he can get away without assaulting them, it would be stupid of him to attempt it ... *It is a risky business to attack an able opponent in a good position.*[28]

Returning to Lind's 1977 *Military Review* article, he was sceptical about the belief that the 1973 war had shown that the defensive had reasserted its supremacy over the offensive. He argued that the "new lethality" of warfare bore no relation to such an assertion, and that the 1976 Field Manual had taken this as given without making any justification for it. Lind made the valid point that certain weapons systems – precision-guided munitions (PGMs), light-infantry anti-tank weapons, and effective ground-based anti-aircraft systems – were just as effective offensively as defensively. FM 100–5 "makes no effort to distinguish what it sees as a new advantage for the defense from the possibility that this could enhance the operational offense".[29]

Lind's critique hinted at the pessimism that had pervaded American thinking at this time. This was a reflection both of the Vietnam experience and an acknowledgement of the conventional superiority enjoyed by the Soviet Union. With everything designed to stop a Soviet advance within the confines of the inner-German border area, Lind pointed out the counter-productive effect of the focus on "winning the first battle", and instead viewed the situation from the enemy's perspective. Soviet forces were organised into echelonear formations with deep operations in mind. Their doctrine countenanced the "defeat" of a heavily attrited first echelon. However, they were prepared to absorb this attrition given that they still had adequate strength in the follow-on echelons to force a second and subsequent battles. The Soviets were, therefore, prepared for a long war. American doctrine had no answer to such an approach. Strategically, a fixation with the initial battle suggested an "all or nothing" approach that betrayed American pessimism about the conventional balance of forces in Europe. Although Starry admitted that the concept of the first-battle thesis was "somewhat controversial", TRADOC informed Lind that it was "an attempt to offset the assumptions which have governed US military policy in the past: that time and materiel will eventually rectify any initial disadvantage".[30]

The penchant for firepower in the 1976 manual was seized on by Lind as evidence that the effectiveness of weaponry such as tanks would not be utilised properly. As he pointed out, the tank was discussed first and foremost as an instrument of firepower, and not of mobility. The manual tended to utilise the worst elements of the thought processes favoured by systems analysts, referring to rates of fire and kill probabilities. The defender was assumed to be at an advantage because of the inherent destructiveness of firepower, while "the weapons of the attacker are not as effective as the weapons of the defender, and his forces are more vulnerable".[31]

Lind used the Clausewitzian tool of historical analysis to illustrate the potential of Soviet doctrine and to highlight the shortcomings of its American counterpart. As well as alluding to German and Soviet experience, he also pointed out that the Israelis had adopted manoeuvre in their Suez counter-attack in the 1973 war to surprise the Egyptians. Basically, Lind was criticising what he saw as a "wrong kind of defence", or shallow defence as opposed to defence in depth. Lind wrote that a shallow defence would require an ability to execute an extremely skilful withdrawal in the midst of the chaos created by the enemy offensive. Defence in depth, on the other hand, would give the defender some room for error. German experience against the Soviets in the Second World War highlighted the advantages of the latter over the former.[32]

Ultimately, however, Lind's main point was that the new doctrine was strategically damaging to the United States and NATO. He interpreted it as an admission that the situation in a conventional war in Europe would be hopeless, with the doctrine papering over the cracks of inevitable retreat. For Lind, FM 100–5 had institutionalised a Maginot mentality, which was epitomised by its focus on linearity:

> the farther forward the battle can be fought, the better … If the active defense can maintain coherence along the FEBA (forward edge of the battle area) or in the tactical zone just behind it,… the more successful the total defense will be.[33]

Clausewitz had written about the way in which space should be traded off for time when campaigning on the defensive, a course that NATO could not follow given its inability to defend in depth: "It cannot be the object of defense to protect the country from losses; the object must be a favorable peace."[34]

DePuy, on the other hand, later rationalised the defensive orientation of NATO strategy as follows:

> [T]here are people who feel that the doctrine of the army is too defensive. They feel that success in battle only comes to the attacker. And, they are disturbed about the amount of time, effort, and concentration that we now have on the defense. I agree with all of that. I think it is too bad. I don't think it is a formula for winning the war. At best, it is a formula for a stalemate or for deterrence. Unfortunately, however, the facts of life in NATO, and the correlation of forces as the Soviets call it, are such that we do not have a general offensive capability in Europe.[35]

Critically, Active Defense completely lacked any means of interfacing with Soviet doctrine. This was inadmissible given its premise that the Soviets would begin the war by attacking, something that would set the pattern for events to come. Lind believed that manoeuvre was the most practical way for the Americans to proceed, and criticised the shortcomings of Active Defense in failing to appreciate intelligence. He concluded that "no examination of the possibility of reform is being undertaken in key areas such as the 'can-do' mentality and the adherence to an attrition/firepower rather than a maneuver doctrine".[36]

Lind's significance lies in the fact that he managed to introduce ideas derived from operational art into the debate over the 1976 field manual. He argued that there was an alternative, and in the process demolished some of the most cherished notions of conventional American military thinking, particularly the belief in superior firepower. Nevertheless, the force of Lind's argument provoked counter-criticism, and not only from the TRADOC establishment. Some of his critics such as Archer Jones, Robert Doughty and Don Holder cited Clausewitz in their conviction that FM 100–5 was sound in its emphasis on the defensive. Jones argued that Active Defense was the last, logical step in a process of improving the theory of the defence, which had begun during the eighteenth century. He alluded to Napoleon's approach to the strategic defensive as one "which was in opposition to the cordon system then in vogue". Clausewitz had written of the need for such concentration:

> [F]or the main force, intended to defend the country, to be strung out in a long series of defensive posts against the enemy's main army – in fact, in a cordon – would be so absurd that one would have to investigate the immediate circumstances accompanying and explaining such an occurrence.[37]

Jones also argued that Napoleon's concentration of all uncommitted forces at the point where the enemy's main thrust was detected eschewed the need for a subtracted reserve. Active Defense implied this in that any forces not engaged in battle were in reserve. Doughty and Holder, who later became converts to operational art, cited Clausewitz in their belief that the defensive was superior to the offensive in modern war. Shimon Naveh has pounced on these criticisms as evidence that Clausewitzian thought is an anachronism when, in fact, the proponents of Active Defense were selective in their use of his thinking. Jon Sumida has recently made a similarly flawed interpretation of Clausewitz's writings on the defence. Dialectic is very much at play in Clausewitz's interpretation of the defence. In effect, he is arguing aloud. Moreover, one must distinguish between the strategic defence and the tactical defence. Janeen Klinger's interpretation is, therefore, much nearer the mark and, in the context of Active Defense, very pertinent: "The validity of Clausewitz's view concerning defense is linked to a distinction he makes between tactics and strategy and the fact that a characteristic could be true of tactics but not true of strategy."[38]

Those critics who followed in Lind's path tended to focus on the manual's overemphasis on defence. DePuy reacted to this criticism by arguing that he was being realistic given the strategic circumstances. However, General Alexander Haig, the Supreme Allied Commander in Europe, made the valid point that the manual was concerned only with the European theatre, and provided no guidance as to how the Americans should approach a conflict that might occur elsewhere in the world.[39] Naveh has summed up the importance of the 1976 field manual, for all its flaws, as being a stepping stone on the way forward to formulating a theory for the operational level of war:

By presenting the American armed forces with a conceptual product, deficient as it might have been, TRADOC managed to provide, for the first time after many years of intellectual drought, a distinctly theoretical foundation upon which a critical discussion could be based.[40]

Defence policy from Schlesinger to Brown

The advent of Mutual Assured Destruction presented strategists with a dilemma in that the development of any feasible strategy involving nuclear weapons, other than that executed in an all-out war, was difficult to articulate. Colonel George Smith, USMC, believed that, in such an event, Clausewitz's notion of absolute war would be a reality: "Accepting the conclusion that war can now be waged in the total form envisioned by Clausewitz,... [m]an must perpetuate, even improve, the means that threaten his destruction while seeking reasoned ways and means to eliminate that threat."[41]

It was a moot point as to what would happen if deterrence failed. Strategists began to consider the possibility that, should the nuclear threshold be passed, a means of limiting the effort required to achieve some rational political purpose should be in place. This approach was tailored to ensure that the political leadership would have a warfighting capability in place that would offer options beside total war. Indeed, it was argued that the existence of such a capability would actually strengthen deterrence. This line of thought required an ability to see international relations as consisting of more than the divide across Europe between NATO and the Soviet bloc. Such an approach had posited that everything revolved around the way in which NATO responded to a Soviet attack on West Germany. This had arguably skewed military planning, as can be seen from analysing FM 100–5 of 1976. However, given the degree to which Soviet interests were being pursued world-wide, it was possible that a crisis could occur anywhere, and at any time.

James Schlesinger's academic background in economics gave him the understanding to criticise the pedantry of the systems analysts. As far as nuclear strategy was concerned, Schlesinger was firmly on the side of those who were sceptical of the credibility of MAD. While working at RAND, Schlesinger had expressed his concern that one consequence of the controversy over anti-ballistic missile (ABM) deployment had been "to turn our thoughts away from city avoidance and minimizing collateral damage to the civil fabric of our opponent's society and towards employment of military capabilities in their most destructive mode".[42]

However, both Schlesinger and Harold Brown, his successor in the Carter Administration, accepted that "essential equivalence" was important for its symbolism in that it would prevent the Soviets from being seen as somehow superior. Lawrence Freedman has argued that this approach was both flawed and potentially counter-productive: "Once subjective factors were accorded crucial importance in the formation of a deterrent posture then all aspects of military power became of potential importance and nothing could be discounted."[43]

Trying to establish an index of military power that could convey the effectiveness of each side's strategic nuclear forces was a futile exercise. Although such an index might provide political capital in arms control negotiations, it would depend on subjective measurements: Would one use numbers of delivery vehicles or warheads; accuracy and yield; or unquantifiable factors such as target strategies? Despite his apparent aversion to such an approach, Schlesinger argued that it would be dangerous to allow any asymmetry to develop between the superpowers in the "basic technology and other factors that shape force effectiveness".[44] In the final analysis, this approach betrayed a penchant for placing confidence in the weaponry involved rather than answering the more abstract question as to how to respond to a situation where deterrence had failed.

Nevertheless, Schlesinger attempted to find some way out of the assured destruction morass, and he developed a strategy broadly based on the concept of escalation dominance. While his National Security Decision Memorandum (NSDM) 242 of 1974 did not radically alter the focus of the Single Integrated Operational Plans established a decade before, it did herald a new approach in its shift from countercity targeting. McNamara had failed to implement a "no cities" policy in the 1960s. However, technology had now advanced to the extent where the required intelligence, precision, and command and control capabilities existed. NSDM 242's emphasis was on controlling escalation through the development of limited nuclear options to counter the Soviet threat in a variety of theatres by utilising these advances. It even mentioned the importance of "non-targets", mainly around population centres, which were places that the Americans should try to avoid damaging. While such options might permit the Americans to fight across the whole range of potential conflict, there was no guarantee that civilian populations would remain unaffected by precision targeting:

> US officials have proclaimed that the US does not target population per se. But, while there are procedures employed for minimising collateral damage, this minimisation is conducted with respect to a basically fixed target set and weapons arsenal. Such constraints allow little flexibility in attempting to significantly reduce collateral damage. Without significant limitations on collateral damage, limited war scenarios have little plausibility.[45]

In 1982, Colonel Nicholas Fritz, USAF, speculated as to how Clausewitz would have analysed the various schools of thought on the best way of deterring the Soviets and concluded:

> He would note the position of those who think that the ability to destroy a finite number of Soviet cities is sufficient to deter any Soviet use of nuclear weapons. Clausewitz would object to this notion on the grounds that destruction of population per se is not useful because the opponent's capability to strike your forces has not been altered.[46]

Schlesinger's emphasis on "flexibility" tended to draw the sting out of any would-be critics. Only Bernard Brodie offered a credible critique, arguing that it was not necessarily the case that "expanding the President's military options is always a good thing" because this would depend on one man's "wisdom". Brodie also made the valid point that Congress had recently enacted legislation to clip the president's wings, given the leeway with which successive presidents had been able to make decisions over Vietnam.[47]

The Schlesinger Doctrine, as it became known, attempted to solve the conundrum facing NATO in central Europe. It underpinned three military objectives: aiding conventional forces engaged in a major conflict; undertaking damage limitation by destroying the remainder of the enemy's strategic forces; and acquiring effective military superiority at any given point on the scale of conflict (i.e., escalation dominance). Schlesinger confirmed that he would not rule out the first use of nuclear weapons to aid NATO in a crisis – such a crisis may well have occurred if the strategy underpinning the 1976 FM 100–5 failed to prevent a Warsaw Pact advance. The rationale behind going nuclear would involve limited strikes at those targets that could be interpreted as supporting the enemy's immediate war-making capability such as submarine bases, airfields, railheads and oilfields. Nevertheless, Schlesinger hoped that advances in conventional weaponry, particularly in terms of precision, would raise the nuclear threshold.

There are some comparisons between the Schlesinger Doctrine and flexible response. Schlesinger's emphasis on flexibility ensured that America's arsenal of tactical nuclear weapons would have to be modernised, given that it had been neglected in recent years. However, this plan triggered a political row within NATO – not only given the potential effects of nuclear fallout over Germany but also because their use would break a taboo. The point as to whether certain members of NATO were more afraid of nuclear war than they were of Soviet aggression was moot, and this came to prominence during the controversies over the deployment of intermediate nuclear forces (INFs) in Europe at the turn of the decade. Clearly, the Americans were banking on their allies having the political *will* to contemplate any eventuality.

In the event, Schlesinger failed in his objective to draw people's attention to a nuclear strategy based on something other than an all-out exchange of nuclear weaponry between the superpowers. The possibility of a Soviet attack with ICBMs against American missile silos could effectively wipe out the US ICBM force given its storage in fixed-site and land-based positions. If, on the other hand, the Americans attempted to inflict similar damage on the Soviet ICBM force, it would fall short of total success because this force was less vulnerable to such an attack. In such a situation, the United States would have no option but to try and annihilate Soviet cities – something that would invite retaliation in kind. As Senator Henry Jackson pointed out, this could undermine deterrence as the Soviets "might conclude that no American President would order such a move".[48]

Colin Gray – a proponent of escalation dominance – wrote in 1978 that the loss of one leg in the American strategic triad would be "an event so momentous that its anticipation should be the occasion for a fundamental review of strategic doctrine".[49] However, Freedman has argued that the fact that ICBM vulnerability was the greatest cause of concern to the Americans could be taken "as a symptom of the underlying stability of the strategic balance".[50] Effectively, American concerns were the result more of a lack of confidence than of a proper reading of the situation. Nevertheless, Ronald Reagan was to exploit concerns over the vulnerability of the ICBM force during the 1980 presidential election.

Jimmy Carter had entered office in 1977 determined to further reduce American reliance on nuclear weapons. He was very sceptical about the possibility of limiting nuclear war. In 1979, Brown criticised the notion of a strategy based on counterforce:

> [C]ounterforce and damage-limiting campaigns have been put forward as the nuclear equivalents of traditional warfare. But their proponents find it difficult to tell us what objectives an enemy would seek in launching such campaigns, how these campaigns would end, or how any resulting symmetries could be made meaningful.[51]

However, American intelligence assessments of Soviet strategic policy suggested that the Soviet approach to nuclear strategy differed from that of the West in that the Soviet Union entertained thoughts of victory. Given this, Carter was forced to introduce a Nuclear Targeting Policy Review to examine Soviet nuclear doctrine closely to allow the Americans to tailor their strategy accordingly. This revealed that the Soviets favoured short, decisive conflicts, whether conventional or nuclear. Carter therefore decided to pursue the possibility of fighting a protracted nuclear conflict to frustrate Soviet war aims. In this context, if in no other, it would be possible to describe Carter's approach as Clausewitzian. His administration's most important pronouncement on nuclear policy was Presidential Directive (PD) 59 unveiled by Brown in June 1980. This directive emphasised the need to target logistic and war-supporting industries ahead of other economic targets. It placed great emphasis on command posts and other C3 facilities, thereby targeting the Soviet political and military leadership so as to paralyse their chain of command. In so doing, PD59 acknowledged that the Soviets' main centre of gravity was their polity. It also confirmed Schlesinger's moves towards escalation dominance by making the reserve force more survivable so as to support a protracted conflict. Brown later justified the underlying emphasis on escalation dominance:

> The countervailing strategy is less of a departure from previous doctrine than is often claimed. It keeps deterrence at the core of US policy. And it implies no illusion that nuclear war once begun would be likely to stop short of an all-out exchange. But it does acknowledge that such a limited war *could* happen, and it seeks to convince the Soviets that if a limited nuclear attack by them somehow failed to escalate into an all-out nuclear exchange, they would not have gained from their aggression.[52]

Commentators such as Gray argued that the West should take PD59's logic further and target the whole Soviet political system. This line of thought was a throwback to that of the inter-war air power enthusiasts who argued that strategic bombardment would cause an enemy to cease its military operations by destroying its infrastructure. Gray believed that the Soviet system of command and control was weak enough to collapse completely if the leadership was removed early enough to ensure that the strategic nuclear forces ceased to function. Gray's thought processes derived from his belief that the Soviets had a more realistic appreciation of the political utility of nuclear weapons than the Americans. One can argue that this derived from Marxism-Leninism's appreciation of Clausewitzian theory, and Gray argued that the West should adopt a similar approach when framing its nuclear strategy. As he wrote in 1980, "nuclear weapons are fully subject to the same logic of strategy that applies to all other weapons".[53]

Both superpowers possessed so-called "rear echelon" or intermediate-range nuclear forces that could be used not only against conventional reserve forces and communications systems but also against cities behind the field of battle. The Soviets were especially active in modernising their capability during the late 1970s. In December 1979, NATO announced, in the face of some vigorous opposition, that 572 American medium-range ballistic and cruise missiles would be deployed in Western Europe. This decision is a perfect illustration of the Clausewitzian relationship between policy and war in that it confirmed the credibility of the link between the defence of Europe and American nuclear power. It also served to reassure the Europeans, and the West Germans in particular, of America's commitment to their defence, and also presented Soviet planners with further food for thought if ever they contemplated a strike against Western Europe.

In 1979, Michael Howard wrote an article in *Foreign Affairs* that was intended to try and shift the debate about US strategy away from what he saw as an overemphasis on weaponry. In addition to the dimension of technology, Howard identified three equally important dimensions of strategy: social, logistical and operational. Taking his lead from Clausewitz, Howard attempted to emulate the way in which *On War* had made the crucial distinction between the logistical and operational dimensions of war. Subsequent experience had taught that social and technological factors were equally valid. (Clausewitz, of course, acknowledged society's role though he did not believe that technology was as significant given the relative technological parity of the armed forces in the Napoleonic Wars.)

Basically, Howard recognised a need to plan in the event of deterrence failing to prevent a Soviet attack on Western Europe. Given the social dimension of strategy, Howard concluded that it would be very difficult for a democracy to initiate a nuclear war, even in response to aggression:

> If this is the case, and if on their side the conventional strength of the Soviet armed forces makes it unnecessary for their leaders to take such an

initiative, the operational effectiveness of the armed forces of the West once more becomes a matter of major strategic importance, both in deterrence and in defense...

The Western position ... appears both paradoxical and, quite literally, indefensible, so long as our operational strategy explicitly envisages the initiation of a nuclear exchange.[54]

Nixon had established Iran and Saudi Arabia as the "twin pillars" of American interests in the Middle East. The former collapsed in 1979 after the Islamic revolution had deposed the Shah. This setback was compounded by the Soviet invasion of Afghanistan later in the same year. These events heightened American concerns about the so-called "arc of crisis" stretching from Angola through the Horn of Africa and Yemen to the Middle East, and along which pro-Soviet and anti-Western forces seemed to be taking control. Carter was therefore forced to announce his own eponymous doctrine in 1980. The Carter Doctrine stated that any attempt by an outside power to gain control of the Gulf region would be regarded as an attack on the vital interests of the United States. A Rapid Deployment Joint Task Force (RDJTF) was formed to give this policy military credibility. The Carter Doctrine had the effect of focusing American minds on those areas of the globe other than Europe where the United States had vital interests at stake. Nevertheless, though this may have satisfied some conservatives, who believed that only the Soviet Union was prepared to use military power to further its strategic interests, it was obvious that the RDJTF – which was about 20,000 strong – was no more than a token gesture. The geographical proximity of the Soviet Union to the Middle East ensured that it was even less likely to be stopped there if it decided to use force than it would be in Europe. In post-Soviet years, however, the successor to the RDJTF, Central Command, would play a crucial role as the military arm of American policy in the region.

That the American geopolitical position vis-à-vis the Soviet Union was not as weak as conservatives supposed can be seen in an analysis of the Helsinki conference of 1975. Although the Soviets seemed to be proceeding with self-assurance and confidence on the world stage, they were in fact very much aware of their own weaknesses and limitations. Their decision to recognise that existing borders should not be changed by force can be interpreted as being driven by caution. From the West's perspective, this was sensible given that there was no possibility of changing the status quo in this manner. In other words, the de facto Soviet occupation of eastern Europe was made *de jure*. The Soviets were quite happy to settle for what they already held, albeit their proxy forces elsewhere in the world would not be prevented by Moscow from advancing the communist cause.[55]

The move away from active defense

The interpretation of contemporary Soviet doctrine by advocates of the Active Defense concept and those who favoured military reform reflected the polemical nature of the debate. While the former defined Soviet doctrine in the narrow terms of lessons learned from the 1973 war and the increase in lethality of modern firepower, the latter interpreted it in its true light, taking it as a template for what was to become AirLand Battle. Basically, the proponents of Active Defense failed to recognise that contemporary Soviet doctrine was the logical outcome of the process begun in the 1920s and resurrected in the late 1960s. The theory of deep operations had now developed to an extent that far outweighed the lessons to be learned from a study of the tactical concepts and deployment of weapon systems as seen in the 1973 war. The reformers, on the other hand, argued that by failing to appreciate Soviet doctrine properly, the 1976 version of FM 100–5 was laying the foundations for failure.

The Soviets had been busy since the late 1960s with preparing an offensive capability spearheaded by Operational Manoeuvre Groups (OMGs) to exploit the shallowness of the NATO rear. OMGs posed not only an operational problem but also a strategic one. By driving into NATO's rear, the Alliance would be deterred from using tactical nuclear weapons to destroy them. Theoretically, this meant that NATO could not deter Soviet forces from entering NATO territory through the threat of nuclear use *after* hostilities had begun. Brigadier-General Huba Wass de Czege, who helped to write the 1982 version of FM 100–5, has confirmed that the US Army learned from Soviet history:

> I think you need to understand that between 1980 and 1985 we studied many things of relevance. We did read the Russians, studied the Battle of Kursk and the final campaigns on the Russian fronts, even the Manchurian campaign [against Japan in 1945] ... Of course, we had to re-interpret what we learned to its relevance to the conditions in Europe in the eighties.[56]

Donn Starry, one of the main contributors to the Active Defense doctrine, quickly began to have doubts about its efficacy as a result of manoeuvres he conducted at the regimental level and above as the commander of the US V Corps in Germany early in 1977. Its narrow focus, combined with his greater appreciation of the Soviet threat, led him into the reform camp. Starry became commandant of TRADOC in July 1977, and was therefore in a position to give practical effect to the ideas being propounded by the reformers. Nevertheless, politics dictated that he present the development of US doctrine as being a continuum of the process that had led to the 1976 manual. His role as one of its writers gave him the leeway to improve on it. Using his tenure with the V Corps as a laboratory in which to develop operational manoeuvre, Starry changed the emphasis on fighting the first battle to accommodate a concept called Central Battle. In August 1977, he defined this as "the place where all the combat systems interact on the battlefield" and later wrote:

> [W]e've got to get out of a defensive mind-set and restore the "spirit of the offense" to our thinking. But, the task is not that simple. We need to reaffirm that the strength of the Active Defense comes from small unit initiatives which are offensive in nature ... Secondly, we need to think through

when larger units (brigades, divisions, the corps) can best transition into more coordinated offensive operations properly supported with effective joint offensive suppression and containment of second echelons.[57]

By experimenting at the corps level, Starry and his staff came to appreciate that manoeuvre was based around a division of the twin dimensions of time and space: the present and the future, and the front and the depth. This led to a process called force generation, which overhauled traditional concerns with force structure and capabilities, and instead focused on the factors of tempo, mobility, fire, surveillance, continuity of operations, and co-ordination. The whole was aimed at neutralising the operational capability of the enemy. This warfighting capability was one of four areas that Starry saw as vital to the army's operational integrity. The others were: training and educating the force for the challenges of modern war, developing and procuring the necessary technologies, and restructuring the force to meet global demands.

Starry entrusted TRADOC's chief of the Combat Development Analysis Directorate, A. G. Pakorny, with the task of further developing the process initiated by the concepts of Central Battle and force generation. Unlike DePuy, whose thinking was shaped by immediacy, Starry gave his analysts eight years in which to complete the enterprise known as the Battlefield Development Plan (BDP). This tailored procurement to doctrine by examining the technological developments that were going to shape the future battlefield as well as Soviet doctrine. Starry furthered this process by initiating a policy whereby doctrine could be shaped not only by TRADOC but across the army as a whole so as to avoid the divisiveness that had characterised the debate over the 1976 manual. Late in 1979, for example, he transferred the responsibility for composing a new FM 100-5 to the Department of Tactics at Fort Leavenworth. The team drafting was to include Major Leonard "Don" Holder as well as Wass de Czege, who was then a lieutenant-colonel.[58]

Starry's evolutionary approach to doctrinal development was illustrated by the iterative development of the Central Battle concept into a more advanced Integrated Battlefield, then an Extended Battlefield, and ultimately AirLand Battle. The Integrated Battlefield provided the means by which close-in operations and operations in depth could be integrated into a single operational theory. Given the echelonear nature of the Soviet armed forces, the Air Force could use interdiction to slow down the momentum of the Soviet advance. In 1978, the Army and Air Force process of collaboration had produced a joint TRADOC-Tactical Air Command document, *Joint Attack of the Second Echelon*. By using the Air Force's mobility, the US armed forces would be able to acquire the space required for manoeuvre in depth without jeopardising NATO's political aim of avoiding offensive operations on the ground across the inner-German border. Striking in depth would present NATO with the time and the opportunity to annihilate the mass of the attacking forward echelon.

The flexibility that operations in depth would afford NATO was compounded by an ability to deploy a tactical nuclear strike if necessary. This would force the

Soviets to increase the intervals between each echelon, thereby disrupting their momentum. It also placed a greater emphasis on the initiative of NATO commanders in that they would have to view the operation through a strategic perspective rather than as being a series of tactical battles. Therefore, although the deliberate spreading of resources throughout the enemy depth appeared to dissipate the tactical advantage of concentration, it in fact served to produce favourable conditions that could be exploited at the tactical level. Thus, a two-way process can be seen: the strategic level drove the impetus down to the operational and then the tactical level, and vice versa.

In a 1979 article, the general tenor of which supported the development of operational art, Edward Luttwak pointed to the lack of any expression of this concept in Anglo-American military thought. He also criticised the American military's approach to warfare as perceived through the traditional prism of an attrition-based, firepower-centred paradigm and through the not-so-traditional penchant for systems analysis:

> To their great discredit, the uniformed military have chosen to play the bureaucratic game, and now have their own models, suitably rigged. Instead of resisting the pressure to conform, and elevating their intellect to the study of war ... the military waste their talents on studies and models which are based on premises which are false, and which they *know* to be false ... Unfortunately, the tactics of bureaucratic conflict in the Pentagon are of no use on the battlefield.[59]

Luttwak wrote another article in 1981 that explicitly damned American strategic thought for its lack of appreciation for the operational level of war and its fixation on attrition as manifested in the inflexibility of certain principles of war. Claiming that US officers lacked the mindset to understand the concept, Luttwak wrote that the operational level was an important element in European strategic thought as evidenced by Clausewitz's work: "The operational level of war, as opposed to the tactical and strategic levels, is or ought to be of greatest concern to the analyst."[60]

Traditionally, the American soldier had viewed firepower as a means of gaining the tactical initiative by attriting the enemy's mass. However, by perceiving momentum to be the driving force behind Soviet doctrine, the Americans discovered that this owed its existence to mass. The reformers therefore identified the follow-on echelon's mass as being the key to depriving the enemy of his operational capability. This lay in the realisation that the enemy's critical vulnerability was the offensive logic of his operational plan. It was now that one interpretation of Clausewitz's centre of gravity came into play at the operational level: "*The center of gravity is the greatest concentration of combat force.*" By combining defence at the front with an offensive in depth, NATO could exploit attrition to preserve the integrity of the territory behind its own front. Therefore, "attrition was portrayed in a new light, and the *deliberate* inter-action between manoeuvre and attrition has become one of the fundamentals of advanced operations".[61]

The impetus behind AirLand Battle was furthered by a grand strategic context in which the United States had suffered the twin setbacks of the Iranian revolution and the Soviet invasion of Afghanistan. These were events that forced the Carter Administration to change its dove-like approach to international relations and ultimately paved the way for the election of Ronald Reagan in 1980. Army chief-of-staff, Edward Meyer, recognising the Clausewitzian relationship between war and policy, pointed to the global situation as proof that the Active Defense concept was inadequate. Rather, the Army needed to consider the operational level of war and the Extended Battlefield. As Starry noted in his seminal article, "Extending the Battlefield", written in 1981: "Deep attack is not a luxury; it is an absolute necessity to winning."[62]

Starry's article confirmed that American theory for the operational level was beginning to mature. His inspiration came partly from a study of deep attack targeting for nuclear weapons. Starry's appreciation of Soviet doctrine and his firm grasp of the strategic imperatives underlying the need for military planning combined to allow him to develop a concept based on the notion of achieving operational shock. Naveh has described the article not unreasonably as "unequalled both in the quality of writing and in the depth of its ideas in the history of modern American military thought".[63]

Naveh's interpretation of operational art as being based on the logic of systems revolves around the interactions, based on operational manoeuvre, between mass and the combined-arms force so as to destroy the rival system through the process of operational shock. Starry advocated this approach as the alternative to the traditional method of wearing down the enemy advance through attrition alone. However, Naveh, in misinterpreting Clausewitz's writings on the defence, goes on to say that the "systems" approach contradicts the Clausewitzian paradigm and that, consequently, Starry is a post-Clausewitzian:

> Starry succeeded in liberating Western military thought from the oppressive domination of the Clausewitzian prejudice of the strategic impotence of the defensive ... By abrogating the last of the Clausewitzian dogmas which guided the Western concept of manoeuvre for more than a century, the emergence of the Extended Battlefield concept indicated, more than any other event, the maturation of the American operational theory.[64]

However, a close reading of Starry's article indicates a very deep appreciation of Clausewitz's teaching about the need to tailor the political aim of the war to the military's means of executing it. While Starry did develop ideas first articulated by theorists such as Tukhachevskii, he did not do so at the expense of Clausewitz's most important contribution to strategic thought. Rather, he complemented this, combining a solid analysis of the operational level of war as it had developed during the twentieth century with the timeless dictum that war is a continuation of policy. In the traditional paradigm of attritional thinking, which focused firmly on the tactical level, the main ingredient that was missing was the need to appreciate the strategic framework. It was this vacuum that Clausewitzian thought was able to fill in American theory. In Starry's words, the Extended Battlefield concept emphasises that

> once political authorities commit military forces in pursuit of political aims, military forces must win something, or else there will be no basis from which political authorities can bargain to win politically. Therefore, the purpose of military operations cannot be simply to avert defeat, but, rather, it must be to win.[65]

For Starry, the key to victory was the deep battle. Given a scarcity of resources it needed to be carefully co-ordinated with the close-in battle to achieve synchronisation, otherwise those resources would be wasted on attacking targets whose destruction would have little impact on the close-in battle. Synchronisation provided a means to combine the entire range of activities being undertaken by friendly forces throughout the depth of the enemy's position so as to induce his collapse through producing the circumstances conducive to operational shock. Starry emphasised the urgency with which US forces at the corps and divisional level needed to start training and planning for the extended battle:

> In NATO, in the Middle East and in Korea, our defensive strategy must extend beyond simply denying victory to the other side. It must, instead, postulate a definable, recognisable (although perhaps limited) victory for the defender. Enemy leaders must be made to understand clearly that, if they choose to move militarily, no longer will there be a status-quo ante-bellum – something to be restored.[66]

Forces in the NATO theatre were not to be treated as a tripwire beyond which the strategic nuclear forces would come into play. Rather, they were to be considered as a means with which to overcome the Soviets' integrated conventional-nuclear-chemical threat. Deep battle arose as a consequence of Soviet doctrine and its emphasis on using the follow-on echelons to maintain the initiative. Starry viewed these echelons as being critical to the outcome. Like William Lind, Starry was concerned that NATO lacked the room in which to conduct a defence in depth because of the restricted geographical space that West Germany afforded. Therefore, the forward defence had to be used as a basis for attriting the enemy assault echelons and then slowing up, dispersing, and ultimately destroying the follow-on echelons so as to seize the initiative and assume the offensive. This concept was reminiscent of Clausewitz's argument about the defence being the stronger form of war *if* properly utilised. Another Clausewitzian piece of rhetoric clinched the argument. "Operative tactics ... must provide for quick resolution of the battle under circumstances that will allow political authorities to negotiate with their adversaries from a position of strength."[67]

It was vital that the battle should occur relatively deep in the enemy's territory so as to prevent the Warsaw Pact from bringing its numerical advantage to bear in the close-in battle. This might also avoid the need to deploy tactical nuclear weapons as a last resort to prevent the NATO front line from being overrun. However, Starry did not dismiss the possibility of deploying nuclear, as well as conventional, firepower throughout the depth of the battle. The full spectrum of land and air weapons systems would have to be integrated into the "air–land battle". Interdiction was the means through which this would be executed, involving not only air (deep) and artillery forces (close in), but also special forces and deception. In other words, it would be almost a carbon copy of the Soviets' own operational rationale. By holding the follow-on echelons long enough, the defence would have time to destroy the front-line echelons and seize the initiative by going over to the offensive. The need for synchronisation throughout the battlefield ensured that unity of command was essential, given the need to repulse the assault echelons and to anticipate the intentions of the follow-on echelons. This would ensure that "the commander is fighting not separate battles, but one well-integrated battle with several parts highly interrelated over time".[68]

Starry was convinced that America's superiority in technology as reflected in advanced sensors, electronic weaponry, and command and control systems could be deployed as a significant force multiplier in the AirLand Battle. Organising these assets into a war-fighting capability became the responsibility of a programme initiated across the Army, involving not only TRADOC but also the Army's schools and units in the field. The opportunities presented by new technologies were, as Richard Lock-Pullan comments, a response to the new understanding of the battlefield as seen by the US Army.[69]

FM 100–5, 1982: the AirLand Battle manual

Starry's article paved the way for AirLand Battle to be incorporated into US doctrine when the new FM100–5 was unveiled in 1982. General Glenn K. Otis, who succeeded Starry at TRADOC in 1981, articulated this reality in *Military Review*:

> AirLand Battle is now the doctrine of the US Army. It states that the battle against the second echelon forces is equal in importance to the fight with the forces at the front. Thus, the traditional concern of the ground commander with the close-in fight at the forward line of own troops (FLOT) is now inseparable from the deep attack against the enemy follow-on forces. To be able to fight these simultaneous battles, all of the armed services must work in close co-operation and harmony with each other. If we are to find, to delay, to disrupt and to kill the total enemy force, we will need the combined efforts of the Air-Army team.[70]

Significantly, DePuy issued a *mea culpa* when he examined the new field manual in the light of its predecessor, which he had made his own:

> Although 100–5 is called operations, we were thinking tactics. That was a

fatal flaw. We were wrong in not grasping that. None of us had studied the military business at the operational level very carefully or thoroughly or well.[71]

In a letter written to Starry in April 1981, Major-General Alexander Weyand had advocated that the draft of the new manual should at least imitate the style of Clausewitz:

> I feel the intellectual tone of the manual should be raised to a level befitting the capstone manual of the major military power in the Free World ... If we must err in focusing FM 100–5 on its audience, I would prefer to err towards a manual which reads more like Clausewitz than an ROTC [Reserve Officer Training Corps] primer. I feel the current draft has very little of Clausewitz in it but a lot of ROTC material.[72]

The manual *was* Clausewitzian in its emphasis on the link between its doctrinal concept and NATO strategy; in its acceptance of a theoretical construct, which can be traced back, at least partly, to *On War*; and in the way in which its emphasis switched from the physical to the moral. For example, the manual cited Clausewitz's observation that the moral element must be considered when undertaking the offensive.[73] However, it should also be noted that Lieutenant-General Richard E. Cavazos, commander of US Army 3rd Corps, was highly influential in emphasising moral elements and, in so doing, he drew freely on the works of Ardant du Picq and John Keegan. Wass de Czege says of the theoretical foundations of the manual:

> In the early days of the School of [Advanced] Military Studies, toward the end of the theory course, I divided the students into two teams. One had to argue that the new doctrine was more influenced by Clausewitz, the other by Sun Tzu. You could make a case for either. I think different theorists emphasise different things and therefore they are difficult to compare. But they all add wisdom.[74]

Holder and Wass de Czege confirmed that not only Clausewitz but also theorists such as Sun Tzu, Liddell Hart and F. O. Miksche, the Czech-born interpreter of blitzkrieg, were consulted. They also examined the campaigns of Sherman, Jackson, Lee, Patton, Clarke and MacArthur.[75]

Otis insisted on incorporating the operational level of war into the manual, which was based around the four tenets of initiative, depth, agility and synchronisation. John Romjue believes these were a combination of what he terms Clausewitz's "violent effect" and Liddell Hart's indirect approach. The operational level of war was defined as:

> [P]lanning and conducting campaigns. Campaigns are sustained operations designed to defeat an enemy force in a specified space and time with

simultaneous and sequential battles. The disposition of forces, selection of objectives, and actions taken to weaken or to outmaneuver the enemy all set the terms of the next battle and exploit tactical gains ... In AirLand Battle doctrine, [the operational level] includes the marshaling of forces and logistical support, providing direction to ground and air maneuver, applying conventional and nuclear fires in depth, and employing unconventional and psychological warfare.[76]

Major Gertmann Sude, an officer from the German Army studying at Leavenworth in 1985, illustrates how the manual deployed Clausewitz's writings on the advantages to be gained from proper use of terrain such as "cover and concealment", "obstacles" and "observation and fire". Sude concludes that "FM 100–5, where the analysis and use of terrain is concerned, completely reflects the ideas written in *On War*."[77] Lock-Pullan, on the other hand, argues that the depth of the opposing force was a more significant influence on AirLand Battle than terrain.[78]

The manual deployed Boyd's notion of the OODA loop to articulate the need for commanders to obtain superiority through swift and decisive decision-making. Brigadier-General Crosbie Saint, commander of the US 7th Army, made clear the need for improvisation in a letter to Wass de Czege:

> The Field Manual reviews our requirement to function in an austere environment. Austerity breeds the necessity for improvisation, especially in the early stages of conflict when lines of communications would be most threatened and the nation has not fully geared for war. The requirement would occur at all levels of command in the theater of war, from squad leader to theater commander. It would be the only solution to scarce personnel and equipment resources needed to prosecute the war.[79]

The purpose behind the deep battle in AirLand Battle was to break up the Warsaw Pact armies into more palatable morsels so as to overcome numerical inferiority in the close battle and therefore to defeat the enemy sequentially. Using the entire depth of the battlefield to hit the enemy and to unbalance his forces would prevent him from bringing his firepower and manoeuvring capability to bear. In a reverse of the Active Defense, AirLand Battle advocated maintaining a substantial reserve, which, as Major Steven Argersinger notes, was advocated by Clausewitz "[so that] the defender [can] fling this body against a part of the enemy forces, thus opening a minor offensive battle of his own ... in order to produce a total reversal".[80]

While the Soviet theory of deep battle involved the deployment of combined-arms units revolving around the OMG, any deep operations undertaken as part of the AirLand Battle would essentially comprise an independent effort on the part of the Air Force. US Army logisticians did not seriously consider the implications of a deep drive on the ground. As far as interdiction from the air was concerned, the experience of the Second World War had shown this to be ineffective unless it was combined with rapid ground manoeuvre. That interdiction was therefore viewed as being an essentially defensive means can be gleaned from a paper by the US Air Force officer, Lieutenant-Colonel David Alberts:

> Interdiction is most likely to be effective against an enemy on the offensive and relying on rapid maneuver and massive firepower for success ... As these are expended they must be replenished, or the unit's effectiveness will diminish. Under the Soviet concept, as units themselves are worn out, they are replenished. The faster the pace of fighting and the more intense the battles, the greater is the theoretical importance of interdiction and the greater is Soviet vulnerability to it.[81]

This defensive emphasis was necessary as any hope that joint air and ground offensive operations could take place would run into the political obstacle of European objections. Therefore, any belief in using pure air power as a tool for victory may have been shown to be wishful thinking if conflict had occurred between NATO and the Warsaw Pact on the inner-German border. Nevertheless, the manual applied Clausewitz's notion of using the defensive as a launching pad for the offensive, citing his concept of the defence as "a shield of blows".[82]

Argersinger, writing as if he were Clausewitz, emphasised the need for the manual's readers to understand the concepts contained therein:

> Broad concepts, such as synchronization, depth, and economy-of-force, were introduced without the theoretical background I would have thought necessary. Your description of how to fight the AirLand Battle flows quite easily from these concepts, and it is an understanding of the concepts that should be the objectives of an army's educational system.[83]

AirLand Battle's aim at "fighting outnumbered and winning" was only a milestone towards overcoming the inadequate legacy left by Active Defense. Advocates of operational art tend to criticise the 1982 manual for its lack of maturity, which is perhaps understandable given that it was only the next step on the long road to the full realisation of this genre in US strategic thought. Leonhard, for example, has criticised AirLand Battle as a "half-way house" between the tactical intransigence of the 1976 manual and the adoption of operational art. Colonel John Rodgers argued that the manual did not fully grasp the significance of synchronisation for operations, and that practitioners in the field were in danger of failing to realise this. Wass de Czege, however, saw the new manual as being antithetical to the previous one, while Martin D'Amato says that Starry "allowed the free flow approach to the writing of doctrine that helped quell the resistance created in the development of Active Defense".[84]

The AirLand Battle concept was briefed to all service chiefs and their deputies, and also to many politicians, including the Congressional Military Reform Caucus and Vice-President George Bush. AirLand Battle affected strategy in that it provided a way of wresting the initiative from the Soviet Union, "disabusing it of any perception that shifting strategic power had opened for it a new freedom of action at theater levels".[85]

Also in 1982, a School of Advanced Military Studies (SAMS) was founded under the combined influence of Meyer and Starry at Fort Leavenworth to educate and train high-ranking officers. This was soon followed by the Air Force with its School for Advanced Airpower Studies at Maxwell Air Force base, Alabama, and the Marine Corps with its School of Advanced Warfighting at Quantico, Virginia. The SAMS took the brightest and best students from the year-long course run by the Army Command and General Staff College (CGSC) and allowed them to remain at Leavenworth for another year to study the operational level of war in more depth. SAMS was Wass de Czege's brainchild and he believes that "[w]hat is taught [there] is a greater influence on doctrine than anything outsiders might speculate about".[86]

Elsewhere in the US Army's education system, the role of Clausewitz and the teaching of operational art was growing apace. During the 1980s, between 8,000 and 10,000 copies of *On War* were being sold in the United States each year. All CGSC students were given a copy of *On War* to read prior to joining their class in 1978/79. Politically, Clausewitz was taken beyond the armed forces through Harry Summers's *On Strategy*, a copy of which was sent to each member of Congress by Representative Newt Gingrich in 1982.[87]

Conclusion

In the mid-1970s, the post-Vietnam military began to read Clausewitz more widely than ever before when a new generation of junior officers were introduced to *On War* at the various services' colleges. Almost simultaneously, a steady stream of articles began to appear in military journals that referred to Clausewitz as a guide in the debate over US strategic thinking and doctrine, whether through a historical evaluation of his thought or through its application to contemporary problems.

The Arab–Israeli conflict of 1973 affected the manner in which the US Army thought about modern war at the tactical level, and helped to stimulate the debate that produced the 1976 edition of FM 100–5, *Operations* and continued thereafter. At the strategic level, the Soviets had a firm grasp of the Clausewitzian relationship between war and policy, something that the US armed forces would only slowly begin to appreciate. It is therefore no surprise that the 1976 manual took the political aim – deterrence or, failing this, achieving a stalemate to restore the status quo – too much for granted. The Army's concept of Active Defense was far too restrained by this factor and consequently the United States would not have enjoyed the superiority assigned to the defence in Clausewitz's writings. The belief that Active Defense doctrine would allow the US Army to fight outnumbered and win the first battle was ill-founded.

America's geopolitical position in the late 1970s vis-à-vis the Soviet Union was not as weak as many thought at the time. In its final year in office, the

Carter Administration utilised the existence of nuclear weapons and used them as a strategic instrument through the deployment of INFs in Europe, thereby making the link between the United States and the defence of Europe crystal clear. In the same context, one can see the way in which the military's adoption of operational art to bridge the strategic–tactical chasm actually supported this process through giving the United States a credible war-making capability that would raise the nuclear threshold.

The US Army's doctrine writers adopted a more manoeuvrist approach within the context of the operational level of war, which would overcome the constraints imposed by the narrowness of the inner-German border by advocating operations in depth through the aid of interdiction by the Air Force. The Clausewitzian notion of the defensive was now properly emphasised. AirLand Battle was founded on the idea that the operational plan must fulfil the objective of the political authority, which would need to negotiate any post-war settlement from a position of strength. No clearer example of Clausewitz's dictum that war should serve a political purpose could be put forward.

The 1982 version of FM 100–5 was underpinned by a number of Clausewitzian concepts and also acknowledged the necessity of fighting at the operational level of war. Nevertheless, the manual's understanding of Clausewitz and the operational level was immature – a fact that reflected the radical change in approach that was required to overhaul the deficiencies of its Active Defense predecessor. Moreover, it should be noted that the use of Clausewitz's ideas compared to other thinkers was by no means exclusive. Sun Tzu and Liddell Hart, in particular, were studied in some detail at the service schools.

5 American strategic thought under Reagan

Strategy under the first Reagan administration

The extension of the battlefield at the operational level was mirrored by a revival in American geopolitical thinking, which was also changing from containment to going on the offensive. Reagan's election coincided with the end of *détente* and the beginning of a "second cold war". While this interpretation tends to point towards movement on the American side, it should be pointed out that the Soviets, having husbanded their military strength for a number of years, had begun to promote aggression more openly, either directly as in Afghanistan or indirectly as in Angola and Ethiopia. This had coincided with a decrease in US defence spending during the 1970s of 20 per cent in real terms.[1] Reagan intended to confront Soviet expansionism and to reverse it through a large arms build-up, thereby confronting the Soviets with the reality of strategic bankruptcy. The Brezhnev Doctrine was to be overturned by the Reagan Doctrine, which combined idealism with realism and aimed to defeat communism by confronting its geopolitical offensive through providing aid to anti-communist counterinsurgency forces in Africa, Afghanistan and Central America. Secretary of State George Shultz summed up this policy in February 1985:

> Today ... the Soviet empire is weakening under the strain of its own internal problems and external entanglements ... The forces of democracy around the world merit our standing with them. To abandon them would be a shameful betrayal – a betrayal not only of brave men and women but of our highest ideals.[2]

Certain commentators used Reagan's election to propound a conservative worldview, which recognised that the Soviets' belief in deploying nuclear weapons as a means to victory should be reciprocated in the West. There was an underlying assumption that the Soviets were able to use the existence of nuclear weapons as a political tool, given that the West seemed to fear nuclear war more than they did. This was rooted in the prevalent liberal view that nuclear weapons were an abomination and, as such, could not be considered to be a rational tool of international relations. On the other hand, some conservatives such as Colin Gray recognised that while all-out nuclear war was irrational, the very existence of these weapons meant that they had to be adapted in some sort of meaningful way to the West's foreign policy. This realistic mindset found an outlet in the Reagan Administration and was Clausewitzian in its logic.[3]

Reagan's achievement was to complete the West's victory in the Cold War. In Henry Kissinger's words, it was:

> [A]n astonishing performance – and to some academic observers, incomprehensible. Reagan knew next to no history, and the little he did know he tailored to support his firmly held preconceptions ... When all was said and done, a president with the shallowest academic background was to develop a foreign-policy of extraordinary consistency and relevance. Reagan might well have had only a few basic ideas, but these also happened to be the core foreign-policy issues of his period, which demonstrates that a sense of direction and having the strength of one's convictions are the key ingredients of leadership.[4]

Reagan understood the underlying weaknesses of the Soviet system and this fed his natural self-confidence, which arose to some degree from his belief in American exceptionalism. He used his constitutional position as the only directly elected official in the Federal Government to drive foreign policy, thereby setting the tone of the debate in Congress and among the wider public. His ability to appeal to the latter over the heads of the former was invaluable. His rapport with the armed forces consolidated this facet of his leadership. Michael Handel has written that this "undoubtedly led to the US military's interest in and trust of politics", and, by extension, Clausewitz.[5]

The strategic lessons of the Vietnam War were absorbed by the Services' War Colleges, which now taught their students the value of the Clausewitzian linkage between war and policy. The military should, therefore, have become aware of the truism, reflected in the Clausewitzian trinity, that a war, particularly if it was drawn out, requires the sustained and active support of the people. However, it is still not clear to this day if the American military (and policy-makers) realise that when the decision to go to war is made, the aim for which the war is fought should be crystal clear. Whilst Reagan almost certainly never read Clausewitz, he showed Clausewitzian instincts when he warned that the United States should not commit its armed forces to conflict in the Third World "unless we are prepared to let them win".[6]

In some ways, however, Reagan poses a challenge to a Clausewitzian interpretation of his administration. His rhetoric was based on exceptionalism, just like Woodrow Wilson's, Franklin Roosevelt's and Jimmy Carter's. But, the end he desired – the peaceful collapse of the Soviet Union – was decidedly Clausewitzian. Furthermore, his means – an arms build-up – was also Clausewitzian. Reagan was never a practitioner of *realpolitik* in the way that Theodore Roosevelt or Richard Nixon had been. But such an approach was inappropriate at that moment in history. The practitioner of *realpolitik*, while always probing for weaknesses in his opponent's armour, is nevertheless wary lest he reveal his own shortcomings. He is very much a non-zero-sum game player. Reagan, on the other hand, was extremely sure of America's position. It is not a cliché to suggest that he arrived at just the right moment in history:

> A decade earlier, his rhetoric would have driven domestic civil disobedience out of control and might have led to confrontation with a still confident Soviet Union; a decade later, it would have appeared antiquated. In the conditions of the 1980s, it laid the foundation for a period of unprecedented East–West dialogue.[7]

Reagan's arms build-up was undertaken in the face of a widely held belief that such a move would be counter-productive as the Soviets would only respond in kind. While this had certainly been the case earlier in the Cold War, the reality in the 1980s was different. The Soviet leadership had been aware of the inherent weaknesses of their system for a number of years and knew that any attempt to keep up with a further expansion in the arms race was economically impossible. The advance from mechanical to electronic engineering confronted the Soviets with a technological chasm that they were incapable of bridging. As Norman Friedman has written, Reagan, perhaps without knowing it, was engaging in an "economic attack" on the Soviets.[8]

The most significant decisions of the whole Reagan presidency were to push through NATO's deployment of intermediate nuclear forces in Europe and the announcement of the Strategic Defense Initiative (SDI). From the beginning, the main kernel in Reagan's thought was that the source of international tension lay in the Soviets' seemingly insatiable appetite for defence spending, a fact corroborated by intelligence inputs. This issue was constantly emphasised during his first administration, thereby mobilising public support and confounding his critics. The move away from mutual assured destruction (MAD) signalled by Schlesinger and Brown was made more urgent under Reagan. Basically, he was prepared to think the unthinkable and to ask "what happens if deterrence fails?" In October 1981, his administration announced a strategic modernisation programme to improve America's nuclear capability. The Missile Experimental (MX), the Trident D5 Submarine Launched Ballistic Missile (SLBM), air- and sea-launched cruise missiles, and the B1 bomber were all to be procured. Emphasis was also placed on overhauling America's capability in command, control, communications and intelligence (C3I) so as to provide for operating the American nuclear deterrent at a more sophisticated level than hitherto. The thinking behind these changes was revealed in a leaked copy of defence guidance obtained by the *New York Times* and *Washington Post* in 1982:

> Should deterrence fail and strategic nuclear war with the USSR occur, the US *must prevail* and be able to force the Soviet Union to seek earliest termination of hostilities on terms favorable to the US.
>
> The US must have plans that assure US strategic nuclear forces can

render ineffective the total Soviet military and political power structure ...
and forces that will maintain, throughout a protracted conflict period and
afterward, the capability to inflict very high levels of damage against the
industrial/economic base of the Soviet Union ... so that they have a strong
incentive to seek conflict termination short of an all-out attack on our cities
and economic assets.[9]

The emphasis under Reagan had therefore shifted from a *counter*vailing to a
*pre*vailing strategy. As his secretary of defense, Caspar Weinberger, put it: "You
show me a Secretary of Defense who's planning not to prevail and I'll show you
a Secretary of Defense who ought to be impeached."[10]

The outcome of the administration's review was National Security Decision
Directive No. 13 (NSDD13), which was taken as the basis for Single Integrated
Operational Plan 6-D (SIOP6-D), which contained plans to target some 40,000
major Warsaw Pact military, economic and political sites. Stephen Cimbala has
criticised this as a plan driven by policymakers unfamiliar with the requirements
of military operations. Basically, most of the civilian officials who had a hand in
this process had no knowledge of the weapons with which they were dealing and
consequently no idea of how to optimise the number of warheads at their disposal to intended targets. Hence the need for 40,000 "potential" targets. Nevertheless, the guidance for the SIOP was jointly agreed by the president and the
NSC before cascading down to the offices of the defense secretary and the Joint
Chiefs-of-Staff (JCS), and eventually the Joint Strategic Target Planning Staff
(JSTPS) headed by an Air Force officer. As Clausewitz wrote:

> [W]hen people talk ... about harmful political influence on the management
> of war, they are not really saying what they mean. Their quarrel should be
> with the policy itself, not with its influence. If the policy is right – that is,
> successful – any intentional effect it has on the conduct of the war can only
> be to the good. If it has the opposite effect the policy itself is wrong.[11]

Despite the apparent increase in nuclear options allowed by NSDD13, Reagan
was still faced with the dilemma of deciding how to react if deterrence failed.
His public utterances suggested that he knew there could be no "victory" in a
nuclear war. Moreover, despite his criticism of past arms control agreements and
his wariness of the Soviets, he continued to keep open the option of arms
control. Such a course was necessary to keep Congressional and public opinion
onside, given the difficulties involved in taking an approach to nuclear strategy
that could be interpreted as rational. Colonel Nicholas Fritz, USAF, speculated
that Clausewitz would have approved of arms reduction as a means of bolstering
deterrence: "He would view any way of reducing enemy armaments as an
appropriate strategy."[12]

NATO's decision to deploy Pershing II and Cruise intermediate range
nuclear missiles in Europe was purely political. It was criticised by many Europeans who misinterpreted it as part of the American desire to limit nuclear war,

which, as Lawrence Freedman has pointed out, was nonsense as "these weapons were wholly unsuited to such a strategy".[13] On the contrary, they provided a means of embedding the American nuclear guarantee to Europe by coupling the link between a conventional land war in central Europe and strategic nuclear war as these weapons were capable of hitting targets in the Soviet Union. Policy therefore drove force structuring and the potential for escalation dominance ensured that although the Americans would be unable to limit nuclear war in the territory of their allies, the Soviets likewise would be unable to do so.

Reagan's "zero option" offer of November 1981, whereby he offered to remove the Intermediate-range Nuclear Forces (INFs) in exchange for a Soviet promise to do likewise, proved to be a risk worth taking. At the time, the NATO INF force was still a paper one while the Soviet SS-20 force actually existed on the ground. Gradually, Reagan backed away from the "zero option" in a show of accommodation, and the Soviets exposed the feebleness of their position by walking out of the Geneva talks in late 1983 as the first Pershing and cruise missiles arrived in Europe. Such intransigence allowed NATO governments to deploy these forces without as much internal strife as they had expected, given that public opinion fell in behind them. The West Germans, who had previously been looked upon by the Soviets as potentially lukewarm to NATO, were galvanised by this behaviour. "Neutralisation" of West Germany and opposition to INF deployment were central facets of Soviet foreign policy. When the Soviet bluff was called, their strategic, as well as moral, bankruptcy was unmasked. Ultimately, the INF treaty of 1987 removed all of these missiles from Europe thereby vindicating Reagan's approach to nuclear diplomacy.

Alexander Bessmertnykh, Gorbachev's deputy foreign minister, has conveyed the impression that was cast on the Kremlin when the United States made the decision to go ahead with the INF deployment:

> [T]here was a certain mood suddenly cast on Moscow that we [had] failed[,] in that ... the situation had tremendously deteriorated as far as Soviet interests were concerned. But if it were not for that [deployment,] which was negative to us, maybe the developments would have been slower, took many more years ... So it kind of pushed the whole process into much higher speed and finally brought us to a solution.[14]

In 1982 the administration articulated its national security policy by issuing NSDD32, which looked to provide a capability for fighting a prolonged conventional war. The advent of AirLand Battle and the Navy's Maritime Strategy was part of a two-pronged thrust that was intended to enable the United States to modify its planning for nuclear war. The other prong was the SDI announced by Reagan in March 1983. His SDI broadcast centred around the rhetorical, even idealistic, question:

> What if free people could live secure in the knowledge that their security did not rest upon the threat of instant US retaliation to deter a Soviet attack,

that we could intercept and destroy strategic ballistic missiles before they reached our own soil or that of our allies?[15]

Although Reagan did not write any memoirs, we can extrapolate both from his deeds and from the words of key players in his administration that SDI was both a genuine attempt to end the nuclear arms race and also a tool with which to coerce the Soviets into retaliating in the knowledge that this was impossible given their dearth of resources. Weinberger has confirmed that SDI *was* Reagan's idea and not a proposal by his staff.[16] Reagan's learning of the targeting options of the SIOP during the mandatory presidential briefing on the plan almost certainly brought the terrible reality of nuclear war home to him, and certainly played a part in his approval of NSDD32: "There is ... some evidence that in a very real sense, the President had been repelled by the full implications of the policies his own administration had been pursuing and so sought to push policy in a quite different dimension."[17]

That SDI may have been a stick with which to beat the Soviets can be interpreted from the offer Reagan made to share the technology (but not the cost) with the Soviets. Far from being an "out of character promise", as interpreted by Freedman, this was a natural conclusion to the administration's long-term strategic aim, which was to end the Cold War without going to the brink of nuclear war. In practical terms, however, the SDI concept, which would rely on space-based systems was years, if not decades, ahead of its time. It is difficult to see how Reagan could believe that it was feasible to implement SDI in the near-to-medium term, despite his plea to the scientific community to make nuclear weapons useless.

The majority of strategic defence analysts in the United States reacted sceptically to SDI, as did Congress, which would have to approve any funding. There was a fear in some quarters that in attempting to ensure that nuclear weapons were no longer a useful tool in international relations, the safety catch of deterrence might be jeopardised in the process. Harold Brown, while supporting some initial research efforts, argued that the concept was impractical. McGeorge Bundy, George Kennan and Robert McNamara wrote an article for *Foreign Affairs* criticising it as a flight of fancy and singling out Weinberger for particular vitriol.[18] Weinberger, in turn, criticised the closed mindset of many in the community of strategic thinkers:

> [T]o those who traipse from resort to resort reading each other's papers on security and strategy, the idea of proposing that we, or any other country, try to defend ourselves against the nuclear missiles of any other country, was not only revolutionary, it was sacrilegious.[19]

Robert Osgood argued that SDI would contravene existing treaty obligations, particularly the ABM Treaty of 1972. Paul Nitze, a leading arms negotiator in the administration, believed that the acid tests of SDI were cost-effectiveness and survivability. The Soviets could simply increase their nuclear arsenal to the extent where it would overwhelm the defence or else develop alternative ways of delivering ICBMs, which would be far cheaper than implementing their own version of SDI:

> It is ironic that Paul Nitze should have become so taken with what came to be called the 'Nitze criteria' as a means to retard or arrest the momentum of the SDI program. In fact, the criteria of military effectiveness, survivability and cost-effectiveness were ... adopted by the Reagan Administration months prior to their articulation by Nitze, [and] are routinely assigned to weapons systems of any kind.[20]

Cimbala has pointed out that "the temptation for both Americans and Soviets is to make what appears to be a Clausewitzian move toward relative advantage in strategic nuclear, or non-nuclear, weapons technology, on the assumption that this temporary advantage can be exploited for future coercion."[21] However, in so doing, some offensive means of coercion would also be required as no defence is ever absolute. As W. E. Burrows remarked, "there is every indication that, far from removing strategic missiles, ballistic missile defence would force both sides to find more inventive ways to attack the other".[22] Such strategic realities have always existed, making incorrect Freedman's assertion that technological trends had rendered Clausewitzian thinking obsolete.[23]

Cimbala's assertion that a "true window of opportunity" might be opened up by SDI could have applied equally to either superpower despite Reagan's public statement that he was not intent on gaining military superiority. From the Soviet perspective, they might decide to take the Western Europeans "hostage", a fear that fuelled European opposition to SDI. Therefore, the defence of the American homeland and its strategic nuclear forces would not necessarily improve NATO's situation. As Cimbala argues, this could only be achieved as it had always been through "the Clausewitzian supremacy of shared political values and expectations to military defense commitments".[24]

There was even a fear that hawks within the Soviet polity might argue for a pre-emptive strike lest they lose the advantages that nuclear power granted them in the field of international relations. In the event, Reagan succeeded in prompting the Soviets to return to the arms control talks they had abandoned over the INF issue. He overcame his critics by deploying a political acumen that put Clausewitz's concept of policy into practice. The scourge of nuclear war had cast a shadow over humanity since 1945, and any politician who made a gesture towards removing this would gain popular support. The American people realised that their defence was safe in Reagan's hands: on the one hand, he was prepared to face down Soviet attempts to gain conventional and nuclear superiority by building up American strength in these areas; on the other hand, he spared no effort in trying to find a way out of the nuclear maze. As Kissinger has remarked of SDI, "no weapon would ever have been developed if it first had to submit to [a] perfectionist criterion".[25]

The Weinberger doctrine

It is perhaps significant that one of the administration's most powerful advocates, Caspar Weinberger, gave Clausewitz practical expression during a speech he made at the National Press Club in Washington on 28 November, 1984, shortly after Reagan had been re-elected. Weinberger's speech centred around six tenets, which highlighted the need for the United States to balance military force with political requirements. These tenets became known as the "Weinberger Doctrine".[26]

The Weinberger Doctrine was formulated partly as a response to the legacy of the Vietnam War, and partly in reaction to an internal debate in the administration involving Weinberger and Secretary of State George Shultz concerning American military involvement in Lebanon and Central America. Whereas Weinberger had drawn the lesson from Vietnam that the United States should be wary about entering into conflicts with no guarantee of a swift resolution, Shultz argued that force should be used to bolster American diplomacy in these areas. Shultz therefore advocated an approach based on *realpolitik*, given that he believed American national interests were at stake. Weinberger, on the other hand, argued that without firm public support and clear policy objectives, the United States would be vulnerable to being sucked into long and costly conflicts with heavy casualties and finally inevitable withdrawal or defeat. It was a danger that confronted the US forces deployed in Lebanon at that time.

Richard Lock-Pullan has commented that the Weinberger Doctrine was "greatly influenced" by Summers's *On Strategy* while Donn Starry, who was now commander of US Readiness Command, lobbied Weinberger to set the sort of criteria that was outlined in the latter's speech.[27] Conrad Crane has also argued that the military drove the rationale behind the Weinberger Doctrine, the very antithesis of Clausewitz's view that policy should be ascendant. As Major John Otis, USMC, put it: "Clausewitz ... would view Mr. Weinberger's reluctance not only as an overly cautious hesitancy to commit US forces to combat, but as the judicious exercise of his responsibilities as our Secretary of Defense."[28]

Weinberger and the US military were clearly concerned about the effects on military morale of the memories of Vietnam and the realisation that there were limits to US military power. Weinberger was also concerned about the undermining of America's ability to wage the Cold War in that it might drain itself of strength by becoming involved in peripheral conflicts: "We must be prepared, at any moment, to meet threats ranging in intensity from isolated terrorist acts, to guerrilla action, to full-scale military confrontation."[29]

The six tenets of the Weinberger Doctrine were:

1   *The vital interests of the United States or its allies must be seen to be at stake.* Despite this, Weinberger was aware that the United States might need to fight for lesser interests in order to safeguard its vital interests: "We must ... be farsighted enough to sense when immediate and strong reactions to

apparently small events can prevent lion-like responses that may be required later. We must never forget those isolationists in Europe who shrugged that 'Danzig is not worth a war' and 'why should we fight to keep the Rhineland demilitarized'."[30]

2 *Once the decision to fight is taken, the effort should be wholehearted so as to reflect the intention of winning.* This reflected the US military's fear that it might go to war insufficiently equipped to accomplish its goals, with later reinforcements being fed in piecemeal thereby ensuring a long, drawn-out and costly conflict. In other words, they did not want a repetition of Vietnam.

3 *Political and military objectives must be clearly defined.* This is the most explicitly Clausewitzian of the six tenets. It is also the acid test that the United States failed to apply in Vietnam and which Weinberger and the military feared was being overlooked in Lebanon. Weinberger cited Clausewitz in evidence: "No one starts a war – or rather, no one in his senses ought to do so – without first being clear in his mind what he intends to achieve by that war and how he intends to conduct it."[31]

4 *Political and military objectives must be continuously reassessed to maintain a balance between ends and means.* In other words, one needs to be ready for the possibility that the ends no longer justify the means, and that it may be worth abandoning a conflict if its cost is becoming prohibitive. Clausewitz, of course, believed that war is a political act and therefore one should not expend an effort that exceeds the goal. He wrote of two reasons that might force one to cut short a conflict: "the first is the improbability of victory, the second is its unacceptable cost".[32]

5 *Before troops are sent abroad, there must be some reasonable assurance of Congressional and public support.* This was another vital lesson of Vietnam, and clearly reflects Clausewitz's trinity. Of course, there may be occasions when the public does not interpret an interest as being vital even although their leaders may. As Michael Handel writes, "leaders must do their best to mobilise public opinion, educate and lead it – but, if necessary, also take action even without a clear consensus".[33]

6 *The commitment of US forces to war should be undertaken only as a last resort.* This tenet may contradict the first tenet in that by dithering over whether or not to use force the opportunity may pass, leaving the vital interest shorn of protection. However, in Clausewitzian terms, the polity should not sanction a war that is alien to the nature of the policy in question.[34]

David Twining has described the Weinberger Doctrine as representing "a maturation and sophistication of our strategic judgement; more importantly, it adapts and clarifies defence policies of a different time and slower world to the exigencies of the present and the challenges of the future".[35]

However, while the Weinberger Doctrine confirmed that post-Vietnam America had adopted elements of Clausewitzian thought when developing its grand strategy, it did so in a haphazard manner. While the focus on objective was sound, "Weinberger's emphasis on the militarily achievable renders obsolete the Clausewitzian emphasis on the priority of political aims, rather than objectives, in setting military strategy".[36]

To advocates of *realpolitik* such as Shultz and Kissinger, the Weinberger Doctrine boxed policymakers into a corner. They argued that America's hands would be tied by a pledge to fight only "popular, winnable" wars rather than wars based on a calculation as to whether vital national interests were at stake. Together with the War Powers Act, the Weinberger Doctrine would make it almost impossible for the United States to use force in exercising its responsibilities as a great power, surely a disavowal of Clausewitz. To some extent this would come to pass in the American response to the international crises of the 1990s and, again, after Iraq was occupied in 2003. On the other hand, many of the tenets of the doctrine were evident during the First Gulf War when domestic and international opinion was successfully mobilised in support of that conflict. Finally, one should acknowledge the circumstances in which Weinberger framed his doctrine. The Soviet Union was America's main enemy, and Weinberger was rightly cautious lest American military power should be dissipated by fighting in peripheral engagements.

Air and maritime power

The US Air Force was quick to distil lessons from the Vietnam War. Tactically, it learned from the way in which the North Vietnamese had conducted their air campaigns, and these lessons were incorporated into the "Top Gun" programme for training fighter pilots. As Benjamin Lambeth has written:

> It was finally recognized by airmen for the first time in years, at least in American practice, that the pilot and his personal attributes and skills, rather than the aircraft or the weapon system, constituted the main ingredient in the formula for success in air combat.[37]

In 1975, the Air Force's Tactical Air Command (TAC) had begun to work in tandem with TRADOC so as to enhance joint operations between the Army and Air Force tactical units, a process culminating in the latter's contribution to AirLand Battle. During the same year, the "Red Flag" exercises, which simulated a conflict in central Europe, began. These exercises became "the largest, most sophisticated simulated battlefield in the world".[38]

As far as using airpower as an instrument of war was concerned, the Air Force remained convinced of its validity despite the mixed fortunes of the use of strategic bombing over South-East Asia. The continuing importance of strategic nuclear forces ensured that the Strategic Air Command (SAC) would continue to have a primary role to play in the execution of a strategy designed to win a global conflict. In 1982, "Project Warrior" was instigated with the intention of "[improving] the warfighting spirit and perspective of air force people [and encouraging] an improved understanding of the theory and practice of war".[39]

In 1984, the Air Force updated its manual, Air Force Manual (AFM) 1–1, *Basic Aerospace Doctrine of the United States Air Force*. Harold Winton has described it as a more coherent view of the theory and application of airpower than any of its predecessors. However, the tactical and strategic levels of war were seen as being separate: TAC would help to fulfil the tenets of the conventional AirLand Battle, while SAC concentrated on its plans to launch a nuclear war against the Soviet Union, much as it had been doing since the 1950s. This ensured that Air Force doctrine was contradictory and hence inflexible. Indeed, while SAC might advocate the primary role of airpower, there were those in TAC such as General Robert Russ, its commander, who "believed that the air force's main role was to support the army".[40]

According to AFM 1–1, the Air Force's primary role was to concentrate on neutralising and destroying the enemy's warfighting capability, thereby breaking his will to continue the war. This Clausewitzian tenor was reflected in Lieutenant-Colonel Barry Watts's *The Foundations of US Air Doctrine: The Problem of Friction in War* (1984). This work revolved around the application of Clausewitz's concept of friction to airpower. Watts was on the staff at Maxwell Air Force base, which was home to the Center for Aerospace Doctrine, Research and Evaluation established in 1983. A colleague of Watts, Major Mark Clodfelter, later wrote *The Limits of Airpower: The American Bombing of North Vietnam* (1989), and based it on a "Clausewitzian analysis" of the use of airpower in that conflict.[41]

The US Navy and Marine Corps were not to be left behind by their sister services in the search for innovative ways of defining their roles. Indeed, they were to initiate a theory of warfare that went beyond that which the army could achieve in the 1980s in terms of linking operations with grand strategy. Under Carter, the Navy had been neglected. A five-year ship-building plan was compromised by the refusal of the president and his secretary of defense, Harold Brown, to allow the construction of any more full-sized or "Nimitz"-class aircraft carriers. This was based on the administration's belief that the Navy's main role was to protect the sea lines of communication (SLOC) between the United States and Europe. However, the crises of the late 1970s in the Middle East persuaded Carter to expand his naval building plans to include the construction of a new "Nimitz"-class carrier. Reagan, by contrast, had approved the construction of three more of these vessels by 1983.

While the Army and tactical air forces thought about prolonging a conventional war in Europe, the Navy was given the leeway to look at how American interests elsewhere might be protected simultaneously to fighting in Europe. It also studied the question of diverting Soviet attention from central Europe by striking at the Soviets' vulnerable flanks. In so doing, however, the Navy began to cast adrift from concerns about coalition warfare and to adopt a more unilateralist tone with an emphasis on power projection. A global maritime strategy was sure to raise questions about the American commitment to Europe. Even within Europe itself, the emphasis placed on NATO's northern flank, which was close to the bases of the Soviet Northern Fleet in the Arctic Circle, could well leave NATO's southern flank in the Mediterranean dangerously exposed;

From the global perspective of a superpower, the argument for a maritime-based grand strategy is faultless. From the viewpoint of European allies in immediate proximity to the Soviet Union, it could appear substantially less attractive, especially when combined with the robust ideological stance of the Reagan Administration.[42]

The Maritime Strategy was taken forward with enthusiasm by Reagan precisely for this very reason – there was a perception in America that the United States was somehow beginning to lose its influence in NATO in relation to the Europeans. It is therefore not difficult to disagree with James Nathan's Clausewitzian interpretation of it: "The Maritime Strategy has always been ... a political strategy in a military guise."[43]

The origins of the Maritime Strategy are to be found in work done by the Center for Naval Analyses, which was based on deciphering unclassified information about the Soviet Navy during the 1970s, and in US intelligence assessments that overturned previously held assumptions about both the Soviet Navy's strength and its doctrine. Rather than taking the offensive on the open seas and attacking SLOCs, it was now assumed that the Soviet Navy would be deployed in home waters to defend the "bastions" within which Soviet SSBNs would operate.[44]

In 1981, NATO developed a Concept of Maritime Operations (CON-MAROPS) through which operational concepts and planning could be developed in preparation for a prolonged conflict with the Soviet Union. It centred on five major campaign scenarios: the Norwegian Sea, the Atlantic SLOC, Shallow Seas, the Mediterranean SLOC, and the eastern Mediterranean. CONMAROPS was actually developed at the same time as the Maritime Strategy, but was publicly acknowledged five years before it. While both strategies emphasised forward operations, the Maritime Strategy was bolder, given its global reach and its advocacy of power projection and amphibious warfare through taking the conflict into Soviet waters. Whereas CONMAROPS fitted comfortably within the paradigm of flexible response, the Maritime Strategy was seen by the Alliance as supplementing rather than complementing conventional war in Europe. As with the Army's transition to AirLand Battle, the Maritime Strategy enabled the Navy and the marines to concentrate on offensive warfare. The strategy's most persuasive advocate was Reagan's secretary of the Navy, John Lehman, described by Nathan as "the most influential Naval Secretary since Theodore Roosevelt" and by James Kitfield as someone who "in his first four years almost single-handedly redefined the role of the civilian service secretary".[45]

In 1978, Lehman had described what he saw as the Navy's primary mission:

[It] is to ensure the unimpeded use of the seas by the US and its allies in peace and if need be [to prevent] hostile military attempts to deny such use. In war this mission also includes active denial to the enemy of the use of the seas, harbors, and adjacent airspace. Sea control does not mean what the term seems to imply, control of all seas simultaneously. To carry out its mission the navy must only prevent hostile denial of use of needed areas during the times of their need and no more. To achieve this the navy must be able to project power under the sea, on the surface, in the air above, and over land.[46]

The Maritime Strategy was as much a tool to be deployed during peace as during war. It served to improve American counterforce capabilities and to allow the US Navy to overcome its quantitative inferiority to the Soviets by building its strength up to a projected force of 600 vessels, including 15 carrier-based battle groups and 100 nuclear-powered submarines. Essentially, the Maritime Strategy reinforced deterrence at every level on the ladder of escalation. This included the nuclear level, given that it was planned to have forward deployed forces within striking distance of those Soviet nuclear assets scattered around the periphery of the Soviet Union. As Lehman put it:

All weapons are most valuable when their existence prevents the need for their employment. All of the categories of the carriers' primary and secondary missions have been exercised in battle, but vastly more numerous have been the occasions when their deployment to conduct such missions has achieved political objectives without hostilities.[47]

The Maritime Strategy emphasised seizing the initiative as soon as war was declared. Eric Grove, the naval commentator, interpreted this approach as being the Maritime Strategy's fundamental driving force. In so doing, he drew upon the writings of Sir Julian Corbett, a noted early twentieth-century disciple of Clausewitz:

As Corbett put it, "the offensive must not be confused with the initiative [though it may include offensive elements]. It is possible to seize the initiative under certain circumstances by taking a defensive position from which the enemy is bound to acknowledge us or abandon the operation." This summed up the forward strategy as actually put into effect.[48]

Taking the battle to the Soviets would involve offensive operations carried out by carrier battle groups through the use of carrier-based aviation, nuclear-powered submarines, conventionally equipped cruise missiles, and possibly even amphibious assault by marines against important Soviet bases. The ultimate objective of this, as defined by Admiral James Watkins, chief of naval operations, was that the danger posed to the Soviet submarine-based nuclear reserve would force the USSR to sue for peace on American terms, a very Clausewitzian aim. As Watkins put it, "the real issue is not how the Maritime Strategy is influenced by nuclear weapons, but the reverse: how maritime power can alter the nuclear equation."[49]

However, it was a high-risk strategy and there were some who criticised it as potentially dangerous. Former commander of the 6th Fleet and president of the

Naval War College, Admiral Stansfield Turner, was among the sceptics. Writing in 1982, he expressed incredulity that "thoughtful military planners would actually [bottle up the Soviet Navy]".[50]

Unless nuclear force was used, any attacks on port facilities and associated airfields would be futile as the damage could easily be repaired. Turner further contended that there was a distinct possibility that the Navy could lose around a third of its carriers during such a campaign, a rate of attrition which no president could allow, given the need to cover other theatres of war – particularly the North Atlantic.[51] Moreover, any notions that the Maritime Strategy might lead to large-scale Soviet troop withdrawals from Europe were blinkered by the fact that the strike force the United States could send ashore consisted of two divisions of marines, while the strike aircraft deployed by the carriers would make little impact against the Soviets' land-based defences.

Nevertheless, the Maritime Strategy heralded the beginnings of a change in the concept of amphibious warfare. Until now, amphibious operations had emphasised the need for a frontal assault. However, the manoeuvrist approach was beginning to enter the kernel of naval thought:

> The basic requirements of an amphibious assault, long held to be vital to success, may no longer be attainable … In recent years, military reformers have advocated an approach [manoeuvre warfare] to land tactics [*sic*] that may offer an alternative … Success in such a venture could forestall a return to Gallipoli-like syndrome … Combining maneuver and amphibious warfare impels a new way of thinking about a doctrine that, after nearly fifty years of existence, has become deep rooted in both the Navy and Marine Corps.[52]

While there was a degree of inter-Service politicking behind the Maritime Strategy in that the Navy used it as a lever for more funding, its roots were strategic rather than economic: "The Maritime Strategy was Clausewitzian even though Mahan was the Navy's patron saint."[53]

The debate over the Maritime Strategy went beyond the traditional paradigm in American strategy between those who favoured a maritime-based or Mahanian approach and those who favoured a continental-based or Clausewitzian approach.[54] The Maritime Strategy contained elements of the expeditionary warfare strategies associated with the latter and elements of the former in its global sweep. Rather, it centred in the debate between those who favoured a Eurocentric approach, which recognised that the Soviet centre of gravity lay in its conventional *strength* in central Europe, which could best be overcome by providing SLOC protection for ground and air reinforcements from the United States, and those who favoured attacking the Soviet periphery whereby the Soviet centre of gravity was perceived to lie in its *weaknesses* on the flanks, particularly the vulnerability of its submarine-based nuclear forces to a surprise attack from the sea. NATO's maritime objectives in the north were to contain the Soviet Northern Fleet; to deny the Soviets access to northern Norway's air bases; to defend northern Norway against air and land attack; and to prevent a Soviet amphibious assault on northern Norway. With the exception of the first of these objectives, all were linked to fighting on land.

> [T]he Soviet–US competition is not a contest between land power and sea power, as it sometimes appears. That kind of fallacious thinking misdirects people into debating the false alternatives of continental land power versus maritime strategies. Nations do not inhabit the sea. Wars cannot be won at sea.[55]

While the Maritime Strategy was predicated on the basis of wartime operations in the North Atlantic and Arctic oceans, most of the United States's naval power was being committed to the Pacific and Indian oceans during peacetime. Therefore, as Turner testified to Congress in 1985, any execution of the Maritime Strategy would require a weakening of American strength elsewhere in the world.[56] This was the Maritime Strategy's Achilles' heel in that allies situated around those seas would find themselves having to distract Soviet attention in support of the US Navy's forward operations against the northern Soviet coast. Given this, would these nations then be willing to participate in a superpower conflict that could conceivably end in nuclear war? Furthermore, US naval power was vulnerable during peacetime in these areas, particularly the Middle East. In that region, the need to defend oil shipping lanes against possible Soviet interdiction was jeopardised through having no access to any air bases among the potentially friendly states of the Gulf littoral. This was despite the American policy of containment in the region since 1980. The problem was highlighted during the 1987–88 "War of the Tankers" when the Americans found themselves restricted to using carrier-based aviation, the range and payload of which is inferior to that of aircraft based on land.

In 1986, Colin Gray cautioned against an aggressive execution of the Maritime Strategy. If the US fleet was to fail in its mission and suffered heavy losses in the process, then NATO would be in serious danger of losing any conventional war:

> Common sense has been an early victim in the contemporary US debate over maritime strategy. It should be obvious, given the geographic scope of its tasks, the technical sophistication of the prospective enemy, and the likely desperate strategic circumstances of a future war, that the US Navy must be very large, technically capable, and prepared – within reason – to sail in harm's way.[57]

However, it is clear that like all the other conventional strategies adopted by the US military in the 1980s, the efficacy of the Maritime Strategy was restricted by the overbearing influence of the grand strategic situation, particularly the nuclear balance. Ultimately, this central feature of the Cold War would be resolved by peaceful means.

The strategic context: rolling back communism

Ronald Reagan's presidency was in sync with the notion that the Executive should, in harness with Congress, seek and win the support of the American people in the pursuit of the administration's objectives. Such an approach complemented Clausewitz's notion of the fascinating trinity, given that the political authority was responsible for channelling the passion of the people along a rational course. Reagan's intention to preserve peace through strength struck a chord with the American people, but it still required his ability as a communicator to translate this aim into reality. His "democratic revolution" speech to Congress of 14 March 1986, whereby he pledged to reverse the seemingly immutable Brezhnev Doctrine, epitomised this approach. Weinberger, meanwhile, argued that the Americans could negate the improvements in Soviet capabilities made since the early 1970s by exploiting their technological superiority:

> Where possible, we should adopt strategies that make obsolete past Soviet defense investments. We should devise programs for which an effective Soviet response would be far more costly than the programs we undertake. If possible, we should try to move the competition into areas in which we have natural advantages and to channel Soviet defense effort into areas that are less threatening to us and less destabilising to the overall military balance.[58]

Building military strength – even in the pursuit of maintaining peace – is a risky course for a democratic politician to take. However, the administration's overt determination to resist Soviet aggression earned public support. Weinberger summed up the position in 1986:

> Strength is the price for peace. If peace seems expensive, consider the alternatives. By scrimping on strength we will reduce our security and increase the risks of war. But if we fail to keep the peace, the costs will be incalculable.[59]

The administration's reading of the Soviet threat enabled it to think from a Soviet perspective. Weinberger believed that deterrence had to be informed by such thinking. To build up sufficient forces to deter an attack that simulated an American attack on the Soviet Union would be counter-productive. Rather, it was necessary to reinforce deterrence by acquiring the level of strength that the Soviets themselves believed was necessary to deter an attack by the United States on the Soviet Union. In other words, the administration was taking a novel approach to answering the old question "how much is enough?" As Weinberger put it:

> We seek to deter war by maintaining forces and demonstrating the determination to use them, if necessary, in ways that will persuade our adversaries

that the cost of any attack on our vital interests will exceed the benefits they would hope to gain.[60]

This rationale was as applicable to conventional deterrence, and a policy of buttressing US conventional forces, as it was to nuclear deterrence. It confirms Clausewitz's belief that mankind, not weapons, cause war. As Colonel Richard Swain wrote in 1986:

> [C]onditions and weapons technology have changed dramatically, but Clausewitz retains much of his original relevance. He does so because, in 1827, rather than seeking to answer the question of whether war ought to exist, Clausewitz asked why, or to what end, war exists as a feature of man's experience.[61]

The political imperative of nuclear decision-making in relation to the existence of theatre nuclear forces overshadowed any operational deployment of these weapons in the event of a conventional war going wrong in Europe. The escalatory relationship between operational art and the use of low-yield nuclear weapons came firmly within the realm of the political leadership and was therefore not the concern of the operational commander on the scene. Strategy dictated that a defeat at the operational level might be a better alternative than a failure to come to terms with the enemy on the basis of the gains he had made during the opening stages of a conventional conflict. "[T]he operational commander should recognize that war for a strategically defensive, status quo power like the United States normally represents the collapse of policy, not its continuation, as the most famous, but misunderstood, dictum of Clausewitz appears to maintain."[62]

On the other hand, the deterrent effect of having forces on the ground was a valuable political tool. The introduction of the light division to the US Army's order of battle provided an ability to project flexible forces around the world. In West Germany, for example, the light division could be utilised to defend urban and other rear areas. Such an operational asset could play its part in fulfilling the aims of American strategy, which, according to Weinberger, sought "the earliest termination of conflict on terms favourable to the United States, our allies, and our national security objectives, while seeking to limit the scope and intensity of the conflict".[63]

In 1986, the United States enhanced its ability to wage warfare at the strategic level when Congress passed the Department of Defence Reorganization Act, better known as the Goldwater–Nichols Act after its sponsors, Senator Barry Goldwater and Representative Bill Nichols. This was the first real bureaucratic attempt to impose "jointness" upon the US armed forces and was also intended to iron out the problems that had nullified effective command on the ground in Vietnam by empowering the respective commanders-in-chief through widening the remit of the chairman of the Joint Chiefs-of-Staff. The intention was to improve campaign planning at the theatre level by effectively translating the broad, sometimes ambiguous advice, coming from political decision makers into a strategy for winning the war. This was to be done through improving the quality of the military advice the president received, given the disproportionate weight that civilian advice had enjoyed since the 1960s. Given this, it is not surprising that Weinberger and the Defense Department fought hard to prevent the legislation being passed. Charles McFetridge was correct to interpret these moves as a "[desire] to reassert the importance of [military] advice and move it back into the field of foreign-policy and national strategy formation. This would be congruent with Clausewitz's philosophy."[64]

Goldwater–Nichols also resulted in a requirement for the Executive to submit an annual report to Congress concerning the national security strategy of the United States. The first, in 1987, identified the Soviets "as the most significant threat to US security and national interests". However, it also acknowledged the threat of international terrorism as being "particularly insidious in nature and growing in scope".[65]

The Reagan Administration's foreign-policy was beginning to have a significant effect on Soviet conduct. By 1986, the Soviets had begun to tone down their support for those proxy forces that were fomenting revolutionary situations in the Third World. At the same time, Mikhail Gorbachev was hinting at a Soviet move towards accepting the "zero option" for INFs first put forward by Reagan in 1981 when Soviet strength appeared to be in the ascendancy. The Reagan Administration's refusal to accept Gorbachev's proposal at Reykjavik in October 1986 that an effort be made to abolish all nuclear arsenals allowed the Americans to sign the INF Treaty in 1987 without jeopardising SDI. Finally, but perhaps no less significantly, the change in Soviet military doctrine to a posture of "defensive defence" in 1987 illustrated that the changes in American doctrine and improvements in conventional forces made during the first half of the decade had also had a desired outcome.

FM 100–5, 1986

Although FM 100–5 of 1982 constituted an advance in army doctrine, shortcomings remained. NATO erroneously interpreted AirLand Battle as being strategic, rather than operational, because of its references to "defeating the enemy" and "decisive action". Given this, General William Richardson, now the commandant of TRADOC, stressed that the next manual would directly address these concerns by aligning US doctrine as closely as possible to that of the Alliance. Above all, he stressed that cross-border operations would be implicitly ruled out where the political leadership rejected such an approach.[66] Like Clausewitz, Richardson was aware of the subordinate role operations played to strategy: " 'Winning' in AirLand Battle doctrine means defeating the enemy on the field of battle and destroying his will to resist in engagements and battles of major operations and campaigns that are governed by strategy and national policy."[67]

NATO had developed a concept of Follow-On Forces Attack (FOFA) in the mid-1980s. It was designed to allow the Alliance to overcome its deficiencies in conventional strength by exploiting the Warsaw Pact's echelonear structure through the use of emerging technologies that increased the range of fires and improved targeting capabilities. However, ground units could not encroach Warsaw Pact territory for political reasons. AirLand Battle, on the other hand, provided for the use of pre-emptive strikes and incursions by ground forces into enemy territory. But, if it was applied in Europe, AirLand Battle would come within the confines of the Allied Command in Europe's operational plan, which would restrict its utility to the limits of engagement under which FOFA would be deployed.[68] There was, therefore, a dichotomy between FOFA and operational art. As David Jablonsky put it:

> If NATO is truly to function at the operational level, it must take the advice of Clausewitz to heart. "Even when the only part of [the] war is to maintain the status quo", he wrote, "the fact remains that merely parrying a blow goes against the essential nature of war, which certainly does not consist merely in enduring."[69]

FM 100–5 of 1986 constitutes the high water mark of Clausewitzian influence in US Army doctrine since Vietnam. It was written by Don Holder, Wass de Czege, and the latter's successor as director of the School of Advanced Military Studies (SAMS), Colonel Richard Sinnreich. Both Holder and Wass de Czege had developed their thinking since 1982. Wass de Czege believed that FM 100–5 was a guide, and not a doctrinal cookbook, to be read by officers who wished to *learn* how to act, and not be *told* how to do so in the Jominian tradition. Wass de Czege's intentions therefore fitted Clausewitz's perspective on the didactic properties of theory. As Richardson put it: "Every officer must understand that the great value of our doctrine is not the final answers it provides but, rather, the impetus it generates toward creative and innovative solutions to the problems of combat."[70]

The new manual extolled a number of "concepts central to the design and conduct of campaigns and major operations".[71] The four tenets of initiative, agility, depth, and synchronisation remained from the 1982 manual. While at first glance synchronisation appears to be an inherently unClausewitzian concept, given its systematic nature, it is not incompatible with an approach that attempts to accommodate friction in the planning of a campaign, *if properly applied*. As Colonel Clinton Ancker says: "Synchronisation is of itself neither a good or a bad thing."[72] Synchronisation as understood as a tenet in the 1982 manual was seen as a tool that merely allowed the commander to co-ordinate the rear, close-in, and deep battles. The revised manual eradicated the distinctions between the three types of battle and therefore provided an opportunity to examine synchronisation properly. It correctly discussed synchronisation as a concept to be applied in an environment where friction existed:

> Synchronization need not depend on explicit coordination if all forces involved fully understand the intent of the commander, and if they have

developed and rehearsed well-conceived standard responses to anticipated contingencies. In the chaos of battle, when communications fail and face to face consideration is impossible, such implicit coordination may make the difference between victory and defeat ... Most of all, it requires unambiguous unity of purpose throughout the force.[73]

The manual placed great emphasis on identifying enemy centres of gravity, describing them as the "key to all operational design".[74] Wass de Czege explained that the centre of gravity was incorporated into the manual not because Clausewitz had specifically formulated it but rather because of its perceived applicability to contemporary conditions. Wass de Czege saw the centre of gravity arising from the particular mission, enemy, terrain, troops available and time (METT-T) that influenced operations in the theatre at all levels of command. It also served as a way of clarifying the 1982 manual's hints at getting close to enemy vulnerabilities. "Trying to approach the problem from the perspective of a center of gravity leads you to see very quickly that some vulnerabilities are interesting but a waste of resources because they do not lead anywhere useful in the end."[75]

Major Thomas Kriwanek, a SAMS student at the time the manual was published, argued that Clausewitz's definition of the centre of gravity does not apply to the operational level. Given the dynamism of a manoeuvre campaign, several potential sub-centres of gravity might need to be attacked to undermine the enemy's campaign plan. In this respect, Kriwanek argued that Clausewitz did not develop the idea beyond the boundaries imposed by the conditions of his time:

> [*On War*] is not complete enough. It suggests an attritional style of warfare with two opposing centers of gravity in a death struggle on the open battlefield, influenced only by their intrinsic power ... [It] does not take into consideration the dominant characteristics of the opposing forces ... the complexity of the modern operational battlefield assumes field armies of different capabilities.[76]

Antulio Echevarria has recently argued that, for Clausewitz, the centre of gravity was a holistic concept, one that treats the enemy as an entire system, or structure, and does not apply to any particular level of war. The centre of gravity concept therefore "focuses on achieving a specific effect, the collapse of the enemy. Hence, it is an effects-based approach, rather than a capabilities-based one."[77]

There is no set formula for determining the centre of gravity during planning and, given the dynamism and fluidity of operations, it is easier to detect it in hindsight. Although Clausewitz discusses the centre of gravity in detail in Book VIII of *On War*, a problem in interpreting his argument is presented by what he writes elsewhere in the work: "A center of gravity is always found where the mass is concentrated most densely." Unfortunately, critics such as Shimon

Naveh have cited this statement to suggest that Clausewitz's thought could be reduced to the single concept "of a destructive trend aimed and directed towards the main body of the enemy army". Professor James Schneider and Lieutenant-Colonel Lawrence Izzo, on the other hand, criticise Clausewitz for carrying "the analogy too far" by suggesting several centres of gravity beyond the enemy army. It is difficult to agree with this line of thought given the manner in which theorists such as John Warden have since further refined the concept.[78]

Many of Clausewitz's interpreters have believed the centre of gravity (*schwerpunkt*, translated as "point of main, or critical, emphasis") to be synonymous with the decisive point. Naveh has written that the US Army failed to define the centre of gravity clearly in FM 100–5, 1986, because of "the unintelligible manner in which it was initially introduced by Clausewitz". On the contrary, the US Army's interpretation of the centre of gravity is actually closer to what Jomini described as a decisive point. Jomini believed that all strategic "combinations" were flawed if they did not operate "with the greatest possible force in a combined effort against the decisive point". This "point" was one "whose attack or capture would imperil or seriously weaken the enemy". William Lind and Schneider and Izzo have rightly criticised the manual for implying that decisive points and the centre of gravity were interchangeable. "FM 100–5 arrives at a meaning of center of gravity that can be applied to anything worthy of being attacked."[79]

FM 100–5 described geographic features such as terrain, the boundary between two army groups, and lines of communication as centres of gravity when in fact they were decisive points. Clausewitz, however, wrote: "Operating against the enemy's line of communication ... seldom leads to the *decision* that we have assumed to be the object of the campaign."[80]

In discussing his concept of genius, Clausewitz observed that there are no particular rules governing the conduct of war. This therefore requires a need for initiative on the part of subordinate commanders, a quality that the Prussian military had articulated in the form of *Auftragstaktik*. This was emphasised in the 1986 manual as a means by which the operational commander could avoid being distracted by tactical matters at the expense of his more strategic role. His subordinates on the spot were better able to deal with the potential chaos of an uncertain battlefield. The junior commander should therefore "conduct his operation confidently, anticipate events, act fully and boldly to accomplish his mission without further orders".[81]

Paradoxically, technology was ensuring that the junior commander's role in events was having more of an impact on the campaign itself given the increased firepower, lethality and range of modern weaponry. It was therefore crucial that small-unit actions should be conducted within the framework of a coherent campaign plan that could withstand the effects of friction through allowing subordinates to use their initiative. However, it can be argued that initiative is only one aspect of the *Auftragstaktik* concept. In this respect, the manual failed to examine it in the context of such elements as the commander's "genius"; wider command and control issues (though the manual recognised the need for this at the nuclear level and discussed its potential impact on operations); the relationship between the operational commander and his subordinates; training and education; and, above all, its part in the construct of an American theory of war. While the allusion was there, the manual did not fully grasp the possibilities offered by a proper application of *Auftragstaktik*. J. L. Silva was correct to suggest that:

> *Auftragstaktik* was a product of German social and cultural traditions ... This concept worked so well ... that we in the US Army now idolize it without fully comprehending the totality of what it was, why or how it developed, or how it worked as a system.[82]

Another Clausewitzian concept that informed the 1986 manual was that of the culminating point. Clausewitz wrote that the identification of the culminating point of the attack is "[t]he natural goal of all campaign plans" as it encompasses the moment when attack becomes defence and vice versa. Wass de Czege justified its inclusion in the manual as recognition of the need for manoeuvre at the operational level. The actual passages in the manual more or less reflect *On War*:

> Unless it is strategically decisive, every offensive operation will sooner or later reach a point where the strength of the attacker no longer significantly exceeds that of the defender, and beyond which continued offensive operations therefore risk overextension, counterattack, and defeat. In operational theory, this is called the culminating point ... Once operations begin, the attacking commander must sense when he has reached or is about to reach his culminating point, whether intended or not, and revert to the defense at a time and place of his own choosing.[83]

Where FM 100–5 and Clausewitz diverge, however, is in the former's conviction that the offensive may continue even after the culminating point is passed, albeit risking the possibility of defeat through overexposing oneself to a counterattack. Clausewitz, on the other hand, argued that by now the opportunity for victory has passed unless the enemy somehow fails to take advantage: "An attacker may ... take on more than he can manage and, as it were, get into debt; a defender must be able to recognise this error if the enemy commits it, and exploit it to the full."[84]

Dr Frederick Kagan has argued that it is not necessarily the case that all offensive operations end in a transition to the defence. Many, of course, end in victory. In this sense, he was advocating the inter-war Soviet theorist Georgiy Isserson's concept of "consecutive operations", which was intended to overcome the problem of the "operational pause". Isserson advocated the need to tailor the campaign plan to take account of the whole of the enemy's depth. This line of argument suggested that one could not plan for operations in depth by using the same formulae as one would if contemplating a linear operation. FM 100–5, according to Kagan, "rejected the advance made by Soviet operational art and returned to the age of Napoleon [and, by implication, Clausewitz] in its thinking".[85]

Nevertheless, the 1986 manual did caveat its discussion of the culminating point by implying that, where possible, the campaign should be separated into phases so as to enable the attacker to regain the initiative before continuing. Wass de Czege recalls:

> I always advised that one needs to be aware that offensives tend to culminate due to an array of factors which need to be taken into account to the extent possible in operational design. Good operational design ensures that operationally significant objectives are reached before the forces of culmination have full impact.[86]

Major Mark Redlinger has articulated the distinction between the culminating point and an operational pause:

> The culminating point by Clausewitzian definition is a moment of balance within the operational plan. To proceed beyond this equilibrium would lead to a reaction – counterattack – by the defender ... The culminating point marks the end of an operational plan ... An operational pause, on the other hand, occurs when the attacker has come to a momentary suspension in the attack, but not in the operational plan. The overall strength of the attacker is still sufficient to achieve the ends.[87]

While Kagan recognises, as Clausewitz did, that this issue is central to operational art, he overlooks the fact that both Clausewitz and FM 100–5 factored the influence of friction into their discussions. One must always have a plan in reserve in case of failure. What Kagan, following Isserson, describes is an ideal, not necessarily something that is always realistic. One can argue that this ideal occurred in the Gulf War of 1991 but that planning to fight the Warsaw Pact in 1986 was another matter altogether.

When comparing the 1982 and 1986 manuals, Naveh has argued that the fundamental difference between the two lay in the former's advocacy of the destruction of the enemy force as the operational aim while the latter believed it should be to concentrate superior strength against enemy vulnerabilities at a decisive time and place. Both, however, were Clausewitzian in that they were explicitly framed in the context of achieving a strategic and political objective. While the 1986 manual was more in tune with operational art than its predecessor, it is hyperbole to suggest that it "was actually an entirely new approach to warfare. This approach was based on a systematic and holistic approach to war that recognised the primacy of operations."[88]

FM 100–5, 1986 complemented the Goldwater–Nichols reforms of the same year in recognising the need to develop a force structure to conduct joint operations. The manual perceived the importance of "jointness" in that future operations would acknowledge the developing battlespace through the involvement of elements from across the land, sea and air environments. It therefore looked beyond single service operations conducted in support of unilateral actions by the United States. This would impact upon strategy and campaign planning in that the commander would need to take account of political cohesion, particularly in allied operations, in addition to his other functions. Despite this, the US Air Force continued to have misgivings about Army doctrine. For example, the Army saw synchronisation as being restricted to the battlefield and did not consider the interface between ground manoeuvre and air interdiction. However, both services appreciated the existence of friction: "Clausewitz's concept of friction in war has direct application in a multitude of undertakings today: the AirLand Battle, C3I design, space doctrine, nuclear employment concepts, and joint doctrine."[89]

There can be no doubt that FM 100–5, 1986 was influenced by Clausewitz's writings. The extent to which this is so was debated by American military commentators. Major John Saxman wrote in 1992: "Clausewitz, more than any other theorist, has had a significant impact on current US military operational thinking and warfighting doctrine." Glenn Harned, on the other hand, has written that while Clausewitz was more influential than Jomini and Sun Tzu in informing the manual, its real theoretical significance was its reapplication of the principles of war as "combat imperatives", surely a more Jominian approach. Galloway, balancing these views, dismissed the belief that Clausewitzian "extremism" had overcome a prescriptive approach to American strategic thought. Wass de Czege himself took a pragmatic view and contended that Clausewitz was one of many thinkers who were reference points in the formulation of the manual, and that their influence lay in the contemporary relevance of their ideas. "[W]hat I said in my 1988 [*ARMY*] article still holds. What Clausewitz says about method relating to early 19th century warfare needs to be reevaluated and reinterpreted. We did the best we could. I think we improved on Clausewitz."[90]

The fact is that Clausewitz was useful not because of any dogmatic application of his theories but because of the way in which the allusions to his work might make officers ponder their subject, therefore reflecting Clausewitz's ideal of the utility of theory as study. Unskilled application of his theories would render any doctrine useless. An accurate summation was made by Richard Swain, who wrote in 1990:

> In his day, Jomini's works satisfied the need filled by doctrine today. Jomini has been superseded not by modern theorists, but by contemporary doctrine writers. Clausewitz sought to fill another need, one like that Jakob Burkhardt saw for history: "Not to make men clever for next time;… to make them wise forever."[91]

Further interpretations of Clausewitz

The study of Clausewitz came to assume even more importance in the services' colleges during the 1980s. Colonel Thomas Vaughn articulated the need for this upward trend in 1982: "[C]onversation with Clausewitz is a valuable aspect of the total education and preparation required for true military professionalism."[92]

An analysis of the US Army Command and General Staff College's annual prospectus between the years 1974 and 1992 reveals that the use of Clausewitz as a study tool gradually increased. This was especially so after the foundation of SAMS at Leavenworth. Wass de Czege had written a detailed study guide to the Howard and Paret edition of *On War* for SAMS students, which looked at Clausewitz from a soldier's, rather than a social scientist's, perspective. SAMS used Clausewitz for didactic purposes in the wider context of teaching military theory rather than looking at his theories in isolation. Lectures revolved around concepts and included references to a number of military theorists.

In 1986, a "Military Classics" course examining the evolution of the military art from antiquity to the Korean War was introduced at Leavenworth, and included a seminar on Clausewitz. In 1989, a course on the "Evolution of Modern Warfare" was added to the Regular Course curriculum. This included an analysis of Clausewitz, with an emphasis on American military experience since 1941. In the same year, a discretionary course, "Clausewitz for Commanders", was introduced to enable officers to evaluate Clausewitz's hypotheses through a critical analysis of historical campaigns. This would "allow SAMS students to get their feet wet with Clausewitz and to provide those unable to attend SAMS exposure to Clausewitz".[93]

The latter course was disbanded in 1991 in the aftermath of the Gulf War. This tailors with the experience of Dr Earl Tilford, formerly of the Strategic Studies Institute at Carlisle. He recalls classes that centred on the teaching of Clausewitz at the Army War College in the 1980s being oversubscribed as officers attempted to face the post-Vietnam challenges to the United States. However, after the Gulf War, the numbers attending dwindled rapidly as officers felt that there was nothing more for them to learn.[94]

A number of monographs written by students at SAMS and the CGSC during this period revolved around analyses of Clausewitz's thought and its application to the contemporary strategic environment. Subjects ranged from treatments of Clausewitzian concepts such as the trinity, the defence, culmination, and the centre of gravity to an analysis of Hegel's influence upon *On War*. Many of these works concluded that Clausewitzian thinking remained relevant to present and future operational and strategic problems. Following Clausewitz's lead, many students alluded to historical examples, mainly drawn from the twentieth century, to illustrate their arguments.[95]

Clausewitzian studies were also of significance at the Air War College's School for Advanced Air Power, thanks to the efforts of Lieutenant-Colonel David MacIssac. A military history course was introduced in the 1980s with some emphasis on Clausewitz. The extent to which his work has permeated Air Force minds cannot be properly ascertained in the post-Gulf War era, given that conflict's significance for zealous advocates of airpower. "[T]he techno-wonks believe that technology has now made old forms of warfare obsolete. Of course

Clausewitz is about a great deal more than the clash of land armies, but Air Force people generally do not read."[96]

The Army War College's curricula during the 1980s and 1990s followed a similar pattern to the above schools. "We here at the Army War College of course use Clausewitz in our curriculum. Interestingly enough, the page count has dropped significantly over the years. Currently the students digest about 40 pages in the core curriculum."[97]

Disagreement continued among US military commentators as to the utility of Clausewitz. Colonel Lloyd Matthews, the editor of *Parameters*, journal of the Army War College, wrote: "[I]t remains difficult to articulate to an outsider exactly what we have learned from the Prussian about fighting wars ... I am convinced that the raw, undigested text of *On War* is insufficient for that purpose."[98]

Others criticised him on moral grounds, taking the liberal view that war is an abomination. Eric Alterman, a political scientist, criticised what he saw as Clausewitz's glorification of the role of war in society: "I ... find Clausewitz's rhetoric on the subject sufficiently inflammatory ... to assert that this man did not sufficiently value the human lives lost and destroyed in warfare relative to the values he did profess."[99]

While this is a stinging critique, Alterman understood, and agreed with, much of *On War*. He appreciated certain Clausewitzian concepts such as the centre of gravity and the need to limit war as being of value to American strategic thought. However, he did not agree with Clausewitz's "world view" and is one of the few commentators writing in US military periodicals at the time to have taken this wider perspective. Many critics also misunderstood Clausewitz's philosophical style and failed to see that his use of theses and antitheses – for example, offence and defence, and ends and means – did not necessarily lead to contradictions. Therefore, Matthews was being slightly disingenuous in saying that "an enterprising dissenter, if he scours far enough, can always find a Clausewitzian quotation to contradict your own".[100]

Clausewitz's relevance was constantly questioned throughout the period under review. Major John Shepherd argued that "Clausewitz's concept of war needs substantial modification, though not complete overhaul, if it is to be sufficiently comprehensive for modern American warriors and statesmen".[101]

In 1988, General William DePuy wrote an essay for *ARMY*, "Concept of Operations: The Heart of Command, the Tool of Doctrine", in which he argued along similar lines to Shepherd:

It is currently popular to consult the writings of ... Clausewitz for insights into the operational art. Indeed, Clausewitz has much to offer, but the structure of armed forces in his time was relatively simple...

Commanders must now cope with three times the complexity that confronted Clausewitz, and he described the difficulty of operating when even the simplest action became difficult and when "friction" beset every battlefield endeavor. Of course, Clausewitz was correct. How much more correct would he be today?[102]

FMFM 1, *Warfighting*, 1989

Of the four services, the one that came closest to adopting a Clausewitzian approach, other than the Army, was the Marine Corps. Like the Army, it had gradually moved from an attritionist stance during the 1980s. The Marines could claim that Colonel John Boyd, and in particular his civilian advocate William Lind, were the inspirations behind this transformation. In his introduction to Lind's *Maneuver Warfare Handbook* (1985), Colonel John Studt explained the need for his fellow Marines to understand the theoretical basis of war:

> I served over 31 years' active duty with the Marine Corps, saw combat in both Korea and Vietnam, and attended service schools from the basic school to the Naval War College. Yet only toward the end of my military career did I realise how little I really understood the art of war ... commanding a battalion at Khe Sanh, I was resolved that none of my Marines would die for lack of superior combat power. But we were still relying on the concentration of superior firepower to win ... For the first time in our history we face a potential enemy with superiority in men and materiel. Against such an enemy we cannot win with the firepower doctrine we embrace today.[103]

Lind was convinced that the Marine Corps was unprepared for the demands of modern warfare, given its failure to develop the thought processes required to deal with these. He drew an analogy with the Falklands War, a conflict in which the warfighting ethos that the Marine Corps needed to practise and understand had succeeded: "In terms of the priority the Marine Corps gives to winning in combat, it is closer to the Argentines than to the British. That should deeply concern every Marine."[104]

The Marine Corps' inter-war *Tentative Landing Operations Manual* described in Chapter 2 was initially superseded by a series of Landing Force Manuals (LFMs) in the 1940s and 1950s, and then, in 1964, by the first Fleet Marine Force Manual (FMFM) 6–1, *Marine Division*. This was the first publication to articulate the organisation, doctrine and tactics which a Marine Division required to fulfil its mission. However, FMFM 1, *Warfighting*, published in March 1989, was the first Marine Corps text that encouraged its readers to *think* about war. As the Corps' commandant, General Al Gray, explained: "This book explains my philosophy on warfighting ... The thoughts contained here represent not just guidance for actions in combat, but *a way of thinking* in general." The manual itself was written by Captain John Schmitt, who had read widely but was particularly interested in the concepts of Clausewitz and Sun Tzu. Schmitt made the bold claim that FMFM 1 was the first manual to translate properly the ideas of theorists from the past 2,500 years "into a cohesive doctrine".[105]

Among those who advised Schmitt in his writing of the manual were Boyd and Lind, as well as high-ranking Marine Corps officers. Boyd had criticised Clausewitz for, in his eyes, overemphasising the decisiveness of battle and underestimating the utility of strategic manoeuvre; and for seeking to exhaust the enemy by encouraging him to increase his expenditure of effort, which would obviate the possibility of paralysing him. Nevertheless, Boyd's biographer, Grant Hammond, writes that Boyd's ideal of manoeuvre warfare "is Clausewitzian in approach, about war as art and, therefore, non-linear".[106]

FMFM 1 expressed the tactical and operational levels of war in Clausewitzian terms: "Tactics can be thought of as the art and science of winning engagements and battles ... The *operational* level of war is the use of tactical results to attain strategic objectives." These were strictly subordinate to strategy, the definition of which closely echoed *On War*'s: "The single most important thought to understand about our theory is that war *must serve policy* ... Of course, we may also have to adjust our policy objectives to accommodate our means; we must not establish goals outside our capabilities."[107]

The correct application of manoeuvre warfare principles was important to a relatively small service such as the Marine Corps. The probability was that a Marine Expeditionary Force (MEF) would be outnumbered by its opponents and this made it vital to economise on the use of that force, thereby making manoeuvre warfare a force multiplier. Furthermore, the emphasis on operational art ensured that the Marine Corps was beginning to look beyond the traditional amphibious *assault*. The emphasis was shifting to an amphibious *campaign*, and in this respect the Marines were following the logic not only of Goldwater–Nichols and FM 100–5, 1986 in their emphasis on jointness but also of the opportunities being afforded by technological change, which was increasing the size of the battlespace to make littoral operations part of the land campaign and vice versa. The advantages that the Marines had from being based at sea gave them an opportunity to conduct manoeuvre that outweighed any forcible entry capability. The amphibious warfare conducted in the Pacific during the Second World War would no longer serve as a template. Rather, the Marines needed to think in the wider context of, for example, the British campaigns in the Peninsular War. In this can be seen the origins of the Corps' development of "Operational Maneuver from the Sea" in the late 1990s.

FMFM 1 was conscious of the need to develop the commander's grasp of the art of war. As Lind put it:

> [Maneuver warfare] requires commanders and operations officers with what Clausewitz called a "talent for judgement", composed of imagination, creativity, and intuition. It requires study of the enemy, his weapons, techniques, doctrines, and, if at all possible, his commander's tendencies. It adds up to a good deal more than is usually meant by "just common sense".[108]

However, there were critics of FMFM 1 who lamented its lack of attention to what they perceived to be the main business of the Marine: fighting. Lieutenant-Colonel Jeffrey Lloyd commented that the manual's obsession with manoeuvre warfare diverted it from any worthwhile discussion of the need to close with and destroy the enemy in combat. This was something that could not be avoided indefinitely by constant manoeuvring. "Maneuver warfare is so concerned with being able to 'fight outnumbered and win' it sometimes forgets that fighting outnumbered is precisely the challenge we seek to give our enemies."[109]

In fact, the manual did discuss what it saw as the continuing relevance of firepower and violence to achieve operational objectives; it was just that it placed a manoeuvrist emphasis on these. "The greatest value of firepower is not physical destruction – the cumulative effects of which are felt only slowly – but the moral dislocation it causes ... Once gained or found, any advantage must be pressed relentlessly and unhesitatingly."[110]

Other critics, such as Lieutenant-Colonel Edward Robeson and Major Craig Tucker, condemned the manual for implying that everything in the past was being dismissed in the quest for a panacea – that of manoeuvre warfare. However, the manual did not diminish the Marine Corps' proud history, rather it was written in a context where there was an urgent requirement to overhaul an attritionist mentality.[111]

Christopher Bassford has described FMFM 1 as being essentially a distillation of *On War*. While this may be an exaggeration, it was as full of Clausewitzian concepts as FM 100–5, 1986. "John Schmitt ... always tells me [FMFM 1 is] essentially Sun Tzu. The formal logic, however, and indeed the chapter and section structure, are blatantly Clausewitzian. On the other hand,... the emphasis on maneuver is not at all Clausewitzian."[112]

FMFM 1 cautioned against a direct read across from *On War* in its discussion of the centre of gravity. Acknowledging the different conditions prevailing in Clausewitz's time, the manual explained that the emphasis should now be on pitting one's strength against enemy vulnerabilities and not enemy strengths. This was a manifestation of the need to husband scarce resources in the face of a numerically superior foe. Nevertheless, FMFM 1, like FM 100–5, 1986, has been criticised for distorting Clausewitz's original intention. Major Patrick Strain, USMC, wrote that the Marine Corps "has a strong misunderstanding of centers of gravity as a source of strength using the decisive point as a conduit through which it can be successfully attacked". Tucker argued that the manual inadvertently referred to critical vulnerabilities because of the centre of gravity's attritionist connotations. He wrote that "Clausewitz ... never intended for his theory to have practical application on the battlefield ... To determine a 'critical vulnerability' one must determine what makes a vulnerability critical ... To find a critical vulnerability we must first determine a center of gravity."[113]

FMFM 1 stipulated that the *focus of effort* should be against those enemy vulnerabilities identified as being the key to unravelling his position. This was related to the notion of seeking surfaces and gaps:

> Gaps may in fact be physical gaps in the enemy's dispositions, but they may also be any weakness in time or space: a moment in time when the enemy is overexposed and vulnerable, a seam in an air defense umbrella, an infantry unit caught unprepared in open terrain, or a boundary between two units.
>
> Similarly, a surface may be an actual strongpoint, or it may be any

enemy strength: a moment when the enemy has just replenished and consolidated his position or an integrated air defense system.[114]

Robeson criticised the use of surfaces and gaps, implying that this term is an imperfect translation of the German *Lücken und Flächentaktik*. While the manual spoke of avoiding enemy strengths, it also implied that to achieve a decisive result a gap would have to be created. The only way of doing this was to attack a surface directly – something the manual cautioned against. "We should delete all references to 'surfaces and gaps' and discuss 'soft spots' or 'exploitation opportunities'. Particularly annoying is the use of the word 'gap' [which] loses *any* preciseness in definition."[115]

Much of FMFM 1 was informed by an awareness of the existence of friction, which it defined in its own strikingly Clausewitzian language as well as citing *On War*. As the aim of the campaign is to achieve operational shock, exploiting friction is a means of doing this.

> If we are to win, we must be able to operate in a disorderly environment. In fact, we must not only be able to fight effectively in the face of disorder, we should seek to generate disorder for our opponent and use it as a weapon against him.[116]

Lind noted that one way of exploiting the confusion and chaos of the battlefield is through the use of mission-type orders that place great responsibility on subordinate leaders. FMFM 1 likewise emphasised the need for decentralised control in the pursuit of campaign objectives. Its definition is interesting: "Mission tactics are just as the name implies: the tactic of assigning a subordinate mission without specifying how the mission must be accomplished."[117]

Despite FMFM 1's recognition of friction, it did not embrace synchronisation. This led to a fundamental doctrinal difference with the US Army for which synchronisation was defined in FM 100–5, 1986 as a concept that brings order to the battlefield. Schmitt explained the Marine Corps' view in a 1994 article:

> [S]ynchronization reflects an extremely deterministic and methodical approach to military operations. We can understand the appeal it has for the American mind. It is organized, orderly and logical ... FMFM 1 tells us that war is inherently uncertain, unpredictable, frictional, fluid, disorderly, imprecise, and somewhat random. The problem is that these truths do not sit well with Americans in the current culture ... Unfortunately, the nature of war described in FMFM 1 is inconsistent with – no, make that contradictory to – this culture.[118]

There is an argument that whereas the Marine Corps treated war as an art, the Army was still occasionally inclined to view it as a science despite its emphasis on the operational "art". Such an approach would not complement Clausewitzian thought in that it almost tried to make warfare predictable. Nevertheless, one would argue that the Army has been unfairly criticised in respect of synchronisation. The Marine Corps, and more particularly Schmitt, viewed synchronisation as a dogma. The Army did not.

The notion of the culminating point was defined by FMFM 1 as the means by which the relationship between offence and defence could best be understood. Like Clausewitz, the manual described the defence as the stronger form of war. Mounting an attack required an ability to generate enough force to overcome the inherent superiority of the enemy's defence. Hayden, however, argued in his commentary to FMFM 1 that the element of "resistance" inherent in the defence is an attribute of a weaker military power. In this view, manoeuvre warfare dictated that "if you're on the defense you have lost or may be losing the initiative. Most Great Captains of history have used the defense to draw out their enemy – not to 'preserve and protect' themselves."[119]

Conclusion

The Reagan Administration's policy of peace through strength relied on a perceptive balancing of the three elements of Clausewitz's paradoxical trinity, especially given the ability of the polity to persuade the people to support it. The administration's success in forcing the Soviets to sign the 1987 INF Treaty without its giving up SDI was the ultimate strategic benefit of this approach.

AirLand Battle and the Maritime Strategy complemented strategy, thereby emphasising the importance of the strategic–operational interface.

While the Weinberger Doctrine had shaky Clausewitzian foundations, it was the culmination of the American military's soul-searching following the Vietnam War. Basically, the US armed forces would not be committed to conflict unless there was a national interest at stake that could be used to convince Congress and the American people of the necessity of fighting. "This advocacy, rather bizarrely, reversed Clausewitz's intention as it made policy a continuation of the nation's operational tools of war, rather than a continuation of strategic policy. It was the 'operationalisation' of strategy."[120]

The Maritime Strategy renounced the Navy's Mahanian heritage to the extent that it emphasised littoral, as well as deep water, warfare. Ultimately, the forward strategy was intended to force the Soviets into negotiating for peace on NATO's terms. To this degree, it could be described as Clausewitzian given its political impetus and its emphasis on seizing the initiative from the Soviets. In reality, however, one must be sceptical about the utility of the strategy in the event of a war ever taking place.

Williamson Murray has recently described FM 100–5, 1986 and FMFM 1 as "the two greatest doctrinal manuals that the American military has ever produced".[121] FM 100–5, 1986 is the ultimate doctrinal expression of Clausewitz's influence on the US Army. It should be noted that Clausewitz tended to be viewed as a thinker whose thought could be adapted to the present day, which perhaps explains why some of his concepts were not entirely understood. For example, the manual's notion of the centre of gravity could be conceived of as being similar to Jomini's decisive point. References to Clausewitz were also useful for didactic purposes – he might stimulate officers to think more deeply about the problems posed by their profession.

The Marine Corps' manual, FMFM 1, *Warfighting*, 1989, confirmed that Clausewitz's thought had spread beyond the Army. It was a manual that comprehended the operational level of war and its role between tactics and strategy. Its espousal of manoeuvre warfare, while not based on Clausewitz, did require an understanding of war as an art; that friction is ever-present in war; and that intuition and "genius" are fundamental requirements of the officer as Clausewitz had written in *On War*. The manual's references to the centre of gravity took Clausewitz's concept as a starting point and adapted it to what it believed to be the manoeuvrist aim of seeking out the enemy's critical vulnerabilities. While this may have lost the sense of Clausewitz's original meaning of the phrase, the manual was dealing with a changed nature of warfare, whereby one had inferior resources to the enemy. Furthermore, unlike the Army, the Marine Corps did not misread the centre of gravity for a decisive point.

6   The Gulf War

Desert Shield: the military build-up

Saddam Hussein's invasion of Kuwait on 2 August 1990 took the world by surprise. In less than a day-and-a-half, his forces had occupied the country. Nothing now seemed to stand in the way of the Iraqis reaching the Saudi oilfields. The initial reaction of the United States reflected the shockwaves reverberating from Saddam's coup. Politically, British prime minister, Margaret Thatcher, bolstered President George Bush's resolve to challenge Saddam. Militarily, however, the United States was impotent. No agreement existed with Saudi Arabia to station US troops on its soil, while the force earmarked to defend the region, the 3rd Army, more or less existed only on paper. "When asked by Lt.-Gen. Charles A. Horner, the Air Force component commander, what the [3rd] Army had to protect the deploying United States Air Force, a small pen knife was all the [3rd] Army commander [Lieutenant-General John Yeosock] could produce."[1]

Despite the distance separating the Arabian peninsula from the continental United States, the strategic objectives of any campaign to liberate Kuwait were immediately apparent. The need to remove Iraqi forces from Kuwait instantly allowed a coherent military plan to take shape. Bush's decision of 7 August to set in place Operation "Desert Shield" and to deploy more than 200,000 troops to Saudi Arabia suggested to Saddam that any plans he had of continuing his conquests southward would be met with a robust response. Furthermore, Bush fulfilled the criterion of the Weinberger Doctrine's second tenet – to mobilise all efforts towards victory – when he declared: "I will not, as Commander-in-Chief, ever put somebody into a military situation that we do not win – ever. And there's not going to be any drawn-out agony [like] Vietnam."[2]

Bush therefore showed that he understood the Clausewitzian concept of utilising military force to fulfil a clear political objective. As Lieutenant-Colonel Thomas DuBois points out, the structure of the forces being deployed in the Gulf illustrated the purpose for which they were being sent: "Significant by their absence were military advisers, observers, or small-scale peacekeeping forces ... there could be no doubt that the strategy to employ the military instrument had winning armed conflict as its objective."[3]

A significant factor in enabling the United States to shift vast forces to the

Gulf was, of course, the end of the Cold War. The Americans were able not only to commit XVIII Airborne Corps, already earmarked for "out-of-area" operations, but could also utilise those heavy forces based in the United States that were intended to reinforce NATO. Most significantly of all, they could afford to deploy VII Corps (the 1st and 3rd Armored Divisions, and the 2nd Armored Cavalry Regiment) from Europe, a force with the offensive "punch" required to evict the Iraqis from Kuwait. The arrival of the first heavy tank units in late August illustrated that the "window of vulnerability" was beginning to pass for the Allied coalition. Indeed, from around this time, the Iraqi order of battle in Kuwait began to substitute offensively oriented tank divisions with infantry units best suited for the defensive.

The uncertainty within the Iraqi leadership as to what to do once it became clear that the United States was serious in its intention to liberate Kuwait helped the Americans to gain that most important of factors in war: time. If, on the other hand, Saddam had acted decisively and had decided to attack US forces as they were deploying on the ground in Saudi Arabia, there is no doubt that the United States would have taken casualties out of all proportion to those eventually suffered. The political consequences of this scenario could have gravely affected Bush's ability to conduct the war.[4]

The US commander-in-chief, CENTCOM, General Norman Schwarzkopf, realised at an early stage that the objective to liberate Kuwait would require a large-scale ground offensive. He believed that airpower would be required to soften up the opposition to allow for the successful execution of an offensive on the ground. On 25 August 1990, he predicted the pattern of the events that lay ahead:

> We will offset the imbalance of ground combat power by using our strength against his [Saddam's] weakness. Initially execute deception operations to focus his attention on defense and cause incorrect organization of forces. We will initially attack into Iraqi homeland using airpower to decapitate his leadership, command and control, and eliminate his ability to reinforce Iraqi forces in Kuwait and southern Iraq. We will then gain undisputed air superiority over Kuwait so that we can subsequently and selectively attack Iraqi ground forces with air power in order to reduce his combat power and destroy reinforcing units. Finally, we will fix Iraqi forces in place by feints and limited objective attacks followed by armored force penetration and exploitation to seize key lines of communication nodes, which will put us in a position to interdict resupply and remaining reinforcements from Iraq and eliminate forces in Kuwait.[5]

Although Desert Shield was a time of preparation for military conflict, one can still identify a Clausewitzian culminating point for the Iraqis. This occurred when the Allies changed from a defensive to an offensive posture. It involved a commitment on the part of Bush to allot the necessary resources to Schwarzkopf, via the Joint Chiefs-of-Staff (JCS), to conduct an offensive operation into Kuwait. In mid-November 1990, the arrival in the Middle East of extra ground forces, three more carrier battle groups and another Marine Expeditionary Force, as well as additional airpower, illustrated this point. Schwarzkopf outlined his campaign plan to his commanders on 13 November. This centred around VII Corps, which would be tasked with attacking and destroying the Iraqi Republican Guard Forces Command, identified as a key centre of gravity.

Saddam was naive to think that he could prevent the United States from reversing his gains in Kuwait. He believed that Iraq's experience in its recent war with Iran stood it in good stead for the forthcoming ordeal. Yet, as Jeffrey Record remarks, the most pertinent comparison that Saddam should have drawn was "not the slaughter of Iranian teenagers in the swamps outside Basra, but rather the Arab–Israeli Wars, which demonstrated the futility of Arab attempts to best the Israelis in conventional combat".[6]

By consolidating his forces inside Kuwait, Saddam believed that his numerical advantage would tell in repulsing a frontal assault across the Kuwaiti border. In fact, this deployment was a gift to an enemy that was now ready to conduct manoeuvre warfare on a huge scale, and opened up the possibility of a gigantic replay of the ancient battle of Cannae with all the deadliness of modern ground and air firepower. Deception added to Saddam's eventual woes: CENTCOM briefings made great play of massed assaults and breaching attacks while coalition forces were deployed in heavy formations along the Saudi–Kuwaiti border, ready to be moved to the north-west and the Saudi–Iraqi border as soon as the air campaign began.

Nevertheless, estimates of Iraqi strength by American intelligence bordered on the cautious. Military intelligence tends to concentrate on quantifiables, such as numbers of troops and hardware, rather than intangibles, for example, morale and training. Moreover, the Iraqi armed forces had recently fought a long, high-intensity conflict whereas the United States had not. Therefore, the Iraqis looked good on paper. In the event, the utility of Clausewitz's apparent warning as to the untrustworthiness of intelligence was to be confirmed: "Many intelligence reports in war are … false, and most are uncertain."[7]

Sea power was highly significant in Desert Shield. The coalition had almost complete maritime supremacy from the outset – the Iraqis lacked any proper sea denial capability – and the presence of carrier-based aviation provided the allies with their initial suite of airpower. Furthermore, it was a Marine Expeditionary Brigade that provided the first element of a credible ground defence in Saudi Arabia. Naval power also contributed significantly to the blockade of Iraq itself, a useful lever with which to put domestic pressure on Saddam's regime. In essence, the US Navy fulfilled the out-of-NATO area objective of the Maritime Strategy. As Schwarzkopf remarked to the graduating class of the Naval Academy in 1991: "It was the quickest and largest military buildup since World War Two, an 8,000 mile, 250-ship, haze gray bridge, one ship every 50 miles from the shore of the United States to the shores of Saudi Arabia."[8]

The concept of Mission, Enemy, Terrain, Tactics and Time available (METT-T) was the means by which the US military translated its doctrine into practice during the build-up. The *mission*, as interpreted by the military from the objective set by the political authority, was to generate enough initial combat power to defend Saudi Arabia, and then to evict Iraqi forces from Kuwait. The *enemy* was, of course, the Iraqi armed forces, and in particular its central pillar, the Republican Guard Forces Command whose removal would help to fulfil the campaign's objective. The *terrain* in the Arabian Peninsula was perfect for manoeuvre warfare: the desert was huge, flat and open. Saudi Arabia had good port facilities. The only drawback was the lack of a decent road network, which potentially ensured the existence of transportation bottlenecks. Overall, however, the terrain features of the theatre would complement the coalition's technological advantages in air reconnaissance and precision munitions. As far as *troops* were concerned, the US 3rd Army was the major force in theatre. It initially lacked reinforcements, which in itself posed a severe logistical problem. However, the willingness of the Saudi authorities to provide a base allowed it to deter Iraqi aggression successfully and then to form the basis for the effort to defeat the Iraqis in the Kuwait theatre of operations. Finally, the *time available* was, as has been already noted, a critical factor. The need to rely on strategic air and sea lift ensured that the enemy had the opportunity to inflict a defeat on forces already in theatre and, later on, to hamper the build-up. Moreover, the lead time required to call up US reserve forces (six months) was another factor in influencing the overall tempo of operations. Fortunately, the enemy proved to be compliant enough to allow the coalition to use time to its advantage.

The planning of the military operation had to overcome the conceptual problem of an operational pause. Lieutenant-General Frederick Franks, commander of VII Corps, rightly believed that allowing an operational pause to occur would be tantamount to surrendering the initiative. Lieutenant-General Yeosock, 3rd Army commander, likewise rejected the possibility of a pause in operations, focusing instead on the need for relentless attack. He believed that any pause should be no more than an exercise in taking stock of the situation. It might be necessary, for example, to react to the Republican Guard's response to the VII Corps' initial penetration of its position:

> Operational pauses, which are designed to avoid the [Clausewitzian] sin of culmination, are one of the tricks of the trade that have received no small attention in the SAMS [School of Advanced Military Studies] education, a sort of unwritten doctrinal construct. In theory, however, such pauses are spaced to follow achievements of major objectives ... In this sense, Yeosock's anticipation of a pause *after* the destruction of the Republican Guard would seem most appropriate.[9]

While Schwarzkopf's staff were busy preparing their plan for the forthcoming campaign, Secretary of Defense Richard Cheney almost jeopardised civil–military relations by formulating a plan of his own. This involved an airdrop of the 82nd Airborne Division on top of Scud missile sites in western Iraq, and then a link up with the 101st Air Assault Division and the 3rd Armored Cavalry

Regiment to threaten Baghdad from the west. Furthermore, having had his plan formalised by staff in the JCS, he revealed it to Bush prior to informing Schwarzkopf, the commander on the ground. Once he had seen the plan, Schwarzkopf convinced JCS chairman, General Colin Powell, as to its logistical inapplicability and had it quashed. This contravention of Clausewitz's dictum that the military authority should be responsible for framing the military plans to fulfil the political objective was well summed up by Schwarzkopf: "Put a civilian in charge of professional military men and before long he's no longer satisfied with setting policy but wants to outgeneral the generals."[10]

Desert Shield: the political build-up

Bush set out America's political objectives in an address to Congress on 5 August 1990. These were: to ensure that all Iraq's forces unconditionally withdrew from Kuwait; that the government of Kuwait be restored; that Saudi Arabia and its Gulf neighbours should be protected; and that American citizens living abroad should be safeguarded. Of these objectives, the need to protect Saudi Arabia was an overriding American national interest and can be seen as an outgrowth not only of Weinberger's first tenet but also of the Carter Administration's decision to earmark forces for the region in 1980. Moreover, the stability of the region was at stake, as was America's reputation. Failure to reverse Saddam's annexation of Kuwait, a blatant contravention of international law, would give succour to aggressors everywhere.

Bush had to overcome several initial challenges. Not only did he have to rapidly build up a military force capable, first of deterring the Iraqis, and then of driving them from Kuwait, he also had to mobilise international opinion. Political and economic sanctions were enforced against Iraq, while at the same time diplomatic pressure was to be brought to bear on Saddam to withdraw unconditionally from Kuwait. Scepticism about the efficacy of sanctions was overcome, at least in the short term. "[T]he principal difference between the porous sanctions that had proved ineffective in past crises and the virtually airtight sanctions against Iraq was the enforcement by coalition naval power and the co-operation of nations sharing land borders with Iraq."[11]

Assimilating the strategic lessons of half a century of experience, the United States undertook to marshal as many allies as possible in its desire to isolate Iraq. This was achieved through Bush's judicious use of the United Nations (UN), and his careful attempts to appeal to the inviolability of international law. In the process he, together with Secretary of State James Baker, gathered together a coalition that was as disparate as that which the Duke of Marlborough had brought together within the Grand Alliance against Louis XIV almost 300 years earlier. Twenty-five countries formally joined the allied coalition, nine of which participated with the United States in the air campaign that began in January 1991. The remaining members played some role in the maritime and land campaigns or, as in the case of Japan, helped to finance the whole operation. Politically, the support of the Arab nations, particularly that of Egypt and Syria, was vital in preventing Saddam's attempts to appeal to pan-Arab nationalism.

Alliances mitigate against creating favourable opportunities to achieve high tempo in military operations as they tend to slow down decision-making. This owes much not only to differences in opinion but also to the issue of achieving interoperability in doctrine, force structure and equipment. The Americans had to work within these parameters when framing the plans that would decide the conduct of the war, a process of the type that Clausewitz rightly saw as being laborious:

> There is a decided difference between the cohesion of a *single* army, led into battle under the personal command of a *single* general, and that of an *allied force* ... In the one, cohesion is at its strongest and unity at its closest. In the other, unity is remote, frequently found only in mutual political interest, and even then rather precarious and imperfect; cohesion between the parts will visually be very loose, and often completely fictitious.[12]

Bush also needed to be wary of any attempt on the part of Saddam to try and weaken the coalition through exploiting its potential vulnerability as a centre of gravity. In this respect, Saddam took a Clausewitzian perspective, particularly regarding his attempts to wrest the Arab nations away from the coalition when he tried to draw Israel into the conflict in January 1991 with a series of Scud missile attacks on its cities: "Among alliances, [the center of gravity] lies in the community of interest ... It is against [this] that our energies should be directed."[13]

Obviously, if Israel had joined the conflict, the "community of interest" binding many of the Arab states to the alliance – fear of Iraq – may have unravelled. Saddam also believed that, like the Vietnamese communists before him, he could exploit the centre of gravity of American domestic opinion. Indeed, he remained convinced until the very last moment that the United States would not resort to war because of its fear of casualties. As he explained to the American ambassador to Baghdad, April Glaspie: "Yours is a society that cannot accept 10,000 dead in one battle."[14]

Ultimately, the attempts to make Iraq leave Kuwait peacefully through economic sanctions, diplomatic pressure, and the bringing together of a coalition under UN auspices, failed. Nevertheless, in keeping with the sixth tenet of the Weinberger Doctrine, the United States could legitimately claim that the use of force was a "last resort".

As the threat of conflict escalated, Bush showed that he had the political will to ride the logic of escalation dominance when, in response to the threat of the Iraqi use of weapons of mass destruction, he informed Baghdad that such a step would provoke a nuclear response from the United States. In this respect, Bush avoided repeating the mistake of the Truman Administration in Korea, which, although admittedly wary of Soviet action, failed to mobilise the utility of its nuclear deterrent to deter the Chinese communists. Bush's move also pre-empted any attempt by Saddam to use his unconventional weapons for purposes of blackmail.[15]

Domestically, Bush had to square the Clausewitzian trinity – revolving around its constituent elements of government, people and armed forces – through gaining Congressional support for any armed conflict in the Middle East. The objectives of American policy were fiercely debated. Some questioned whether there was a goal beyond the liberation of Kuwait – namely, the forcible removal of Saddam and the destruction of Iraq's military capability. Others questioned the need to adopt an offensive strategy while simultaneously pursuing all "peaceful means" to prevent a conflict. Senator Sam Nunn, for example, argued in November 1990: "We're committed [to defend Saudi Arabia], but I do not think that means we have to build up an offensive force to liberate Kuwait."[16]

Bush embarked on a public relations effort to reconcile the American people with the military build-up. Opinion polls showed that whereas 82 per cent of the public had supported Bush's policy in August only 51 per cent did so in November. This can be seen against a background of the call-up of Reserve and National Guard components and its bringing home to the American people of the sacrifices involved. Nevertheless, Bush continued to emphasise that a vital US national interest was at stake. He also pointed to the multilateral nature of the venture, and the role that the United States was playing as a leader of world opinion in confronting aggression. He did this by appealing to American exceptionalism, perhaps the one deviation from what was a Clausewitzian approach on his part. His rhetoric about a "New World Order" was in fact a throwback to Woodrow Wilson, and he used this as the centrepiece of his speech announcing the commencement of hostilities on 16 January 1991: "We have before us the opportunity to forge for ourselves and for future generations a new world order, a world where the rule of law, not the law of the jungle, governs the conduct of nations."[17]

Bush had to be decisive in his actions or else the impression that the same slow, uncertain build-up that had led to the Vietnam quagmire might be given. Crucially, he ensured that Congress supported him by asking it for permission to go to war in January 1991, thereby ensuring that he had "squared" the trinitarian triangle. In this way, a schism between the Executive and Legislature was avoided, although the important caveat that this was not an actual declaration of war should be noted. As the *Washington Post* observed in November 1990:

> If Mr Bush wants the latitude to start a war by invading Iraq, the approval of King Fahd or the UN will mean nothing without the approval of the American people. And that approval can only come through an open debate in Congress.[18]

Desert Storm: the air campaign

The decision to launch an air offensive in advance of any ground campaign was made so as to provide the conditions that would make the latter a success. The initial objectives of the air campaign were, therefore, to paralyse the Iraqi system of command and control; to achieve overwhelming air superiority; to destroy the Iraqis' lines of communication; to nullify the Iraqis' nuclear, chemical, and biological weapons capability; and to negate the fighting power of the Republican Guard. These objectives reflected a radical change that had very recently taken place in the US Air Force's doctrine. Colonel John Warden, US Air Force, a veteran of Vietnam, served on the air command staff when Saddam invaded Kuwait. He had written a tract, *The Air Campaign: Planning for Combat*, which argued that the Clausewitzian concept of the centre of gravity should guide the US Air Force's selection of targets in its offensive campaigns. Warden saw five concentric, strategic rings that formed the enemy's centres of gravity: leadership, production, communications, population and military forces. In this respect, he depicted the enemy as a system, with the notion that the destruction of the central ring – leadership – would lead to the paralysis of the whole given the dependence of the outer rings on the centre. "The aim of all military action, then, is not the destruction of enemy armed forces but the manipulation of the enemy leadership's will."[19]

Lieutenant-Colonel Timothy Reese, US Army, has rightly written that such a conception led to a false dichotomy between the enemy's will to resist and his physical strength, whereas Clausewitz would have said both needed to be destroyed.[20]

The JCS appointed Warden to head a joint working group, and he succeeded in persuading Horner to formulate a plan based on a conventional strategic air campaign that would utilise the technological superiority of the Air Force in destroying Iraqi centres of gravity. For example, the advantages accrued from the allies' space-based intelligence assets allowed them to have a clear picture of Iraqi dispositions. Warden defined the centre of gravity as "that point where the enemy is most vulnerable and the point where an attack will have the best chance of being decisive".[21]

Warden's argument illustrates the degree to which the concept of the centre of gravity was still not properly defined in American military doctrine. In other words, should it be a source of strength or vulnerability? Like Reese, Major Collin A. Agee has argued that Warden's paradigm tended towards what he calls Clausewitz's treatment of cohesion, rather than his emphasis on destruction:

> Warden's perception of the center of gravity, focused on vulnerability, is remarkably similar to the US Marine Corps doctrinal approach ... and remarkably different from the Army's. His center of gravity is the point where the enemy is most vulnerable and where an attack will be decisive. In a passage that portends Desert Storm, he contends that if there is more than one center of gravity, force must be applied to all of them.[22]

The operational order for Desert Storm stated that the Iraqis possessed three centres of gravity: their national command authority; their nuclear, biological, and chemical weapons capability; and the Republican Guard. Clearly, the centres of gravity identified at the strategic level in the Gulf War were strengths in the Clausewitzian mould, and not vulnerabilities. Antulio Echevarria has argued that CENTCOM spent far too long trying to identify the Iraqi centres of gravity when, if they had been cognisant of Clausewitz's meaning, they would have realised that the concept was superfluous as "the Gulf War was not a war of annihilation".[23]

Warden also believed that friction had been rendered an anachronism by advances in technology:

> The whole business of action and reaction, operations, friction, et cetera, was a function of serial war and the imprecision of weapons … [These nineteenth-century concepts are] an accurate description of the way things were, but not a description of how they ought to be or can be.[24]

On the contrary, there was clear evidence of friction occurring on several occasions during Desert Storm, most notably the destruction of the Al Firdos air raid shelter in central Baghdad when some 300 civilians were killed. Warden argued that technology would allow for the execution of a limited war with minimal collateral damage. In this respect, he was taking his systems analysis to its logical conclusion. As Major Howard Belote writes: "Strategists cannot allow a quantitative focus to obscure their understanding of the human interaction that constitutes both war and politics. Despite Warden's claim to the contrary, technology has not invalidated Clausewitz; war is still unpredictable."[25]

The decision to launch the air offensive on 16 January, as soon as the UN deadline for Saddam to leave Kuwait had expired, was politically sound: it showed that Bush had the courage of his convictions. Militarily, it also allowed the ground forces to continue their, as yet incomplete, build-up. The air campaign provided the cover for Schwarzkopf to carry out his deception plan, which involved moving the US XVIII Airborne Corps and VII Corps 200 miles to the north-west, poised to invade Iraq itself. By 17 February, CENTCOM had moved some 100,000 troops and 1,200 tanks an average of 200 miles west from their original positions.

On 29 January, Saddam attempted to disrupt the success of the air campaign by launching an assault into Saudi Arabia using three armoured brigades at Al Khafji, an undefended village some nine miles inside the border. The Iraqis were swiftly ejected by a combination of land and air forces, and Al Khafji remained the Iraqi Army's one act of defiance as its homeland was pounded day after day for a period of almost seven weeks. What Al Khafji illustrated was the importance of joint operations in modern warfare: space-based assets such as the Global Positioning System (GPS) pinpointed the invaders; US Army and Marine Corps units fixed the enemy in place – though it was Saudi and Qatari forces who did most of the fighting; and air and artillery assets were used to pulverise the Iraqis. Michael Gordon and Lieutenant-General Bernard Trainor, USMC (Retd.) note that CENTCOM failed to recognise the significance of Al Khafji:

> Those on the ground saw only the tip of the military iceberg because most of the Iraqi troops committed to the battle never made it to the front [having

been destroyed from the air]. And the ground generals who controlled the war – Schwarzkopf and Powell – were not inclined to accept the notion that an invading army could be destroyed from the air. Confounded by Khafji, CENTCOM did not make a single substantive change in its plan for a land offensive as a result of the battle.[26]

Clausewitz appreciated the principle of concentrating mass against the enemy at the perceived decisive point.[27] To do so required superiority of numbers on the part of the attacking force. In the Gulf War, PGMs made it possible to concentrate against a target with very few aircraft, thus utilising a contradictory principle: economy of force. During the strategic bombing campaigns of the Second World War, the necessity of massing at the tactical level, whereby several hundred aircraft attacked only a single target each day, allowed the enemy time to make good the damage suffered. Therefore, targets had to be revisited in the effort to wear down the enemy's powers of recovery. Hence, attrition set in. In the Gulf, however, precision attacks, particularly where stealth was involved, were successfully carried out by so few aircraft that other aircraft could carry out sorties against other targets. Missions could be planned to inflict moral as well as physical damage. The cumulative effect was to fulfil the higher strategic goals of the campaign. "Desert Storm not only demonstrated the tremendous leverage available to war planners who apply new technologies under ancient principles, but also revealed the phenomenal cost of failing to do so."[28]

The air campaign contributed greatly to damaging the capability of the Iraqis to support their forces in the field. The national electric grid was greatly damaged, as was 80 per cent of Iraq's oil-refining capacity. By the end of the conflict, less than 40 per cent of the Iraqi Air Force remained intact. On the other hand, the effect of attacks on the Iraqi communications network was partly nullified by the response of the Iraqis. Imaginative mechanisms such as alternative routing, prioritisation of traffic, and artificial bridging were used to counteract the effects of the bombing. In the final analysis, however, it must be said that the doctrine the US Air Force deployed in the Gulf War was vindicated, though one must not subscribe to the belief that airpower alone won the campaign. For example, Air Force chief-of-staff, General Murrill McPeak, said in testimony to Congress in March 1991: "That is the first time in history that a field army has been defeated by air power."[29]

Rather, air power was a means to an end, paving the way for the ground campaign that completed the task. As Benjamin Lambeth has said:

> There is ... a case to be made that the contribution of US airpower to the allied victory in Desert Storm constituted enough of a departure from past experience to suggest that a new relationship between air and surface forces in joint warfare may be in the offing.[30]

The allies had many advantages: air supremacy, favourable weather, and flat terrain that offered little cover for moving targets. The Air Force was right to isolate the battlefield and to carry out deep interdiction strikes against economic and military targets. However, high-altitude bombing of the Iraqis' dug-in defensive positions in Kuwait did not result in much damage or casualties. The air campaign failed to eject a single division from Kuwait. What the air campaign did illustrate was the need to win air superiority and to nullify the enemy's ability to wage war. It also severely dented enemy morale, with the effect that many Iraqi front-line troops deserted at the first opportunity. Thomas Keaney has summed up the hyperbole surrounding the effects of the air campaign. "There was nothing in the Gulf War data that supported the existence of quantifiable measures of operation, much less strategic effectiveness … In this sense, Clausewitz had it right [in his critique of relying on intelligence reports]."[31]

Desert Storm: the ground campaign

Despite the protestations to the contrary of airpower enthusiasts, the strategic objectives of the campaign could only be achieved with the aid of forces on the ground. By mid-February, Bush sensed that the air campaign had softened Iraqi capabilities to the point where the ground campaign could commence. Nevertheless, he continued to view the war within a wider context, publicly praising the efforts made by the Soviet Union to mediate, thereby ensuring that the escalation of the conflict to the ground could be portrayed once again as a measure of the last resort. As Sir Michael Howard noted at the time, public opinion had to remain in step with the allied campaign:

> However skilful may be American statesmanship, however successful the allied armed forces in the field, if American public opinion is so horrified by the sight of slaughter that it ceases to be supportive of the whole enterprise, Saddam Hussein might still not lose the war. In this, as in much else, the Clausewitzian analysis remains starkly relevant.[32]

The deployment of the Iraqi mass of troops within Kuwait allowed the allies to plan an enveloping operation around it that would forgo the need to break through the heavily fortified, deeply echeloned linear defence on the Kuwait–Saudi Arabia border. This would enable the allies to conduct simultaneous attacks against the echelonear flanks throughout the depth of the Iraqi deployment. The allies' supremacy in artillery and airpower, coupled with the damage already inflicted on the Iraqi command and control system, ensured that the Iraqis' artillery assets were virtually non-existent. Indeed, there was no indication as to whether the Iraqis actually had any plan in mind to defend Kuwait other than to rely on the static tactics that had been effective in the war against Iran, but would prove futile against a technologically advanced foe. As Major Armor Brown points out: "[E]ven if Saddam Hussein had turned all of Clausewitz's criteria [for the defense] into advantages and had given sound strategic guidance that was properly translated into operational engagements and tactical battles he probably still would have lost."[33]

The other point to note about the system of Iraqi command and control was its centralised nature. Saddam exercised direct control over decision-making at the lowest levels, thereby discouraging initiative and making it easier for the coalition to paralyse the Iraqis. With their command and control assets either destroyed or disrupted, subordinate commanders did not have the will to make decisions of their own. Lieutenant-General Franks noted that "by the time [anyone] called Baghdad, on their broken down communication system that the Air Force had destroyed, and got that to the field and they reacted to it, we'd be on them".[34]

Robert Leonhard has argued in his *Art of Maneuver* that the fixation with the Republican Guard as a centre of gravity was a manifestation of attritionist thought rather than manoeuvre doctrine because it involved a desire to destroy rather than defeat. Leonhard says that the belief that the Republican Guard was the fulcrum of the Iraqi armed forces led the coalition to think that its destruction would result in the paralysis of the Iraqis. However, as he points out, the Iraqis had already been paralysed long before VII Corps had made contact with units of the Republican Guard. Retrospectively, the logic of Leonhard's argument leads to the conclusion that the Republican Guard was not a centre of gravity. While this may appear to be the case with hindsight, it overlooks the fact that when the campaign was planned the Republican Guard was identified as the most important element in the Iraqi order of battle, and not only for military reasons. Politically, the Republican Guard was Saddam's Praetorian Guard and existed as much to put down internal threats to the regime as it did to fight as a conventional military force. Therefore, allied planners saw the neutralisation of the Republican Guard as a precursor to Saddam having to surrender Kuwait. Schwarzkopf identified the Iraqi centres of gravity as Saddam and the Republican Guard: "The center of gravity is plain and simply that thing that, if destroyed, will destroy the will of the enemy to fight."[35]

Schwarzkopf faced some initial opposition to his plan to envelop the Iraqis in Kuwait. This was partly due to the fixation that many commanders continued to have with confronting mass head-on rather than seeking to create an opportunity to dislocate the enemy in the manner that Schwarzkopf's plan intended. In the event, the decision to move VII and XVIII Corps to the west after the beginning of the air campaign, which has been described as "the most audacious" in American military history,[36] ensured that the ground campaign was a formality and that allied casualties would be minimal. The allies were able to manoeuvre both in space (through envelopment) and in time (by penetrating the Iraqis' depth faster than they could respond). Desert Storm was therefore the modern equivalent of Caesar's bloodless victory at Ilerda and Napoleon's similarly cheap victory at Ulm. The allies lost some 146 men in battle, with another 500 wounded. Iraqi losses were over 100,000, with another 100,000 taken prisoner. As Lieutenant-Colonel H. T. Hayden, USMC, remarks: "You cannot argue with success ... [Schwarzkopf] provided superb examples of deception, pre-emption, dislocation, and disruption."[37]

Leonhard, who was deployed with a task force of the 3rd Armored Division, cautions that the weakness of the opposition means that one cannot possibly

conclude from Desert Storm that the United States fought a textbook manoeuvrist campaign, particularly at the tactical level:

> [O]perational successes (themselves born of strategic successes) obviated
> any reliance upon tactical perfection. Such a relationship is a paradox, for
> on the one hand maneuver theory applauds operational art that preordains or
> avoids the need for tactical success, while on the other hand it looks scepti-
> cally on the boasts of a successful ground force that in reality was never
> seriously tested in battle.[38]

Another paradox in the conduct of the campaign was the way in which attrition was used to create the opportunity for the manoeuvre to succeed. Tactical
manoeuvre, when it was practised, relied on the support of massed fires.
However, it was the logistical support that the US Army provided that was the
real catalyst in ensuring the Desert Storm plan succeeded. Working with only
a limited number of ports as conduits for supplies, the Army had to rely on
forward logistics bases to conduct the ground war. It is certain, as
Schwarzkopf recognised, that without this support, his plan of manoeuvre
would not have succeeded. "During wartime, you must be a logistician.
Without logistics, you are going to lose ... [it] was the biggest challenge of the
war."[39]

As has already been noted, the allies succeeded in achieving information
dominance during Desert Storm. It is worth examining this in light of Clausewitz's critique of intelligence in *On War*. Clausewitz did not actually criticise
intelligence *per se*, rather he wrote of the serious potential for friction emanating from the constant flow of information at the commander's disposal,
much of which might be contradictory and all of which had to be disseminated
to provide worthwhile intelligence regarding the enemy's intentions. Therefore, there is a cause-and-effect relationship between information and intelligence. Howard and Paret's 1984 edition of *On War* translates the German
Nachrichten as "intelligence" when in fact it can also be translated as
"information". Therefore, rather than say "many intelligence reports in war are
contradictory", the translation should read "much information in war is contradictory".[40]

It is not necessary to note, as Major Victor Rosello does, that Clausewitz
"fought on the wrong side of the war" and was unaware of the skill with which
Napoleon put his intelligence to use. However, Rosello is right to suggest that
the distinction between information and intelligence is more than an exercise in
semantics: "The decision to regard intelligence as simply information on the
enemy might be a purely academic argument, but in light of today's tendency to
quote Clausewitz as an authority on modern military matters, the issue tran-
scends academic boundaries."[41]

In an article for *ARMY* published in 1996, Lieutenant-Colonel Anthony
Coroalles attempted to portray Clausewitz's ideas in the context of information
age operations by imagining that he is a contemporary:

In my day, cohesion was principally a function of the will of the commander and the morale of the troops. Today, your forces not only achieve cohesion through the will of the commander and the morale of the troops, but
also through information...

Without doubt, information can be considered the hub of a modern
army's operational power and strength. In modern operations, destroying an
opponent's ability to gain, process and transmit information may be the
surest way to destroy that enemy.[42]

One of the features of the Gulf War was the way in which American intelligence greatly overestimated the capabilities of the Iraqi armed forces. The disparity between the expected threat and the actual threat was enormous, and gave
the lie to the claims by some that modern intelligence was slowly unveiling the
shroud of the fog of war. A more serious point is that overestimating the
enemy's strength can lead to a loss of tempo by inducing caution in the framing
of one's plans. This might mean, for example, that plans to exploit break-
throughs and to pursue the enemy might not be in place, arguably a problem that
arose at the time the ground campaign was brought to a halt in the Gulf. According to Leonhard, even reports on the weather were either late or plain wrong.
"Fortunately, many of the soldiers could listen to commercial radio stations and
get the accurate weather."[43]

The Americans practised deception at all levels: strategically, the dispositions
during Desert Shield, as well as political talk of "liberating" Kuwait if diplomacy failed, convinced Saddam that the coalition would invade Kuwait head-on
therefore ensuring that he concentrated the mass of his forces within the
Emirate. Operationally, American deception convinced the Iraqis that an
amphibious assault by the Marines was planned along the coast (some 20,000
Marines thereby tied down 125,000 Iraqis), while the VII and XVIII Corps,
together with the three other operational corps groupings, were initially positioned opposite the Kuwaiti border before moving west under the cover of the
air campaign. Nevertheless, the omnipresence of the media made it difficult to
achieve complete deception, given their ability to emphasise coalition capabilities and to estimate coalition intentions in real time. Schwarzkopf overcame
this by drip-feeding the media with information about events along the Kuwaiti
coast and border. "Schwarzkopf did not give false information; he merely gave a
misleading emphasis to true information."[44]

In assessing operations during Desert Storm, TRADOC concluded that the
US Army was becoming more accomplished in its practice of *Auftragstaktik* or
mission command. In fact, the combination of vast amounts of information and a
propensity for oversupervision by higher headquarters actually ensured that
small-level units had little opportunity to display initiative. The impact of
advanced technology was a significant factor in this. For example, the Small
Lightweight GPS Receiver, a hand-held commercial position locator, allowed
commanders at every level to receive specific orders concerning operations.
Major Anthony Garrett concludes: "Clearly, while the Army planned and

executed maneuver warfare at the operational level, tactical level performance adhered to traditional set piece, centralised operations."[45]

Leonhard's battalion and brigade commanders observed after the conflict that they had not been called upon to make any tactical decisions. Centralised command meant that concern with exposing flanks ensured that the advance struck along the entirety of the enemy's own flank rather than looking to exploit the concept of surfaces and gaps. Thus, while centralised command was not actually a hindrance to the success of Desert Storm it worked against an enemy that was even more constrained by command and control at the higher levels. If the Iraqis had been able to exercise more initiative at the small-unit level there would have been more of a contest between coalition manoeuvre and Iraqi mass. There were some instances of mission command on the allied side. For example, the 2nd Armored Cavalry Regiment of the VII Corps overwhelmed the "Tawakalna" Division by a combination of small-unit initiative, aggression and firepower. However, as Leonhard notes, "[t]he break between our written doctrine and our practice has never been more clearly demonstrated than in Desert Storm, despite the politically safe statement that our doctrine has been vindicated".[46]

Both the US Army and the US Marine Corps made important contributions to the coalition's victory. From a theoretical point of view, there are some interesting observations to be made when comparing the performance of the two services. The I Marine Expeditionary Force's role involved an amphibious force lying off the Kuwaiti coast, while the 1st and 2nd Marine Divisions were to drive straight through the Iraqi defences towards Kuwait City. While Marines interpret their performance in the Gulf War as being a vindication of their manoeuvrist doctrine, some in the Army have come to the opposite conclusion. Colonel Clinton Ancker has remarked that while the Army conducted a manoeuvrist campaign by enveloping the Iraqis, the Marine Corps used attritional means by conducting a head-on assault into Kuwait.[47] However, it should be noted that while the Marine Corps were prepared to take casualties, the effects of the air campaign had destroyed Iraqi morale to such an extent that the Marines rolled over the defences with little loss, a result not normally associated with such tactics.

The Marines, who had witnessed the Iraqis' performance at Al Khafji, changed their plan to a simultaneous attack with each division making its own breach from the original intention of a sequential attack through a single breach. The 3rd Army, on the other hand, kept to its original timetable, starting its attack a day after the Marines. It was only once the campaign had begun, on 24 February, that Schwarzkopf ordered the 3rd Army to bring forward the start of its campaign by 15 hours, but still 11 hours after the beginning of the ground attack. The time already lost was to prove crucial, being compounded by adverse weather conditions and the divergence in perceptions between the field commanders of the 3rd Army and Schwarzkopf in Riyadh, which would continue to increase.[48]

Barry Watts has written of the way in which the performance of the 3rd

Army, particularly its VII Corps, illustrates the eternal validity of Clausewitz's concept of friction. According to Keaney, who taught at the National War College, this is the one aspect of Clausewitz's work that is familiar to all US military officers. Nevertheless, many of Clausewitz's readers, including Gordon and Trainor, perceive friction to impact only on tactics, a result perhaps of Clausewitz's description of conditions affecting battle, when in fact it applies at all levels of warfare.[49]

The degree to which synchronisation is an issue in the theoretical construct of operational level warfare gave practical effect to the concept of friction during the campaign. Watts, alluding to Clausewitz's observation of the battles of Jena-Auerstadt where the Prussian command chain consisted of three commanders-in-chief and two chiefs-of-staff, illustrates that synchronisation failed to accommodate the existence of separate service commands under a nominally joint commander:

> In Clausewitzian terms, ... synchronization focused above all else on mini-mizing the internal friction of *one's own* military 'machine'. As such, it exemplifies friction in the narrow sense and harks back to Clausewitz's first-known use of the term *friktion* in 1806.[50]

The Marine Corps has criticised the US Army's VII Corps for failing to close the gap on the road to Basra through which the Iraqi forces managed to extricate themselves from being trapped inside Kuwait. Seventh Corps' rationale was the need to create an operational pause to allow it to synchronise its forces so that 1st Infantry Division could reorient its attack from the north-east to the east across the Basra–Kuwait City highway.[51] This was the outcome of a campaign plan that was expressed in phase lines, whereby once a certain point was reached the advance would stop. Thus, rather than criticise the tenet of synchronisation, the real issue here is the extent to which centralised command prevented the commander on the spot from initiating the closing of the ring around the Iraqis. Seventh Corps' operational order explicitly stated that "once we reach the objec-tive, there will be a planning/decision cycle".[52]

The Marine Corps, on the other hand, used thrust vectors instead of phase lines, and constantly adjusted the focus of their effort to the nature of the sur-faces and gaps they encountered in the enemy's defences. The point to bear in mind is that the US Army and Marine Corps were key players in executing CENTCOM's plan, together with their coalition partners. Each vindicated the doctrines expressed in FM 100–5 and FMFM 1 to the extent that was possible *given* the ineptitude of the opposition. Each played a part in ensuring that Bush was able to bring the ground offensive to a successful conclusion on the morning of 28 February, exactly 100 hours after it had begun, by which time XVIII Airborne Corps' 24th Infantry Division had covered 230 miles – the fur-thest and fastest advance in history at that time.

Schwarzkopf has, not surprisingly, interpreted the decision to stop differ-ently. He believes that his aim of repeating Cannae was fulfilled:

The gate was closed. Very important point ... We chose to open it again when the ceasefire was declared ... We had them completely surrounded just like Cannae.

I agreed with the decision to stop ... At that given instant in time no-one thought Saddam Hussein could survive this incredible defeat and therefore we had written off Saddam Hussein. That's why the decision was made.[53]

Comparisons with Cannae are slightly flawed. At the tactical level, Schwarzkopf did not repeat the double envelopment that Hannibal executed. A single envelopment was deployed to outflank the Iraqis west of Kuwait, while a threat of envelopment on the amphibious flank east of Kuwait was forgone in favour of a frontal assault. Strategically, however, Desert Storm's results were more favourable to the victor than Cannae's. Whereas Rome recovered to eventually defeat Carthage, Desert Storm achieved its objective of liberating Kuwait. The fact that Saddam Hussein remained in power for another 12 years is beside the point.

It seems clear that Schwarzkopf lacked a complete picture of what was happening at the front. Indeed, his memoirs tend to contradict the previous citation in that they hint at his frustration as the campaign continued regarding the ability of the Republican Guard to avoid being trapped: "Until we'd destroyed the Republican Guard, our job was only half done, and all of us felt the window of opportunity was rapidly slamming shut."[54]

Decisive victory?

The decision to call a halt to the campaign has been the subject of intense speculation among military commentators. One thesis suggests that the media's graphic portrayal of the carnage on the highway between Kuwait City and Basra was significant. Rick Atkinson of the *Washington Post* has written that Powell "anticipated that Americans and allies alike would soon see televised images of the carnage ... and react with outrage. To blight the dazzling performance of the US military with images of a 'turkey shoot' was both unnecessary and foolish."[55]

Gordon and Trainor have suggested that the decision to end the war was "political" (which, in Clausewitzian theory, should always be the case), and that Schwarzkopf, without having any true grasp of the scene at the front, concurred with this. Leonhard, on the other hand, puts the halt down to what he sees as the US military's age-old problem of failing to exploit tactical success and pursuing the enemy so as to create a strategic victory. Michael Handel believes that the United States concentrated on the wrong centre of gravity. Rather than targeting the Iraqi armed forces for destruction, he argues that Saddam Hussein should have been the main focus of effort. In this sense, Handel adopts Warden's approach: the central, command ring is the key centre of gravity. Destroying the Iraqi armed forces did not eradicate the problem of Iraq in US foreign policy. However, this argument overlooks the limited nature of the war. Unlike the

Second World War, where unconditional surrender was demanded of Germany, the more limited aims of the Gulf War did not warrant the extra effort and resources required to depose Saddam.[56]

Handel has cited Clausewitz to support his argument:

> [T]he importance of the victory is chiefly determined by the vigor with which the immediate pursuit is carried out. In other words, pursuit makes up the second act of the victory and in many cases is more important than the first. Strategy at this point draws near to tactics in order to receive the complicated assignment from it; and its first exercise of authority is to demand that the victory should really be complete.[57]

Handel overlooks the fact that this passage was written prior to the time when Clausewitz concluded that there is more than one type of war. What applies to one set of circumstances does not necessarily apply to another set. Clausewitz would have recognised the decision to end the Gulf War as perfectly rational given the political parameters involved. Moreover, one must bear in mind the situation in which the ground forces found themselves after four days of combat. Maintaining the high tempo that they had created in the previous 100 hours would become more and more difficult as their logistical support system became more stretched. Commanders were concerned that their forces might find themselves entering urban areas and getting bogged down – a process that would have increased both coalition and civilian casualties, thereby taking the gloss off the victory. Finally, returning to the strategic level, there was no contingency beyond that which existed for liberating Kuwait – driving on to Baghdad and completing the destruction of the Iraqi armed forces and the Saddam regime was not an option.

As Bush and his national security adviser, Brent Scowcroft, wrote after the war:

> The end of the effective Iraqi resistance came with a rapidity which surprised us all, and we were perhaps psychologically unprepared for the sudden transition from fighting to peacemaking. True to the guidelines we had established, when we had achieved our strategic objectives (ejecting Iraqi forces from Kuwait and ending Saddam's threat to the region) we stopped the fighting. But the necessary limitations placed on our objective, the fog of war, and the lack of "battleship 'Missouri'" surrender unfortunately left unresolved problems, and new ones arose.[58]

The Gulf War perfectly illustrates the differences between limited and unlimited war. While moral considerations may have demanded the removal of Saddam and his trial for crimes against humanity, political and military realities, not least the difficulty in maintaining Arab support, dictated that the war ended when it did. Although the administration made some ambiguous noises that encouraged the Iraqi opposition, the subsequent uprisings in the north and south of the country cannot be viewed in retrospect as offering an opportunity for a seamless continuation of the war. They presented a completely new set of circumstances to those that had existed when the Iraqis occupied Kuwait. Major Frederick Rudesheim therefore misunderstands the Clausewitzian paradigm when he writes of the experience of the Gulf War: "If one subscribes to the notion that winning a battle is not always everything, then the Clausewitzian maxim that 'the destruction of the enemy's armed forces is the overriding principle in war' must be revisited in modern context."[59]

Most commentators agree that the conduct of the Gulf War was Clausewitzian. DuBois, for example, has argued that US policy and strategy met the standards of both Clausewitz and the Weinberger Doctrine. Handel has written that the Gulf War met all the tenets of the Weinberger Doctrine with the possible exception of the tenet that war should be a last resort. Finally, if one accepts his adaptation of Clausewitz's trinity, Summers is correct to say that the Gulf War represented a return to America's trinitarian roots in that the people, government and armed forces were very much in sync in executing the war.[60]

Shimon Naveh is in no doubt that operational art was fundamental to the coalition victory, arguing that the conflict closed a broader historical circle extending back to the Napoleonic era. In fact, he might have gone further. The Gulf War surely marks the last attempt by a non-Western polity to attempt to defeat technologically advanced and doctrinally sophisticated Western armed forces at conventional warfare in conditions that favour the latter. Naveh cites the Final Report to Congress by the Department of Defense as proof of his thesis:

> Evolving joint operations doctrine guided the planning and conduct of the ground offensive. The basic principles of initiative, depth, agility, synchronization and combined arms are understood and practised by all services.[61]

Where Naveh's argument is flawed, however, is in his contention, cited in the introduction to this work, that the war served to disprove Clausewitz. As Robert Citino says: "It is difficult ... even to entertain the plausibility of an argument that Saddam Hussein's 'generalship' has somehow invalidated Clausewitz."[62]

Despite some of the problems inherent in executing joint warfare in the Gulf, Christopher Bassford is convinced that Clausewitz provides the common conceptual base for jointness:

> Clausewitz has provided the intellectual common ground that formal doctrine has always sought but – because of its unavoidably narrow focus, usually single-service orientation, and prescriptive intent – failed to provide. The value of that common ground lies in the very flexibility of Clausewitzian theory that many have found so frustrating.[63]

General Robert Scales has taken a more rounded view, albeit from the army's perspective, as to the significance of the doctrine deployed during Desert Storm:

AirLand Battle … continues as a viable foundation for the development of future war-fighting doctrine … the 1986 version of AirLand Battle was a vision of what was possible rather than an owner's manual for the equipment and force structures available at the time … the conditions of combat and the dynamics of the Desert Storm battlefield proved to be modelled with remarkable fidelity to FM100–5.[64]

Wass de Czege, on the other hand, argues that what was taught at SAMS was probably more influential than FM 100–5, 1986 on the conduct of operations during Desert Storm. Dr Stephen Blank believes that Desert Storm showed the US military to be better students of Tukhachevskii and Ogarkov than the Soviets.[65]

Technology undoubtedly played a part in the Coalition victory. Stephen Biddle has gone as far as to say:

[T]he [Gulf War] changed the whole course of American military thought – the revolution in military affairs thesis that now dominates the defense debate is a product of the radically surprising nature of the Desert Storm loss rate. Though the RMA thesis had been presented before the war, few were persuaded.[66]

However, as General Donn Starry, father of the AirLand Battle concept, notes, technology was only one of several elements required for the campaign to succeed:

The military force fought outnumbered and won its first and succeeding battles … The part of the force that brought the war to a successful termination was a corps-sized combined arms mechanized force employed with lightning-like speed and devastating lethality … In summary, the equipment, organization and training designed to support AirLand Battle doctrine was an unqualified success.[67]

Conclusion

Prior to the beginning of Desert Storm, the perceived significance of Clausewitz in the American preparations for conflict was best articulated by Joel Achenbach of the *Washington Post* in December 1990:

A dead Prussian haunts the Pentagon, the White House and Capitol Hill. Lately, he's been in those Senate hearings on the Persian Gulf crisis, swaggering among the experts, whispering in their ears, seizing their tongues, making them parrot the ideas of a book from another century – *his* book.[68]

At the strategic level, the Gulf War highlighted the importance of Clausewitz's notion that strategy should serve policy. It was a conflict that was very much limited by political circumstance despite later protestations that the Iraqi regime could have been overthrown. The allies had a strategic aim – the eviction of Iraqi forces from Kuwait – that influenced the conduct of the campaign at the operational level. The Gulf War also illustrated the importance of Clausewitz's centre of gravity at the strategic level, as modified by Warden and his notion of concentric rings, though it was also applied to the operational level through the planning to nullify Saddam's most effective military asset, the Republican Guard. Although the overall US treatment of the centre of gravity was ambiguous, their use of the concept provides an adaptation of Clausewitz to the Gulf War. Among the many lessons learnt from the conflict, the realisation that friction is a recurring theme in warfare is one that has exercised the minds of military practitioners and theorists alike.[69] The belief that information age operations and digitisation of the battlespace will help to eradicate friction must be tempered by the reality of a campaign where, even when one side enjoyed overwhelming superiority, the "fog of war" still played havoc with planning and operations.

The Gulf War served as a vindication of the efforts made by the American armed forces to refine their doctrine in the aftermath of Vietnam. Above all, it served as a pay-off for their reappraisal of the importance of the intellectual side of war. FM 100–5 served as the keystone manual for the Army's doctrine as practised in the Gulf War. The corps, which had long been envisioned as a focal point for planning, bridged the tactical and operational levels of war. The VII and XVIII Corps' campaign plans were designed to accord with FM 100–5, and were supported in turn by the 3rd Army's and CENTCOM's plans, which bridged the operational and strategic levels in accordance with Clausewitz's conviction that war plans be tailored to fulfil a political objective.[70]

7 The problem of low-intensity conflict from Vietnam to Panama

The theoretical and historical background

Contrary to the general perception of Clausewitz as a prophet of conventional warfare, he did devote some attention to the issues of guerrilla warfare and what he called "the people in arms". In formulating his thinking on this subject, Clausewitz drew on the lectures he gave on small-scale warfare at the Prussian War College in 1810 and 1811. These were partly influenced by the writings of Scharnhorst and the Hessian light infantry officer Johann von Ewald, who had, rarely among his contemporaries, studied the American Revolutionary War. The lectures discussed the deployment of small units of regulars that could conduct *kleine krieg* – also translated as the "war of detachments". Such operations would involve patrols, raids, ambushes and information gathering; in other words, elements of what we now call special operations. Peter Paret is convinced that these lectures did not constitute the origin of Clausewitz's later thinking about unconventional warfare. Instead, he argues that by referring to "partisan" (*Partheygänger*) Clausewitz meant regular soldiers rather than guerrillas conducting small war. Werner Hahlweg, on the other hand, identifies these lectures as a "starting point" in the development of Clausewitz's study of guerrilla warfare.[1]

The real origin of Clausewitz's thinking about irregular warfare lies in his *Bekenntnisdenkschrift* – "statement of conviction" or "memorial of confession" – of spring 1812. The *Bekenntnisdenkschrift* reflected Clausewitz's thinking about the dire circumstances in which Prussia found itself at that time, having been turned into a vassal of France. It emphasised the potential of arming the population to resist the occupier. Clausewitz drew on the examples of the Vendée and Spain to discuss guerrilla warfare fought in conjunction with the regular army. During the Peninsular War, for example, Wellington found the combination of his regular forces and the Spanish guerrillas to be crucial in defeating the superior numbers of French regulars. Clausewitz's line of thought was further developed when he witnessed partisan warfare in Russia later in 1812 and when the *Landwehr* (militia) was mobilised during the struggle to liberate Prussia from the French in 1813.

In Book VI of *On War*, "The Defence", Clausewitz examined the emerging phenomenon of the people in arms. He did so within the context of a conventional strategic defensive in which an insurrection would be a last resort after a defeat in battle or else a prelude to a decisive battle. In common with the *Bekenntnisdenkschrift*, these writings recognised that the support of at least some sections of the regular army was essential to success. Clausewitz argued, both intuitively and from experience, that a nation that is on the verge of catastrophe will use any means at its disposal to save itself. Despite this, he did not see the initial impetus for unconventional warfare coming from the government. Rather, it would arise as a result of the spontaneous motivations of those on the spot, the efforts and sacrifices of local populations in encountering the enemy. Clausewitz described a popular uprising in *On War* as being "an outgrowth of the way in which the conventional barriers have been swept away in our lifetime by the elemental violence of war".[2]

Clausewitz went on to remark that he was unsure "whether mankind at large will gain by this further expansion of the element of war; a question to which the answer should be the same as to the question of war itself. We shall leave both to the philosophers."[3]

Steven Metz suggests that it is difficult to make a connection between Clausewitzian thought and the contemporary definitions of LIC:

> Clausewitz would have been uncomfortable with the notion of LIC being applied to the conditions of his day given his aristocratic outlook. He considered guerrilla warfare only in the direst of circumstances. He focused on partisan action rather than what we would understand as insurgency. Nevertheless, Clausewitz influenced Mao from the perspective that war and politics go together.[4]

As has been discussed in Chapter 1, Clausewitz's concept of real war is compatible with the notion of "intensity" in explaining the ferocity or otherwise of conflict. Given that Clausewitz only came to this realisation in 1827, one must approach what he writes in Chapter 26 of Book VI with a degree of caution as this precedes the Note of July 1827. Domicio Proença Junior and E. E. Duarté rightly see the conviction that there is more than one type of war as a crucial aspect of Clausewitz's thought: "This is such a paramount component of the theory of war that major adaptation would be required before the contents of VI-26 could be used authoritatively."[5]

LIC encompasses insurgency/counterinsurgency (CI), terrorism/counter-terrorism, and peace enforcement (though not peacekeeping, which emphasises consent, not force). Frank Hoffmann, writing on the American tradition of "small wars", has recently defined the latter as involving "protracted and extremely lethal conflicts of the most savage and persistent violence, and cannot be classified as small in scale or by arbitrary distinctions between high-, medium- or low-intensity conflict".[6]

Colonel David Hale, a Task Force commander who served in Panama in 1989, has summed up the traditional indifference of the American military to LIC:

When I was a student at Leavenworth, I said that [LIC] is too complicated, there are no rules in it,... it's too much an art and not much of a science. It's too unpredictable and uncontrollable, it's too tough. And, by the way, the chances are so low that I'm going to have to do any of that.[7]

Russell Weigley has opined that the US Army lacks an institutional memory of LIC, requiring it to improvise each time it conducts this form of conflict. Despite the experience of fighting Indian tribes on the frontier, it was only in 1911 that army doctrine for so-called "minor warfare" first emerged. It was recommended that aggressive small-unit activity be undertaken against irregulars, and this was put into practice during General John Pershing's expedition against Pancho Villa in Mexico in 1916. The Marine Corps produced a comprehensive *Small Wars Manual* in 1940 that appreciated the non-military roots of many insurgencies by emphasising the need for stable government. Though not of much utility in the Second World War, practitioners of counterinsurgency read this manual in Vietnam and when aiding the Contras in Nicaragua during the 1980s. "The Marine authors drew attention to the fact that the time-honored Clausewitzian dictum of destruction of the enemy armed force often would not be the prime objective."[8]

In stark contrast to the Marines, the Army's *Field Service Regulations* of the 1940s devoted a fraction of their space to small wars. The Army's Infantry School did produce a substantial tract on counterguerrilla warfare in 1950 that encapsulated the lessons provided by the resistance movements of the Second World War in Europe, though significantly it did not examine the Maoist model that had just proved so successful in China. There was a sudden increase in interest in counterinsurgency during the Kennedy Administration in the early 1960s. The increased emphasis on "situations short of war" in the Army's Field Manual 100–5, *Operations* took the role envisaged by the Marines further when it stated in 1968: "The fundamental purpose of US military force is to preserve, restore, or create an environment of order or stability within which the instrumentalities [*sic*] of government can function effectively under a code of laws."[9]

At that time, the US Army was still expected to bear the brunt of counter-guerrilla operations with some support from the host nation's forces. The importance of intelligence in surveying the threat, and the need to provide economic assistance to the indigenous population to win "hearts and minds", was also emphasised. The chastening experience of Vietnam, however, led to an emphasis on the host nation taking the military lead in counterinsurgency. FM 100–20, *Field Service Regulations: Internal Defense and Development*, acknowledged this requirement in 1974. As Colonel Rod Paschall noted: "Counterguerrilla warfare is highly political in nature. The ability to win is based on both military and political actions of the beleaguered host government."[10]

Throughout the period of the Cold War, the United States viewed LIC in the context of the wider struggle between the superpowers. The bipolar nature of that conflict made the Americans believe that wherever national or allied interests were threatened by insurgency, the Soviet Union stood to gain. Robert

Leonhard has criticised the way in which this distorted attempts by the United States to confront such situations:

> [S]uch a perspective has lent an irrational, disproportionate emphasis upon LIC within the US. Coupled with the unfathomable complexity and difficulty of conducting successful low-intensity operations, the imperatives of bipolarity have conspired to cause American politicians and soldiers alike to commit great resources to optimizing the army and other services for LIC.[11]

A contrary view has been propounded by Michael Smith. In this view, the requirements of the Cold War dislocated LIC from the mainstream of strategic thought. The consequence was that, after the Cold War ended, both military and political policymakers were unable to adjust from dealing with contingencies that involved clearly defined states and their armed forces. Such rigidity in thinking impacted upon the United States' (and, by extension, the West's) very slow, and unsatisfactory response to the type of warfare witnessed in the former Yugoslavia. As Smith says:

> [T]he deficiency of strategic studies with regard to the study of low intensity conflict has nothing to do with the supposedly malign influence of Clausewitz and everything to do with the legacy of twentieth century warfare ... It is this that accounts for the state-orientated, means-addicted, strategic mentality that was ill at ease in comprehending anything that did not encompass the massive clash of organised armed forces.[12]

Nevertheless, the superpower dichotomy is a useful yardstick in measuring American success in countering LIC. Because the United States is a democracy, its means of engaging in this form of conflict tend to be restricted when compared to the means available to an authoritarian state. There is a need to inform public opinion of the issues at stake prior to involvement so as to justify the inevitable sacrifices in lives, weapons and money that must be made. This is especially true when fighting against an enemy, such as the Viet Cong, that appreciates the importance of public opinion to its opponent.

Unfortunately, the US government failed to take such a course prior to Vietnam and this led to a lack of resolve being shown by the political and military leadership at important stages of the conflict. The Soviet Union had no such problems prior to its Afghan campaign and, although they ultimately suffered a Vietnam-type humiliation, the Soviets were less constrained in deploying draconian measures against their irregular opponents. In a democracy, something as benign as increasing intelligence gathering can draw opposition. This has unfortunate consequences in that when attempting to penetrate a terrorist organisation, for example, human intelligence is of far more significance than technological superiority.

A study published by the US Army Military History Institute in 1982, John Tashjean's *The Transatlantic Clausewitz*, relayed the contemporary significance of Clausewitz's discussion of the "people in arms" to the US military. Tashjean alluded to Dr Alexander Atkinson's *Social Order and the General Theory of Strategy* (1981), which had examined Clausewitz's interpretation of people's war in the wider context of his axiom that war is a continuum of policy. Atkinson rightly saw Clausewitz as viewing war as a "social" phenomenon, affecting society as a whole. Avi Kober has recently reminded us of Clausewitz's analysis of war's dynamism and its propensity to assume many forms. The social aspect of LIC, although also important in other types of conflict, compounds the issue making LICs "much more difficult to capture and conceptualize in the framework of a comprehensive and coherent theory".[13]

Unfortunately, despite the Vietnam experience, some American military commentators overlooked the importance of several of Clausewitz's teachings for LIC. As early as 1974, for example, Lieutenant-Colonel James Johnson failed to take account of Clausewitz's whole theory of war: "[T]he equivocal results of Indo-China and Algeria – where modern armies with classical Clausewitzian doctrine met people's armies armed with Maoist doctrine – remain to confound our peace of mind." A decade later, Dr Sam Sarkesian displayed a very narrow understanding of the centre of gravity: "[The] Clausewitzian notion [is] that the center of gravity in war is the defeat and destruction of the enemy armed forces." As noted elsewhere in this work, there is much more to this concept than that. Clausewitz's defensive–offensive paradigm is also of great significance in LIC given that invariably the CI must begin on the defensive. It must then gradually shore up its position before taking the war to the insurgent, something that the Reagan Administration appreciated in its support of El Salvador's government against communist insurgency during the 1980s. The paradoxical trinity revolving around government, people and armed forces is also highly relevant. While Clausewitz's trinitarian perspective is vital from the counter-insurgent's perspective, Major John Buckley reminds us that it also serves as a powerful driver of those who would wage "people's war":

> Insurgency creates a mirrored image of Clausewitz's model with the people joined at the surface of the mirror ... Viewing insurgency in this Clausewitzian framework, military operations to support or counter insurgency remains subordinate to political direction.[14]

Post-Vietnam operations: from the *Mayaguez* to Desert One

Writing about LIC in 1983, Edward Luttwak alluded to the legacy of Vietnam in the context of what he saw as America's need to defend Western interests in peripheral areas such as Angola more vigorously:

> [T]he nation acquired its phobia of involvement in the most prevalent form of conflict, and the one form of conflict unlikely to lead to nuclear escalation. The toll that irrational fear has exacted from interests large and small thereby left undefended has continued to grow.[15]

As we have already seen, the main focus of US defence policy after Vietnam shifted firmly to preparation for a conventional war in Europe. In the meantime, the US military's preparedness to fight LIC withered on the vine. Non-military organisations were also affected with the CIA, for example, being forced to cut its capabilities in human intelligence drastically. The first post-Vietnam operation that could be described as low intensity was the *Mayaguez* incident of 1975. Some 250 US Marines landed on the Cambodian island of Koh Tang to rescue the 39 crew members of the SS *Mayaguez*, which had been seized by a Cambodian gunboat. The operation became a fiasco when it was realised that the ship's crew was not on Koh Tang and when the Marines themselves were evacuated after encountering severe Cambodian resistance. It later transpired that at the time the assault began, the Cambodian government had already announced that the *Mayaguez* had been released, together with its crew. In the event, the United States lost 38 dead, 50 wounded and three missing.

In the wake of the *Mayaguez*, Lieutenant-Colonel Donald Vought detected the first signs of what would become known as "Vietnam syndrome": "The new elite rising to power in the US reflects an abhorrence of involvement where there is cost – that is, it is acceptable to tamper so long as no sacrifice is called for."[16]

Given its focus on a conflict with the Soviet Union in Europe, the 1976 version of FM 100–5 paid no more than lip service to LIC. Gone were the three chapters on "sublimited war" that its 1968 predecessor had included. It also continued the doctrinal tradition of separating special operations from conventional operations, with the latter being tactical in nature and focused at the corps level, and the former being strategic and very much the prerogative of the National Command Authority and theatre commanders. The 1976 manual's mantra of "winning the first battle" was at odds with the need for patience required in any CI operation. Though the manual reflected the military's obsession with highly sophisticated technology and equipment, it also betrayed a desire to forget Vietnam. In August 1976, General Donn Starry remarked: "After getting out of Vietnam, the Army looked around and realised it should not try to fight that kind of war again elsewhere."[17]

Ironically, despite the Army's best efforts to refocus on conventional war in Europe, the majority of its officers were convinced that given the danger of any such conflict escalating to the nuclear level, the most likely form of future conflict would be of a low-intensity nature somewhere in the Third World. This was in spite of a complete rundown in CI instruction at Leavenworth and Carlisle from the mid-1970s.

Aside from Europe, the Gulf region continued to attract the attention of American strategic planners. According to Secretary of State Henry Kissinger in 1975, the United States would feel compelled to intervene in the Middle East if some national interest – notably Western access to oil – was threatened. Though of a different political hue, the Carter Administration continued to pursue a similar rationale with regard to the region:

> The continuation of US support for its friends in the Middle East, coupled with the genuine interest expressed by the Carter Administration in redu-

cing tension in the Arab–Israeli theater, promises to bring the Middle East closer to the West and is a national strategy worth pursuing as vigorously as possible.[18]

Unfortunately, American preparations to fight in the Middle East were based on the notion of a "limited contingency", whereby there would be a rapid deployment of a small force to a particular trouble spot. The problem was that the re-emphasis on a high-intensity conflict in Europe was jeopardising the ability of the United States to fight extra-European conflicts of a more limited nature as the military muscle required to execute any such contingencies was not in place. Moreover, there was a question mark over the public's response to situations where US forces might be deployed, but where no particular US interest was at stake. This post-Vietnam shift towards non-intervention began to move back again when the US Embassy in Teheran was seized in November 1979 during that country's Islamic Revolution.

The overthrow of the Shah of Iran had seriously unbalanced US policy towards the Middle East. The new Khomeini regime was deeply hostile to the West in general and the US in particular. Although this could be portrayed as being a symptom of the sort of initial fervour that characterises all revolutions, clearly it represented a longer-term threat. Though also ideologically unfriendly to the Soviet Union, the fact that the revolution had overthrown a Western ally was clearly to the benefit of the Soviets in a region close to their southern borders. The holding of 66 American hostages inside the embassy compound was a severe humiliation for the United States, and the Carter Administration's response would be crucial in sending a message to potential enemies and allies alike. Initially, the Americans tried to negotiate the hostages' release by trying to bring economic pressure to bear on the Iranians. The United States sought consent and when this was not forthcoming they adopted a course of achieving their end without consent – a rescue operation codenamed "Eagle Claw".

The military's recent rundown of its preparations to conduct special operations jeopardised the rescue attempt. There was no proper command and control organisation in place to plan, train for, and execute the mission. Forces had to be provided by each of the separate services, with no one body co-ordinating a joint effort to adapt these to the task at hand. Some six months passed before the operation took place and ended in disaster at Desert One in south-western Iran, some way short of the objective in Teheran, when an attempt by airborne forces to rendezvous went wrong. Eight servicemen lost their lives and it is a moot point as to whether the effort would have been worth while even if it had succeeded; the revolutionary cadres could have searched the streets of Teheran and rounded up more Western hostages. Nevertheless, the operation's failure was highly damaging in terms of US prestige and international standing. Yet, surprisingly, Soviet military analysis of the operation put the failure down to bad luck – Clausewitzian friction – more than anything else. As James Kitfield put it: "From the first moment, the imponderables that lurked in any combat mission had whipsawed Eagle Claw mercilessly."[19]

In a review of the Desert One disaster, Harry Summers cited Clausewitz to illustrate the dilemma facing Colonel Charlie Beckwith, the commander of the Delta Force unit that was involved in the rescue attempt. The moment of truth for Beckwith arrived when he realised that only five of his helicopters were operational, rather than six as originally intended. As Clausewitz had written when describing the qualities underpinning military genius:

> [O]nce conditions become difficult, as they must when much is at stake, things no longer run like a well-oiled machine. The machine itself begins to resist, and the commander needs tremendous willpower to overcome this resistance ... Only to the extent that he can do this will he retain his hold on his men and keep control.[20]

The failure at Desert One did concentrate American minds on the question of special operations forces again, particularly their organisation, training, and command and control. Colonel J. J. A. Wallace, British Army, has pointed out that the operation was manoeuvrist in that forces took the indirect approach and used speed to exploit both tempo and surprise while dispensing with mass, a critique of traditional US LIC operations. Perhaps the best way of dealing with the hostage situation would have been prevention rather than cure. In 1978, future secretary of the Navy, John Lehman, argued persuasively that the notion of deterrence applied across the whole spectrum of conflict and not just to nuclear strategy:

> Deterrence is simply dissuading a potential adversary from taking action hostile to US interests, perhaps by persuading the adversary that the consequences would outweigh the benefits. Political adversaries abound, from the Soviet Union to Black September, and the range of hostile actions we might wish to dissuade is infinite, from all-out nuclear first strike to kidnapping of US tourists.[21]

The publication of FM 100–20, *Low-Intensity Conflict*, in January 1981, represented an attempt by the US Army to ensure that the disparate guidance on the subject provided by a number of different field manuals, such as FM 31–20, *Special Forces Operations* (1977), was consolidated into one doctrinal manual. Its purpose was to provide soldiers with a number of principles to guide them in the conduct of what were called Internal Defense and Development (ID&D) operations. However, the Army continued to misunderstand LIC. FM 100–20's definition was unsatisfactory in that it did not properly encompass those non-military elements – political, psychological, and economic – that must be addressed when conducting CI operations. This was despite the emphasis placed on psychological operations as a basis for ID&D elsewhere in the manual. FM 100–20 defined LIC as:

> [T]he limited use of power for political purposes by nations or organizations ... to coerce, control or defend a population, to control or defend a territory

or establish or defend rights. It includes military operations by or against irregular forces, peacekeeping operations, terrorism, counter-terrorism, rescue operations and military assistance under conditions of armed conflict. This form of conflict does not include protracted engagements of opposing regular forces.[22]

This definition is also notable for its use of the word "limited". It is not necessarily the case that a nation or an organisation will treat a LIC as limited and hence tailor its means accordingly. In many instances, the protagonists involved may well view the conflict as "total", something Clausewitz realised back in the early nineteenth century when he began to explore people's war, and something that the experience of Vietnam should have taught the military. They also continued to fail to see that their role should exist alongside that of non-military organisations and not necessarily be predominant. The manual had other shortcomings. Further up the escalatory ladder, it did not discuss the value of conventional operations in LIC and thus failed to give credence to the notion that such operations might be launched against an insurgent's base or against sanctuaries provided by a contiguous nation. At the lower end of the conflict spectrum, counter-terrorism was ignored. As Paschall commented: "The prime deficiencies of the 1981 manual stem from a highly restrictive definition and the absence of subordinate and supporting doctrinal literature."[23]

Low-intensity operations under the first Reagan administration

After assuming the Presidency in 1981, Reagan began the process of raising the profile of special forces to ensure that his administration's objective of opposing Soviet expansionism in the Third World did not lack a military edge. However, although some inroads were to be made in improving LIC capabilities, other, more pressing concerns – both conventional and nuclear – were to dominate the administration's strategic thinking. This ensured that Reagan and his advisers did not challenge the Army to shift its ethos from one solely concerned with high-intensity conflict to one that also embraced LIC. Rather, they relied on the "trinitarian" view that the government and people would support the Army in times of conflict. Doctrinally, FM 100–5, 1982 alluded to LIC operations and attempted to sum up a diversity of roles by stating: "The US Army must ... be ready to fight light, well-equipped forces ... insurgents or sophisticated terrorist groups ... Soldiers and units must prepare for such battles, and the Army's operational concept must enable it to win."[24]

Major-Generals Donald Morelli and Michael Ferguson argued that the tenets of AirLand Battle – initiative, synchronisation, agility, and depth – were relevant to LIC.[25] Disappointingly, the 1982 manual did not develop its discussion of Clausewitz's centre of gravity beyond conventional warfare. If it had done so, it would have noted that, in LIC, the major centre of gravity is the people, whether the indigenous population or else public opinion within the intervening nation.

Events such as the Soviet invasion of Afghanistan, the Sandinista victory in Nicaragua, and gains by communist insurgents in Guatemala and El Salvador prompted Secretary of State Alexander Haig to comment:

> We cannot ignore Soviet activity in the developing nations because our pas-sivity alters the calculations of other countries. It makes further Soviet expansion or Soviet-backed destabilization appear to be inevitable. It gives the appearance – and it is no more than an appearance – that Marxism in the Soviet mode is the wave of the future.[26]

As it turned out, Afghanistan was to be the crucial theatre, though no US mili-tary action ever took place there. Rather, the United States covertly supported the Mujahedin guerrillas, helping to turn them from a ragbag mixture of rebels into a competent fighting force by the early 1980s. The supply of anti-air Stinger missiles through the CIA, for example, helped to counter the threat posed by Soviet airborne forces. By 1985, it had become clear to the Soviet Union that it was bogged down in a morass with no satisfactory way out. This, as much as anything, brought home to the Kremlin the bankruptcy of its grand strategy.

One of the first tests that the Reagan Administration faced in the Third World was in Lebanon, where the civil war continued to rage in the aftermath of the Israeli invasion of mid-1982. In July 1982, a force of 1,800 Marines was sent to the country to participate in a multinational peacekeeping effort together with French and Italian troops. The Marines were to stay for 30 days and did not take any offensive weapons ashore so as not to provoke an unnecessary confronta-tion. Unfortunately, the Americans failed to recognise Clausewitz's wisdom that: "[T]he original political objects can greatly alter during the course of the war and may finally change entirely *since they are influenced by events and their probable consequences.*"[27]

The American deployment in Lebanon was opposed by Secretary of Defense Caspar Weinberger, who criticised the State Department for believing that "many situations in the world required the 'intermixture of diplomacy and the military'".[28]

The White House repeated some of the fundamental mistakes made in Vietnam: it never established a clear objective for the Marines' mission nor did it devise an exit strategy; and it interfered in the conduct of tactical operations. Permission to use fire support, for example, was dependent on the National Command Authority's sanction.[29] It is therefore not surprising that perceptions of the mission's objectives varied at different levels of the command chain. Fur-thermore, the volatile situation in Lebanon ensured that others' perceptions of the Americans changed. In September 1982, the Shi'ite population looked favourably on the Americans' presence as a safeguard against further massacres of civilians. Twelve months later, however, the Americans were seen as hostile, given their overt support for the Lebanese government. The United States had made the fundamental mistake of being seen to take sides in a civil war, and would pay the price in blood.

Major Daniel Schuster, USMC, has shown how Clausewitz's culminating point applied to the US operation in Lebanon. Clausewitz gave five reasons for culmination in his chapter on "The Culminating Point of Victory":

1 Besieging and investing fortresses leads to friendly attrition, which weakens the force (the analogy in a peace enforcement operation might be stop and search raids).
2 Establishing a theatre of operations in enemy territory makes the force vulnerable to attack, while measures to oppose such an attack invariably weaken the force over time.
3 Long lines of communication place a burden on logistics and *increase* the difficulties inherent in political control of the operation thereby lengthening the time taken to make decisions on the part of commanders.
4 The balance of political alignments can shift over time.
5 Finally, a defeated opponent may gain time to recover and mount fresh resistance to foreign invasion. This would very much depend on the character of the people, the nature of the country, and in political affiliations, which in Lebanon's case were extremely volatile.[30]

Identifying the culminating point is crucial to all campaign plans. However, as we have seen, Clausewitz realised that wars differ in intensity and do not necessarily lead to the destruction of one side by the other. Therefore, the culminating point "is bound to recur in every future war in which the destruction of the enemy cannot be the military aim, and this will presumably be true of most wars".[31]

Schuster went on to write:

Applying Clausewitz's factors leading to culmination when a peacekeeping [or peace enforcement] force is no longer perceived as being neutral, the force is vulnerable to culmination from (i.) friendly attrition, which adversely influences the cost–benefit formula necessary to maintain popular support for peacekeeping; (ii.) a change in political alliances as one or more belligerents seek alliances to counter the perceived threat of subjugation by the peacekeeping force; and (iii.) increased popular resistance to the foreign forces once seen as saviors and now seen as invaders.[32]

As opposition to the American presence grew among the indigenous population, so there was a commensurate increase in the terrorist threat. In 1986, Noel Koch, who had been the Department of Defense's senior official for special operations and counter-terrorism, informed a number of congressmen that a general disdain for special operations and a bloated command structure, which was totally unsuited to low-intensity operations, were responsible for American inaction in the face of this threat. In the event, on 23 October 1983 a lorry packed with a 12,000-pound bomb exploded at the Marine barracks in what was believed to be the largest non-nuclear device ever detonated. Two hundred and forty-one US servicemen were killed and another 128 wounded. In February 1984, Reagan announced the withdrawal of the Marines from Lebanon. The United States had finally decided, after much prevarication, that the costs of being drawn into a bloody civil war outweighed any benefits that might accrue to the national interest.

There is a school of thought that suggests that the only way to have thwarted the terrorist threat in Lebanon would have been to have struck directly at its centre of gravity, which many suspected to be Iran. It is a manifestation of the administration's completely ambiguous policy in Lebanon that a peace enforcement mission could have been expanded into one where an act of war was committed against a sovereign state. On the other hand, the Americans could have followed the examples of the Israelis and French in bombing Iranian training camps in Lebanon as retaliation for terrorist attacks on their forces. Colonel Richard Swain has argued that such actions are similar in nature to what Clausewitz termed "wars of observation". In the event, as Eric Hammel notes: "The US carried out no known direct reprisals for the battalion headquarters bombing."[33]

General William DePuy wrote of the Lebanon intervention that: "Vague, exploratory deployments like 'showing the flag' or 'presence' are doubly dangerous because they permit incremental, flabby thinking in Washington." In a similar vein, Schuster has portrayed Beirut as an instance where the United States failed to apply Clausewitzian thinking: if "victory" in Beirut was to mean maintaining a US presence there, then the obverse of this was that the withdrawal of that presence constituted a "defeat".[34]

Concurrent with the Beirut operation, US special forces found themselves operating closer to home when a crisis in Grenada suddenly erupted in October 1983. Prime Minister Maurice Bishop and four of his Cabinet ministers were murdered by the Soviet-Cuban sympathisers of the People's Revolutionary Army. Showing the same concern for US interests in the Caribbean that had driven the policy of previous US administrations, Reagan decided to use the subsequent unrest on the island as a pretext for removing a potential thorn from America's side. The US intervention, code-named "Urgent Fury", had three objectives: to protect the lives of American citizens, notably a group of 800 students held hostage; to restore order on Grenada; and to eradicate Cuban and Soviet influences from the island.

The role of special forces on Grenada was crucial. They executed 13 missions, ten of which were designated "special" rather than conventional. Captain Daniel Bolger has written that previous experience of special operations indicated that some 60 per cent of these missions would abort. In the event, the figure was nearer 20 per cent. The Americans did not have enough information as to where all potential hostages were situated. Therefore, they decided to go for the jugular by capturing the whole island. The Americans exploited the element of surprise, with on-site intelligence and reconnaissance paving the way for conventional forces to come in and complete the operation. American restraint with regard to the civilian population greatly aided the intelligence effort. Speed was vital. When Lieutenant-Colonel Ray Smith's Marine Corps

Battalion Landing Team 218 captured the operations officer of the Grenadian Army, the latter said: "You appeared so swiftly in so many places where we didn't expect you that it was clear that resistance was hopeless, so I recommended to my superiors that we lay down our arms and go into hiding."[35]

Bolger has praised the performance of special forces on Grenada, partly putting this down to the leeway given them by their superiors: "The conventional commanders and staff for Urgent Fury did as well as they did because, by and large, they remembered the nature of their elite forces ... Special warriors led the way in the Grenada fighting."[36]

Nevertheless, the operation was not without its critics. William Lind, in his role as an adviser to the Congressional Military Reform Caucus, pointed to the poor integration of special forces and conventional units at the beginning of the operation and also to shortcomings in intelligence. As the operation progressed, special forces capabilities, such as operations at night, had to be curtailed because conventional forces lacked commensurate capabilities. However, the operation was a success and the critics tended to focus on those imperfections that affect every military operation. They failed to appreciate the time factor in that the landings were planned in the space of less than a week and also the fact that any attempt to take all of the island in the first wave might endanger the lives of the hostages held inland. In the event, all major objectives were achieved by the third day of the operation. Lind's critique also overlooked the joint nature of the operation, which encouraged the use of surprise and deception, and also capitalised on good intelligence.[37]

In his assessment of the Grenada operation, which he judged to be a success despite what he saw as its rather rugged execution, DePuy believed the most important element was its jointness:

> The study of neither Clausewitz nor Napoleon reveals easy answers to this [joint] dimension of operational art in the era of limited wars and nuclear deterrence. It seems to be the classic operational trap of the last half of the 20th century.[38]

At the tactical and operational levels, Urgent Fury accelerated the process of improving America's special forces capabilities in the wake of the Iranian hostage rescue attempt and integrating these into the Joint Task Force commander's plan of operations. At the strategic level, Grenada provided Weinberger with a Clausewitzian example of the successful use of US military power: "If the measure of success is attaining our political objectives at minimum cost, in the shortest possible time, then the Grenada operation has to be judged to have been a complete success."[39]

The State Department and the NSC were also urging that US troops be sent to Central America to oppose the communist regime in Nicaragua and communist guerrillas in El Salvador. Weinberger again opposed them, arguing that the commitment of troops without a clear objective would lead to long and costly drawn-out involvements that might undermine public support and ultimately damage US grand strategy. Instead, Reagan decided to support the Contras in Nicaragua and the El Salvadorean regime through military aid and overt shows of force through large training exercises in the region.

Reagan intended to undermine Nicaragua's Sandinista regime from the periphery, a policy that would take time to bear fruit, but which would avoid the costs inherent in direct military intervention. He was therefore able to undermine the Sandinista regime without undertaking military action and thus illustrated Clausewitz's maxim that the ultimate objective in any conflict is political. As Captain Kevin Dougherty put it: "Instead of raging against the seeming lack of definition [of LIC], soldiers are better off accepting the dominance of political considerations in LIC and realising that military decisions will be driven by political objectives."[40]

Low-intensity operations under the second Reagan Administration

The US military continued to try and address LIC throughout the 1980s, and still struggled to define it properly. In an address to the School of Advanced Military Studies in April 1985, General Paul Gorman stated simply that LIC was "war turned upside down". In other words, it required the reversal of the order of deployment of resources traditionally used to fight war, with security assistance being the initial method and warfighting, if necessary, coming later. As Lieu-tenant-Colonel John Fulton argued: "In attempting to provide definitions and identity ... the doctrine community may be creating a doctrinal foster home for orphaned warfare concepts, including counter-insurgency, antiterrorism, peace-keeping, contingency operations, rescue and foreign military assistance."[41]

The 1986 version of FM 100–5 pointed out that AirLand Battle doctrine "applies equally to the military operations characteristic of low-intensity war". Professor Steven Metz propounded the view that the *core logic* of FM 100–5 could be applied to LIC, and that its general principles would also apply in LIC.[42]

Libya, under its enigmatic leader Colonel Muammar Qaddafi, was viewed by the Reagan Administration as a prime sponsor of terrorism in the mid-1980s. The increasingly violent and random nature of terrorist attacks staged by groups based in the Middle East persuaded the administration that, rather than try and deal with each attack as it came in a piecemeal, reactive manner, policy would be better served by striking pre-emptively at the centre of gravity of the threat – Libya and, in particular, Qaddafi. This was not to imply that Libya was the only state sponsor of terrorism – Syria and Iran were others. However, Qaddafi's volatile rhetoric compounded the danger being spread by his acolytes beyond the confines of the Middle East.[43]

The events leading to the US bombing of Libya in April 1986 are easily summarised. In March, US military exercises in the disputed Gulf of Sidra off the Libyan coast, during which two Libyan patrol boats were destroyed by US aircraft after the latter were targeted by missiles, provoked Qaddafi into ordering terrorist strikes against US targets. On 5 April, a Berlin night club frequented by US servicemen was bombed, killing two Americans and a civilian, and wounding 229 others, including 79 Americans. Western intelligence sources immediately confirmed Libya's guilt. The administration decided to strike at Libya itself despite a lack of support from its European allies (with the notable exception of the United Kingdom).

On 14 April, US forces conducted Operation "Eldorado Canyon", a night air raid against several targets in Tripoli and Benghazi. Militarily, the raids were not an overwhelming success – only four of the 18 aircraft involved actually hit their intended targets – and there was some collateral damage, with 37 people, mainly civilians, being killed. Politically, however, it was successful. Qaddafi went to ground for months having narrowly escaped with his life. His image as a fearless protector of Arab interests was severely damaged and his terrorist machine was made moribund – with the exception of the 1988 Lockerbie bombing. Internationally, Qaddafi was isolated. Suitably impressed, the Europeans resumed their co-operation with the Americans by imposing sanctions and expelling Libyan diplomats. Despite inevitable condemnation of the raid, the Soviets did nothing to help Qaddafi, while most Arab nations had little sympathy for his plight.

In the United States itself, Congress supported the raid, as did the public, thereby ensuring that the elements of Clausewitz's trinity were in sync. Weinberger has summed up the effects of what was the first example of a US military response to state-sponsored terrorism:

> Our allies and potential foes now had a far more accurate realization that neither threats nor terrorism could succeed against a newly strengthened America. Our people and our allies took comfort from this and another step had been taken to demonstrate how military strength is vital for peace.[44]

In 1985, the Army began its Joint LIC project, which involved the military, the Department of State, the JCS and the CIA. Its final report was issued in 1986 and concluded that the United States lacked a coherent CI strategy. Another initiative was the establishment by the Army and the Air Force of a Center for LIC at Langley Air Force Base, Virginia. Also in 1985, a number of members of Congress, from both parties, urged that the United States improve its ability to fight what they believed to be the most likely form of conflict on the horizon. In 1987, despite the Defense Department's misgivings, the National Defense Authorization Bill established a unified combatant command for special operations, the US Special Operations Command (USSOCOM), which dovetailed with Congress's establishment of an Office of the Assistant Secretary of Defense for Special Operations and LIC (ASD/SOLIC) to provide a basis for planning defence policy and military strategy for LIC. As a way of giving practical effect to the Reagan Doctrine, the administration articulated its policy for LIC in the first *National Security Strategy* of January 1987. It stated that the major causes of LIC were "instability and lack of political and economic development in the

Third World" providing "fertile ground ... for groups and nations wishing to exploit unrest for their own purposes".[45]

Critics of Reagan's LIC policy, such as Professor Stephen Sloan, have argued that Reagan tended to take dramatic, short-term measures – Grenada, the Libyan raid – without considering the long-term approach needed in CI, and that the administration also ignored existing doctrine. Such analysis tends to underestimate the success of the administration's policy in Central America, which followed a long-term design but which Sloan argues was not conveyed convincingly enough to Congress or the public. Steven Metz, on the other hand, praised the Reagan Doctrine for initiating an improvement in LIC capability:

> Since strategy drives doctrine, only the consummation of the process begun with the Reagan Doctrine – in other words, a real revolution in US security strategy – would open the way for operational and tactical initiatives in the insurgency/counterinsurgency environment.[46]

Peter Schraeder has put the strategic impetus behind the Reagan Doctrine in its wider historical context:

> For the first time in post-World War Two history, the United States publicly adopted and implemented a program that went beyond traditional containment and embraced instead the need to roll back already established communist Third World regimes.[47]

When the administration decided to oppose Cuban and Nicaraguan-backed rebels in El Salvador, many in the military welcomed the opportunity to put into practice the lessons learnt from the failure of CI in Vietnam. In 1988, "American Military Policy in Small Wars", a report written by Lieutenant-Colonels A. J. Bacevich, J. D. Hallums, R. H. White and T. F. Young, all senior Harvard fellows, articulated this need: "For the US ... El Salvador represents an experiment, an attempt to reverse the record of American failure in waging small wars, an effort to defeat an insurgency by providing training and material support without committing American troops to combat."[48]

Andrew Krepinevich has criticised US policy in Central America, not because of its strategic objective but rather for some of its practical effects at the tactical level, as manifested in training exercises. These were centred around campaigning against the Nicaraguan Army rather than against the guerrilla forces based in the area. When counterguerrilla tactics were practised, they consisted of search and destroy operations similar to those used in Vietnam. The El Salvadorean armed forces were as poorly prepared for CI as their South Vietnamese counterparts had been. The training of El Salvadorean officers at Leavenworth and at Fort Benning's Infantry School was concerned with teaching conventional tactics. Firepower was emphasised as if the enemy was situated in a number of fixed geographical positions, rather than as a guerrilla army constantly on the move.[49]

Nevertheless, the indirect application of American military power vis-à-vis Nicaragua succeeded. The impact of a large training exercise, "Golden Pheasant", in Honduras in March 1988 was to ensure that the 2,000 Sandinista guerrillas inside the country had begun to withdraw and that the communists would seriously enter peace negotiations. Several years of Reagan's military, economic and political pressure had left the Nicaraguan economy in a state of near collapse and demoralised the population. The fall of communism in Eastern Europe in 1989 persuaded the Sandinista regime that the game was up and, in early 1990, elections were held, which the Nicaraguan opposition won.

> In measuring the contribution of the Reagan administration in this remarkable turn of events in Nicaragua,... [one] interpretation would be to view Reagan as a skilled guerrilla warrior who mastered several of the key lessons promoted by such unlikely leaders as Mao and Che [and, by extension, Clausewitz].[50]

In a December 1988 article, Lieutenant-Colonels James Montano and Dennis Long penned an imaginary letter of advice from Clausewitz to the incoming Bush Administration, which was based on their reading of *On War*. In it, they made a comment that puts Reagan's policy in Central America into its proper historical context: "War in your day must be thought of as a constant and continuous competition between you and your enemies. This modern warfare employs a wide variety of instruments and methods in which the stakes are preservation of national interests."[51]

The Bush Administration and LIC

In an effort to encourage a joint approach to LIC by the US armed forces, the JCS produced a draft doctrinal publication, JCS 3–07, *Doctrine for Joint Operations in Low-Intensity Conflict*, in May 1989. Despite its doctrinal purpose, JCS 3–07 was policy-oriented in nature and, as such, it failed to address the need for operational doctrine at the joint level to reflect strategic objectives in LIC. That such a need existed can be inferred from the criticism of the Marine Corps' FMFM 1, *Warfighting*, 1989, by Lieutenant-Colonel H. T. Hayden, USMC:

> The weakest part [of the manual is] in the area of LIC or military operations other than war. Very little of maneuver warfare doctrine ... can be applied in humanitarian/peacekeeping or peacemaking missions. However, the culture of maneuver warfare is applicable, e.g. decentralization, mission-type orders, focus of effort, etc.... [The manual needs] to be revised in order to move beyond Clausewitz and his era (1850–1945).[52]

While Hayden's critique is perfectly valid, he overlooked the fact that Clausewitz does not belong to any particular era and that much of what he wrote is applicable to LIC. This would be acknowledged by the Army and Air Force in their joint publication, FM 100–20/Air Force Pamphlet (AFP) 3–20, *Military Operations in Low Intensity Conflict*, of 1990, which is discussed below. This manual would be a more satisfactory doctrinal guide to LIC than JCS 3–07, and built on the two services' close relationship, which had developed with the advent of AirLand Battle.

Much of the debate about joint operations was stimulated by the US experience in Panama after 1987. The United States had long treated Panama as lying firmly within its sphere of influence and had maintained a military presence there. In June 1987, opposition forces mounted demonstrations against General Manuel Antonio Noriega, the commander of the Panama Defense Force (PDF) and the *de facto* ruler of Panama despite its "democratic" government. Noriega resorted to repression to quell the disturbances. At this stage, American forces maintained a low profile in Panama. In February 1988, two federal grand juries in Florida indicted Noriega for drug-related offences. At a stroke, the Panamanian political situation was transformed into one involving the United States. Noriega now questioned the right of the US Southern Command (SOUTHCOM) to remain inside Panama.

Throughout the following year and a half, US–Panamanian relations deteriorated as Noriega intensified his anti-American rhetoric and allowed the PDF to intimidate US citizens within Panama. Meanwhile, the new chairman of the JCS, General Colin Powell, authorised SOUTHCOM to start making plans for an American intervention in the country as the United States found itself in a situation that inhabited the grey realm between war and peace. It was a situation that perfectly illustrates Clausewitz's political–military paradigm and its applicability to LIC. Acting under political constraints, the US military had to restrain itself from any actions that might cause collateral damage and therefore harm the American cause. At the same time, however, the PDF could continue to harass US interests almost with impunity.

> Commanders who were already acclimated [*sic*] to the LIC environment best understood the constraints political–military interactions placed on them. Commanders wedded to the tradition of military officers being left alone to make decisions once political leaders have decided to employ armed force to achieve political objectives experienced difficulty, even some mental agony, as they were forced to adapt to a very untraditional situation.[53]

Matters came to a head in December 1989 when Noriega was named head of state by the Panamanian legislature. President George Bush immediately decided to reconcile competing political considerations and military desires by giving the go-ahead for Operation "Just Cause", the US intervention in Panama. Bush propounded four strategic objectives: to protect US citizens in Panama; to restore proper democracy there; to keep the Panama Canal open to international traffic; and to capture Noriega. Fortunately for the United States, the majority of Panamanians wanted rid of Noriega, ensuring that this was one enemy centre of gravity – public opinion – that was already in its hands. At the operational level, the PDF's centre of gravity lay in the Canal Zone, where US forces were swiftly to capture the cities of Colon and Panama City. The aim was to ensure that, having lost this key area, the PDF would be paralysed and the rest of the country would offer little resistance. Operations were designed to fulfil this strategic objective: no fewer than 27 objectives were assaulted on the first night.

Robert Leonhard has written that the approach adopted by the United States in Panama was the correct one in a LIC environment and completely at odds with the ethos of AirLand Battle:

> Simply put, AirLand Battle doctrine was bankrupt in such a scenario. With no Soviet second echelon, without the convenience of being the defender, without the joyously open terrain of the North German plain to hurl our antitank missiles at, and without the benefit of "high payoff" targets to saturate with artillery fires, AirLand Battle was confounded. It left no guidance for a contingency operation, no theory concerning the means of defeat, and no advice on the physics or psychology of war.[54]

Despite this, much of the fighting in Panama was clearly conventional. American forces used their superior numbers vis-à-vis the PDF to execute operations combining manoeuvre with firepower. The widespread use of Army aviation encouraged this approach, while the F-117 Stealth bomber saw action for the first time. Certainly, the use of overwhelming force, as illustrated in Panama, was a radical departure from the tempo of operations associated with LIC. As Just Cause continued, the military found itself unilaterally conducting stability operations (Operation "Promote Liberty") to restore law and order given that civilian specialists had not yet arrived in theatre. This ensured that US troops had to comply with restrictive rules of engagement, a problem that Captain Steven Collins, commander of C Company, 2nd Battalion, 7th Infantry Division (Light) during Just Cause perceptively put in a Clausewitzian context:

> Where before, Clausewitz's concept of marriage between military force and political policy was thought to operate primarily in the realm of politicians and generals, it is clear today that every soldier in a low-intensity conflict must comprehend the concept before he can undertake the action to see that it is realised. Otherwise, restrictive rules of engagement may appear to the soldiers as mere obstacles and hindrances to be circumvented.[55]

One could argue that the recent experience of Iraq shows that the need to plan what have become known as Phase IV operations was not learnt by the US military after Panama. Indeed, John Fishel has argued that Promote Liberty was poorly executed because of a lack of planning.[56]

Operation Just Cause itself was a resounding success precisely because its objectives were achieved so swiftly, even allowing for the fact that protracted negotiations were required before Noriega entered American custody. The use of overwhelming force combined with an adroit combination of manoeuvre and firepower obviated against the curse of incrementalism. This ensured that any adverse international reaction was smothered by the cushion of US military success. Indeed, there was praise for US successes at the operational level from the Soviet Union. One Soviet military commentator was impressed by the "professional efficiency" of US special forces and suggested that this would serve as a model for his own nation's armed forces as it illustrated the leverage to be gained from the swift deployment of a mixture of light and special forces.[57]

Edward Luttwak, the experienced military commentator, felt compelled to offer a critique of Just Cause. In an article for the *Washington Post*, published on 31 December 1989, he praised the campaign plan for its clarity and boldness. Luttwak believed that the large size of the initial American force, which gave them numerical superiority, effectively ensured a *coup de main* and prevented a repetition of the need to build up forces over several days as in Grenada. However, he criticised what he viewed as "grossly excessive" firepower, arguing that what was appropriate in a large-scale conventional war was not appropriate in Panama where public opinion, both at home and abroad, would be upset by images of destruction in what was ostensibly a contingency operation. Yet this analysis was self-contradictory – the use of firepower ensured that US forces completed the swift victory that the plan that met Luttwak's approval had intended. Tom Donnelly, the editor of *Army Times*, replied to Luttwak by illustrating examples where US Rangers had clearly avoided the unnecessary use of firepower and where US forces in general had taken great care to avoid collateral damage. Captain Mike de Mayo commented of Luttwak that he "allowed his perception of events to be skewed by the speculative reporting of a media absorbed itself in the fog which inevitably accompanies the tactical execution of operational design".[58]

The Army continued to separate its treatment of LIC from its mainstream doctrinal manuals by publishing FM 100–20, *Military Operations in Low Intensity Conflict*, in December 1990. In belated recognition of the joint nature of such operations, the manual was published in conjunction with the US Air Force, which termed it AFP 3–20. FM 100–20/AFP 3–20 incorporated Clausewitz into its treatment of LIC. It also offered a more satisfactory definition of the genre than previous doctrinal publications:

> Military operations in LIC may include tactically direct actions such as direct assistance, strikes, raids, and shows of force or demonstrations. However, political, economic, or psychological objectives shape the way in which even these tactically direct operations are executed.[59]

The manual followed FM 100–5 in its use of imperatives (though not of tenets), which served as the basis for the planning and conduct of LIC operations. The five imperatives of FM 100–20/AFP 3–20 were political dominance, unity of effort, adaptability, legitimacy and perseverance. Of these, political dominance is the most obviously Clausewitzian. The soldier is required to understand the political objective that affects military operations at all levels from the strategic to the tactical. Unity of effort entailed the requirement for jointness, not only among the military services but also with other government agencies. Adaptability illustrated the need to be able to respond effectively in whatever situation the United States found itself. Legitimacy referred to the willing acceptance on the part of those involved as to the right of a government to govern or of a group to take decisions. Genuine authority was all important, and it was this that each side in a LIC needed to achieve.[60] Finally, perseverance reflected the protracted nature of LIC and emphasised the need for patience in pursuing strategic objectives.

FM 100–20/AFP 3–20 acknowledged Clausewitz's aphorism that war is not an autonomous activity but is always an instrument of policy. The state is required to decide what sort of conflict it is embarking upon "neither mistaking it for, nor trying to turn it into, something that is alien to its nature".[61]

Nevertheless, American commentators continued to take a sceptical view of Clausewitz's relevance to LIC. Major John Shepherd, for example, wrote just prior to the publication of FM 100–20/AFP 3–20:

> Combating modern terrorism or large drug-dealing enterprises may require nations to mount warlike efforts against amorphous and shadowy trans-national networks – an idea rather far removed from the Clausewitzian concept of war between states obliging the clash of opposing field armies.[62]

While FM 100–20/AFP 3–20 was undoubtedly the most comprehensive statement to date of the US Army's (and Air Force's) doctrinal effort regarding LIC, there was a feeling that many of the Vietnam-era lessons embodied within it were becoming outdated with the end of the Cold War. Steven Metz articulated this concern: "[S]uch doctrine indicates that we are beginning to understand forms of LIC, especially Maoist-style protracted rural insurgency, that are fading in strategic importance."[63]

Conclusion

At first sight, there appear to be tensions between Clausewitz's thought and LIC. However, Clausewitz's ability to perceive war as a social phenomenon and as an instrument of policy is very compatible with the drivers behind insurgency and terrorism where the will of the people plays such a fundamental role. US doctrine for fighting LIC and its policy in practice has not been inconsistent with a Clausewitzian approach, though it is more difficult to determine connections between American strategic thought and Clausewitz in this respect than it is in more conventional areas. Nevertheless, having virtually ignored counterinsurgency after the Vietnam War, with arguably disastrous results in Lebanon, the US military and polity began to pay more attention to it in the late 1980s. Indeed, the military used Clausewitz as a means of doing so in the Army–Air Force manual, FM 100–20/AFP 3–20, *Military Operations in Low Intensity*

Conflict, of 1990. Moreover, the military's understanding of Maoist theory, albeit driven by circumstances, was, in its own way, an indirect adaptation of Clausewitz. Successful operations against Grenada and Libya may have been impressive in the short term, but in the longer term were overshadowed by America's counter-revolutionary activities in El Salvador and Honduras, which provide a textbook example of successful CI. In the final analysis, however, US advances in understanding requirements for conducting LIC were to be undone by subsequent events in the 1990s and beyond.

8 Strategy and policy during the 1990s

The Powell Doctrine

The Bush Administration responded to the end of the Cold War by developing a strategy based on pre-empting crises through the forward presence of US military forces. This strategy paved the way for US forces to be used in multinational peacekeeping duties. As the administration's "National Security Strategy" (NSS) of 1992 put it: "The most desirable and efficient security strategy is to address the root causes of instability and to ease tensions before they result in conflict."[1]

There was a tension between the administration's desire to intervene in regional problems and General Colin Powell's reluctance to commit US forces in anger born out of his experience as a junior officer in Vietnam. To this end, the chairman of the Joint Chiefs-of-Staff (JCS) published a "National Military Strategy" in 1992 that included reference to "decisive force", a principle that has been described as an addendum to the Weinberger Doctrine of 1984 but could just as easily be interpreted as continuing the tradition of American strategic thought that had evolved after the Civil War and had been utilised in the recent conflict in the Gulf. Decisive force was propounded as a means to "overwhelm our adversaries and thereby terminate conflicts swiftly with a minimum loss of life".[2]

However, Powell diverged from Weinberger in that he did not refer to military power solely as an option of "last resort". Rather, it was an asset to be used interchangeably with the other tools available to the statesman: diplomatic and economic power. After the former Yugoslavia started to fragment in 1991, Powell argued that any intervention on America's part would have to be determined by a very careful consideration of political and military objectives, which would have to be continually scrutinised and made clear to the armed forces. In an article for *Foreign Affairs* in 1992, Powell warned in Clausewitzian vein that there are "no fixed set of rules for the use of military force". It is little wonder that one commentator described the Powell Doctrine as a continuation of the US military's predilection for determining the types of wars it would fight.[3]

Powell articulated a number of questions that would have to be answered in the affirmative before military force could be used:

Is the political objective we seek to achieve important, clearly defined and understood? Have all other non-violent policy means failed? Will military force achieve the objective? At what cost? Have the gains and risks been analyzed? How might the situation that we seek to alter, once it is altered by force, develop further and what might be the consequences?[4]

When he reflected on US military operations since 1989, Powell concluded that they had succeeded across the spectrum of conflict from the Gulf War to humanitarian relief because each mission "carefully matched the use of military force to our political objectives".[5]

Critics of Powell made the valid point that his thinking was more relevant to the type of inter-state warfare envisaged at the time Weinberger was defense secretary. By 1991–92, however, a different type of international relations was being shaped in which many conflicts would take place within states, which were, in the main, peripheral to US security interests. The protagonists in these conflicts were not as vulnerable to threats of economic sanctions nor were they suitable candidates for punitive military operations. Jeffrey Record argued that the Weinberger–Powell Doctrine, as it came to be known, actually stood Clausewitz on his head "by holding force to be a substitute for rather than a companion to diplomacy".[6]

FM 100–5, 1993

The Gulf War had been the first major test of the reforms initiated by the Goldwater–Nichols Act of 1986, particularly the attempt to introduce a more joint approach to warfighting by the US armed forces. After the conflict had ended, the drive towards jointness continued. In November 1991, Joint Publication 1, *Joint Warfare of the US Armed Forces*, was commissioned by the JCS. Powell was convinced that it would take a decade or more for the armed forces to become truly joint. Without wishing to dilute the uniqueness of each service's *esprit de corps*, JP1 was designed to start eradicating some of the distinct approaches to operations taken by the forces. The recent conflict had only served to highlight the degree to which the services still operated independently. For example, the Army and the Air Force differed in their interpretations of the deep battle area: what was deep to the Army was not deep to the Air Force. JP1, therefore, deliberately eschewed traditional Air Force terminology such as strategic attack in favour of the phrase "direct attack of enemy strategic centers of gravity".[7]

Trying to discern any Clausewitzian influence in this or any other joint publication is no easy task, as Colonel Paul Herbert points out: "Army doctrine and doctrinal development was the paradigm that most influenced joint doctrine ... the process of putting together a joint publication makes it difficult to identify a coherent, underlying theory of war, whether Clausewitzian or something else."[8]

In June 1993, the first defence review of the new Clinton Administration committed the military to continue to prepare to fight two regional conflicts simultaneously. However, it was the changed nature of the threat facing the United States in the early 1990s that prompted the Army to produce another version of FM 100–5, *Operations*, in 1993. With an emphasis on force projection and joint operations, the main purpose of the manual was to articulate the Army's requirement to fight as part of a joint, combined, United Nations or interagency force, and to be able to conduct full-dimensional operations, which were defined, in language reminiscent of Weinberger–Powell, as "applying all means available to accomplish any given mission decisively and at the least cost".[9]

The manual described five basic tenets: initiative, agility, depth, synchronisation and versatility. Of these, all but versatility had been included in the previous version of FM 100–5. Versatility was now introduced as a recognition that the Army had to prepare itself for a multitude of tasks. It was described as "the ability of units to meet diverse mission requirements. Commanders must be able to shift focus, tailor forces, and move from one role to another rapidly and efficiently..."[10]

Given a background of increasing involvement in peacekeeping and other such activities, the manual defined three distinct strategic environments: war, conflict and peace. In peace, the United States would "influence world events through those actions that routinely occur between nations"; conflict "is characterized by hostilities to secure strategic objectives"; and war involved "the use of force in combat operations against an armed enemy".[11]

Army activity in "peace" and "conflict" was swept up under the umbrella of "operations other than war" (OOTW). This concept had been introduced in the contemporaneous joint doctrine manual, Joint Publication 3–0, *Doctrine for Joint Operations*,[12] which made the distinction between "war" or large-scale warfighting and OOTW, which incorporated a whole gamut of operations from humanitarian assistance through counter-terrorism and peace enforcement to counterinsurgency. Not surprisingly, the appearance in FM 100–5 of OOTW, and the attendant, bogus distinctions between war and peace, was heavily criticised. Robert Citino went as far as to describe the concept of OOTW as "the most ridiculous development of the era [the 1990s]. [T]here is absolutely no place in FM 100–5 for the intricacies of hurricane relief or the details of the 1991 antimeningitis campaign in the Cameroons."[13]

By discarding the admittedly imperfect concept of low-intensity conflict, which had been articulated most recently in FM 7–98, *Operations in Low Intensity Conflict*, of 1992, and incorporating the confusing notion of OOTW, FM 100–5 lacked the essential clarity required for the dissemination of sound doctrine. There was also the usual doctrinal allusion to the need for "decisive victory" achieved through the use of "overwhelming combat power", with the manual making it clear that "[v]ictory is the objective, no matter the mission".[14] Quite how the objective of victory was to be reconciled with some of the more arcane missions that came under the rubric of OOTW was not so apparent.

Drawing on the work of writers who disputed Clausewitz's relevance in the post-Cold War world, Robert Bunker criticised the concept of OOTW as being a derivative of the Army's Clausewitzian definition of war.[15] As far as Bunker was concerned, the OOTW concept was being applied to a world in which Clausewitz's paradigm no longer held firm given that non-Western adversaries would fight indirectly, using deception and flexibility. In recommending that a dual doctrinal model should be developed by the US Army, Bunker erroneously restricted Clausewitz's relevance to preparing for war between states: "[A] revolutionary non-Clausewitzian one for operations in the non-Western world and a traditional Clausewitzian model for operations in the Western and Western-influenced world."[16]

When it came to a discussion of more traditional military matters, FM 100–5, 1993 proved to be a retrograde step in the development of Army doctrine, a reversion to the Jominian cookbook approach. As with all previous manuals, the principles of war, described as having "withstood the test of time", were included.[17] But, the manual's use of historical vignettes was restricted in the main to conflicts during the twentieth century, particularly post-1945. There was no mention of Clausewitz at all; nor, indeed, was Jomini referred to. However, the manual did maintain three obvious Clausewitzian concepts: friction, centre of gravity and culmination.

Friction was described as an "accumulation of chance errors, unexpected difficulties, and confusion of battle that impede[s] both sides". Although the manual rightly acknowledged that friction is a permanent element in war, it stipulated that applying the tenet of agility could lessen its effects as agility allows "friendly forces to react faster than the enemy ... disrupting the enemy's plans and leading to late, uncoordinated, and piecemeal responses". In other words, maximise the enemy's friction and minimise your own.[18]

The centre of gravity was described as "the hub of all power and movement upon which everything depends". It might not be immediately recognisable – for example, the mass of an enemy formation that has not yet formed. Alternatively, it might be abstract – for example, the enemy's will – or it might be something concrete such as a strategic reserve. The manual was correct to say that the centre of gravity is not synonymous with a decisive point, but then made the mistake of saying that the latter holds the key to attacking the former.[19] Decisive points cannot, in any way, be related to the more abstract centres of gravity recognised in the manual. It was a typical oversight of FM 100–5, 1993, in that there was no discussion of the origins of the concept nor any attempt to understand Clausewitz's intent when he formulated it. Much the same could be said of the manual's discussion of culmination:

> In the offense, the culminating point is the point in time and location when the attacker's combat power no longer exceeds that of the defender ... A defender reaches culmination when he no longer has the capability to go on the counteroffensive or defend successfully.[20]

The manual's interpretation of the culminating point was confusing in that Clausewitz had written only of the culminating point of the attack. It was not possible for the defender to reach culmination, in Clausewitz's conception, because to do so he would have to be attacking in the first place. Such an interpretation misses the point. FM 100–5, 1993 lacked its 1986 predecessor's understanding of Clausewitzian terminology, which while not perfect had at least laid a foundation for the reader to develop an understanding of Clausewitz's teachings on these subjects. On the whole, the manual was very much a period piece in that 1993 was the first year of the Clinton era, which promised to herald a foreign policy based on the principles of Wilsonian internationalism. In the event, it would only serve to prove the wisdom of Clausewitz's aphorism that every strategic approach reflects the spirit of its age.[21]

Strategic atrophy, 1993–2000

Bill Clinton's preparation to be president of the United States and, consequently, commander-in-chief of the US armed forces has been pithily summed up by Williamson Murray and Major-General Robert Scales: "Knowing little about US military institutions and having no hands-on experience in foreign affairs, Clinton was poorly prepared to deal with the complex issues of war and peace."[22]

Clinton assumed office in January 1993 with a conviction that, in the post-Cold War world, considerations of national interest should not be allowed to override humanitarian concerns. Weinberger–Powell would be swept aside. Ignoring the lessons of history, and in particular the failure of the League of Nations to impose collective security on the world in the 1930s, Clinton placed his faith in "assertive multilateralism", which was driven by the interests of an amorphous entity referred to as the "international community", embodied by the United Nations. It was to be a new era, one in which, as Clinton's second secretary of state, Madeleine Albright, put it, the question determining American policy was "what are the consequences to our security of letting [ethnic and religious] conflicts foster and spread", regardless of whether they were located in areas peripheral to American interests.[23]

Ironically, one of the last acts of the outgoing Bush Administration was to intervene in Somalia on purely humanitarian grounds. It was an intervention that was to lead to the disintegration of Clinton's idealistic approach to foreign policy as expediency replaced all other considerations in his administration's thinking. Operation "Restore Hope" began in December 1992 amid a blaze of media publicity as US forces were filmed making an unopposed landing on the Somalian coast. Somalia had been riven by famine and internecine conflict since mid-1991 with rival factions of the United Somali Congress under its military commander, General Mohammed Farah Aideed, and political head, Ali Mahdi Mohamed, at loggerheads. The UN had first become involved in January 1992, and Operation Restore Hope was the US contribution to a UN operation conducted by a United Task Force (UNITAF) to ensure the safe distribution of aid. It was commanded by Lieutenant-General Robert Johnson, USMC, and, at its peak, consisted of troops from 20 nations, including 37,000 Americans.

Although the UN wanted US forces to disarm the rival Somali factions, Bush restricted American involvement to humanitarian relief. Powell's influence could be detected in the planning of Restore Hope. He was convinced that, given the media's coverage of the situation, the American people would support the operation. Therefore, its objective – to open supply routes and get aid moving, and to pave the way for a UN peacekeeping force – was compatible with Powell's insistence on having clear and achievable objectives. The UN secretary-general, Boutros Boutros-Gali, on the other hand, wanted the aid operation to be extended into a commitment that would address Somalia's underlying socio-economic problems. In Clinton, he found an American president who was willing to support such a policy. Clinton accepted a widening of the US *modus operandi* out of a desire to shore up the credibility of the UN and to showcase the virtues of multilateralism. The incoming secretary of state, Warren Christopher, informed the Senate Foreign Relations Committee that "the United Nations cannot be an effective instrument for sharing our global burdens unless we share the burden of supporting it".[24]

In January 1993, it was announced that UNITAF would intensify its operations, particularly in the capital Mogadishu. This led to clashes with Somali gunmen as UN troops attempted to disable their armed pick-up trucks and to confiscate their weapons. In late February, Aideed, now at the head of his splinter group the Somali National Alliance (SNA), instigated anti-UN riots in Mogadishu. The following month, the UN Security Council passed Resolution 814 allowing UNITAF's successor, United Nations Operation in Somalia (UNOSOM) II, to disarm the Somali militias. This decision took place despite the concerns of commanders on the ground about the impracticalities of such a mission. It was a clear departure from the rules of engagement under which UNITAF had deployed. These had depended on the consent of the gunmen, and could only use force if humanitarian supplies were jeopardised. In other words, the UN had crossed the threshold from peacekeeping to peace enforcement. Nevertheless, Albright, the then US ambassador to the UN, described UNOSOM II as "an historic undertaking. We are excited to join it and we will vigorosly support it."[25]

UNOSOM II assumed control of operations in May 1993, and was immediately hindered by convoluted command and control arrangements. US forces remained outside the UN chain of command but were divided between CENTCOM and the Special Operations Command. Despite being controlled from Florida in the case of CENTCOM, and despite the Clinton Administration's desire to support the UN, it was considered more expedient to keep US forces independent. As Mats Berdal has made clear, this command structure reflected an American concept of operations "and was not an example of the US accepting UN command".[26]

Moreover, UNOSOM II was far too weak to execute the task for which it was deployed. The large American force that had contributed to UNITAF had been stripped to the bones. Only 4,500 American military personnel were left, of which only a Quick Reaction Force (QRF) of 1,150 troops from the 10th Moun-

tain Division was capable of conducting robust operations. "In reality, the political and military objectives were beginning to outstrip the means for achieving
them. Just as the mandate got tougher, the force got weaker."[27]

UNOSOM II's mandate to disarm the warring factions inevitably led to conflict with Aideed. His SNA militia shot dead 24 Pakistani troops on 5 June as
they were being deployed to uncover suspected weapons caches. This incident
led the Security Council to pass Resolution 837, which authorised UNOSOM II
to bring to trial those responsible for attacks on UN personnel. Effectively,
UNOSOM II became involved in a manhunt for Aideed. It did so at the instiga-
tion of the Clinton Administration. In 1996, the deputy chief of mission at the
US embassy in Somalia, Walter Clarke, wrote that all the major Security
Council resolutions on Somalia "were written by US officials ... and handed to
the United Nations as faits accomplis".[28]

Between June and August, Aideed's forces escalated their operations despite
the efforts of UNOSOM II to curtail them through the use of raids backed, in
some cases, by airpower. The mission to capture Aideed rested with the QRF,
which was augmented with some Cobra attack helicopters and C-130 gunships.
It was also bolstered in late August by the arrival of 400 Rangers and a small
Delta Force troop known collectively as Task Force Ranger.[29] The QRF, which
was under direct American command, launched several abortive missions to
capture Aideed before 3 October when an intense firefight with Somali fighters
in Mogadishu led to the incident that has been immortalised on screen as "Black
Hawk Down". Task Force Ranger raided an SNA meeting of high-ranking
Aideed aides, which resulted in the capture of 24 prisoners. As the task force
pulled out, rocket-propelled grenades brought down two helicopters, leaving
them stranded. The QRF and elements of the UNOSOM II force were deployed
to rescue the task force and, in the ensuing battle, 18 US soldiers were killed and
74 wounded. Somali casualties stood at over 300 dead and 700 wounded.[30]

The demise of Task Force Ranger and the spectacle of dead US servicemen
being paraded in the streets of Mogadishu persuaded Clinton that US forces
should desist in the hunt for Aideed and stop all other aggressive operations. On
6 October, with congressional and public support for the mission rapidly slipping away, Clinton announced that all US personnel would leave Somalia within
six months. It would be simplistic to conclude that an aversion to casualties
among the US public was responsible for this decision as their support had been
declining for months. The truth is more complex. There was a clear inability on
the part of the UN to meet its objectives in Somalia, which had basically
changed from supplying aid to nation-building. Congressional support had also
become increasingly fragile, particularly after Resolution 837 was passed. By
the end of September, Congress was resolved to ensure that Clinton would seek
their approval to continue operations in Somalia. Moreover, one cannot absolve
George Bush, Snr of some of the blame. As Jeffrey Record later wrote:

It was naïve to believe that the United States could simply dart into the
anarchy of Somalia, pass out some food, and then leave without at least

attempting to deal with the primary source of starvation, which was political, not meteorological or logistical.[31]

While Somalia had illustrated that the Weinberger–Powell Doctrine could only be applied to conflicts where there was a clear mission, it also, ironically, induced a fear of "mission creep" that would come back to haunt Clinton as his administration struggled to define clear objectives for deploying forces elsewhere in the world.[32] However, perhaps the most significant legacy of Somalia was its influence on the War on Terror launched almost a decade later. The success of Aideed in facing down the US and the UN was not lost on other rogue elements in the world, who drew their own conclusions from the humiliating debacle. It is perhaps no coincidence that the leader of al-Qa'eda, Osama bin Laden, was based in neighbouring Sudan between 1991 and 1996. Just as it had assumed strategic significance during the Cold War, the Horn of Africa would once more make its mark on world affairs.

Far from being chastened by his defeat in the Gulf War, Saddam Hussein would continue to be a thorn in America's side until he was ousted from power in 2003. Clinton's response was to indulge in what became known as "cruise missile diplomacy", beginning in June 1993 with strikes against targets in Baghdad after an attempt by the Iraqis to assassinate former president Bush had been thwarted. In the main, Clinton followed a policy of enforcing no-fly zones in the Kurdish north and Shi'ite south of the country, and supporting UN sanctions, which only increased the suffering of the Iraqi people while enriching the regime at their expense and impressing on it the feebleness of the UN. Powell had presciently written of the problems that would arise should clear strategic objectives not be in place to deal with the type of regime typified by Iraq's:

> Decisive means and results are always to be preferred, even if they are not always possible. We should always be sceptical when so-called experts suggest that all a particular crisis calls for is a little surgical bombing or a limited attack.[33]

Cruise missile diplomacy came about as a result of effects-based thinking, which was heavily influenced by the US Air Force in the early 1990s. The belief was that strategic effects could arise through striking those targets that were critical to an enemy's functioning by using discrete air strikes. This would then lead to paralysis. Effects-based operations were a logical extension of John Warden's systems approach, which had influenced the air campaign in the Gulf War. However, isolated strikes on Iraq, Afghanistan and Sudan during the 1990s were to have no impact on those regimes whatsoever. Without inflicting pressure at the operational, strategic and political levels to at least moderate the behaviour of these regimes, the use of such raids was pointless. "Such a one-dimensional approach to the search for effect in military strategy led to the paradox that physical destruction failed to yield political decision."[34]

In an acknowledgement that he had learnt at least some of the lessons from

Somalia, Clinton signed Presidential Decision Directive (PDD) 25 in May 1994. PDD 25, which described "Key Elements of the Clinton Administration's Policy on Reforming Multilateral Peace Operations", emphasised that, rather than taking the lead in multilateral operations, the US would have a more limited role. It stated that the president would always maintain command authority over US forces but would consider placing them under a UN commander when supporting an operation sanctioned by the Security Council. Shortly after this, the administration published its first NSS in June 1994. Betraying a lack of coherence in responding to the dislocation of the post-Cold War world and believing that there were no obvious threats to the nation on the horizon, the NSS defined security in an anodyne sense as "protecting our people, our territory, and our way of life". Such an approach was to endure for the rest of Clinton's period in office. For example, the Quadrennial Defense Review of 1997 cryptically stated that the main purpose of the armed forces was to "meet the demands of a dangerous world by shaping and responding throughout the period from 1997 to 2015".[35]

The first test of PDD 25 came in September 1994 when the United States participated in a UN operation in Haiti. The island's president, Jean-Bertrand Aristide, had been deposed in a military coup by Lieutenant-General Raoul Cedras in September 1991. In April 1993, the JCS ordered US Atlantic Command to begin planning for operations in Haiti, a process that eventually saw the US Army's XVIII Airborne Corps being despatched in September 1994 under Operation "Uphold Democracy". The intention was to help stabilise the island until Aristide returned. The experience of Somalia led the US military to insist that their rules of engagement would not extend to participating in a peacekeeping exercise, thereby heralding something even more restrictive than the precepts of Weinberger–Powell: casualty avoidance. The consequences of this process were immediately highlighted when US forces were unable to prevent two demonstrators being shot dead by Haitian police on 20 September. By March 1995, the situation had been stabilised to the extent that elections could be held. The last American troops left in April 1996 but, soon after, the situation on the island began to deteriorate once more. With no desire to make a long-term commitment to securing stability on Haiti, the administration's policy goals were not achieved.

The fragmentation of the former Yugoslavia and the subsequent conflict that raged in Bosnia from early 1992 posed a continual dilemma to US foreign policy. Even allowing for the euphoria engendered by the victory in the Gulf and the rhetoric about a "New World Order", Bush had baulked at the prospect of intervening in the Balkans. In Warren Christopher's words, Bosnia was "the problem from hell".[36]

US policy towards Bosnia was conducted at arm's length for three years as it avoided making any major contribution to the UN forces in the country, while at the same time congressional and public support for contravening the UN arms embargo to restore some symmetry to the conflict by arming the Bosnian Muslims was ignored. In April 1993, national security adviser, Anthony Lake, had proposed a policy of "lift and strike" whereby the arms embargo would be lifted and air strikes would be launched against the Serb forces besieging the Bosnian capital, Sarajevo. It was rejected by France and the United Kingdom. The United States was unwilling to intervene unilaterally. There then followed several occasions on which Clinton considered more direct intervention as the Serbs continued to launch sporadic attacks on towns designated "safe areas" by the UN. Finally, in the summer of 1995, the Bosnian Serb massacre of 8,000 unarmed Muslims at Srebrenica in close proximity to an impotent force of Dutch peacekeepers forced the administration to act. Conscious of events in Rwanda in 1994, where hundreds of thousands had been massacred while the world stood by, Clinton decided to deploy airpower against the Bosnian Serbs in conjunction with offensives on the ground by the Croats and the Bosnian Muslims. Rather than rely on the UN, the operation was commanded by NATO.[37]

Operation "Deliberate Force" began at the end of August 1995 and lasted two weeks. During that time, over 3,500 sorties were flown by aircraft from eight NATO countries against 56 targets. Sixty-five per cent of all sorties were flown by the US Air Force. The capitulation of the Serbs owed much to their defeats on the ground, which led to the expulsion of their people from the Croatian Krajina. Nevertheless, Benjamin Lambeth has commented that Deliberate Force was an avowal of the efficacy of airpower:

> [It] did not constitute an especially historic event in the evolution of air power [but] it provided a textbook illustration of air power in action not to "win a war", but rather to achieve a discrete and important national goal.[38]

Despite the success of Deliberate Force, Clinton was anxious that the subsequent deployment of US forces to enforce the Dayton Peace Accords in December 1995 would be over within a year. In the event, US forces remain in Bosnia. Interestingly, the chairman of the JCS at the time, General John Shalikashvili, was keen to reiterate the spirit of the Weinberger–Powell Doctrine: "[W]hen you commit the military force of the United States you must do so in a decisive way. We talk about such things as overwhelming force."[39]

The 1990s proved to be a short interlude between the Cold War and the rise of Islamic fundamentalism into something that was more than a peripheral threat to American interests. Yet, arguably, the dangers posed by militant Islamic groups such as al-Qa'eda should have been obvious to the Clinton Administration from its first days in office, which came after the first attempt to destroy the World Trade Center in January 1993. As the administration continued to follow a liberal, idealistic foreign policy, al-Qa'eda's operations became increasingly daring. In 1996, 18 US servicemen died after a bomb was detonated at the Khobar Towers in Saudi Arabia; in 1998, two massive bombs ripped through the US embassies in Kenya and Tanzania, killing 240; and in 2000 a dinghy packed with explosives, ripped a hole in the side of the naval destroyer USS *Cole*, which killed 17. While alluding to the dangers posed by international terrorism, the administration's NSS of 1998 continued to place faith in multilateralism:

The security environment in which we live is dynamic and uncertain, replete with a host of threats and challenges that have the potential to grow more deadly, but also offer unprecedented opportunities to avert those threats and advance our interests.[40]

In the meantime, Saddam Hussein continued to have a malign impact on US foreign policy. Efforts since 1991 to contain him had not had any effect on his behaviour. An attempt by the CIA to sponsor an uprising against him was an abject failure and, by 1998, he was confident enough to extend his game of brinkmanship against the UN to the point where he would expel the last UN weapons inspectors from Iraq. In January 1998, Clinton aborted planned air raids on Iraq, codenamed "Desert Thunder", as Saddam made a later, unfulfilled, promise to the UN to allow inspections to continue. Saddam was thus given more breathing space to make a mockery of the UN until December 1998 when US and British aircraft were deployed as part of Operation "Desert Fox", which was less ambitious in scope than Desert Thunder. At this stage, the UN had given Saddam an almost clean bill of health with respect to weapons inspections, with the exception of one building. At the outset of Desert Fox, Clinton announced that it was

> designed to degrade Saddam Hussein's capacity to develop and deliver weapons of mass destruction, and to degrade his ability to threaten his neighbors. At the same time, we are delivering a powerful message to Saddam Hussein: if you act recklessly, you will pay a heavy price.[41]

Desert Fox lasted for 70 hours, though air operations against Baghdad were revived intermittently throughout 1999. The administration claimed that Iraq's ballistic missile programme was set back by up to two years and that important command and control facilities had been destroyed. But it was another half-hearted effort, typical of Clinton's presidency:

> Clinton met Saddam Hussein's refusal to verifiably destroy his weapons of mass destruction by accepting Hussein's expulsion from Iraq of UN weapons inspectors. He met murderous attacks by al-Qa'eda on two US embassies in Africa and an American warship with the most token efforts at reprisal and capture. He shrugged at Iran's nuclear program and dealt with North Korea's nuclear and missile programs by agreeing to deals that remain uncompleted and unverified.[42]

MCDP 1, *Warfighting*, and MCDP 1–1, *Strategy*, 1997: Clausewitz condensed

The process of integrating the capabilities of the services continued in 1995 with the publication of *Joint Vision 2010* (JV 2010). Concentrating on the operational level of war, JV 2010 emphasised the need for "full spectrum dominance", which entailed four elements: dominant manoeuvre, precision engagement, full dimensional protection and focused logistics. The common denominator of the four concepts was information technology. As Steven Metz wrote, JV 2010 "represented the codification of the idea that a RMA [Revolution in Military Affairs] was underway".[43]

Underpinning JV 2010 were individual initiatives by each of the services: the Army's Force XXI, the Air Force's AF 2025, the Navy's Strategic Studies Group, and the Marines' "Sea Dragon" and "Urban Warrior" concepts. The Marines were flourishing as a service under the shrewd leadership of its commandant, General Charles Krulak. He was instrumental in adapting the Marine Corps to the realities of the post-Cold War world by undertaking the aforementioned programmes of experimentation and developing new operational concepts, which would exploit new technologies. Most notably, "Operational Maneuver from the Sea" foresaw an ability to launch forces from the sea to capture operational and strategic objectives deep inland through bypassing enemy resistance on the shore. The increasing importance of the littoral in world affairs presented the Marines with their opportunity. Krulak was also aware that the recent conflict in the Gulf would not necessarily provide a template for future operations: "[t]he future may not be 'son of Desert Storm' but 'Stepchild of Somalia and Chechnya' ".[44]

The Marines made a very important contribution to the development of Clausewitzian thinking by replacing FMFM 1, *Warfighting*, of 1989 with Marine Corps Doctrinal Publication (MCDP) 1, *Warfighting*, and its sister publication, MCDP 1–1, *Strategy*, in 1997. Captain John Schmitt, who had been heavily involved in writing FMFM 1, was the primary author of MCDP 1 while MCDP 1–1 was authored by Christopher Bassford, a Clausewitzian scholar from the National Defense University. Bassford's influence could also be detected in the definition of politics in MCDP 1, where it was emphasised that "war is an extension of both politics and policy with the addition of military force". This definition deliberately avoided the ambiguity in using either politics or policy when translating the word *politik* from German and is, therefore, faithful to the argument propounded by Clausewitz in *On War*.[45]

In his introduction to MCDP 1, Krulak explained that the objective of the manual was to foster an understanding of the nature of war and to emphasise the importance of concepts associated with the philosophy of manoeuvre warfare:

> One goal of the revision is to enhance the description of the nature of war – for example, to emphasize war's complexity and unpredictability and to widen the definition of war to account for modern conflict's expanding forms. Another goal ... is to clarify and refine important maneuver warfare concepts such as commander's intent, main effort, and critical vulnerability.[46]

The dominance of Clausewitzian concepts in the manual is illustrated by the fact that he was mentioned 21 times, as opposed to Sun Tzu who was mentioned only five times and Liddell Hart just twice. Jomini was not referred to at all. MCDP 1–1 was a very Clausewitzian document that accurately described Clausewitz's dichotomy between war and politics:

> Clausewitz's reference to war as an expression of politics is … not a prescription, but a description. War is a part of politics. It does not replace other forms of political intercourse but merely supplements them.[47]

Likewise, MCDP 1 closely followed Clausewitz's argument that war is a continuation of political intercourse: "It is important to recognise that military force does not replace the other elements of national power but supplements them."[48]

MCDP 1 argues that total war and perfect peace rarely exist. Rather, following Clausewitz's philosophical approach, these are described as extremes between which lie the most familiar forms of relationship between political entities. "The decision to resort to the use of military force of some kind may arise at any point within these extremes, even during periods of relative peace."[49]

Continuing the Clausewitzian theme, but also drawing on Delbrück's bipolar theory of strategy, the manual describes the tendency to and from destruction in war. Where policy wishes to achieve extreme political ends, the intensity of the effort will tend toward destruction with fewer political restrictions on the way in which the war is conducted. Rather than use the term "strategy of annihilation", the manual prefers "strategy of incapacitation", which equates to the destruction of the enemy's military capability to resist. Where the motive for conflict is more limited, military force will be increasingly constrained by political considerations. Again, the manual discards Delbrück's terminology of "strategy of attrition" and replaces it with "strategy of erosion" to illustrate the intention to erode the will of the enemy's leadership.[50]

This approach to describing the varying intensity of warfare, founded as it was on classical strategic thought, was in stark contrast to that adopted in JP 3–0 and FM 100–5, which had introduced the notion of OOTW. MCDP 1–1 criticised OOTW as being a manifestation of an approach that "lumps many forms of political conflict that clearly satisfy Clausewitz's definition of war with other events – such as humanitarian assistance – that do not".[51]

MCDP 1–1 inserted an important caveat about the relationship between the military and political objectives of war when, using the Gulf War as an example, it stipulated that even where a political objective is limited, the military means to achieve that end need not necessarily be limited. It also clearly articulated the importance of the Clausewitzian trinity. Citing the trinity in full from *On War*, and therefore avoiding the confusion engendered by the use of the "people, army, government" shorthand description, MCDP 1–1 described its underlying dynamics:

> At any given moment, one of these forces may dominate, but the other two are always at work. The actual course of events is determined by the dynamic interplay among them.[52]

If a criticism of MCDP 1 can be made, it is that it continued the trend of US doctrinal publications that misinterpreted the concept of centres of gravity, which were defined as being any important sources of enemy strength and were contrasted to critical vulnerabilities, which were described as enemy weaknesses that could be exploited to reduce his ability to resist.

> We should try to understand the enemy system in terms of a relatively few centers of gravity or critical vulnerabilities because this allows us to focus our own efforts ... [M]ost enemy systems will not have a single center of gravity on which everything depends ... It will often be necessary to attack several lesser centers of gravity or critical vulnerabilities simultaneously or in sequence to have the desired effect.[53]

Rather than being an effects-based approach as this interpretation would imply, MCDP 1 actually takes more of a capabilities-based approach and overlooks the centripetal quality of the centre of gravity as a focal point for the enemy's physical and psychological force.[54] MCDP 1–1, meanwhile, stated that an understanding of centres of gravity and critical vulnerabilities formed

> the core for the development of a particular military strategy. Among the centers of gravity, strategists find military objectives appropriate to the political objectives and the war fighting strategy being pursued. Among the critical vulnerabilities, strategists find the most effective and efficient means of achieving those military objectives.[55]

One doubts whether this is actually the case. It is not clear that strategists deliberately draw up a list of targets that could be reconciled with a purist's definition of centres of gravity and critical vulnerabilities. Given that the former term was not coined until Clausewitz's time, one would not find any historical examples to illustrate the point before the nineteenth century nor would one find many during the period since.

MCDP 1 highlighted the importance of friction in war, a reality that clearly affected the thinking behind the manoeuvre school of warfare. It suggested that strength of mind and spirit were needed to combat its effects, much as Clausewitz had emphasised the commander's genius. "The very essence of war as a clash between opposed wills creates friction. In this dynamic environment of interacting forces, friction abounds [...] One essential means to overcome friction is the will..."[56]

Friction and centres of gravity were, of course, contributions made by Clausewitz to the lexicon of war. However, he did so at a time when the prevalent understanding of science was based on the work of Sir Isaac Newton (1642–1727). Newtonian science was linear in nature, allowing a direct connection to be made between the cause and effect of a phenomenon. If this is extended to command and control arrangements by a military force, one is left with a process that is very much "top-down" based on a desire to bring some order and control to the process of fighting on the battlefield. For example, Schmitt has described the operational concept of synchronisation as "the example nonpareil of Newtonian War".[57]

MCDP 1 and MCDP 1–1 were underpinned by the conviction that war was non-linear in nature and that the precepts of Newtonian science were no longer relevant to an understanding of modern warfare and all its complexities. Instead, the manuals embraced complexity theory, which emphasises a universe that is driven by chaos in stark contrast to the Newtonian view of an ordered existence. It is particularly relevant to the study of biology and ecology where nature reveals the existence of "complex, adaptive systems". The social phenomenon of war is ripe to be analysed according to this way of thinking because of the existence of friction and the realisation that military organisations are also complex systems. Although Bassford confessed that a doctrinal publication was not an orthodox place to present what he rightly called a "world view", he argued that it would help officers understand war's place in a complex world as well as the nature of the organisations in which they served. As MCDP 1 described it:

> War is a complex phenomenon,… In reality, each belligerent is not a single, homogeneous will guided by a single intelligence. Instead, each belligerent is a complex system consisting of numerous individual parts … At the same time, each has its own mission and must adapt to its situation. Each must deal with friction, uncertainty, and disorder at its own level, and each may create friction, uncertainty, and disorder for others, friendly as well as enemy.[58]

The key to control in such an environment was to take decision-making out of the hands of one individual to the maximum extent possible and to decentralise it, thus building on the notion of mission command that had entered US military doctrine in the 1980s. Command was to be exercised by a disparate group of individuals who could interpret the overall objective of the campaign according to the circumstances in their particular locality.

The incorporation of complexity theory into the doctrine of the US Marine Corps contrasted sharply with the complete lack of original intellectual thought embodied in the doctrinal publications of the Army. Clearly, whereas the latter had turned away from Clausewitz, the former had embraced him more tightly than ever. The Marines took their cue not only from Krulak but also General Paul van Riper, the commander of Marine Corps Combat Development Command, who, in April 1996, had urged the Marines' doctrine writers to look beyond the confines of traditional military thought and to embrace the ideas being propounded by scientists in the world at large. Such an approach was very reminiscent of Clausewitz's in his day.[59]

Operation Allied Force, March–June 1999

Although the irredentist aspirations for a Greater Serbia had been thwarted with the signing of the Dayton Accords in 1995, the former Yugoslavia was to return to prominence in international relations in 1999 after Kosovo, the historical cradle of Serb nationalism, which was now 90 per cent Albanian, attempted to break away from Serbia and Montenegro. Diplomacy failed to provide a solution when Slobodan Milosevic, the Serb president, rejected the terms of the Rambouillet Agreement in February 1999. As a consequence the Yugoslav Army and Serb paramilitaries overran the province, leading to the beginnings of an exodus of Kosovo Albanians. In March 1999, the United Nations passed Resolution 1199, which called on the Serb government to end hostilities forthwith and withdraw its forces from the province. When the Serbs refused to comply with the UN's terms, NATO set in train a plan, codenamed "Allied Force", to expel the Serbs from Kosovo by force. Clinton described NATO's objectives:

> [We will] demonstrate the seriousness of NATO's purpose so that Serbian leaders understand the imperative of reversing course, to deter an even bloodier offensive against innocent civilians in Kosovo and, if necessary, to seriously damage the Serbian military's capacity to harm the people of Kosovo.[60]

Allied Force began as a demonstration of airpower that was expected to force the Serbs back to the negotiating table after a few days. However, nothing of the sort occurred. The brutal Serbian campaign of ethnically cleansing Kosovo actually intensified after the first NATO sorties were flown on 23 March with up to a million people being displaced from the province. Despite the endless repetition in US doctrine of the need to apply decisive, if not overwhelming, force, the approach to the campaign over Kosovo began with barely a whimper. The initial attacks were concentrated against Yugoslavia's integrated air defence system, which was mainly concentrated around Belgrade, and its air force even though it was not involved in conducting operations in Kosovo. As Benjamin Lambeth, commenting on the US Air Force, would later write: "The way the air force commenced [the campaign] violated two of the most enduring maxims of military practice: the importance of achieving surprise and the criticality of keeping the enemy unclear as to one's intentions."[61]

The incremental approach adopted by NATO to the campaign in Kosovo was Vietnam all over again in microcosm. Moreover, traditional strategic airpower theory, which emphasised the use of aerial bombing to erode the will of the enemy population, was very difficult to apply in a limited campaign. The result was that, at the outset, the Serbs were actually handed the initiative: they could decide at what point they no longer wished to continue the conflict. Like Vietnam, Allied Force would expand its target set over time with the caveat that political considerations would impinge upon what could and could not be targeted. The problem was that by that time NATO could have been rendered impotent by cracks within the coalition and by a lack of support among its peoples.[62]

One of the most abject features of Allied Force was the way in which the mere existence of Yugoslavia's Air Force and air defence system restricted

NATO aircraft to fly only above 15,000 feet thereby seriously degrading their effectiveness. Moreover, for all the rhetoric emanating from the Clinton Administration and the Alliance about the nobility of the campaign, such a restriction was in its own way immoral given that more Kosovars were dying after bombing began than before. Restrictive rules of engagement also led to incidents in which civilian convoys were inadvertently targeted by NATO aircraft. Targeting procedures were further tightened in April to ensure that pilots received authorisation before attacking military convoys. This change occurred after the accidental bombing of the Chinese embassy in Belgrade on 6 April, which could have had even more drastic political repercussions than was actually the case. By this stage, the main objective of the campaign quickly crystallised into maintaining the credibility of NATO. Nevertheless, General Klaus Naumann, chairman of NATO's Military Committee, confessed that avoiding casualties among Alliance forces was the main driver behind its strategy:

> [W]e have no reason at this point in time to change the strategy which is focused to some extent on the philosophy of our democracies that we should avoid casualties, we should avoid the loss of life. That is the basic point.[63]

NATO's problems were compounded by the decision not to commit a single soldier to the theatre while hostilities continued. With the exception of the use of the proxy forces from the Kosovo Liberation Army (KLA), which aided the targeting of Serb forces from the air, NATO remained reluctant to launch a land campaign. This owed much to the US Army's ambivalence over becoming involved in a potential quagmire in the Balkans. In April, the Army had deployed 24 Apache attack helicopters as part of Task Force Hawk in response to a request from SACEUR, but the nature of their deployment had been a fiasco. Some 5,000 support troops, including ground defence forces to protect them from Serb artillery, were deployed with the aircraft. This cumbersome tail considerably slowed down events and rendered useless any attempt to surprise the Serbs through utilising the shock value of the Apaches. Moreover, the 15,000 feet limit imposed on the use of NATO air assets was above the altitude at which they could operate. Strategically, the deployment was conducted in such a manner as to render it no more than an empty threat. Operationally, it illustrated that the army had not yet adapted to having a flexible and responsive organisation that could conduct expeditionary warfare. Furthermore, as Lambeth notes, it highlighted "a breakdown in joint doctrine for the combat use of helicopters that was disturbingly evocative of earlier competition for ownership and control of coalition air assets ... during Desert Storm".[64]

Given a reluctance to use ground force, the only way in which NATO could bring the Serbs to heel was through intensifying the air campaign to target the Yugoslav power grid and transport network. Certainly, there is evidence that the Serbs eventually gave in because they feared NATO would escalate the bombing to the extent where there would be mass civilian casualties and

Serbia's economic infrastructure would be destroyed.[65] Therefore, one can agree with Lambeth's conclusion that airpower worked only in a tautological sense in that it was used exclusively and, in its absence, ethnic cleansing would have continued regardless.[66]

The consequence of these constraints meant that even when the campaign was intensified, the focus was not on neutralising the Yugoslav Army and para-militaries in Kosovo but rather on Serbia itself. Attacks on oil refineries and such facilities in Serbia were of no use in preventing gunmen from killing civil-ians in Kosovar hamlets and villages. There, Serb armoured vehicles were able to draw on local supplies of fuel and use ruses such as setting up decoy tanks to avoid targeting from the air. Dispersing widely across Kosovo and making the most of the cover provided by the topography of the land, the Serbs could con-tinue their campaign more or less with impunity. Milan Vego has criticised NATO, and, in particular, the Supreme Allied Commander in Europe (SACEUR), General Wesley Clark, for dogmatically following Warden's approach of identifying critical centres of gravity to be attacked. Clark went as far as to demand that 5,000 targets be identified by his planners only to be told that there was nowhere near this number in Serbia. Demonstrating an ignorance of Clausewitz, Clark takes the view that there is a "political level of war" in addition to the strategic, operational and tactical levels of war as if politics and war are completely distinct.[67]

With more aircraft arriving in theatre, it was only during what is generally referred to as the third phase of bombing, beginning in May 1999, that NATO attempted to target the Serb forces in Kosovo systematically.[68] However, one needs to be careful when speaking of a third phase of bombing because there were no clearly defined differences between the nature of the targets now being attacked with the exception of the new emphasis on the Serb forces on the ground. NATO was still targeting Yugoslavia's air defence system, its command and control structure, and its oil industry, much of which had already been destroyed.

There is little doubt that a joint air and land campaign could have brought Milosevic to the negotiating table sooner, but NATO's reluctance to commit land forces encouraged him to believe that the Alliance lacked the stomach for a protracted campaign. In the event, it took 78 days before Milosevic finally capit-ulated. There have been various theories propounded as to why he did so: the threat of a joint air and ground operation is one, but the most convincing is the intervention by Serbia's traditional Slav ally, Russia. The Russians may have been convinced that NATO was about to launch a ground offensive. Such an outcome would place Russia in a quandary: should it stand by and allow its fra-ternal cousin to be overrun or should it intervene on the side of the Serbs with who knew what consequences for its relations with the West? As it was, Milose-vic came back to the negotiating table and actually benefited more than he would have done had he given in at Rambouillet. NATO would have to deploy some 25,000 troops to maintain the peace, including a contingent from Russia.[69]

On the one hand, the NATO campaign had brought an end to ethnic cleansing in Kosovo and allowed refugees to begin to return home. On the other, however, it had seriously undermined the credibility of NATO and the West. For US defense secretary William Cohen to describe it as an "overwhelming success" because it eventually forced Milosevic to withdraw was completely disingenuous. Richard Lock-Pullan has described Allied Force as being a "parody of strategy; suffer no casualties" while Peter Herrly has cited Clausewitz to illustrate that it should not have been too difficult for NATO to devise a strategy to deal with the Serbs:

> If the political aims are small … a prudent general may look for any way to avoid major crises and decisive actions, exploit any weaknesses in the opponent's military and political strategy, and finally reach a peaceful settlement.[70]

The Kosovo campaign has aptly been described as "war in a time of peace", which entailed a careful use of stand-off, precision weaponry to avoid casualties and to manage a campaign in accordance with erroneous perceptions of public opinion. Remarkably, in testimony made to the Senate Armed Forces Committee in July 1999, Clark opined that NATO had got it wrong and that it could have used legal means to block Yugoslav ports to bring pressure to bear on Milosevic. Taken together with other non-military measures, including the use of electronic means to isolate the Serb leadership, NATO might not have needed to resort to force at all. In his memoirs, Clark was even more damning: "[A]ny first year military student could point to the more obvious inconsistencies between our efforts and the requirements posed by the principles of war."[71]

While Clark's diagnosis was correct, his prescription was depressingly reminiscent of the Jominian mindset that had settled upon much of the US Army in the late 1990s: "Using military force effectively requires departing from the political dynamic and following the so-called 'Principles of War' identified by post-Napoleonic military writers a century and a half ago."[72]

When analysing the way in which the campaign appeared to be unravelling in April 1999, Daniel Johnson was right to argue that it had distorted Clausewitz's understanding of the relationship between ends and means in that the "end" of expelling the Serbs from Kosovo had become subordinate to preserving the unity of NATO whose military force was ostensibly providing the "means" to this end:

> [O]ur leaders lack the theoretical and practical knowledge to make proper use of the forces at their disposal.
>
> In short: NATO needs statesmen who know their Clausewitz, but it does not have them.[73]

Conclusion

Lock-Pullan has written of a "debate between the Clausewitzian model of the Army and the broader Creveldian viewpoint" as being a microcosm of the debate about US foreign policy in the 1990s.[74] Objectives in Somalia seemed to be clear initially from a Weinberger–Powell perspective. These then became muddled as the Clinton Administration tried to shore up the credibility of the UN. This involved an escalation of the mission from one of humanitarian assistance through peacekeeping to peace enforcement, for which the vacuities of OOTW could not prepare the military. Failure in Somalia induced a fear of casualties that was to constrain the execution of American foreign policy whenever force was contemplated. Its most pernicious effects could be seen in Kosovo – where an absurd restriction was placed on the conduct of air operations and where it was clear that no ground troops would be deployed as long as hostilities continued – and in the incoherent response to the twin dangers of rogue states, epitomised by Iraq, and international terrorism, which was being radicalised by al-Qa'eda.

While the 1993 edition of FM 100–5 recognised that the emerging strategic environment would require an army that could project force over long distances and conduct operations as part of a joint campaign, the capstone operational manual of the US Army was reduced in some places to a prescription for social work. It marked a milestone on the army's turn away from Clausewitz. General Eric Shinseki, Army chief-of-staff, used the experience of Kosovo to illustrate the need for a more deployable and flexible army called the "Objective Force". Citino provided a damning critique:

> It is nearly inconceivable that a proven high-quality force of unparalleled mobility and destructive power, such as the US Army in 1991, would decide to transform itself completely based on the size of the bridges in Albania, but nevertheless it seems to be happening.[75]

However, while the Army continued to turn its back on the thinking that drove the reforms of the 1980s, the Marines produced two manuals of outstanding quality in MCDP 1 and MCDP 1–1. These went beyond the traditional bounds of a doctrinal tract and described the way in which a paradigm based on cause and effect had been superseded by one based on probabilities and trends. In doing so, they demonstrated that Clausewitz is a theorist who is as suited to this new understanding as he was to the old. The centre of gravity, for example, is associated with mass, which epitomised war in the industrial age; but the theories that interpret military forces as complex systems sit comfortably with Clausewitz's notion of friction in war.[76]

Airpower enthusiasts, meanwhile, having been emboldened by the exclusive use of airpower in small-scale operations in Bosnia and Iraq, were deluded by Milosevic's eventual capitulation into thinking that effects-based operations were a panacea, something that fed the wider delusions about the possibilities of a Revolution in Military Affairs driven by technology.

9 American strategy and policy in the age of terror

Transformation and the revolution in military affairs

The most important factor in the development of post-Cold War strategic theory has been the phenomenon of globalisation, which had already been underway for some time prior to the end of the twentieth century.[1] Globalisation is the increasing process of interdependence and connectedness that has arisen in economic, social, political and military affairs. Consequently, even more so than their predecessors, contemporary military theorists must strive to understand the relationship between their subject and the undercurrents of change affecting the wider world. Unfortunately, many theorists have misread these changes as being the product primarily of what they perceive as an increasing need to rely on information technology. Americans, in particular, have been culpable of placing their faith in the notion of information dominance:

> American strategic and military culture is incapable of offering much resistance to the seductive promise of a way of war that seeks maximum leverage from the exploitation of information technologies.[2]

There has been much debate as to whether these changes have sparked a Revolution in Military Affairs (RMA), the origins of which can be traced to Soviet writings about a military–technical revolution.[3] What is clear is that, since the early 1990s, the US military has attempted to meet the challenges posed by change through undergoing a process of transformation, which was defined by the Quadrennial Defense Review Working Group of 2001 as "the set of activities by which the Department of Defense attempts to harness the Revolution in Military Affairs to make fundamental changes in technology, operational concepts and doctrine, and organizational structure".[4]

Andrew Marshall, who has served as the head of the Pentagon's Office of Net Assessment since 1973, argued that the United States had to continue to invest in advanced technology at the expense of what he saw as the services' penchant for maintaining what he believed to be obsolescent platform-based systems. He drew an analogy with the 1920s in arguing that the United States needed to exploit information technology to the degree that the Germans had done with mechanisation. However, he overlooked the fact that the German Army had made the most of mechanisation because it further developed tactical and operational concepts that were already apparent in the latter stages of the First World War. Moreover, these concepts were only part of a wider theoretical construct that encompassed the work of theorists such as Clausewitz.

In his book, *Lifting the Fog of War* (2000),[5] Admiral William Owens foresaw a battlespace of unprecedented transparency arising as a result of exploiting new information technologies, which would enable Command, Control, Communications, Computers, Intelligence, Surveillance, Target Acquisition and Reconnaissance (C4ISTAR) systems, and precision force, to interact seamlessly as a "system of systems". As the title of his work suggests, Owens was propounding a vision that could overcome the problem of friction, which had been conceptualised by Clausewitz. While acknowledging that there would always be some friction in war, Owens argued that the RMA presented Clausewitzian thinking with a "profound challenge" in that the revolution could "introduce such a disparity in the extent to which fog and friction apply to each side in war as to give one unprecedented dominance".[6]

Such a technocentric view, which paid lip service to developments in countries outside the United States, was to be given a severe jolt by experience in Kosovo.[7] Despite possessing a panoply of C4ISTAR systems, NATO was vulnerable to Serbian deception measures such as camouflage and fake targets. With little awareness of what was happening on the ground, NATO's information superiority was severely compromised.[8] Rather than being the driving force behind transformation, information is nothing more than an enabler. Kenneth McKenzie has warned against falling into the trap of overly relying on information technology:

> Technological innovation is unruly, spasmodic, and to a certain extent uncontrollable – the opposite of developing force structure and doctrine which tends to be highly predictable, cautious, and self-regulating.[9]

Given the influence of Owens, the Navy found itself at the forefront of articulating operational concepts for the RMA. The most influential of these was network-centric warfare (NCW) developed by Admiral Arthur Cebrowski. NCW would link platforms and command structures together so as to permit rapid information sharing through the medium of an information infrastructure underpinned by C4ISTAR. The objective would be "to achieve shared awareness, increased speed of command, higher tempo of operations, greater lethality, increased survivability, and a degree of self-synchronization".[10]

When all is said and done, the argument made by proponents of the RMA that it will change the nature of war is absurd. If this happened, then war as we know it would no longer exist. Nevertheless, commentators make free play with the words "the changing nature of war" when, in fact, they are describing evolutionary change in some of the elements that are at play in the conduct of war, whether it is information or new weapons systems. Major John Schmitt has described the thinking of Owen, in particular, as being locked in a "Newtonian" mindset, making exaggerated claims about technological change that cannot address the complexity inherent in the nature of war.[11]

There has undoubtedly been an exponential increase in the speed and volume of information available to commanders. During Operation "Iraqi Freedom" in 2003, for example, US forces used 30 times as much bandwidth as they had during the Gulf War of 1991.[12] However, countering the friction of war requires more than information dominance. It requires an ability to disseminate the meaning of information, to sort out the wheat from the chaff, and to exploit knowledge in its widest sense. This is embodied in the role of the commander, who must call upon all his training, learning and experience when making decisions in the heat of battle. As Clausewitz wrote, friction can never be eradicated but it can be ameliorated to some degree by what he termed the commander's "genius".[13]

A fundamental problem in the thinking of those who make information warfare synonymous with the RMA is that there is no general agreement on just what is meant by information. Is it the exploitation of information technology; the use of intelligence that has been gathered; or something else? All the information-gathering technologies in the world might fail to locate an Osama bin Laden or to uncover a rogue nation's weapons of mass destruction programme. One can only agree with Richard DiNardo and Daniel Hughes who have argued that the term "information warfare" has been overused to such an extent that it has become a tautology.[14]

Nevertheless, theories of information warfare found an outlet in the syllabuses at some of the military's service schools. To give one pernicious example, the populist tract by Alvin and Heidi Toffler, *War and Anti-War*, found favour at the US Air Force Academy. The Tofflers' work is a simplistic Marxian analysis that describes war as having evolved in three "waves" from agricultural through industrial to information societies. In essence, the Tofflers see war as an extension of the prevailing means of production in a given society rather than of politics in the Clausewitzian sense. In today's terms, this means that war is based on the information-age economy. One Air Force officer went as far as to say that the Tofflers constituted "mandatory reading for any US military leader today" and that they provided "the clearest and most accurate explanation of how this new type of warfare [for the information age] evolved".[15]

Although he erroneously referred to "post-Clausewitzian" war, Dr Robert Bunker warned against a wholesale acceptance of the Tofflers' thesis by the US military. Noting that the "third-wave war" theory had also influenced some in the Army such as the chief-of-staff, General Gordon Sullivan, Bunker wrote that the Tofflers' "'civilisation waves' are flawed and therefore improperly articulate the historical process that is now taking place".[16]

US military schools were also increasingly infatuated with the writings of Sun Tzu, the ancient Chinese theorist who had lived at some time between the sixth and fifth centuries BC, partly because he was perceived as a theorist who advocated the use of intelligence. In contrast to Clausewitz, a slim volume, *The*

Art of War, is all we have to work with when analysing Sun Tzu's thought. Nevertheless, this has not stopped many of Sun Tzu's readers from depicting him as the very antithesis of Clausewitz, when, in fact, there are many similarities between the two. Both men might reflect different "world-views", but their works are as much complementary as they are contradictory. Unfortunately, the aphoristic style of Sun Tzu is more suited to the age of the soundbite than the deep philosophising of Clausewitz. Indeed, one of the most senior politicians in the United States, Newt Gingrich, the then Speaker of the House of Representatives, suggested in a speech to the National Defense University in May 1994 that Sun Tzu should be preferred to Clausewitz, both because the latter's work is far longer and, being linked to Napoleonic warfare, is outdated![17]

Fortunately, the teaching of Clausewitz survived in pockets of the American system of military education. In 2000, the syllabus of the National War College stated that Clausewitz had articulated four fundamental truths about war: it is an act of violence; it is a clash of opposing wills; it is dominated by "fog" and "friction"; and it is an instrument of policy. At the same institution in 2003/04, Professor Ilana Kass taught the course, "Military Thought and the Essence of War". Teaching guidance for the course described *On War* as "an indispensable part of the intellectual arsenal we provide to the nation's future strategic leaders".[18]

Neo-conservatism

The coming to age of an information world in which the United States held sway encouraged the neo-conservative movement to propound the idea that the nation should use this to its advantage in international relations, acting unilaterally if necessary. Given the growth of the knowledge-based economy and the consequent increase in American economic power, such strength could easily be translated into diplomatic influence and more.[19]

The neo-conservative movement had originally arisen in response to the strides made by liberal interests in the US during the 1960s and 1970s. The "neo" in the name was used to draw a distinction with the traditional conservative movement that had been eclipsed in the 1970s. In June 1997, the figureheads of neo-conservatism made its agenda clear via the think-tank "Project for the New American Century". Boasting such future worthies of the Bush Administration as Richard Cheney, Donald Rumsfeld and Paul Wolfowitz, their "statement of principles" offered a radical alternative to the incoherencies of Clinton's foreign policy. Arguing that America would pay the price for a foreign policy that lacked focus and a military that was being increasingly neglected, they argued for a "Reaganite policy of military strength and moral clarity". Such a policy would involve a significant increase in defence spending; challenging regimes perceived to be hostile to US interests; and promoting political and economic freedom throughout the world.[20]

The election of George W. Bush in late 2000 allowed the second generation of neo-conservative thinkers to come to prominence. Their stark view of the use of force, seeing it as something to be used as a first resort, if necessary, contrasted with the traditional conservative view that force should be a last resort, as embodied in the Weinberger–Powell Doctrine. However, the appointment of Powell as secretary of state appeared to be a sign that Bush would proceed pragmatically, rather than dogmatically, in foreign policy. Bush made a play during the election of his opposition to nation-building, which would logically have to be pursued if neo-conservative views were to succeed. He pointed out that he would avoid "missions without end" and would not intervene militarily "to stop ethnic cleansing and genocide" if it was not in the American national interest. "When America uses force in the world, the cause must be just, the goal must be clear, and the victory must be overwhelming."[21]

The simultaneous appointment of Rumsfeld as defense secretary, however, gave the neo-conservatives an influential figurehead in the administration. Rumsfeld became the first man to serve in this post twice, having previously been at the Pentagon during Gerald Ford's presidency. He was determined to reform the Pentagon and, in particular, to cut some of the fat out of the military. He was an enthusiast for the transformation agenda and would not be intimidated by what he saw as vested interests in the officer corps or the Pentagon bureaucracy. To this end, he almost immediately oversaw the ditching of the "two-war" scenario that had influenced military planning during the previous decade. Rumsfeld was convinced that the range of threats facing the United States was far wider than such a scenario could deal with. An address made to the House Armed Services Committee in February 2003 illustrates the extent of Rumsfeld's support for transformation:

> We are fighting the first wars of the 21st century with a Defense Department that was fashioned to meet the challenges of the mid-20th century ... We have an industrial age organization, yet we are living in an information age world, where new threats emerge suddenly, often without warning, to surprise us. We cannot afford not to change, and rapidly, if we hope to live in that world.[22]

Given this fixation with the transformation agenda, it was no surprise that the concept of rapid decisive operations (RDO) was incorporated in the administration's first *Quadrennial Defense Review* of 2001. Like NCW and effects-based operations, the objective of conducting RDOs is to paralyse an adversary's ability to fight through both physical and psychological means by utilising information and networks. The promise inherent in RDO allowed the Pentagon to reduce the force structure that had underpinned planning when the two-war scenario was in place. The administration also placed considerable faith in a system of ballistic missile defence that would bring to fruition Reagan's "Star Wars" vision of 1983, which foresaw the end of mutual assured destruction. John Bolton, US under-secretary of state for arms control, articulated the administration's thinking by stating that where "arms control treaties are ineffective or counterproductive or obsolete, they shouldn't be allowed to stand in the way of the development of our foreign-policy".[23]

JP 3–0, 2001

Technological change and the expanded battlespace have ensured that joint warfare is a necessity and no longer the luxury that led some servicemen to view it as anathema as recently as the late 1980s. The military replaced Joint Vision 2010 with Joint Vision 2020 in 2000. JV 2020 emphasised the need for full spectrum dominance, which was to be arrived at through the four concepts of dominant manoeuvre, precision engagement, focused logistics and full-dimensional protection. However, it has been criticised for jeopardising joint-ness by exacerbating the differences between the Army and the Air Force through propounding dominant manoeuvre and precision engagement, which were derived from German and Soviet theories of land warfare and from strategic bombing theory, respectively.[24]

In September 2001, the Joint Chiefs-of-Staff codified the process being driven by JV 2020 by publishing a new edition of Joint Publication 3–0, *Doctrine for Joint Operations*.[25] Unfortunately, just when there was a need for cogency and clarity, JP 3–0 resembled nothing more than a doctrinal cookbook. Following JV 2020, JP 3–0 refers to full spectrum operations across the full range of military operations. This included the notion of operations other than war, which was defined as "an aspect of military operations that *focus on deterring war and promoting peace*". JP 3–0 erroneously cited Clausewitz to illustrate the threshold between war and OOTW, which it said would occur where the use of "military force of any kind comes into play". Yet, if one goes back to Clausewitz's writing regarding the intense nature of warfare, this threshold surely exists between what the manual terms OOTW involving force and OOTW that do not involve force. By eschewing the notion of LIC, the manual lacked the clarity required for the sound dissemination of doctrine.[26]

JP 3–0 listed a number of fundamental elements of operational art. Among these were *synergy*, which emphasised integrating and synchronising the actions of air, land, sea, space and special operations forces; *simultaneity*, which was described as a key characteristic of the American way of war as it involved the simultaneous application of force against key enemy capabilities and sources of strength; and leverage, which would allow joint force commanders to impose their will on the enemy and maintain the initiative.[27] In the context of joint operations as a whole, JP 3–0 drew on Clausewitz's analogy of war as a duel:

> In joint operational art, effective symmetrical attack (fully supported by all components of the joint force) and asymmetrical attack constitute the dueler's sword; the actions of air, land, sea, space, and special operations forces to protect each other is the dueler's shield; and, in its broadest sense, logistics and basing are the dueler's footing, affecting the reach of the sword and the strength and resiliency of the shield.[28]

JP 3–0 described centres of gravity as the "foundation of capability". It saw them as a useful analytical tool during planning and as being the source of the most direct path to victory should they be destroyed or neutralised. Centres of gravity were defined as *"those characteristics, capabilities, or sources of power from which a military force derives its freedom of action, physical strength, or will to fight"*.[29]

By equating the centre of gravity with sources of power, JP 3–0 was diverging from Clausewitz's notion of the centre of gravity as a focal point. What JP 3–0 was describing was, in Antulio Echevarria's words, more akin to centres of critical capability.[30] Moreover, by focusing on single entities such as "characteristics", the manual was falling into the trap of ascribing a linear-based relevance to centres of gravity. In the complex environment of the post-Cold War world, such an approach is inappropriate to the conduct of operations in a non-linear battlespace. Drawing an analogy with the Wright brothers attempting to fly an F-15E, Major Darfus Johnson has argued that planners need to go beyond having a linear understanding of the concept and, instead, approach it from a systems perspective: "The [Wrights] would understand the concept of flight, but the complexity of the plane's systems would be overwhelming."[31]

Johnson, therefore, argued that a centre of gravity should not be seen as a physical strength or weakness but, rather, as a "nexus point" with redundant, self-supporting elements contributing to it. He argued that unlike Clausewitz's "hub of all activity", from which everything emanates, a nexus is a binding point into which everything flows. However, a more literal translation than that of Michael Howard and Peter Paret shows that this was, in fact, what Clausewitz originally implied:

> Everything depends upon keeping the dominant characteristics of both states in mind. From these emerge a certain center of gravity, a *focal point* (*Zentrum*) of force and movement, upon which the larger whole depends.[32]

JP 3–0 described the identification and control of decisive points as giving a commander great influence over the course of events. They were explicitly differentiated from centres of gravity but, rather than limit their existence to geographical objects, the manual also described systemic objects such as command and control systems or refuelling capabilities as decisive points when, in fact, they could be interpreted as centres of gravity. Moreover, JP 3–0 made a leap of faith when it went as far as to describe key events such as the attainment of air or naval superiority as being decisive points. Such a definition would change the nature of a decisive point from a physical to a temporal element.[33]

FM 3–0, 2001

In August 1994, the Army's Training and Doctrine Command published Pamphlet 525–5, *Force XXI Operations*. In his foreword, General Gordon Sullivan described the document as being one of ideas rather than a doctrinal tract. To Sullivan, Force XXI was not a theoretical construct: "We need to think of Force XXI as a mind-set and an orientation rather than an end product of the present process of change. The Force XXI mind-set, however, accepts various degrees of ambiguity, and a very wide spectrum of operations, as routine."[34]

TRADOC's Army After Next project, which began in 1995, encompassed study, conferences and war games with the intention of tailoring the Army's capabilities to the RMA at a strategic level for the period 2020 to 2025. The centrepiece of the Army's experimentation was digitisation of the battlespace, which was given its ultimate expression in the Force XXI Battle Command, Brigade and Below (BCB2) system, a wireless internet system that was trialled in the vehicles of the 4th Infantry Division.

In October 1995, the commandant of TRADOC, General William Hartzog, set in motion a further revision of FM 100–5, *Operations*, as a result of the Force XXI programme. When this revised edition finally emerged in June 2001 it was given a new designation, FM 3–0, to emphasise its relationship with JP 3–0 and joint doctrine. Making it clear that joint doctrine had precedence should any conflict with army doctrine arise, FM 3–0 described the latter as authoritative, not prescriptive.[35]

FM 3–0 set out its strategic context by articulating six dimensions making up the operational environment: the multiple threats to American interests; the influence of political decision-making; unified action with the other services, other government agencies, and coalition partners; land combat; information; and technology. FM 3–0 referred to the Army's need to conduct full spectrum operations to meet its role across all the operational environments. However, while this approach appeared to offer some substance in terms of continuity between different types of operation, it also made the artificial distinction between "military operations in war" and OOTW.[36]

Full-spectrum operations would depend upon certain fundamental elements, including the nine principles of war and the five tenets of army operations. The principles of war were described as the "enduring bedrock of army doctrine" and were applicable across the strategic, operational, and tactical levels of war. The principles of war were "not a checklist" but were a valuable tool in professional military education. The tenets – initiative, agility, depth, synchronisation and versatility – were unchanged from the previous FM 100–5. They were described as building on the principles of war.[37]

FM 3–0 also discussed the emerging concept of asymmetry, which had made a lot of headway in academic circles. Taking the view that asymmetrical warfare allowed one to avoid enemy strengths, the manual defined asymmetry as "dissimilarities in organization, equipment, doctrine, capabilities, and values between other armed forces (formally organized or not) and US forces".[38]

Asymmetric warfare was first mooted as a concept in 1975 as a reaction to the Vietnam War.[39] The 1990s saw an array of thinking that used this phrase to encapsulate the way in which warfare was changing. Yet such thinking only served to highlight the futility of the concept. Any war that has ever been fought has been asymmetric in one shape or another, a fact at least partially acknowledged in FM 3–0.[40] Professor Beatrice Heuser has suggested that Clausewitz himself laid the foundations of current thinking on asymmetry because he discussed the relationship between a stronger opponent and a weaker one.[41] Nevertheless, political scientists, many of whom pay lip service to history, have produced a steady stream of work that tries to provide a definitive definition of asymmetry. Colin Gray, a political scientist who is well read in history, has written of the need to dispense with such arcane debating and to concentrate instead on the need for plain strategic thinking.[42]

Lieutenant-General William Steele, the commanding general of the US Army CAC, described FM 3–0 as the most radical change in army doctrine since AirLand Battle was unveiled in 1982. "For the first time, the Army [doctrinally] talks about itself as a member of a joint team." Steele went on to describe the inclusion of full-spectrum operations as giving the Army the flexibility to do stability and support operations in addition to war fighting. "Doing them simultaneously and concurrently is what is new in this document."[43]

Conrad Crane has rightly criticised FM 3–0 for being dominated by quotations from generals with very little input from theorists.[44] Clausewitz is mentioned only twice, once in relation to training and once in relation to the principle of the objective.[45] This is perhaps surprising given the manual's inclusion of the influence of political decision-making as a dimension of the operational environment. An articulation of Clausewitz's discussion of the relationship between war and politics would have greatly helped the audience at which the manual was aimed. Moreover, there was no discussion of the concepts of centre of gravity and culmination, an astonishing oversight given the amount of attention devoted to these subjects in previous manuals and, indeed, their inclusion in the contemporaneous JP 3–0. Undoubtedly, as Williamson Murray suggests, the increased tempo and number of military operations in recent years has had a detrimental impact on intellectual pursuits within the US military, but, nevertheless, a neglect of this aspect of command makes the need for cogent doctrine more important than ever.[46]

11 September 2001 and its aftermath

There is no doubt that the remarkable events of 11 September 2001, when 19 terrorists belonging to al-Qa'eda hijacked four passenger aircraft and attacked targets in New York and Washington, served to strengthen the hands of those who argued that the emphasis in international relations was moving away from states and, consequently, from regular to irregular forces. Writing immediately after 11 September, Professor Roy Godson argued that half of the world's states no longer controlled substantial portions of their own territory. The initiative in these places had effectively passed over to sub-state forces, such as the Revolutionary Armed Forces of Colombia and the Tamil Tigers in Sri Lanka, or else to transnational forces such as NATO and the United Nations.[47]

Godson was following in the footsteps of earlier anti-Clausewitzian tracts by Martin van Creveld and John Keegan. In *On Future War* (1991), van Creveld expressed the conviction that fighting war in the Clausewitzian manner is dangerously obsolescent. He questioned the notion of "interest" that lies at the centre of policy-oriented war. To van Creveld, the notion that war should only be waged because there is an interest at stake is anachronistic, a legacy of the period between the Treaty of Westphalia of 1648 and the end of the Second World War in 1945 when the state was king. Keegan not only took issue with Clausewitz's continued relevance but questioned the very essence of his thought by suggesting that it had had a malign influence in the past, and could not continue to do so in the future.[48]

In 1999, Mary Kaldor continued the trend by suggesting that war was being transformed from a mainly inter-state affair of the type described by Clausewitz into one where sub-state actors were becoming the predominant force.[49] Yet, if one examines the Europe of Clausewitz's time, shifting patterns of allegiance are apparent with many states being contested by one or more powers, particularly during the Revolutionary and Napoleonic Wars; and states such as France had to deal with subversive movements, notably the anti-republican forces in the Vendée region. Clausewitz was aware of all of this and incorporated it into his work. In his essay, "Agitation" (*Umtriebe*), believed to have been written in the early 1820s, Clausewitz showed that he understood both the concept of sovereignty as vested in the state and the causes of revolution as they had transpired in France.[50]

Kaldor argues that "new wars" are based on "identity politics", which are practised by movements that base themselves on ethnic, religious or racial identity. For example, while al-Qa'eda has exploited some of the elements of globalisation – ease of world-wide travel, information technology, and the international banking system – it rejects totally the apparent universalist philosophy that underpins it. Al-Qa'eda sees this philosophy as endangering the traditional values of Islam, and has consequently spread its influence in those areas of the world that have benefited least from globalisation. Kaldor repeats the erroneous assertion made by van Creveld that Clausewitz's theories apply only to the age of statecentric warfare between, say, 1648 and 1989. This is absurd both because Clausewitz penetrated to the very nature of warfare and because a sub-state actor such as al-Qa'eda still requires states to function in so as to survive and flourish. Unlike terrorist groups that functioned during the Cold War and were the beneficiaries of funds and equipment from "strong" states, al-Qa'eda, which is largely self-financed and equipped, thrives in weak states. Such states possess just enough power to remain sovereign, which – certainly prior to 11 September – deters other states from intervening. The connivance of the Taliban regime gave al-Qa'eda its foothold in Afghanistan, though Lawrence Freedman is not being ironic in stating that this was "not so much a case of state-sponsored terrorism but of a terrorist-sponsored state".[51]

For William Lind, 11 September provided affirmation of a theory he had developed back in 1989 with several US officers – that of "fourth-generation warfare". In sum, fourth-generation warfare would be non-linear in nature and would eradicate the distinction between the civilian elements of society, which writers such as Bunker and Steven Metz mistakenly implied would transcend the Clausewitzian trinity. In the aftermath of the al-Qa'eda attacks, Lind felt compelled to describe those events as being more than terrorism, which he saw as merely a technique. Rather, following the thinking of van Creveld, he wrote:

> Fourth-generation warfare is broader than any technique ... [It] is the greatest change in war since the Peace of Westphalia in 1648, and it undoes what that treaty established: the state's monopoly on war.[52]

Although many commentators tried to draw a natural comparison between 11 September and the Japanese attack on Pearl Harbor in December 1941, perhaps the only similarity was the achievement of surprise by the aggressors. Colin Gray has made the point that the *effects* of surprise are more significant than the actual surprise itself. John Lewis Gaddis argued that whereas Roosevelt had to insist on a war effort that would deprive American citizens of any semblance of normality, Bush had to somehow ensure that the American people continue their normal day-to-day lives. In the new strategic environment, Cold War notions of deterrence were clearly inadequate. The administration's *Quadrennial Defense Review*, published just three weeks after 11 September, made this clear: "If deterrence fails, decisively defeat an adversary ... Such a decisive defeat could include changing the regime of an adversary state or occupation of a foreign territory until US strategic objectives are met."[53]

Given the huge loss of life on 11 September, the United States was now prepared to return to a style of warfare more in keeping with the traditional American way of war, which would be characterised by offensive operations and, if necessary, close-in fighting, in contrast to the pusillanimity of the Clinton years. There would also be less reluctance to take military casualties in the wake of an event that had cost the lives of almost 3,000 civilians.

Diplomatically, the Bush Administration paved the way for operations in Afghanistan by ensuring that Pakistan, until now the major state sponsor of the Taliban, renounced its support for the Afghan regime. Afghanistan was too remote and lacking in decent communications links for there to be a long build-up prior to the insertion of US forces in the country. Therefore, the Afghan campaign, codenamed Operation "Enduring Freedom", began with air attacks from 7 October and the insertion of US and Allied special forces into the country by the middle of the month. Airpower had its limits in a country as impoverished of targets as Afghanistan, but the presence of special forces who operated within a decentralised system of command and control, and were equipped with navigation and designation equipment, allowed for precision strikes to be directed against hostile elements with next-to-no warning. After four weeks of the air campaign, the average number of sorties being flown each day was only 63 compared to 500 at a similar stage in Kosovo and 1,500 during the Gulf War. Although the contiguous countries of Pakistan, Tajikistan and Uzbekistan allowed the Coalition some facilities for conventional and special forces, aircraft had to fly in from afar, being based on aircraft carriers, and in Oman, Diego Garcia and the United States.[54]

The main objective of the Afghan campaign was to destroy those elements of al-Qa'eda based in the country. The removal of the Taliban regime was a secondary aim. The campaign consisted of campaigns in the north centred around Mazar-i-Sharif and in the south around Kandahar; and then operations against al-Qa'eda and its Taliban allies at Tora Bora and in the Shah-i-Kot Valley. In the north, Mazar was taken on 10 November, three days before the capital Kabul fell. By the end of the month, the besieged city of Kunduz was taken in an operation that resulted in 5,000 al-Qa'eda and Taliban captives. The fall of Kandahar on 6 December signalled the end of Taliban rule in the country as Mullah Muhammad Omar, its leader, went into hiding. Attention then switched to the far south of the country where the Tora Bora caves complex, believed to be concealing bin Laden, was attacked and captured in a two-week battle ending on 17 December.[55]

As had been the case in Kosovo, the United States and its Coalition partners seemed to have a natural ally on the ground in the shape of the anti-Taliban Northern Alliance. However, as with the Kosovo Liberation Army, the Northern Alliance was not the most reliable of forces. For a start, it could not be said to represent all the Afghan people, given that the Taliban were mainly drawn from the Pashtuns in the south. Moreover, its 15,000-strong "army" was of dubious quality, having struggled during the past five years to oust the Taliban. However, by operating with special forces, the indigenous allies provided invaluable assistance during close-in operations against al-Qa'eda and the Taliban. Rumsfeld rather extravagantly described the combination of technologically advanced US forces and Afghan fighters operating on horseback at Mazar-i-Sharif as the day "the 19th century met the 21st century and defeated a dangerous and determined adversary".[56]

The failure to capture bin Laden at Tora Bora tarnished the campaign's success. Biddle has argued that the reliance placed on local Afghan and Pakistani allies was to blame as their own interests overrode the desire to encircle and capture the fighters within the caves. Colin Gray has suggested that the operation at Tora Bora exuded such incompetence, given the failure to do anything as basic as block escape routes into Pakistan, that it raised suspicions as to whether there was a political desire to avoid the high casualties that might have arisen had bin Laden and his acolytes staged a last stand. Max Boot argued that the lack of reliable ground forces showed the limitations of the transformation of the US military.[57]

In March 2002, a number of al-Qa'eda redoubts in the Shah-i-Kot Valley became the focus of Operation "Anaconda". US conventional forces, notably 900 men from the 10th Mountain Division, now entered the fray, joining indigenous allies backed by special forces from a number of Coalition nations to make up a force of about 2,000. By now, Taliban and al-Qa'eda forces had adapted to the demands posed by facing an enemy with huge technological advantages. They had learnt to adopt countermeasures to avoid surveillance and consequent destruction from the air by concealing their positions and movements, which meant that they would have to be neutralised through close-in fighting. As Biddle points out, during Anaconda, fewer than half of all enemy positions were known to Coalition forces prior to contact on the ground. General Tommy Franks, commander of Central Command, gave a flavour of the type of fighting involved: "We might find five enemy soldiers in one place and then perhaps some distance away from there we may find three and then some further distance we may find 15 or 20."[58]

In the event, many of the al-Qa'eda fighters were killed but many others managed to escape. However, Anaconda brought an end to major combat operations in Afghanistan. A peacekeeping force had already been despatched in October 2001 to try and maintain a truce among the many Afghan factions as the Taliban's rule was brought to an end. NATO soon assumed responsibility for this force. The Coalition used an institutional approach to try and bring stability to the country, with elections being held in 2004. However, al-Qa'eda and the Taliban continue to pursue operations, particularly in the remote areas of the south-east of the country.

The wider war on terror

On 29 January 2002, Bush made his first State of the Union Address since hostilities in Afghanistan had begun. Looking beyond the immediate future to the longer-term execution of the War on Terror, he referred to an "Axis of Evil" consisting of Iran, Iraq and North Korea: "States like these, and their terrorist allies ... threaten the peace of the world."[59]

In making it clear that the War on Terror would be prolonged and would involve countering not only terrorist groups but also their state sponsors and states that were intent on developing weapons of mass destruction, Bush was giving the American people notice that they could be involved in a conflict of similar proportions to the Cold War. Bush himself has recently described his thinking about the conflict:

> The key thing in the war on terror is, in order to prosecute the war, you've got to understand the nature of the enemy. There's a debate about whether this is a law-enforcement operation or is it a war, and, obviously, I believe it is a war and it requires all tools at our disposal, whether it be military or intelligence or cutting off the finances.[60]

Perhaps most significantly, Bush made it clear that it would be a conflict against regimes not against nations or their peoples. Colin Powell later recalled that the reference to an Axis was designed to capture the world's attention: "I approved it ... European audiences rebel against this kind of direct language, but they need to recognise that when Americans speak in a way that occasionally seems moralising, there may be a moral in there."[61]

The momentum generated by the "Axis of Evil" speech was maintained when the administration produced its "National Security Strategy" the following September. In his introduction to the report, Bush wrote:

The United States will use this moment of opportunity to expand the benefits of freedom across the globe. We will actively work to bring the hope of
democracy, development, free markets, and free trade to every corner of the
world.[62]

The mantra about the beneficial effects of democracy reflected the neo-
conservative agenda. However, the National Security Strategy of 2002 also
reflected other strands of thinking within the administration. Rice's *Realpolitik*
was given emphasis when the document mentioned the need for "building good
relations among the great powers". Moreover, Rumsfeld's desire to see America
prevent threats by taking them out at source and Powell's more measured
approach of relying on deterrence and relationships with allies were also there.
In Rumsfeld's case, the document was quite stark: "[T]he United States will, if
necessary, act pre-emptively."[63]

The National Security Strategy, therefore, revived theories of preventive and
pre-emptive war that had been developed to explain approaches to nuclear
warfare in the late 1950s. The legalistic approach to international relations that
found favour after 1945 tended to categorise any conduct of war other than that
taken in self-defence as an act of aggression.[64] Pre-emptive war, which involves
eradicating a specific threat just as it is about to materialise, can be justified
within the bounds of international law. Preventive war cannot because the perceived threat is not imminent nor even obvious. In his work on nuclear strategy,
Lawrence Freedman has described the common misperception that the distinctions between these notions is "no more than a couple of letters and a hyphen".[65]

In order to avoid being seen to break international law when its very policy was
to challenge those states and terror groups that were willing to act illegally, the
Bush Administration emphasised pre-emption even where it actually pursued a
policy of prevention. Michael Walzer makes a good point when he says that
"[p]erhaps the gulf between pre-emption and prevention has now narrowed so that
there is little strategic (and, therefore, little moral) difference between them".[66]

On the other hand, Reilly has argued that the erosion of "true" pre-emption
would only create instability in international relations as accepted norms of
behaviour were eradicated: "This current mismatch points to a potential lack of
balance in the ends, ways, and means construct that enables the successful execution of a national security strategy."[67]

Jon Sumida has recently argued that Clausewitz clearly rejected both pre-
emptive and preventive war as legitimate defensive options in Book VI, Chapter
8 of *On War*. Sumida believes that Clausewitz demonstrated the reasoning that
the Bush Administration lacked prior to invading Iraq:

Since defense is tied to the idea of waiting, the aim of defeating the enemy
will be valid only on the condition that there is an attack. If no attack is
forthcoming, it is understood that the defense will be content to hold its own
... The defense will be able to reap the benefits of the stronger form of war
only if it is willing to be more satisfied with this modest goal.[68]

The flaw in Sumida's argument, like so many of the "if Clausewitz were alive today" variety, is simply that times have changed. There are elements of Clausewitz's thought that are immutable, possibly including his view that defence is the stronger form of war. However, in an age when rogue states and terrorists are attempting to acquire weapons of mass destruction, there is a danger of interpreting Clausewitz literally and then taking it out of context and applying it to another time and place.

The emphasis placed by the Bush Administration on pre-emption, first in Afghanistan and then in Iraq, has been criticised for taking place in a strategic vacuum. Of course, the need to act with urgency after 11 September was unavoidable. Indeed, Bush could be said to have acted with some restraint in not beginning his counter-offensive for almost a month despite the impulse to act immediately. Nevertheless, there is some truth in the opinion of Hew Strachan, for example. He perhaps goes too far in accusing the United States of abandoning strategy, but he is right to suggest that pre-emption was taken out of context and became a driver of foreign policy rather than a principle of military operations.[69]

Notwithstanding this critique, containing al-Qa'eda was not an option. Lieutenant-Colonel Michael Morris has correctly interpreted al-Qa'eda as being an insurgent force whose message appeals to significant numbers of Muslims rather than an out-and-out terrorist organisation. The scale of its operations across the globe indicates an insurgency, while its cellular structure is more in keeping with that of a terrorist group. Certainly, prior to 11 September, when it operated with impunity from its main base in Afghanistan, al-Qa'eda could conduct its operations overtly. Once the United States counter-offensive against it began in October 2001, it was forced to operate in a more covert manner. The insurgency model suggests that the rhetoric of a "War on Terror" is mistaken and that what is really required is the sort of approach one would take to dealing with an insurgency.[70]

Christopher Daase has described the War on Terror as "a small war writ large", which comes close to Clausewitz's notion, articulated in his *Bekenntnis-denkschrift*, of "pure self-defence" whereby human dignity and justice are peripheral concerns.[71] Given this erosion in moral and legal constraints, Michael Evans has described a trend in warfare that has seen a blurring of the once-clear distinction between high-intensity and low-intensity conflicts. Such a trend has been seen in Afghanistan and Iraq where the transition to so-called post-conflict operations has been very difficult to control. Evans cites two of the authors of FM 100–5 during the 1980s, Huba Wass de Czege and Richard Sinnreich, in support of his contention:

> Clear distinctions between conventional and unconventional conflicts are fading, and any future major conflict is almost certain to see a routine commingling of such operations. Similarly, once useful demarcations between front and rear or between theater and strategic operations will continue to evaporate as the instrumentalities [*sic*] of war become more

interdependent and, as is increasingly true of communications and space systems, less easily separable from their civilian and commercial counterparts.[72]

The War on Terror seems to have as its objective the removal of the roots of terrorism. The means to achieving this end is a series of campaigns designed to prevent the use of terror tactics by sub-state groups such as al-Qa'eda, and also the removal of any possibility that so-called "rogue" states might use, or proliferate the possession of, weapons of mass destruction. Given that the attacks of 11 September were the origin of this conflict, it could be said that the wider struggle against states with weapons of mass destruction removes the focus from the immediate cause of the conflict. However, underlying everything is the assumption that the anti-Western interests of terrorist networks and rogue states could coalesce so as to make them indistinguishable from each other. As Niall Ferguson has written, "Clausewitz would have had no difficulty in recognizing ... the parallel war ... against states 'harboring' or otherwise supporting terrorist organizations."[73]

As we have seen, Clausewitz identified a number of moral and physical centres of gravity, including capital cities, alliances, public opinion, and the personalities of enemy leaders. It might therefore be assumed that the leadership of al-Qa'eda is the movement's Clausewitzian centre of gravity. However, Echevarria has convincingly argued that the real centre of gravity is an ideological one – that is, al-Qa'eda's hatred of apostasy, a factor that has its roots in a radical interpretation of Islam. The defeat of al-Qae'da would, therefore, require more than just the death or capture of bin Laden and his closest associates. It would need the execution of a strategy based on diplomacy and economic means backed by the will to use military force if required. The centre of gravity is organic, and its destruction relies on effects, whether military, diplomatic or economic.[74]

The ideology of al-Qa'eda is crucial in motivating its members to continue their struggle against seemingly overwhelming odds. While the West possesses large technological and economic advantages, it is the social aspect of war that could prove to be its undoing. In contrast to the generally held perception that Clausewitz saw the physical destruction of the enemy's army as the key to victory, moral factors were of more significance to him. Not only did he allude to the morale of the enemy's army but, in recognition of the wider strategic situation, he paid equal attention to the need to break the will of the enemy people:

> The effect of all this [that is, defeat in battle] outside the army – on the people and on the government – is a sudden collapse of the most anxious expectations, and a complete crushing of self-confidence. This leaves a vacuum that is filled by a corrosively expanding fear which completes the paralysis. It is as if the electric charge of the main battle had sparked a shock to the whole nervous system of one of the contestants.[75]

The 11 September attacks, therefore, simultaneously affected all three dimensions of the Clausewitzian trinity. Its continuing relevance was obvious from even a cursory examination of contemporary events. While the trinity is vital from the counter-terrorist's perspective, al-Qa'eda is aware, in the words of Clausewitz, of the importance of the people's "violence and passion". This can be seen in its use of the al-Jazeera satellite television station to broadcast its propaganda videos.[76]

Conclusion

Whether or not a Revolution in Military Affairs is the military manifestation of globalisation, advocates of transformation have set the pace in contemporary American military thought at the turn of the twenty-first century by formulating concepts such as effects-based operations and asymmetrical warfare. The doctrinal publications, JP 3–0 and FM 3–0 of 2001, drew on this thinking. However, while each manual confirmed the importance of conducting joint operations, neither provided evidence of developing joint thinking to the extent where a joint theory of war could be developed beyond platitudes about "full spectrum" operations. For example, Echevarria has commented that in trying to achieve a consensus from the services' diverse interpretations of the centre of gravity, JP 3–0 "defined CoGs too broadly and offered no real method for determining them".[77]

The events of 11 September 2001 provided the neo-conservatives of the Bush Administration with an opportunity to put into practice their vision for a "new American century" that would see democratic values spread across the world. However, whereas Clinton had sought to do this through "assertive multilateralism", the Bush Administration was emboldened by the events of 11 September to take unilateral pre-emptive action if necessary. But self-defence, rather than pre-emption, was the justification for invading Afghanistan in October 2001 so as to attack the centre of al-Qa'eda's operations. The use of special forces, airpower and indigenous forces on the ground was extolled by Max Boot as demonstrating a "new American way of war". However, the age-old problems of conducting war that had exercised Clausewitz's mind remained. General Franks, for example, commented that Operation Anaconda "showed heroism, it showed fog, uncertainty, it showed friction – elements common to every war I think we've ever fought".[78]

More generally, the War on Terror being waged by the United States and its allies can be accommodated within Clausewitz's concept of real war, particularly the extent to which war's intensity varies by degree. In developing a strategy to counter al-Qa'eda, the Bush Administration had to tailor limited means – placing constraints on the degree of force that could be used – with decisive ends – the neutralisation, if not the destruction, of al-Qa'eda and like-minded terrorist organisations. For al-Qa'eda, the conflict would end successfully only with the total defeat of the enemy. For example, bin Laden spoke of the pursuit of the acquisition of weapons of mass destruction by his organisation as a "religious duty".[79]

10 Iraq – invasion and insurgency

Operation "Iraqi Freedom"

At the time of writing, US and British armed forces have been in Iraq for three years. The invasion and occupation of that country has caused more controversy in US foreign policy than any other single event since the Vietnam War. With the benefit of hindsight, it is easy for critics to point to the difficulties the Coalition has faced in trying to counter a violent insurgency as a reason why the invasion should never have occurred in the first place. Moreover, it has become evident that one of the major justifications for invading Iraq – thwarting the regime's attempt to revive its weapons of mass destruction programme – was based on a false premise, deliberate or otherwise. Nevertheless, one should avoid falling into the trap of historical determinism, and instead base any assessment of the reasons for invasion on what was known at the time. Unless, or until, new evidence emerges, perhaps from key members of the Bush Administration, any other approach would be ahistorical and likely only to feed those intent on seeing conspiracy theories in every action of the administration.

Paul O'Neill, former Treasury secretary, has said that war against Iraq was on the Bush Administration's agenda prior to 11 September. However, one needs to go back much further in time for the origins of the conflict. Operation Iraqi Freedom was the culmination of a series of events that had begun with the Iraqi invasion of Kuwait in August 1990. These events had included full-scale warfare to oust Iraq from Kuwait; punitive air strikes to intimidate Saddam Hussein; a stringent inspections process to ensure that his regime's WMD were being destroyed; a sanctions regime intent on punishing Saddam without harming the Iraqi people; and countless resolutions by the UN Security Council to rein the Iraqis in. By early 2003, however, Saddam remained firmly in power. The strategy of sanctions backed by the threat of force in the shape of airpower had been a failure, while the expulsion of UN weapons inspectors from the country had left unanswered the question as to what had happened to Saddam's arsenal of biological and chemical weapons. As Niall Ferguson succinctly puts it: "[T]he overthrow of Saddam was as much post-emption as pre-emption, since Saddam had done nearly all the mischief of which he was capable some time before March 2003."[1]

In November 2001, President Bush apparently asked Donald Rumsfeld to review the military's planning for an invasion of Iraq. Over the coming months, this process was encouraged by those within the administration who were intent on deposing Saddam, notably Vice-President Cheney and Under-Secretary of State for Defense Paul Wolfowitz. Indeed, the latter has been described by Bob Woodward as "the intellectual godfather and fiercest advocate for doing so". Publicly, Bush's "Axis of Evil" speech of January 2002 served more notice on Saddam.[2]

Despite its determination to act unilaterally if necessary, the Bush Administration did make some attempts to ensure that it received the blessing of the UN for its policy. In November 2002, the Security Council was unanimous in its view that Iraq had failed to disclose fully details of its nuclear, biological and chemical weapons programmes as well as repeatedly obstructing efforts to gain access to its weapons sites and being in breach of the disarmament demands made on it by the UN. Security Council Resolution 1441 was therefore passed, stipulating that the Iraqi regime come clean about its weapons programme. Colin Powell later explained the rationale behind this:

> In Resolution 1441 ... we gave Saddam an entry-level test: give us a declaration that answers all the outstanding questions. He failed the test of the resolution. It became a question that he was hiding something, that he was going to drag this out until the international community lost interest.[3]

However, the Security Council failed to explicitly authorise military action to force the Iraqis to comply. Over the next few months, UN weapons inspectors were involved in a game of cat and mouse with the Iraqi regime as they attempted to audit the Iraqis' inventory of unconventional weapons. In March 2003, the US and the United Kingdom returned to the Security Council only to find that France and Germany had mobilised opposition to any military action, which effectively ruled out any hope of obtaining UN authorisation to invade Iraq.

The intelligence assessments of Saddam's WMD programme have been heavily excoriated by those opposed to the war in Iraq. Certainly, there was some misuse of intelligence, which was exaggerated to make it look as if Saddam had a capability to launch missiles tipped with biological or chemical warheads at short notice. Examined objectively, and without the benefit of seeing the raw intelligence presented to policymakers, one can only agree with Robert Jervis who argues that Clausewitz was right to warrant caution about intelligence:

> It is clear that Iraq was a case of collection failure in that the evidence collected was scattered, ambiguous, and often misleading. But this is just what Clausewitz would lead us to expect, and so it is harder to say whether it was a failure in terms of what is usual and whether reforms are likely to produce marked improvement.[4]

In an imperfect world, intelligence is ambiguous and can be interpreted to suggest that the object of the intelligence is acting in a way that accords with one's worst fears. In the case of Iraq, this could be corroborated by pointing to the regime's history, which showed that it was willing to deploy chemical weapons as well as going to great lengths to conceal its having them. In June 2003, McGregor Knox made a very telling observation about this question:

> "Regime change" in Iraq seemed imperative not because Saddam necessarily still had WMD – although the Coalition, judging by the rubber suits the troops initially wore, genuinely feared that he did – but because his continuance in power and his oil wealth guaranteed that he *would* have them again if he survived.[5]

Melvin Laird, Nixon's secretary of defense during the Vietnam War, has cogently argued that, whatever the truth about WMD, no one could accuse the United States of gradually and incrementally slipping into war with Iraq as had been the case in Vietnam.[6]

Central Command was charged with overseeing planning for Operation Iraqi Freedom but found that its initial option of a repeat of Desert Storm, albeit with a two-week air campaign prior to the land assault, was not in keeping with Rumsfeld's belief that transformation had dispensed with the need to deploy the huge numbers of manpower required to mount such a campaign. It was an attitude that believed mass could be replaced by effects. The commander of CENTCOM, General Tommy Franks, was certainly in tune with Rumsfeld's preference for a "lite" option: "This is not 1990. The Iraqi military today is not the one we faced in 1991. And our own forces are much different. We see that in Afghanistan. We need to refine our assumptions."[7]

The Allied land force that invaded Iraq on 20 March 2003 would number less than 100,000 men. It consisted mainly of 3rd Infantry Division, which had some 200 M1A1 Abrams tanks and 250 M2 Bradley fighting vehicles, and the 1st Marine Expeditionary Force, which deployed 120 Abrams tanks. These forces were supplemented by the 11th Aviation Regiment, the 101st Airborne Division, and a brigade from the 82nd Airborne Division as well as the British 1st (Armoured) Division. The plan had envisaged an entry into northern Iraq from Turkey by 4th Infantry Division. However, the Turkish parliament refused to admit American troops on its soil and, in the end, the 4th Infantry Division ended up serving as a deception force whereby the Pentagon encouraged the Iraqis to believe that there would be no attack prior to the arrival of this unit in the south.

Anthony Sidoti has speculated that, given his exposure to Clausewitz's theories as a graduate of both the Army War College and the Armed Forces Staff College, as well as 35 years of experience in the army, Franks must have influenced his planners "to use the framework described in *On War* when developing the combat plans" for Iraqi Freedom.[8] This is perhaps a leap of faith, though the plan undoubtedly supported a clear political objective: that of regime change. The plan itself dispensed with the need for an independent air campaign. Instead, air operations would be conducted simultaneously to the land invasion as part of a truly joint effort. Saddam would, therefore, have no opportunity to gather support internationally to "halt the air bombing", while at the same time it would reduce his ability to prepare to defend Iraq through setting his oilfields alight and deploying his forces in a defensively effective manner. It also ensured that there would be some element of surprise to be derived from the offensive. Franks predicted on the eve of the campaign that it would be "unlike any other in history ... characterized by shock, by surprise, by flexibility, by the employment of precise munitions on a scale never before seen, and by the application of overwhelming force".[9]

The opening aerial assault, which looked to decapitate the regime by destroying a target at which Saddam was apparently meeting his top aides, was launched 24 hours before the operation was due to begin. One of the most overused soundbites about the way in which the Revolution in Military Affairs has allegedly changed the American way of war is "shock and awe". This term originated in a work written by Harlan Ulman and James Wade, jun. in 1996 called *Shock and Awe: Achieving Rapid Dominance*.[10] Yet, when Bush approved the use of cruise missiles and F-117 aircraft to attack the target on the basis of intelligence reports, this was precisely the intended effect. However, it failed to kill Saddam and it was not until the night of 21 March that the full force of the airpower available to the Coalition was unleashed against Baghdad. Even then, some 500 targets were off-limits because of the fear of collateral damage, which was in keeping with the political purpose of the war that it was intended to liberate the Iraqi people. Many air attacks were pre-planned, though some were planned after the aircraft involved had taken off as "targets of opportunity" became apparent. Colonel Howard Belote, USAF, has argued that the air campaign saw Clausewitz's view of physical destruction and psychological paralysis go hand in hand. For example, on the night of 25–26 March, five of the six Republican Guard divisions defending Baghdad tried to move south of the capital to confront the advancing Coalition land forces. The Iraqis were attrited by the use of surveillance and targeting from the air. The air component commander, Lieutenant-General Michael Moseley, had actually returned to the theories of Clausewitz in his war plan and deviated from those of John Boyd and John Warden. Moseley was as interested in destruction as he was in paralysis: "I find it interesting when folks say we're softening them [the Iraqis] up ... We're not softening them up. We're killing them."[11]

The land invasion plan stipulated a twin-pronged assault by V Corps, under the command of General William Wallace, and I Marine Expeditionary Force, under the command of Lieutenant-General James Conway. Fifth Corps was to advance north from the Kuwaiti border towards Baghdad, following the course of the Euphrates River and bypassing the main towns on the way. I MEF would support it by protecting its eastern flank and isolating the capital from the east. CENTCOM accepted the logistical risk involved in going "light" through the conviction that speed, information and precise firepower would overcome any difficulties. Given his simultaneous responsibility for operations in Afghanistan, Franks made Lieutenant-General David McKiernan, commander of the US 3rd Army, the land component commander for Iraqi Freedom. What was remarkable about command and control was the lack of a footprint. For example, Wallace's forward headquarters consisted of only 80 soldiers, three command and control vehicles, and ten other vehicles. The available bandwidth was sufficient to maintain communications with other commanders in the chain of command.[12]

The initial speed of the American advance was unprecedented, with V Corps covering 350 miles in three days before sandstorms (known locally as *shamal*) and the need for resupply caused it to halt. The Marines also advanced swiftly before being held up at Nasiriyah, which required a week to clear. The Americans also encountered resistance from the paramilitary fedayeen, which Saddam had formed after the end of the Gulf War to ensure that any further revolts against his regime would be crushed. The fedayeen's tactics were based on those of the Somali militias that had fought the Americans a decade earlier, using armed pickup trucks mounting machine guns and rocket-propelled grenades. The fedayeen were deployed in the cities that lay along the route of the American advance. Wallace was certainly surprised when the fedayeen emerged from the urban areas "to attack ... our formations, when any expectation was that they would be defending those towns and not be as aggressive".[13]

It has been argued, with hindsight, that the fedayeen turned out to be a more significant centre of gravity than the Republican Guard.[14] When planning the campaign, the Americans saw Baghdad as an important centre of gravity – hence the drive towards the city – and the Republican Guard as being equally significant. Given the regime's reliance on the Republican Guard during the previous decades, its destruction would signal to Saddam that he was about to relinquish his grip on power. In the event, the fedayeen's emergence from the cities of southern Iraq made it a potential centre of gravity whose neutralisation would not necessarily endanger the regime but would make the advance on Baghdad easier. The decimation of the Republican Guard after 25 March dealt a fatal blow to Saddam. He gambled that the *shamal* would ground Coalition aircraft and therefore decided to move his forces forward to confront the threat to Baghdad only to have his forces completely nullified by airpower.

The Coalition had had its own encounter with the effects of friction. On the night of 22 March an air assault, led by 11th Aviation Regiment, had attempted to soften up Iraqi forces prior to their being engaged on the ground by the 3rd Infantry Division. The use of low-flying Apache helicopters in poor conditions caused by the blow-up from the desert sands below reduced the strength of the force by one-third at the outset. The mission was then put back three hours, news of which failed to reach the elements of the Air Force supporting the mission. The result was that the suppressing fire from the Air Force took place some time before the Apaches arrived, alerting the Iraqis who then ambushed the Apache force with a hail of small-arms fire and rocket-propelled grenades. Fortunately, only one helicopter was lost in the operation.

On 29 March, Bush decided that there was no need to reinforce the push for

Baghdad and ordered that it should continue. By this stage, the strength of the Republican Guard's Medina Division defending the approaches to the city had been reduced to only 20 per cent effectiveness, which was typical of the other units operating with it. Indeed, some units had had their radios removed to prevent any revolt against the regime.[15] As the advance resumed, the Republican Guard put up only token resistance. Franks transferred his reserve force – a brigade from 82nd Airborne Division – to V Corps. It was given the task of ending Iraqi resistance at Samawah and Najaf in conjunction with troops from the 101st Airborne Division. The 3rd Infantry Division, meanwhile, was to push north through the Karbala Gap. The main focus for airpower would be switched in the coming days to attacking the Iraqi forces defending the Karbala Gap and the approach to Baghdad. Fifth Corps' assault was backed by I MEF, which would swing due east, cross the Tigris, and approach Baghdad from the southeast. The twin moves of V Corps and I MEF had the effect of drawing the remaining Republican Guard units out of position, allowing them to be attacked from the air, and leaving the capital vulnerable to a land assault. "[O]ne saw a situation where operational maneuver set almost perfect conditions for US forces to fire on their enemy."[16]

With the Iraqis distracted by the operations of the 101st Air Assault Division and the Marines, 3rd Infantry Division was able to seize an opportunity to break through the Karbala Gap by crossing the Euphrates on 2 April despite the fact that the Iraqis had strapped explosives to the bridges. It later transpired that Saddam was convinced the Americans would not seek to take Baghdad and, therefore, he wanted the bridges left intact so his forces could move south and crush any revolt that might take place after the cessation of hostilities. Once it became clear that the Americans were intent on entering Baghdad, Saddam belatedly ordered that the bridges be demolished. However, it was too late to stop the American advance. Williamson Murray and Robert Scales, paraphrasing the Elder Moltke, have said of the breakthrough at Karbala, "the 'Iraqis did not survive first contact with the plan' ".[17]

The Americans were conscious of the danger of becoming involved in protracted urban warfare once their forces had entered Baghdad. As a means of testing the water, it was decided to send some probing forces into the city through the use of "thunder runs". The first of these occurred after dawn on 5 April, when an armoured task force from the 101st Airborne Division entered the city and encountered heavy resistance from fedayeen before returning to base that afternoon. However, only one tank was immobilised while the other vehicles in the task force would be up and running once routine repairs were made. The Americans had demonstrated that they could penetrate to the heart of the city without taking casualties as well as showing the effectiveness of heavy armour in modern warfare. The following day, another task force ran the gauntlet of small arms fire and rocket-propelled grenades. This time, however, it stayed in the city. Robert Citino has described the use of thunder runs as "the one legitimate innovation" of Iraqi Freedom.[18]

The evidence from the thunder runs persuaded the American command that resistance in Baghdad was reeling. The order was therefore given for 3rd Infantry Division and 1st Marine Division to enter the city from the west and east respectively. On 7 April, American intelligence passed on information that Saddam and his sons were meeting at a location in Baghdad's Al Mansur district. A B-1 bomber was ordered to destroy the site with two bunker-busting bombs; but, as had been the case at the outset of the campaign, the quarry had escaped. The following day, central Baghdad was occupied, effectively finishing off Saddam's regime.

After the Turks had rebutted the request to deploy 4th Infantry Division through their territory, a low-level campaign along the lines of that in Afghanistan had been conducted in northern Iraq involving special forces, airpower and Kurdish irregulars. The key cities of Mosul, Kirkuk, and Tikrit were all captured. The fall of the latter, Saddam's home town, on 14 April effectively brought the war to an end.

On 1 May 2003, Bush gave a valediction of the campaign onboard USS *Abraham Lincoln* off San Diego, California. The speech has been castigated for taking place under a banner entitled "Mission Accomplished". Nevertheless, it revealed his thinking behind the campaign's military conduct:

> Today, we have the greater power to free a nation by breaking a dangerous and aggressive regime. With new tactics and precision weapons, we can achieve military objectives without directing violence against civilians. No device of man can remove the tragedy from war; yet it is a great moral advance when the guilty have far more to fear from the war than the innocent.[19]

Iraqi Freedom therefore illustrated the way in which strategic airpower had developed since its conception in the 1920s as a means of terrifying civilian populations through saturation bombing. Now, the emphasis on precision means that it is increasingly possible to spare civilians while attacking targets that are vital to the functioning of the enemy regime. The potential downside to this is the temptation for politicians to interfere in the targeting process.[20] Belote has written that the campaign also illustrated the extent to which the field forces of the enemy were now as much strategic targets as command and control and critical infrastructure: "Seen through a Clausewitzian lens, Iraqi Freedom air operations highlight joint success and recast the airpower debate: fielded forces can be centers of gravity and strategic targets, and paralysis is a means – not 'the perfection of strategy'."[21]

Iraqi Freedom illustrated the benefits of joint effects and the judicious mix of manoeuvre through speed and attrition through firepower. Although much can be made of the technological advantages enjoyed by the Coalition, including the benefits of weapons such as the Joint Direct Attack Munition and unmanned aerial vehicles, victory was as much down to the training, discipline and unit cohesion of American and British troops, which contrasted sharply with that of the Iraqis. These elements were also obvious in the Gulf War, but Iraqi Freedom involved a far larger theatre of operations where a much smaller force achieved its objectives in almost half the time that Desert Storm had taken while suffering one-third of the casualties. Moreover, as Williamson Murray has pointed out:

> Virtually everything in the planning and preparation, the conduct, and the results of the Iraq War underline that Clausewitz's understanding of the fundamental nature of war is much closer to reality than the technological dreams produced in the last decade.[22]

The Iraqi insurgency

With the end of combat operations, the United States and its Coalition partners found themselves in control of a country that had been artificially created in the 1920s. Iraq consists of a Shia majority with two sizeable minorities in its Sunni and Kurdish populations. Trying to reconcile the demands of each ethnic group without allowing the country to fracture would prove to be a much more daunting challenge than removing Saddam from power. Colin Powell had raised this point with Bush in August 2002: "My caution was that you need to understand that the difficult bit will come afterwards – the military piece will be easy. [Iraq] will crack like a crystal goblet and it'll be a problem to pick up the bits."[23]

The US military approached the Iraqi campaign on the basis of a four-phase planning cycle, which encompassed deterrence and engagement, seizing the initiative, decisive combat operations and post-combat operations. Joint doctrine stipulates that the termination of combat operations should be considered from the outset when planning a campaign. In the case of Operation Iraqi Freedom, planning for post-combat operations was the responsibility of the Pentagon's Organization for Reconstruction and Humanitarian Assistance, which was formed in January 2003 and was initially headed by General Jay Garner. Unfortunately, this office was understaffed, poorly prepared, and slow to deploy to Iraq. Moreover, there was little co-ordination between it and the military planners who planned the phase of decisive combat operations even though there is considerable overlap between the two phases. The administration's espousal of neo-conservative thinking, which insisted that the Coalition would be welcomed as liberators and that democracy would, therefore, take root, tended to disfigure any clear planning for what would come after the "liberation".[24]

The American military has traditionally focused on winning wars and not on what comes afterwards. This disjoint between the military and diplomatic phases is a historical legacy of the way in which civil–military relations had developed in the United States. The Bush Administration had somewhat encouraged the military's reluctance to participate in nation-building and peace-support operations by expressing its disdain for such activities in the past. Moreover, there had been a clear inability on the part of the military to pay more than lip service to lessons from previous such activities despite its rich experience in conducting "small wars". Post-combat operations were allocated a low priority by

CENTCOM during the planning for the conflict, given its preoccupation with decisive combat operations.[25]

A major problem also arose in terms of the numbers of troops it was thought necessary to deploy once decisive combat operations had ceased. In February 2003, the chief-of-staff of the US Army, General Eric Shinseki, had informed the Senate that "several hundred thousand" troops would be required to maintain order in Iraq. However, buoyed by the success of the relatively small force that had toppled the Ba'ath regime, the Office of the Secretary of Defense and other officials in the administration were convinced that a post-Saddam Iraq would require even fewer troops to stabilise the country.[26]

Even as Iraq was being liberated, problems were being confronted by the Coalition in terms of having to deal with minor criminals in the form of looters as well as lingering resistance from erstwhile supporters of Saddam. Third Infantry Division (Mechanized), which found itself occupying Baghdad, was forced to improvise having received no instructions regarding the post-combat phase of operations. At the time Baghdad fell there were only 100,000 troops on the ground. If one had a similar ratio of troops to population as existed in Kosovo, then there would have been 480,000 troops in Iraq. Paul Bremer, who replaced Garner in May 2003, later conceded that there were not enough troops on the ground to deal with the transition to post-combat operations. Powell concurred with this view in early 2005 when he said "[m]y own preference would have been for more forces after the conflict".[27]

However, it has been argued that having a large force at the beginning of the occupation may have reduced the ability of the Coalition to maintain such levels through time, given constraints on force structure.[28] Furthermore, the perceived unilateral character of the war severely diminished the prospects of significant Allied contributions beyond those provided by the United Kingdom and Poland. Even after it formally accepted the occupation in May 2004, the UN's involvement was complicated by its traditional model of peacekeeping, which assumes that there is a permissive environment in which to operate. This was not the case in Iraq.

On succeeding Garner, Bremer immediately replaced the Organization for Reconstruction and Humanitarian Assistance with the Coalition Provisional Authority. He also introduced a number of other initiatives that included the "Dissolution of the Entities" Order of 23 May 2003. This decreed a policy of "de-Ba'athification", which, though in keeping with the Bush Administration's desire to hunt down the key members of Saddam's regime who were on the run, had the effect of alienating thousands of ordinary Iraqis who could have assisted the Coalition in getting the country back up on its feet. Although Bremer rescinded his order a month later, the damage had been done. Some 400,000 Iraqi soldiers had been affected by the order. This only exacerbated the problem posed by the Iraqi Army in that there had been no formal surrender. Instead, Iraqi soldiers had simply melted back into the population, creating a condition ripe for an insurgency to flourish. At first, it mainly involved ex-regime elements, but it soon spread to include Sunnis who, though a minority in the country, had traditionally made up the ruling elite. On 16 July 2003, the new commander of CENTCOM, General John Abizaid, confessed that attacks on Coalition forces in Iraq "bear the hallmarks of a 'classic guerrilla-type campaign'".[29]

The insurgency gathered apace during the latter half of 2003. It assumed a particularly brutal nature when foreign jihadists linked to al-Qa'eda began to infiltrate Iraq. Their figurehead became the Jordanian Abu Musab al-Zarqawi and their tactics included the use of improvised explosive devices, small arms, rocket-propelled grenades, mortar attacks, kidnappings, beheadings and suicide operations using motor vehicles. Generally, the insurgents avoided making themselves conspicuous targets for American firepower by operating among the population or by acting in small groups. Excepting the use of night-vision devices and Global Positioning Systems, American troops had no appreciable advantages over insurgents when conducting close-in operations of the type the latter encourage.[30]

Many of those opposed to invading Iraq in the first place had argued that it would shift the focus of American strategy from the more important issue of confronting terrorism. For example, former national security adviser, Brent Scowcroft, had warned that attacking Iraq would result in a "serious degradation in international co-operation with us against terrorism".[31] In the event, the Iraq War and the War on Terror became conflated. While this may have been advantageous to some degree to an administration that had argued that Saddam was a major sponsor of international terrorism, it also gave al-Qa'eda an opportunity to expose the vulnerability of the Iraqi occupation.

A centre of gravity in any insurgency is the people. Winning over moderate Iraqi and Arab opinion would be crucial to the intention of ensuring that Iraq would become a pluralistic society. However, such opinion was alienated early on with the revelations of torture and humiliation of Iraqi prisoners by American troops at the notorious Abu Ghraib prison in Baghdad. American strategy for countering the insurgency was made on the hoof as the administration reacted to what were unforeseen events. Rumsfeld summed up this approach in a memorandum to his senior staff of 16 October 2003: "Are we capturing, killing or deterring and dissuading more terrorists every day than the madrassas and the radical clerics are recruiting, training and deploying against us?"[32]

Gradually, strategy dictated a combination of activities to win hearts and minds, and a determination to neutralise the effectiveness of the insurgent groups. Although intelligence is vital to such an approach, and despite the Americans' superiority in information systems, it is difficult to come by in the midst of a hostile populace and therefore only increases the friction inherent in operating in such an environment. In north central Iraq, the 1st Infantry Division attempted to forge partnerships with local civilian, religious and tribal leaders, as well as undertaking reconstruction of vital infrastructure. Coupled with this were the use of combat operations to kill or capture insurgents while building up indigenous security forces. There was also a conscious requirement to control media interpretations of the insurgency, which focused on "spectacular" attacks by insurgents and any collateral damage inflicted by American firepower. Not surprisingly, comparisons have been drawn with the way in which media coverage of the Tet Offensive undermined the American effort in Vietnam.[33]

Despite the capture of Saddam in December 2003, the insurgency increased in intensity during early 2004. As a Shia insurrection led by the Mahdi Army of the radical cleric, Moqtada al-Sadr, erupted in the south around Najaf, the Americans attempted to stabilise matters in the so-called "Sunni Triangle", which covered the provinces around Baghdad. The key stronghold of the insurgents here was the city of Fallujah. In April 2004, American troops entered the city to deprive the insurgency of the propaganda value of having self-proclaimed "liberated areas". In the event, the operation only bolstered the standing of the insurgents in Iraq and in the wider Islamic world. Rather than storm the city and risk world opprobrium, the Americans negotiated conditions whereby the city would come under the control of the "Fallujah Brigade" of the embryonic Iraqi security forces. In reality, the city would remain a major base from which insurgents could mount attacks on the Coalition. By the summer, it was firmly under the grip of a council of mujaheden, which co-ordinated the activities of a number of insurgent groups that gradually came under the spell of al-Zarqawi. Steven Metz and Raymond Millen described the April standoff as a "galvanizing" point for the insurgency. Lieutenant-Colonel Thomas Hayden was convinced that, in hindsight, it was the point at which the counterinsurgency began in earnest after the "vacillation, indecision, and signs of weakness" that led to the drawback. Meanwhile, by the end of August, al-Sadr's insurrection in the south had been nipped in the bud only by the intervention of the Grand Ayatollah Ali al-Sistani. However, al-Sadr remained free as a result. "[I]t would be difficult to defend the overall record [of the Americans], one of vacillation and inconstancy."[34]

In June 2004, the Americans ostensibly returned sovereignty to the Iraqi people in the shape of the Iraqi Governing Council. However, the country's security remained almost wholly dependent on the foreign military presence. By now, the Americans deployed some 123,000 troops in Iraq supported by 26,800 troops from other Coalition countries.[35] Operations were exerting a considerable strain on those units operating in the most intense areas of the insurgency. For example, one company of the 1st Marine Division had had one-third of its 185 troops killed or wounded during a six-month tour of Ramadi, an insurgent stronghold west of Fallujah, in 2004.[36] While these figures may have paled into insignificance beside the losses in Vietnam, there was another important difference overlooked by those making direct comparisons between the two conflicts. Whereas in Vietnam the Americans had a monolithic enemy, albeit comprised of both the regular North Vietnamese Army and the irregular Vietcong, in Iraq they faced a number of different groups with different objectives besides opposition to the occupation. Sectarian conflict between Sunnis, who had held the upper hand in Iraq since the 1920s, and Shia, who had suffered decades of oppression under Saddam, took place against the backdrop of occupation. Moreover, indigenous insurgents turned their ire on foreign jihadis as well as the Coalition. Trying to formulate a strategy to deal with such a situation is difficult. As Second Lieutenant Samuel Gras recently put it:

> Some groups can be placated by economic development or political inclusion while in other groups, the members must be killed or captured. As there are a variety of groups with disparate goals, there must likewise be a variety of counterinsurgency tactics.[37]

In November 2004, the Iraqi interim government gave its consent to Operation "Phantom Fury", a combined US–Iraqi offensive to clear Fallujah of insurgents. US Army armoured units that had been deployed during the fighting in Najaf during the summer were deployed with units of the I MEF as Task Force Fallujah. Prior to the attack, almost the entire population of 280,000 fled as intended by the Iraqi Governing Council and the coalition. The risk of collateral damage was thereby greatly reduced and meant that blast weapons could be used to enter dwellings. The fighting lasted for more than a week and was the most intense undertaken in an urban environment by the American military since the Vietnam War. The insurgents were crushed "in a swift campaign of coordinated, unremitting battalion-sized movements".[38] The city was cleared of insurgents at a cost of 31 American and eight Iraqi soldiers dead. The number of insurgents killed is unknown but reports suggest that between 1,200 and 2,000 perished. Most of the city's civilian population returned a few weeks later.[39]

A monograph on counter-insurgency written by Lieutenant-Colonel John Nagl, who served as an operations officer with a tank battalion near Fallujah in 2003, was distributed to every general in the army. Nagl's thesis was based on the contrast between US experience in Vietnam and that of the British in Malaya.[40] However, the Americans have been influenced as much by Israeli tactics in the West Bank and Gaza, as can be seen in the use of house demolitions, snipers, and a policy of targeted assassinations of terrorist leaders. Conversely, the insurgents are also adapting tactics used in that conflict. In particular, the use of improvised explosive devices is based on the knowledge acquired by Hizbollah in southern Lebanon.[41]

An article in *Military Review* by Brigadier Nigel Aylwin-Foster of the British Army offering a critique of American counterinsurgency operations in Iraq has recently sparked a debate within the US Army.[42] In spite of its obvious professionalism, Aylwin-Foster thought the US Army in Iraq was weighed down by bureaucracy, centralised command, and a penchant for offensive operations epitomised by the need for "large-scale kinetic maneuver" that was concerned with killing insurgents and not protecting the population. He pointed to the publication of an interim field manual, FM-Interim 3–07.22, *Counterinsurgency Operations*, in October 2004, well over a year after the insurgency began, as an example of the institutional inertia regarding the subject within the Army.[43] American counterinsurgency doctrine has gradually been revised in reaction to the Iraqi experience. A new manual being written at Fort Leavenworth, *United States Counter-Insurgency Doctrine*, will challenge the notion that firepower alone can defeat an insurgency. It will also articulate the paradoxical nature of such operations:

> [T]he more you protect your force, the less secure you are – military forces in compounds lose touch with the people who are the ultimate arbiters of victory; the more force you use, the less effective you are; sometimes doing nothing is the best reaction; and the best weapons for counter-insurgency do not fire bullets.[44]

Strategically, the outcome of major combat operations in Iraq looks irrelevant when compared to what has occurred afterwards. By the end of January 2005, the United States had lost 1,453 dead with another 10,740 wounded.[45] The country had been disrupted to such an extent that the outcomes associated with genuine reconstruction – the regular supply of electricity and water, for example – were only sporadic in some areas. True, elections were held in January and December 2005, but, given the need to defeat the insurgency, the Coalition finds itself at a potentially fatal disadvantage compared to the insurgents who need only avoid defeat. Contrary to his thinking at the time, Clausewitz's discussion about the "posting of guards" has very much become a strategic issue. Elections in volatile countries such as Iraq can also be seen as being a form of conflict derived from the Clausewitzian theory of war.[46]

Conclusion

The decisive combat operations phase during Operation Iraqi Freedom was an overwhelming success for the Coalition at the operational level. However, in the strategic context, it could be argued, in Clausewitzian parlance, that the American culminating point of victory was reached in April 2003. The American goal of regime change may have removed Saddam's regime but, as yet, it has not ensured that a stable regime fills the dangerous vacuum that resulted from the dictator's demise. Hopes that Iraq could be transformed in a manner similar to that of Germany and Japan after the Second World War have been dashed. As Barry Watts says:

> the most troubling manifestation of general friction in America's most recent conflicts has been achieving long-term political ends *after* the cessation of major combat operations ... [The] problem ... involves the recurring difficulties of connecting ends and means in war – difficulties that for Clausewitz were a basic source of friction.[47]

While friction cannot be eradicated, it can be ameliorated by sensible planning for foreseeable circumstances, which in the case of Iraq would have involved ensuring that the number of troops committed to the occupation would suffice to oversee the transition between decisive combat operations and the handover of power to a new Iraqi government.

Given the preoccupation with Iraq, the wider war on terror, now more realistically referred to by the Bush Administration as the "Long War", has been neglected elsewhere.[48] In Afghanistan, for example, stability has not been achieved. Al-Qa'eda and Taliban forces continue to function there, carrying out attacks against Coalition forces with the intention of testing Western political will to remain there for the long term.[49] American attempts to deal with rogue states have also been hindered. Iran, which seems intent on acquiring nuclear weapons, continues to defy international opinion in the knowledge that Iraq has overstretched American resources and also revealed the fissures in the UN Security Council.

Iraqi Freedom has also demonstrated the weaknesses in theories revolving around concepts such as rapid decisive operations. Although the warfighting phase of that campaign was rapid and decisive – though not necessarily an RDO in the purest sense of the term – post-combat operations have been anything but. Nebulous concepts such as RDO offer nothing of note to planners and policy-makers involved in attempting to control and administer vast expanses of terrain containing a hostile populace and concealing a ruthless adversary.

Conclusion

The main object of this work has been to examine American strategic thought since the Vietnam War and to demonstrate Clausewitzian influence upon it. In so doing, the work has also demonstrated a fundamental strategic truth: concerns at the tactical and operational level have as much of an impact upon strategy as vice versa. Cold War thinking tended to overlook this truth, or pay only lip service to it, given the concern with such notions of international relations as deterrence and arms control. Such myopia can also be detected in the contemporary debate over semantics regarding preventive and pre-emptive wars. Such attempts to see the big picture tend to overlook the detail inherent in the reality borne out in Clausewitz's contention that "all strategic planning rests on tactical success alone [and that] only great tactical successes lead to great strategic ones".[1]

Antulio Echevarria has described the way in which the debates held within the Imperial German Army during the late nineteenth century helped to define its thinking. The questions he poses are relevant to the American military of today:

> How should one coordinate the separate combat arms during the conduct of battle? How will new technologies ... impact leadership and command and control? What contributions of Clausewitz are still relevant? How useful are military-historical examples in the education of an officer and the development of doctrine? ... To what extent is it desirable to develop and prescribe principles of war?[2]

Taking each of these issues in turn, when the Vietnam War finished in 1973, the foremost concern of military thinkers with co-ordinating the separate combat arms revolved around the need for combined-arms operations in the land environment. The collaboration between the Army and the Air Force in the development of AirLand Battle advanced such concerns beyond the purview of one service. By the time the invasion of Iraq occurred 30 years later this concern had been transcended by the advent of joint warfare, which aimed to co-ordinate the environments of land, air, sea, and space into one seamless whole. New technologies, meanwhile, have impacted on command and control since Vietnam, but not necessarily in a positive way. The US military has paid lip service to the notion of *Auftragstaktik*, or what it calls "mission command". However, examples of contemporary command and control have been mixed. On the one hand, there are examples of commanders such as Lieutenant-General James Conway, USMC, in Operation Iraqi Freedom who "[a]lmost like a commander in the U.S. Civil War,... wanted to see, and be seen by, his Marines before the battle".[3]

On the other hand, thanks to the advent of C4ISTAR systems, which can detect events thousands of miles away in real time, there have been accusations of interference by the highest political authority in military operations – for example, in Kosovo and in Iraq. It is perhaps unrealistic, in an age of saturation media coverage, to think that the military can conduct operations without their political masters becoming involved in some shape or form. Although in this respect, Clausewitz's distinction between civilian politicians and the military is increasingly blurred, Hew Strachan believes that the military have allowed themselves to be cut off from policy considerations. "Today, the operational level of war occupies a politics-free zone. It speaks in a self-regarding vocabulary about manoeuvre, and increasingly 'manoeuvrism', that is almost metaphysical and whose inwardness makes sense only to those initiated in its meanings."[4]

Strachan highlights a technocratic approach that has been the hallmark of the American military since its inception.[5] John Stone has highlighted the military's continuing infatuation with technological fixes to arrive at a similar conclusion: "[T]he experience of 'Desert Storm' – along with subsequent doctrinal developments – appears to confirm the triumph of the technical tradition of limitation over its political counterpart in US strategic thought."[6]

This disjunction between policy and operations is an unintended consequence of the attempts by post-Vietnam reformers to overhaul what they saw as an attritional mentality within the US military. But, perhaps, it only serves to illustrate that the "American way of war", however interpreted, continues to be more about a way of winning battles rather than a way of winning wars.[7] The latter approach is very much in the Clausewitzian mould whereby military action is carried out to serve a political purpose.

The articulation of the relationship between war and policy is one of those "contributions of Clausewitz" that will always be relevant. Others of relevance today are those of friction, the centre of gravity, the concept of real war, and the fascinating trinity. Friction has revealed itself in many guises. Paul Bremer's fateful decision to disband the Iraqi Army in May 2003 helped to create the conditions of instability in which insurgency has thrived. Actual operations during the warfighting phase of Operation Iraqi Freedom illustrate the rapidity with which events can change, thereby confounding the best laid plans. The abortive air assault by 11th Aviation Regiment on 22 March is an example of this phenomenon. Iraq has shown that those advocates of a Revolution in Military Affairs who believed that technological superiority can lift the veil of the "fog of war" are wrong. Colonel Richard Hooker rightly says that war is inherently "anti-deterministic and non-linear" in character, which ensures that one theorist of war who matters "remains ... Clausewitz".[8]

The centre of gravity has played a key role in the development of American doctrine during the past 25 years. However, the military still lacks a clear and unambiguous definition of the concept. There is no consensus as to whether the centre of gravity is a source of strength or a source of vulnerability; nor is there any agreement on whether the centre of gravity is singular or whether it resides in several sources; nor is there any realisation as to whether it is applicable across the spectrum of conflict or only applies to wars designed to overthrow the enemy completely.

The best way to begin any understanding of Clausewitz is to learn about the nature of war. Only then can one understand that Clausewitz's distinction between absolute war and real war is a theoretical one. As Richard Henrick has written, there is a clear distinction between war's nature and its purpose: "That while the purpose of war is to serve a political end, the nature of war is to serve itself."[9]

Given this context, military men and policymakers need to concentrate on trying to understand all the variables that make up real war. The dualisms of annihilation and attrition at the strategic level, and of attrition and manoeuvre at the operational level have led to unnecessary debates that overlook the need for flexibility across the spectrum of war. War's intensity varies by degree. Clausewitz's most enduring legacy, aside from his interconnection of war and politics, lies in his rethinking of the nature of war: limited war can be just as effective as war waged at a higher level of intensity, something more apt than ever today.

The Clausewitzian concept of the fascinating trinity is applicable to all types of conflict for no conflict makes sense without the contribution of one or more of the trinity's elements. However, a problem lies in the incomplete form of *On War*. There is, for example, no analysis of the application of the trinity to the arming of the people beyond the implicit realisation that the passions of the people come into play. As Robert Baumann has written:

> Clausewitz did not describe in detail how future wars would be fought, but he was a futurist in his own right. In constructing a theory for thinking about war, he assumed that war's essential trinity would remain constant far beyond his lifetime.[10]

Examples of military history remain an important tool in US military education and as a way of illustrating concepts in doctrinal manuals. The problems being faced by the American military in Iraq have been put into historical perspective by commentators such as Lieutenant-Colonel John Nagl, who has used the examples of Malaya and Vietnam to make his case.[11] Nevertheless, there are concerns that the increasing tempo of operations is leaving officers with less time to reflect on their profession. One senior four-star army general informed Williamson Murray in 2004 that the quality of professional military education had reverted to the inadequate standards attained in the mid-1970s.[12]

At around that time, Ward Just wrote: "There has never been a Clausewitz in the American Army because the writing of [*On War*] took time and serious thought. An Army officer has no time to think, and imaginative reflection is discouraged."[13] *Plus ça change.*

These are worrying developments in a world where serious thought is required to deal with the fundamental problems thrown up by the consequences of globalisation, particularly that of international terrorism. Richard Lock-Pullan has described AirLand Battle as arising out of a process of introspection and innovation in the US Army designed to deal with complexity. He believes that a similar process is required in today's military. Moreover, Echevarria has said that the current generation of officers would be receptive to Clausewitz because they recognise the inadequacies of current doctrine as demonstrated in Iraq.[14]

After a period in the 1980s, when its keystone manual, FM 100–5, *Operations* (later renamed FM 3–0) became increasingly Clausewitzian, the American Army has reverted to Jomini's more scientific approach. Consequently, Brigadier-General (Retd.) Huba Wass de Czege wrote that "[t]he 1993 FM 100–5 took a step backward in evolving a sound theoretical basis for evolution into the future".[15]

The Jominian approach is reflected in a continuation of the tradition of "prescrib[ing] principles of war". The result is that quality doctrinal manuals, of which the Marine Corps' MCDP 1, *Warfighting*, of 1997 is the exemplar across the American military, are the exception rather than the rule. Even joint publications, of which JP 3–0, *Doctrine for Joint Operations*, is the most significant, tend to reflect the prescriptive tendencies of a Jominian "cookbook". Again, this is problematic when fighting insurgents and terrorists calls for flexibility. Wrong-headed attempts have been made to distinguish such operations from more traditional warfighting through the advent of "operations other than war". There is a need for the American military as a whole to follow the Clausewitzian approach of the marines in seeing conflict as "a wide range of forms constituting a spectrum which reflects the magnitude of violence involved".[16]

The process of military reform that took place in the United States after the Vietnam War can be compared to the revival in the Prussian military after its defeat by Napoleon in 1806, a revival in which Clausewitz played a practical part. This work has shown that his thought played some part in the American revival. The US military found Clausewitz to be a theorist whose writings were compatible with its desire to adopt the operational level of war and to ensure a seamless link between tactics and strategy. Though he was not the only theorist to influence military doctrine during this period, Clausewitz's work was more commonly drawn upon than anyone else's. Politicians found in him, albeit mainly second hand, a theorist who articulated the requirement that military power should be seen as an instrument of policy that, if wisely used, would benefit the national interest.

The sudden end of the Cold War, which was triggered by the revolutions across the Eastern Bloc in the winter of 1989/90, presented American strategists with a new set of challenges. Peace through strength had been vindicated. Now

American strategy had to adapt itself to the uncertain realities of a post-Cold War world. However, after the Gulf War, Clausewitzian thinking tended to be conspicuous by its absence among policymakers and the military. Events in Somalia, Bosnia and Kosovo were blighted by a reluctance on the part of the United States to become fully involved. Ironically, these half-hearted examples were as much a legacy of the Weinberger–Powell Doctrine, which was at least partly based on an interpretation of Clausewitz, as they were of peripheral concerns such as casualty avoidance.

The events of 11 September 2001 appeared to herald a new wave of decisiveness in American foreign policy. Operations in Afghanistan and during the warfighting phase of Operation Iraqi Freedom seemed to restore decision to the battlefield. However, the unravelling of the Bush Administration's Iraqi policy after May 2003 has once again called into question the efficacy of American strategic thought. Decisiveness on the battlefield does not mean that post-warfighting operations will be a mere tidying-up exercise. On the contrary, they require a degree of strategic dexterity that is lacking at present in American strategy. One can, therefore, only conclude that the Americans have come full circle in Iraq. One critique of the US Army in Iraq, written in 2005, could as easily have been penned in 1965 in relation to Vietnam:

> [T]he characteristic U.S. military intent has remained one of uncompromising destruction of the enemy's forces, rather than a more finely tuned harnessing of military effect to serve political intent – a distinction in the institutional understanding of military purpose that becomes highly significant when an army attuned to conventional warfare suddenly needs to adapt to the more subtle political framework of a [counterinsurgency] campaign.[17]

It is ironic that this is so. First Prussian and then German military men alluded to Clausewitz's concepts without fully recognising his admonition that the political realities behind war should not be ignored. As with their German predecessors, who have been studied relentlessly since 1945 in American military schools, the US military has recently achieved tactical and operational excellence without securing strategic success.[18] Where Clausewitz has been followed, it has tended to be because concepts such as the centre of gravity and culmination are perceived to be of value to tactics and operations. His more fundamental teaching about real war and the role of the trinity within it have been either misunderstood or ignored. Of course, politicians must take most of the blame for strategic ineptitude. At a time when threats to national security range from terrorists and rogue states armed with weapons of mass destruction to recidivist nations armed with high-tech conventional weapons, US military and civilian leaders must develop a way of reconciling operational success with clear strategic objectives across the whole spectrum of conflict. A close reading of *On War* would serve as a sound point of departure.

Notes

Introduction

1 Cited by C. Bassford, "Clausewitz and His Works", Online. Available www.clause-witz.com/CWZHOME/CWZSUMM/CWORKHOL.htm (accessed 19 April 2000).

2 C. Bassford, *Clausewitz in English – The Reception of Clausewitz in Britain and America, 1815–1945*, New York: Oxford University Press, 1994, p. 53. This refers to a lecture given by Luvaas at the US Army War College entitled "Clausewitz and the American Experience" between 1982 and 1987.

3 Bassford, *Clausewitz in English*, p. 6. Emphasis in the original. M. Howard, "The Influence of Clausewitz", introductory essay to C. von Clausewitz, *On War*, 2nd edn, Princeton, N.J.: Princeton University Press, 1984, trans. and ed. by M. Howard and P. Paret.

4 G. T. Hammond, *The Mind of War – John Boyd and American Security*, Washington, DC, Smithsonian Institution Press, 2001, p. 207. D. Moran, "Strategic Theory and the History of War", p. 6, online. Available www.clausewitz.com/CWZHOME/Bibl/Moran-StrategicTheory.pdf (accessed 8 September 2005). B. Brodie, "Strategy as an Art and Science", reprinted in *Naval War College Review*, Vol. 51, No. 1, Winter 1998, p. 27.

5 P. Paret, "Clausewitz: Life and Thought" in P. Paret, *Understanding War – Essays on Clausewitz and the History of Military Power*, Princeton, N.J.: Princeton University Press, 1992, p. 120.

6 Huba Wass de Czege (2000) "Clausewitz and FM 100–5", e-mail (22 June 2000).

7 R. Simpkin, *Race to the Swift – Thoughts on 21st Century Warfare*, London: Brassey's, 1985, p. 11. "Editors' Note", Clausewitz, op. cit., p. xi.

8 B. Fleming, "Can Reading Clausewitz Save Us from Future Mistakes?", *Parameters*, Vol. 34, No. 1, Spring 2004, p. 62.

9 Clausewitz, op. cit., Bk II, Ch. 2, p. 141.

10 Ibid.

11 Ibid.

12 "Disciples" of Clausewitz included such diverse theorists as Herman Kahn and Robert Osgood. H. Kahn, *On Thermonuclear War*, Princeton, N.J.: Princeton University Press, 1961; and R. Osgood, *Limited War – The Challenge to American Strategy*, Chicago: University of Chicago Press, 1957.

13 Cited by L. J. Matthews, "The Uniformed Intellectual and his Place in American Arms", *ARMY*, Vol. 52, No. 8, August 2002, Online. Available www.ausa.org/webpub/DeptArmyMagazine.nsf/byid/CCRN-6CCS56 (accessed 8 September 2005). Bassford, *Clausewitz in English*. B. H. Reid, *Studies in British Military Thought – Debates with Fuller and Liddell Hart*, Lincoln: University of Nebraska Press, 1998.

14 Department of the Army, FM 3–0: *Operations*, Washington, DC, June 2001, pp. 2–3.

15 S. Naveh, *In Pursuit of Military Excellence – The Evolution of Operational Theory*, London: Frank Cass, 1997, p. xx.
16 S. J. Lepper, "On (The Law of) War: What Clausewitz 'Meant' to Say", *Airpower Journal*, Vol. 13, No. 2, Summer 1999.Online. Available www.airpower.maxwell. af.mil/airchronicles/apj/apj99/sum99/waysum99.html (accessed 8 September 2005).
17 Colonel Arthur Lykke, a senior professor of strategy at the US Army War College, cited by Bassford, *Clausewitz in English*, p. 210.
18 F. J. West, "The Fall of Fallujah", *Marine Corps Gazette*, Vol. 89, No. 7, July 2005, p. 57. Kass, cited in J. Achenbach, "Military Theory and the Force of Ideas – From Sparta to Baghdad, Paradigms Have Shifted. Human Nature Has Not", *Washington Post*, 23 March 2003.
19 H. Strachan, "The Lost Meaning of Strategy", *Survival*, Vol. 47, No. 3, Autumn 2005, p. 34. W. Lind, K. M. Nightengale, J. Schmitt, J. W. Sutton and G. I. Wilson, "The Changing Face of War: Into the Fourth Generation", *Military Review*, Vol. 69, No. 10, October 1989, pp. 2–11. W. S. Lind, "4th Generation Warfare and the Dangers of Being the Only Superpower: A Warning from Clausewitz", *CounterPunch*, 8 March 2003. Among military commentators that do not recognise the continuing validity of traditional strategic thought is A. and H. Toffler, *War and Anti-War – Survival at the Dawn of the 21st Century*, Boston, Mass.: Little, Brown, 1993. R. R. Leonhard, *The Principles of War for the Information Age*, Novato, Calif.: Presidio Press, 1998, does recognise the historical validity of such thought but argues in favour of a new approach. M. van Creveld, *On Future War*, London: Brassey's, 1991, argues that Clausewitzian thought, in particular, is anachronistic in the post-Cold War world – as does S. Metz, "A Wake for Clausewitz: Toward a Philosophy of 21st Century Warfare", *Parameters*, Vol. 24, No. 4, Winter 1994–95, pp. 124–32.
20 Clausewitz's most impressive modern-day interpreters include Bassford, Antulio Echevarria, and Colin Gray. Bassford's most important contribution is the internet site www.Clausewitz.com. Among the works of Echevarria and Gray that emphasise Clausewitz's contemporary relevance are A. J. Echevarria, *Globalization and the Nature of War*, Carlisle, Pa.: Strategic Studies Institute, 2003, and C. S. Gray, *Modern Strategy*, Oxford: Oxford University Press, 1999.

1 Clausewitz's theory of war

1 A. Gat, *A History of Military Thought from the Enlightenment to the Cold War*, Oxford: Oxford University Press, 2001, pp. 217–52. P. Paret, *Clausewitz and the State – The Man, His Theories, and His Times*, 2nd edn, Princeton, NJ: Princeton University Press, 1985, pp. 331–55.
2 The most impressive accounts of the development of Clausewitz's thought within the intellectual context of his times are Gat, op. cit. and Paret, op. cit.
3 C. von Clausewitz, "On the Life and Character of Scharnhorst", from C. von Clausewitz, *Historical and Political Writings*, Princeton, N.J.: Princeton University Press, 1992, p. 90, trans. and ed. by P. Paret and D. Moran.
4 The Aufkläring (lit. "enlightenment") was an intellectual movement based in Germany during the late eighteenth century.
5 I. Berlin, *Against the Current: Essays in the History of Ideas*, London: Pimlico, 1997, p. 148. Gat, op. cit., p. 166. Clausewitz was also influenced by Montesquieu and other philosophers, including Immanuel Kant. However, he never openly acknowledged these debts in *On War*, something that Hew Strachan has said adds to the ambiguity of the text. H. Strachan, "Clausewitz and the Dialectics of War", paper presented at Oxford Leverhulme Programme Conference on Clausewitz and the 21st Century, Oxford, March 2005.
6 Clausewitz, op. cit., p. 104.
7 Paret, op. cit., p. 71.

8 C. von Clausewitz, *On War*, 2nd edn, Princeton, N.J.: Princeton University Press, 1984, trans. and ed. by M. Howard and P. Paret, Bk I, Ch. 7, p. 119. Eugenia Kiesling has observed that the modern tendency to allude to fog and friction in war is an adaptation on Clausewitz as he did not mention the "fog of war" in *On War*. E. C. Kiesling, "'On War' Without the Fog", *Military Review*, Vol. 81, No. 5, September–October 2001, pp. 85–7.

9 M. J. Lee, "Clausewitz on Friction", *Marine Corps Gazette*, Vol. 83, No. 2, February 1999, p. 48.

10 Clausewitz, *On War*, VIII, 3, pp. 595–6. Other centres of gravity identified by Clausewitz were the enemy's capital city, the "community of interest" in any enemy alliance, the personality of an enemy leader, and enemy public opinion.

11 J. L. Strange and R. Iron, "Center of Gravity – What Clausewitz Really Meant", *Joint Force Quarterly*, No. 35, 2004, pp. 20–7.

12 A. J. Echevarria, *Clausewitz's Center of Gravity: Changing our Warfighting Doctrine – Again!*, Carlisle, Pa.: Strategic Studies Institute, 2002, p. 14.

13 C. S. Gray, *Modern Strategy*, Oxford: Oxford University Press, 1999, p. 105.

14 M. van Creveld, "The Eternal Clausewitz", in M. Handel (ed.), *Clausewitz and Modern Strategy*, London: Frank Cass, 1986, p. 46.

15 Clausewitz, *On War*, "Note of 10 July 1827", pp. 69–70.

16 Ibid., I, 1, pp. 77, 78 and 80; emphasis in the original.

17 Ibid., I, 1, p. 87.

18 Ibid., I, 1, pp. 81 and 89.

19 Ibid., VIII, 6, p. 610.

20 Ibid., IV, 4, p. 231.

21 Ibid., IV, 10, p. 255.

22 Ibid., I, 1, p. 89. Christopher Bassford and Edward Villacres have shown that the representation of the trinity as "people, government, and army" is too simplistic. E. J. Villacres and C. Bassford, "Reclaiming the Clausewitzian Trinity", *Parameters*, Vol. 25, No. 3, Autumn 1995, pp. 9–19. Bassford translates "wünderlichte" as "fascinating". Michael Howard has argued that "wünderlichte" is untranslatable and that "paradoxical" does not give the sense of what Clausewitz meant. However, it was included in his and Paret's translation despite his opposition. M. Howard, comments made at the Oxford Leverhulme Programme Conference on Clausewitz and the 21st Century, Oxford, March 2005.

23 Clausewitz, *On War*, VIII, 6, p. 605. In the German original, the singular "Plan of War" is used. J. Willem Honig, "Problems of Text and Translation", paper presented at Oxford Leverhulme Programme Conference on Clausewitz and the 21st Century, Oxford, March 2005.

24 I am grateful to Antulio Echevarria for this insight regarding Clausewitz's thinking. Antulio Echevarria, "Clausewitz and LIC", e-mail (7 August 2002).

25 Gat, op. cit., p. 228.

26 Basil Liddell Hart and Hans Delbrück are the most notable examples, and the latter will be discussed on pp. 16–17. More recently, John Lynn, while aware of the difference between absolute war and real war, has imitated Delbrück in saying that Clausewitz propounded two categories of real war, annihilation and attrition, to which Lynn adds a third from the experience of the twentieth century – legitimacy. J. A. Lynn, "War of Annihilation, War of Attrition, and War of Legitimacy: A Neo-Clausewitzian Approach to Twentieth-Century Conflicts", *Marine Corps Gazette*, Vol. 80, No. 10, October 1996, p. 65. Beatrice Heuser misinterprets an earlier, "idealistic" Clausewitz who wrote about absolute war and a later, "realistic" Clausewitz who described real war. B. Heuser, *Reading Clausewitz*, London: Pimlico, 2002, pp. 24–43.

27 Gat, op. cit., pp. 197 and 263–5. Clausewitz, *On War*, "Unfinished [*sic*] Note, Presumably Written in 1830", pp. 70–1. Echevarria is of the opinion that the undated

note was written much earlier than Gat believes, possibly before 1820. Interview with Lieutenant-Colonel Antulio J. Echevarria II at the US Army War College, Carlisle Barracks, Pennsylvania, 19 September 2000.

28 Clausewitz, *On War*, "Unfinished [*sic*] Note, Presumably Written in 1830", p. 71. A. J. Echevarria, "Clausewitz: Toward A Theory of Applied Strategy", *Defense Analysis*, Vol. 11, No. 3, 1995. Online. Available www.clausewitz.com/ CWZHOME/ECHEVAR/APSRAT1.htm (accessed 12 April 2000).

29 P. Paret, "Clausewitz: Life and Thought" in P. Paret, *Understanding War – Essays on Clausewitz and the History of Military Power*, Princeton, N.J.: Princeton University Press, 1992, p. 115. In *On War*, Clausewitz wrote: "If the theorist's study automati- cally results in principles and rules, [these] are intended to provide a thinking man with a frame of reference for the movements he has been trained to carry out, rather than to serve as a guide which at the moment of action lays down precisely the path he must take" (II, 2, p. 141).

30 R. M. Swain, "Clausewitz for the 20th Century: The Interpretation of Raymond Aron", *Military Review*, Vol. 66, No. 4, April 1986, p. 44.

31 J. J. Schneider, "Theoretical Implications of Operational Art", *Military Review*, Vol. 70, No. 9, September 1990, pp. 17–27. S. Naveh, *In Pursuit of Military Excellence – The Evolution of Operational Theory*, London: Frank Cass, 1997. F. Kagan, "Army Doctrine and Modern War: Notes Toward a New Edition of FM 100–5", *Parameters*, Vol. 27, No. 1, Spring 1997, pp. 134–51.

32 Clausewitz, *On War*, III, 1, p. 182 and II, 1, p. 128; emphasis in original. Echevarria interview.

33 H. Rosinski, "Scharnhorst to Schlieffen: The Rise and Decline of German Military Thought", *Naval War College Review*, Vol. 29, No. 1, Summer 1976, pp. 89–90.

34 Echevarria, "Clausewitz: Toward a Theory of Applied Strategy" and Gat, op. cit., pp. 170ff.

35 H. Delbrück, *History of the Art of War within the Framework of Political History*, Vol. 4, *The Dawn of Modern Warfare*, trans. W. J. Renfroe, jun., Westport, Conn.: Greenwood Press, 1975, pp. 454–5. Clausewitz, *On War*, V, 3, p. 282.

36 It would be more accurate to distinguish between the earlier parts of the Napoleonic Wars and the later parts of that conflict. Robert Epstein has convincingly argued that the 1809 campaign, involving France and Austria, provides the first example of oper- ational art being applied on the battlefield by opposing forces. This was achieved owing to the Austrians' use of distributed manoeuvre in imitation of Napoleon. Units now tended to fight a series of sequential actions that had a cumulative effect on the campaign. In this respect, the campaigns from 1809 onwards have more in common with warfare as it was conducted later in the nineteenth century than they do with Napoleon's campaigns prior to that time. R. M. Epstein, *Napoleon's Last Victory and the Emergence of Modern War*, Lawrence: Kansas University Press, 1994. Clause- witz, *On War*, IV, 11, p. 259; emphasis in original. Isserson, cited by J. J. Schneider, "Black Lights – Chaos, Complexity, and the Promise of Information Warfare", *Joint Force Quarterly*, No. 15, Spring 1997, p. 25.

37 Schneider, "Theoretical Implications of Operational Art", p. 20.

38 Geoffrey Herrera has likened the impact of the telegraph and the railroad to that of the internet today. G. L. Herrera, "Inventing the Railroad and Rifle Revolution: Information, Military Innovation and the Rise of Germany", *Journal of Strategic Studies*, Vol. 27, No. 2, June 2004, pp. 243–71.

39 Cited by J. L. Wallach, "Misperceptions of Clausewitz's *On War* by the German Military", *Journal of Strategic Studies*, Vol. 9, Nos 2–3, June–September 1986, pp. 213–14.

40 Rosinski, op. cit., p. 95.

41 D. J. Hughes (ed.), *Moltke on the Art of War – Selected Writings*, New York: Presidio Press, 1993, p. 6.

42 Citations from D. Cranz, "Understanding Change: Sigismund von Schlichting and the Operational Level of War", Fort Leavenworth, Kansa, School for Advanced Military Studies monograph, May 1989, p. 13.

43 Schneider, "Theoretical Implications of Operational Art", p. 21. Where Schlichting used the term *"operativ"*, he was referring to a "kind of activity". Cranz, op. cit., p. 18. Schlichting, cited by A. J. Echevarria, "Neo-Clausewitzianism: Freytag-Loringhoven and the Militarization of Clausewitz in German Military Literature before the First World War", Ph.D. dissertation, Princeton University, 1994, p. 52.

44 Paret, *Clausewitz and the State*, p. 239. W. von Lossow, "Mission Type Orders versus Order Type Tactics", *Military Review*, Vol. 57, No. 6, June 1977, p. 87. *Auftrag* means "task", which, with situation, gives rise to the mission; hence the common, but incorrect, translation of *Auftragstaktik* as "mission orders". R. Simpkin, *Race to the Swift – Thoughts on Twenty-First Century Warfare*, London: Brassey's, 1985, pp. 227–8. The Germans themselves rarely used the term *Auftragstaktik*, but instead emphasised decentralisation.

45 M. Knox, "The Prussian Idea of Freedom and the 'Career Open to Talent': Battlefield Initiative and Social Ascent from Prussian Reform to Nazi Revolution, 1807 to 1944", in M. Knox, *Common Destiny – Dictatorship, Foreign-Policy, and War in Fascist Italy and Nazi Germany*, Cambridge: Cambridge University Press, 2000, p. 193.

46 H. Delbrück, *History of the Art of War within the Framework of Political History*, 4 vols, trans. W. J. Renfroe, jun., Westport, Conn.: Greenwood Press, 1975.

47 The strategies of annihilation and attrition are demonstrated in ibid., vol. 4, *The Dawn of Modern Warfare*, pp. 293–318, 374–83 and 421–48, with particular reference to the campaigns of Frederick the Great and Napoleon.

48 Ibid., p. 379.

49 Cited by Wallach, op. cit., p. 215. Unfortunately, there were serious discrepancies between this edition of *On War* and the original, mainly because several hundred "clarifications" had been inserted into the second edition of 1852 by Clausewitz's brother-in-law, Count Friederich von Brühl. These had not been corrected during the intervening period.

50 R. T. Foley (trans. and ed.), *Alfred von Schlieffen's Military Writings*, London: Frank Cass, 2003, pp. 191–2.

51 H. H. Herwig, "The Prussian Model and Military Planning Today", *Joint Force Quarterly*, No. 18, Spring 1998, p. 72. On the Epigoni, see A. J. Echevarria, "Borrowing from the Master: Uses of Clausewitz in German Military Literature before the Great War", *War in History*, Vol. 3, No. 3, July 1996, pp. 274–92.

52 I. V. Tsybulskiy, "Carl von Clausewitz and the Present", *Voennaya Mysl* (Military Thought), No. 8, August 1991, p. 30.

53 Citation from Heuser, op. cit., p. 47.

54 Nevertheless, William Lind and others have rightly pointed out that the origins of what they call "third-generation" warfare are to be found in the manoeuvre tactics deployed during the Germans' Spring 1918 offensive. They describe third-generation tactics as being "the first truly non-linear tactics". W. Lind, K. M. Nightengale, J. Schmitt, J. W. Sutton and G. I. Wilson, "The Changing Face of War: Into the Fourth Generation", *Military Review*, Vol. 69, No. 10, October 1989, p. 4.

55 D. C. Mock, "A Look at Deep Operations: The Option of Deep Maneuver", Fort Leavenworth, Kansas, School for Advanced Military Studies monograph, December 1987, p. 7. Clausewitz, *On War*, IV, 4, p. 233 and VI, 24, p. 465.

56 Cited by Heuser, op. cit., p. 101.

57 Cited by R. W. Harrison, *The Russian Way of War: Operational Art, 1904–1940*, Lawrence, Kansas: Kansas University Press, 2001, p. 140. According to Bruce Menning, it was N. Varfolomeyev, a Soviet student of operational art, who, in 1928, credited Svechin with the origins of the term. B. W. Menning, "Operational Art's Origins", *Military Review*, Vol. 77, No. 5, September–October 1997, pp. 32–47.

58 Cited by Naveh, op. cit., pp. 10–11.
59 Letter from Clausewitz to Major von Roeder, Prussian Army, 22 December 1827, cited by P. Paret and D. Moran, "Two Letters on Strategy", in Paret, *Understanding War*, pp. 126–7., emphases in original. Roeder was an officer in the Prussian General Staff who requested Clausewitz's advice on an operational problem set by General von Müffling, the chief of the General Staff. These letters have also been examined by W. P. Franz, "Two Letters on Strategy: Clausewitz' Contribution to the Operational Level of War", *Journal of Strategic Studies*, Vol. 9, Nos. 2–3, June–September 1986, pp. 171–94.
60 Harrison, op. cit., p. 181.
61 Cited by R. Simpkin, *Deep Battle: The Brainchild of Marshal Tukhachevskii*, London: Brassey's, 1987, p. 266.
62 J. D. Kelly, "War as a Whole: Operational Shock and Operational Art", *Australian Defence Force Journal*, No. 162, September–October 2003, pp. 19–30.
63 Interview with Dr Stephen Blank at the US Army War College, Carlisle Barracks, Pennsylvania, 19 September 2000. Blank believes that whatever the Soviets learnt from German theorists was overshadowed by their experience of the civil and Polish wars.
64 Cited by Simpkin, *Deep Battle*, p. 105.
65 Heuser, op. cit., p. 12.
66 Clausewitz, *On War*, VI, 8, p. 379.
67 Simpkin, *Deep Battle*, p. 159.

2 The development of American strategic thought and practice

 1 R. F. Weigley, *The American Way of War – A History of United States Military Strategy and Policy*, 2nd edn, Bloomington: Indiana University Press, 1977, p. xx.
 2 Ibid. Weigley described Washington's campaigns as being based on a strategy of erosion rather than one of attrition, which he had interpreted as being on the other side of the Clausewitzian coin from annihilation.
 3 R. F. Weigley, "Response to Brian McAllister Linn", *Journal of Military History*, Vol. 66, No. 2, April 2002, p. 531. B. M. Linn, "*The American Way of War* Revisited", *Journal of Military History*, Vol. 66, No. 2, April 2002, pp. 503–5. A. J. Echevarria, *Toward an American Way of War*, Carlisle, Pa.: Strategic Studies Institute, 2004.
 4 Echevarria, op. cit., p. 13.
 5 M. Boot, "The New American Way of War", *Foreign Affairs*, Vol. 82, No. 3, July–August 2003. Online. Available www.foreignaffairs.org/20030701/faessay 15404/max-boot/the-new-american-way-of-war.html (accessed 28 November 2005). M. Boot, *Savage Wars of Peace: Small Wars and the Rise of American Power*, New York: Perseus Books, 2002.
 6 C. S. Gray, "Strategy in the Nuclear Age", in M. Knox, A. Bernstein and W. Murray, *The Making of Strategy – Rulers, States and War*, Cambridge: Cambridge University Press, 1993, p. 582, emphasis in original.
 7 D. A. Starry, "A Perspective on American Military Thought", *Military Review*, Vol. 69, No. 7, July 1989, p. 3.
 8 Cited by G. A. Craig and F. Gilbert, "Reflections on Strategy in the Present and Future", in P. Paret *et al.*, *Makers of Modern Strategy from Machiavelli to the Nuclear Age*, Princeton, N.J.: Princeton University Press, 1986, pp. 869–70.
 9 H. Kissinger, *Diplomacy*, New York: Simon and Schuster, 1994, p. 46.
10 J. A. Nagl, *Counterinsurgency Lessons from Malaya and Vietnam: Learning to Eat Soup with a Knife*, Westport, Conn.: Praeger, 2002. N. Aylwin-Foster, "Changing the Army for Counterinsurgency operations", *Military Review*, Vol. 85, No. 6, November–December 2005, pp. 2–15.

11 S. J. Lepper, "On (The Law of) War: What Clausewitz 'Meant' to Say", *Airpower Journal*, Vol. 13, No. 2, Summer 1999. Online. Available www.airpower.maxwell. af.mil/airchronicles/apj/apj99/sum99/waysum99.html (accessed 8 September 2005).

12 Cited by Gray, op. cit., p. 593.

13 Cited by Weigley, *The American Way of War*, p. 5. A. T. Mahan, *Naval Strategy Compared and Contrasted with the Principles and Practice of Military Operations on Land*, Westport, Conn.: Greenwood Press, 1975 (reprint).

14 Cited by H. Summers, *The New World Strategy*, New York: Touchstone, 1995, p. 23.

15 H. Strachan, "The Lost Meaning of Strategy", *Survival*, Vol. 47, No. 3, Autumn 2005, p. 49. C. Powell, "US Forces: Challenges Ahead", *Foreign Affairs*, Vol. 72, No. 5, Winter 1992–93. Online. Available www.foreignaffairs.org/19921201faessay5851/ colin-l-powell/u-s-forces-challenges-ahead.html (accessed 29 November 2005).

16 Kissinger, op. cit., pp. 402–3.

17 Cited by M. Handel, *Masters of War – Classical Strategic Thought*, 2nd edn, London, Frank Cass: 1996, p. 246. R. M. Cassidy, "Prophets or Praetorians? The Uptonian Paradox and the Powell Corollary", *Parameters*, Vol. 33, No. 3, Autumn 2003, p. 134.

18 C. von Clausewitz, *On War*, 2nd edn, Princeton, N.J.: Princeton University Press, 1984, trans. and ed. by M. Howard and P. Paret, Bk I, Ch. 1, p. 87. C. Bassford, *Clausewitz in English – The Reception of Clausewitz in Britain and America, 1815–1945*, New York: Oxford University Press, 1994, p. 157.

19 A. Gat, *A History of Military Thought from the Enlightenment to the Cold War*, Oxford: Oxford University Press, 2001, p. 251.

20 Cited by Nagl, op. cit., p. 43.

21 Cited by Summers, op. cit., p. 134.

22 Clausewitz, op. cit., VI, 5, p. 370. Several aggressors since, such as Hitler and Saddam, have also claimed to be "peace-loving"!

23 D. Higginbotham: *The War of American Independence*, New York, Macmillan, 1971. P. Paret, "The Relationship between the American Revolutionary War and European Military Thought and Practice", in P. Paret, *Understanding War – Essays on Clausewitz and the History of Military Power*, Princeton, N.J.: Princeton University Press, 1992, pp. 26–38, provides a good summary of this question.

24 G. E. Rothenburg, "Moltke, Schlieffen, and the Doctrine of Strategic Envelopment", in Paret *et al.*, op. cit., p. 299.

25 R. F. Weigley, *The Age of Battles: The Quest for Decisive Warfare from Breitenfeld to Waterloo*, Bloomington: Indiana University Press, 1991, p. 234.

26 H. Strachan, "Clausewitz and the Dialectics of War", paper presented at Oxford Leverhulme Programme Conference on Clausewitz and the 21st Century, Oxford, March 2005. Literature on the so-called "democratic peace" includes B. M. Russett, *Grasping the Democratic Peace – Principles for a Post-Cold War World*, Princeton, N.J.: Princeton University Press, 1993; M. Doyle, "Kant: Liberalism and World Politics", *American Political Science Review*, Vol. 80, No. 4, December 1986, pp. 1151–69; and F. Fukuyama: *The End of History and the Last Man*, New York, Free Press, 1992. Critiques of this view include C. Layne, "Kant or Cant: The Myth of the Democratic Peace", *International Security*, Vol. 19, No. 2, Fall 1994, pp. 5–49, and K. Waltz, "Structural Realism after the Cold War", *International Security*, Vol. 25, No. 1, Summer 2000, pp. 5–41.

27 Clausewitz, op. cit., I, 1, p. 81. Weigley, *The American Way of War*, p. 60. Linn, op. cit., p. 508. Linn described it as a "third American way of war" beside Weigley's notions of annihilation and attrition.

28 Cited by J. Keegan, *The Mask of Command*, Harmondsworth: Penguin, 1987, p. 181.

29 Cited by Gat, op. cit., p. 288.

30 Clausewitz, op. cit., II, 2, p. 136.

31 Cited by Keegan, op. cit., p. 184. Weigley, *The American Way of War*, p. 72.

32 Clausewitz, op. cit., II, 2, p. 143.
33 Cited by Gat, op. cit., p. 292.
34 Cited by Keegan, op. cit., p. 194.
35 R. F. Weigley, "American Strategy from its Beginnings through the First World War", in Paret *et al.*, op. cit., pp. 430 and 432.
36 Starry, op. cit., p. 4.
37 Cassidy, op. cit., pp. 130–1. Weigley, *The American Way of War*, p. 168.
38 F. G. Hoffmann, "Small Wars Revisited: The United States and Nontraditional Wars", *Journal of Strategic Studies*, Vol. 28, No. 6, December 2005, pp. 913–40. Sherman, cited by Weigley, *The American Way of War*, p. 158.
39 Cited by P. A. Crowl, "Alfred Thayer Mahan: The Naval Historian", in Paret (ed.), op. cit., p. 477.
40 Cited by Kissinger, op. cit., p. 40.
41 Ibid., p. 47.
42 Cited by G. K. Williams, "'The Shank of the Drill': Americans and Strategic Aviation in the Great War", *Journal of Strategic Studies*, Vol. 19, No. 3, September 1996, p. 404.
43 H. T. Hayden (ed.), *Warfighting: Maneuver Warfare in the US Marine Corps*, London: Greenhill, 1995, p. 17.
44 E. O. Goldman, "The US Military in Uncertain Times: Organisations, Ambiguity and Strategic Adjustment", *Journal of Strategic Studies*, Vol. 20, No. 2, June 1997, p. 49.
45 Cited by C. D'Este, *A Genius for War – A Life of General George S. Patton*, London: HarperCollins, 1995, p. 602.
46 Cited by ibid., p. 319.
47 Cited by ibid., p. 349.
48 Mahan, op. cit. Crowl, op. cit. J. S. Corbett, *Some Principles of Maritime Strategy*, ed. E. J. Grove, Annapolis, Md.: Naval Institute Press, 1988. M. I. Handel, "Corbett, Clausewitz, and Sun Tzu", *Naval War College Review*, Vol. 53, No. 4, Autumn 2000, pp. 106–23.
49 H. Rothfels, "Clausewitz", in E. M. Earle (ed.), *Makers of Modern Strategy from Machiavelli to Hitler*, Princeton, N.J.: Princeton University Press, 1943. C. von Clausewitz, *On War*, trans. by J. J. Matthijs Jolles, New York: Random House, 1943.
50 Cited by Weigley, *The American Way of War*, p. 220.
51 W. B. Pickett, "Eisenhower as a Student of Clausewitz", *Military Review*, Vol. 65, No. 7, July 1985, p. 22.
52 Cited by M. Howard, "Influence of Clausewitz", Introduction to Clausewitz, *On War*, trans. and ed. by Howard and Paret, p. 42.
53 M. R. Matheny, "The Roots of Modern American Operational Art". Online. Available www.carlisle.army.mil/usawc/dmspo/Staff%20Publications/modern_operations.pdf (accessed 9 September 2005). Matheny describes *The Principles of Strategy* as being of such quality that they could have been written by a Heinz Guderian or a Tukhachevskii. Weigley, *The American Way of War*, p. 211.
54 This culminated in 1921 when the War Department issued War Department Training Regulations No. 10–5, which included a summary of nine principles of war: objective, offensive, mass, economy-of-force, movement, surprise, security, simplicity, and co-operation. These were adapted by the US Army from the writings of J. F. C. Fuller. Hayden, op. cit., p. 15.
55 Department of the Army, FM 3–0, *Operations*, Washington, DC, June 2001, pp. 4–12.
56 Cited by M. Clodfelter, "Molding Airpower Convictions: Development and Legacy of William Mitchell's Strategic Thought", in P. S. Meilinger (ed.), *The Paths of Heaven – The Evolution of Airpower Theory*, Maxwell Air Force Base, Ala.: Air University Press, 1997, p. 96.
57 T. D. Biddle, "Air Power", in M. Howard, G. J. Andreopoulos and M. R. Shulman,

The Laws of War: Constraints on Warfare in the Western World, New Haven, Conn.: Yale University Press, 1994, p. 157.
58 Goldman, op. cit., pp. 58 and 59.
59 Cited by M. Matloff, "Allied Strategy in Europe" in Paret *et al.*, op. cit., p. 686.
60 Weigley, "American Strategy", p. 443.
61 Cited by D'Este, op. cit., p. 376.
62 Pickett, op. cit., pp. 26–7. Clausewitz, *On War*, trans. and ed. Howard and Paret, VIII, 9, pp. 617 and 619.
63 Cited by Kissinger, op. cit., p. 417. In a student monograph for the US Army War College in 1992, Lieutenant-Colonel H. S. Perry III commented that such a rationale would have "probably caused Clausewitz to roll over in his grave". H. S. Perry, "Clausewitz and Torgau", Monograph, Carlisle, Pennsylvania, US Army War College, 1992.
64 Clausewitz, *On War*, trans. and ed. Howard and Paret, I, 2, p. 91. B. Brodie (ed.), *The Absolute Weapon: Atomic Power and World Order*, New York: Harcourt Brace, 1946.
65 Weigley, *The American Way of War*, pp. 367–8; emphasis in original.
66 The first declassified text of NSC-68 appeared in the *Naval War College Review*, Vol. 27, No. 6, May–June 1975, pp. 51–108.
67 Craig and Gilbert, op. cit., p. 871
68 C. D. McFetridge, "Foreign Policy and Military Strategy: The Civil–Military Equation", *Military Review*, Vol. 66, No. 4, April 1986, p. 26.
69 Clausewitz, *On War*, trans. and ed. Howard and Paret, I, 1, p. 77. C. Crane, "To Avert Impending Disaster: American Plans to Use Atomic Weapons During the Korean War", *Journal of Strategic Studies*, Vol. 23, No. 2, June 2000, pp. 72–88.
70 Kissinger is especially critical of Truman's approach over Korea in this respect. Kissinger, op. cit., p. 488.
71 B. J. Cillessen, "Embracing the Bomb: Ethics, Morality and Nuclear Deterrence in the US Air Force, 1945–1955", *Journal of Strategic Studies*, Vol. 21, No. 1, March 1998, p. 116; emphasis in original.
72 Starry, op. cit., p. 7.
73 R. A. Doughty: *The Evolution of U.S. Army Tactical Doctrine, 1946–76*, Leavenworth Papers No. 1, Fort Leavenworth, Kansas, Combat Studies Institute, US Army Command and General Staff College, 1979, p. 18.
74 Cited by L. Freedman, "The First Two Generations of Nuclear Strategists", in Paret, (ed.), op. cit., p. 740.
75 C. Crane, *American Airpower Strategy in Korea*, Lawrence: University of Kansas Press, 2002.
76 Cited by Bassford, op. cit., pp. 161–2.
77 See, for example, K. Knorr and T. Read (eds), *Limited Strategic War*, London: Praeger, 1962, which discussed the possibility of "limiting" a strategic nuclear war. H. Kahn, *On Thermonuclear War*, Princeton, N.J.: Princeton University Press, 1961. A. Rapoport, "Introduction", C. von Clausewitz, *On War*, ed. A. Rapoport, abridged edn, London: Penguin, 1968, provides an overview of the neo-Clausewitzians. This particular edition of *On War* is flawed in that it is based on an unsatisfactory translation (by Colonel John J. Graham in 1873) and does not include Books VI and VII, which demonstrate some of Clausewitz's more mature thinking.
78 R. Osgood, *Limited War – The Challenge to American Strategy*, Chicago: University of Chicago Press, 1957. B. Brodie, *Strategy in the Missile Age*, Princeton, N.J.: Princeton University Press, 1959. H. Kissinger, *Nuclear Weapons and Foreign Policy*, New York: Harper, 1957.
79 C. S. Gray, *Defining and Achieving Decisive Victory*, Carlisle, Pa.: Strategic Studies Institute, 2002, p. 2, my emphasis. Beatrice Heuser has rightly pointed out that Clausewitz, writing in the context of the 1820s, was familiar with national frontiers

frequently shifting as a result of "limited" conflicts, particularly those he studied from the eighteenth century. However, any attempt to change a frontier in the 1950s might have ended in a war of unprecedented destruction. B. Heuser, *Reading Clausewitz*, London: Pimlico, 2002, p. 181.

80 Cited by Weigley, *The American Way of War*, p. 422.
81 D. A. Rosenberg: "Nuclear War Planning", in Howard, Andreopoulos, and Shulman, op. cit., p. 175.
82 Freedman, op. cit., p. 771.
83 Rosenberg, op. cit. It should be noted that recent research has cast considerable doubt on whether there ever really was a "Schlieffen Plan" in the sense that has traditionally been accepted by historians. A. J. Echevarria, *After Clausewitz – German Military Thought before the Great War*, Lawrence: University Press of Kansas, 2000, pp. 188–97, sums up the debate. A. C. Enthoven and K. Wayne Smith, *How Much is Enough? Shaping the Defense Programme, 1961–1969*, New York: Harper and Row, 1971. D. Ball, "The Development of the SIOP, 1960–1983", in D. Ball and J. Richelson (eds), *Strategic and Nuclear Targeting*, Ithaca, N.Y.: Cornell University Press, 1986.
84 Cited by P. R. Moody: "Clausewitz and the Fading Dialectic of War", *World Politics*, Vol. 31, No. 3, 1979, p. 418.
85 Cited by Gray, "Strategy in the Nuclear Age", p. 611.
86 Cited by A. W. Dowd, "Thirteen Years: The Causes and Consequences of the War in Iraq", *Parameters*, Vol. 33, No. 3, Autumn 2003, p. 53.

3 The legacy of Vietnam

1 J. Shy and T. Collier, "Revolutionary War", in P. Paret *et al.*, *Makers of Modern Strategy from Machiavelli to the Nuclear Age*, Princeton, N.J.: Princeton University Press, 1986, p. 856.
2 Cited by A. Rapoport, "Introduction", in C. von Clausewitz, *On War*, ed. A. Rapoport, Harmondsworth, Penguin, 1968, p. 73. H. S. Summers, *On Strategy – A Critical Analysis of the Vietnam War*, Novato, Calif.: Presidio Press, 1982.
3 R. Paschall, letter to General William E. DePuy, 25 April 1985, DePuy Papers, US Army Military History Institute (USAMHI), Carlisle Barracks, Pennsylvania; emphasis in original. A. Krepinevich, *The Army and Vietnam*, Baltimore, Md.: Johns Hopkins University Press, 1986.
4 W. E. DePuy, transcript of oral history interview with R. L. Brownlee and W. J. Mullen, 1979, USAMHI, pp. 124–5. J. Record, "Vietnam in Retrospect: Could We Have Won?", *Parameters*, Vol. 26, No. 4, Winter 1996/97, pp. 51–65.
5 M. Collins, "Clausewitz and Summers on Vietnam: A Contemporary Analysis of *On Strategy*", *Small Wars Journal*, Vol. 3, October 2005, p. 16.
6 C. C. Crane, *Avoiding Vietnam: The US Army's Response to Defeat in Southeast Asia*, Carlisle, Pa: Strategic Studies Institute, 2002, pp. 7–8. H. R. McMaster, *Dereliction of Duty – Lyndon Johnson, Robert McNamara, the JCS, and the Lies that Led to Vietnam*, New York: HarperCollins, 1997.
7 W. O. Staudenmaier, "Vietnam, Mao and Clausewitz", *Parameters*, Vol. 7, No. 1, Spring 1977, p. 89.
8 Summers, op. cit., p. 69.
9 Cited by H. Kissinger, *Diplomacy*, New York: Simon and Schuster, 1994, p. 646.
10 Cited by Summers, op. cit., p. 59.
11 It appears that no attempt was made to separate CI from the realm of conventional doctrine. R. A. Doughty, *The Evolution of US Army Tactical Doctrine, 1946–76*, Leavenworth Paper No. 1, Fort Leavenworth, Kans.: Combat Studies Institute, 1979, p. 26.
12 P. F. Wynnyk, "Vo Nguyen Giap: A Strategy for Protracted Revolutionary War", in

A. D. English (ed.), *The Changing Face of War: Learning from History*, Montreal: McGill-Queens University Press, 1998, p. 147.

13 J. W. Romjue, "Evolution of American Army Doctrine", in J. Gooch (ed.), *The Origins of Contemporary Doctrine*, Occasional Paper No. 30, Camberley: Strategic and Combat Studies Institute, 1997, p. 66.

14 Cited by Summers, op cit., p. 78.

15 On the origins and early development of the conflict see ibid.; R. S. McNamara, *In Retrospect: The Tragedy and Lessons of Vietnam*, New York: Random House, 1995; R. H. Shultz, "The Great Divide – Strategy and Covert Action in Vietnam", *Joint Force Quarterly*, No. 23, Autumn/Winter 1999–2000, pp. 90–6; Record, op. cit.; and B. Palmer, *The 25-Year War – America's Military Role in Vietnam*, Lexington, University Press of Kentucky, 1984.

16 C. von Clausewitz: *On War*, 2nd edn, Princeton, N.J.: Princeton University Press, 1984, trans. and ed. M. Howard and P. Paret, Bk VI, Ch. 26, p. 479.

17 P. L. Townsend, "Clausewitz Would Have Wondered at the Way We Fought in Vietnam", *Marine Corps Gazette*, Vol. 62, No. 6, June 1978, p. 56. This connection is also shown by Staudenmaier, op cit., p. 79.

18 Crane, op. cit., p. 1.

19 Melvin Laird, secretary of defense under Nixon, has recently written that there was no second attack in the Gulf of Tonkin, meaning that Johnson "and McNamara either dissembled or misinterpreted the faulty intelligence". M. R. Laird, "Iraq: Learning the Lessons of Vietnam", *Foreign Affairs*, Vol. 84, No. 6, November–December 2005. Online. Available www.foreignaffairs.org/2005110184604/melvin-r-Laird/Iraq-learning-the-lessons-of-Vietnam.html (accessed 30 January 2006).

20 R. F. Weigley, *The American Way of War – A History of United States Military Strategy and Policy*, 2nd edn, Bloomington: Indiana University Press, 1977, p. 462. Kissinger, op. cit., pp. 658–9.

21 C. Johnson, *Autopsy on People's War*, Berkeley, Calif.: California University Press, 1973, p. 22; emphasis in original.

22 Cited by Kissinger, op cit., p. 651; emphasis in original.

23 Ibid., p. 652. Material on the conduct and evolution of the war includes Summers, op. cit.; Krepinevich, op. cit.; McNamara, op. cit.; Palmer, op. cit.; R. E. Ford, *Tet 1968 – Understanding the Surprise*, London: Frank Cass, 1995; L. Sorley, *A Better War*, New York: Harcourt Brace, 1999; R. Buzzanco, *Masters of War: Military Dissent and Politics in the Vietnam Era*, Cambridge: Cambridge University Press, 1996; and Anon., "The Longest War", *The Economist*, 29 April 2000.

24 W. C. Westmoreland, *A Soldier Reports*, Garden City, N.Y.: Doubleday, 1976, pp. 35–6.

25 Summers, op. cit., p. 103.

26 Cited by C. D. McFetridge, "Foreign Policy and Military Strategy: The Civil–Military Equation", *Military Review*, Vol. 66, No. 4, April 1986, p. 30. Clausewitz, op. cit., VIII, 6, p. 606. McFetridge actually used a different translation to this but the implication is the same. Since Vietnam, this aphorism has lost some of its truth. In Iraq, for example, "the employment of patrols" has had implications at the highest levels of policymaking.

27 A. Krepinevich, "Recovery from Defeat – The US Army and Vietnam", in G. J. Andreopoulos and H. E. Selesky, *The Aftermath of Defeat*, New Haven, Conn.: Yale University Press, 1994, p. 132.

28 Clausewitz, op. cit., VIII, 4, p. 596.

29 Cited by M. L. Brown, "Vietnam: Learning from the Debacle", *Military Review*, Vol. 67, No. 2, February 1987, p. 51; my emphasis.

30 Cited by H. S. Summers, *The New World Strategy*, New York: Touchstone, 1995, p. 21.

31 Cited by Ford, op. cit., p. 35.

32 Cited by R. M. Swain, book review of H. S. Summers, *On Strategy II*, in *Military Review*, Vol. 72, No. 6, June 1992, p. 80.

33 Forces in river patrol boats operating along the country's inland waterways did engage in psychological operations (psyops), which were limited to countering communist propaganda among the population and attempting to persuade the insurgents to give themselves up.

34 Westmoreland, cited by J. Kiszely, "The British Army and Approaches to Warfare since 1945", *Journal of Strategic Studies*, Vol. 19, No. 4, December 1996, p. 189. Carter Malkasian has offered a contrary opinion to the generally accepted view of American strategy in Vietnam. He argues that commanders at all levels in the command chain had few viable alternatives to attrition because of operational and strategic constraints. C. Malkasian, "Toward a Better Understanding of Attrition: The Korean and Vietnam Wars", *Journal of Military History*, Vol. 66, No. 3, July 2004, pp. 911–42.

35 R. Leonhard, *The Art of Maneuver – Maneuver Warfare Theory and AirLand Battle*, Novato, Calif.: Presidio Press, 1991, p. 162.

36 Ford, op cit., p. 166.

37 Cited by ibid., p. 47.

38 Krepinevich, "Recovery from Defeat", p. 133.

39 J. Kitfield, *Prodigal Soldiers – How the Generation of Officers Born of Vietnam Revolutionized the American Style of War*, Washington, DC, Brassey's, 1997, p. 73.

40 Cited by Ford, op cit., p. 170.

41 CIA cable of 8 December 1967, cited by ibid., p. 76.

42 Ibid., p. 74.

43 R. M. Citino, *Blitzkrieg to Desert Storm: The Evolution of Operational Warfare*, Lawrence: University Press of Kansas, 2004, p. 241.

44 Clausewitz, op. cit., I, 2, p. 91; emphasis in original.

45 Cited by Kissinger, op cit., p. 672.

46 Wynnyk, op cit., p. 144.

47 Lewis Sorley has argued that Vietnamisation and a concurrent change in emphasis from search-and-destroy operations to clear-and-hold operations helped to stabilise the situation in South Vietnam by 1972. L. Sorley, "Courage and Blood: South Vietnam's Repulse of the 1972 Easter Invasion", *Parameters*, Vol. 29, No. 2, Summer 1999. Online. Available www.carlisle.army.mil/usawc/parameters/99Summer/sorley.htm (accessed 2 March 2006).

48 D. Jablonsky, "Strategic Vision and Presidential Authority in the post-Cold War Era", *Parameters*, Vol. 21, No. 4, Winter 1991/92, p. 10.

49 Clausewitz, op. cit., I, 1, p. 77.

50 H. J. Henderson, "Brown-Water Navies and Counterinsurgency Operations", in English (ed.), op cit., p. 165.

51 Sorley, "Courage and Blood".

52 H. Kissinger, *White House Years*, Boston: Little, Brown and Co., 1979, p. 1199; emphasis in original.

53 Summers, *New World Strategy*, pp. 26–7.

54 Documents recently released from the North Vietnamese archives show that the Soviet Union continued to spend more than $1 billion a year aiding the Hanoi regime, a contravention of the Paris agreement. Laird, op. cit.

55 Clausewitz, op. cit., VIII, 3b, pp. 585–6. B. Brodie, "A Guide to the Reading of *On War*", in ibid., p. 702.

56 Ibid., VIII, 2, p. 579.

57 Ibid., III, 1, p. 178.

58 Townsend, op. cit., p. 57.

59 Cited by Summers, *On Strategy*, pp. 115–16.

60 Ibid., p. 95.

61 Ibid., p. 83.
62 Kissinger, *Diplomacy*, p. 658.
63 McNamara, op. cit.
64 Kissinger, *White House Years*, p. 36.
65 R. M. Cassidy, "Prophets or Praetorians? The Uptonian Paradox and the Powell Corollary", *Parameters*, Vol. 33, No. 3, Autumn 2003, p. 136. Summers, *On Strategy*, p. 105.
66 Summers, *On Strategy*, p. 130.
67 Clausewitz, op. cit., II, 2, p. 136.
68 M. Knox, "Continuity and Revolution in the Making of Strategy", in M. Knox, A. Bernstein and W. Murray, *The Making of Strategy*, Cambridge: Cambridge University Press, 1994, p. 621.
69 McNamara, op. cit., p. 311.
70 Summers, *On Strategy*, p. 38.
71 The dilution of Clausewitz's trinity into a simplistic triad of people, government and army originated in Summers's work. Nevertheless, Edward Villacres and Christopher Bassford argue that Summers succeeded in utilising his interpretation of the trinity into a valuable analytical tool and thereby adapted Clausewitz's thought to the Vietnam War. But they also sound a note of caution: "Unfortunately, such adaptations tend to have a counterproductive side effect: When times change, people remember the adaptations and forget the original, fundamental truth to which Clausewitz himself had pointed." E. J. Villacres and C. Bassford, "Reclaiming the Clausewitzian Trinity", *Parameters*, Vol. 25, No. 3, Autumn 1995, pp. 9–19.
72 Clausewitz, op. cit., VIII, 9, p. 626. Kissinger, *Diplomacy*, pp. 672–3.
73 Cited by W. S. Thompson and D. D. Frizzell (eds), *The Lessons of Vietnam*, New York: Crane, Russack and Co., 1977, p. 279.
74 Cited by Summers, *On Strategy*, p. 19.
75 M. T. Brady, "The Army and the Strategic Military Legacy of Vietnam", Master of Military Art and Science thesis, 1990, Fort Leavenworth, Kansas. I am grateful to Dr. Steven Metz of the Strategic Studies Institute, US Army War College, for this insight. Interview with Dr Steven Metz at the US Army War College, Carlisle Barracks, Pennsylvania, 19 September 2000.
76 Summers, *On Strategy*, p. 194.
77 Collins, op. cit., p. 18. Martin van Creveld has, for example, attacked what he calls the "trinitarian" nature of *On War*. M. van Creveld, *On Future War*, London: Brassey's, 1991.

4 The renaissance of American strategic thought

1 R. J. Spiller, "In the Shadow of the Dragon: Doctrine and the US Army after Vietnam", *RUSI Journal*, Vol. 142, No. 6, December 1997, p. 53.
2 S. Turner, "Convocation Address", reprinted in *Naval War College Review*, Vol. 51, No. 1, Winter 1997/98.
3 Dr Earl Tilford, Strategic Studies Institute, US Army War College, letter to the author, 24 June 1999. Interview with Lieutenant-Colonel Antulio J. Echevarria II at the US Army War College, Carlisle Barracks, Pennsylvania, 19 September 2000.
4 M. Howard, comments made at the Oxford Leverhulme Programme Conference on Clausewitz and the 21st Century, Oxford, March 2005. Angus Malcolm had also been involved in the translation but died before it was completed. Paret and Howard then revised the whole text of the translation.
5 H. Rosinski, "Scharnhorst to Schlieffen: The Rise and Decline of German Military Thought", *Naval War College Review*, Vol. 29, No. 1, Summer 1976, p. 83. The citation is from the introduction to the essay by the journal's editor. Two other examples of Clausewitzian articles in the American military press during this period, aside from

Rosinski, are N. H. Gibbs, "Clausewitz on the Moral Forces in War", *Naval War College Review*, Vol. 27, No. 4, January–February 1975, pp. 15–22, and G. F. Freudenberg, "A Conversation with General Clausewitz", *Military Review*, Vol. 57, No. 10, October 1977, pp. 68–71. The latter was typical of the genre of writing, of which Summers's *On Strategy* is the most famous example, that examined the lessons of Vietnam through a Clausewitzian prism. Robert Citino has written that in "intellectual tone and breadth of interests [*Military Review*] was fully the equal of the interwar German journal, the *Militär-Wochenblatt*". R. M. Citino, *Blitzkrieg to Desert Storm: The Evolution of Operational Warfare*, Lawrence: University Press of Kansas, 2004, p. 260.

6 C. von Clausewitz, *On War*, Princeton, N.J.: Princeton University Press, 1984, trans. and ed. by M. Howard and P. Paret, Bk I, Ch. 3, p. 112. P. H. Herbert, *Deciding What Has to Be Done: General William E. Depuy and the 1976 Edition of FM100–5, Operations*, Leavenworth Paper No. 16, Fort Leavenworth, Kans.: Combat Studies Institute, US Army Command and General Staff College, 1988, p. 79.

7 Citation by Spiller, op cit., p. 46.

8 Ibid., p. 46.

9 Cited by Major-General Cushman, commandant of the Combined Arms Center, Fort Leavenworth, in a note to generals Creighton Abrams and William E. DePuy, 4 May 1974, DePuy Papers, US Army Military History Institute (USAMHI), Carlisle Barracks, Pennsylvania.

10 J. Kitfield, *Prodigal Soldiers – How the Generation of Officers Born of Vietnam Revolutionized the American Style of War*, Washington: Brassey's, 1997, p. 153.

11 D. A. Starry, "A Perspective on American Military Thought", *Military Review*, Vol. 69, No. 7, July 1989, p. 8. Kitfield, op. cit., p. 154. H. R. Winton, "An Ambivalent Partnership: US Army and Air Force Perspectives on Air–Ground Operations, 1973–90", in P. S. Meilinger (ed.), *The Paths of Heaven – The Evolution of Airpower Theory*, Maxwell Air Force Base, Ala.: Air University Press, 1997, p. 437.

12 Cited by Spiller, op. cit., p. 50.

13 Clausewitz, op. cit., VI, 5, p. 370.

14 J. E. King, "On Clausewitz: Master Theorist of War", *Naval War College Review*, Vol. 30, No. 2, Fall 1977, p. 31.

15 Interview between Dr Michael Pearlman and DePuy, 15 January 1987, Group US Army Command and General Staff College, file CTAC-027, p. 10.

16 Department of the Army, FM 100–5: *Operations*, Washington, DC, July 1976, pp. 5-13–5-14; my emphasis.

17 Clausewitz, op. cit., VI, 5, p. 370.

18 Spiller, op. cit., p. 50. Aside from a general chapter in FM 100–5 on the use of tactical nuclear weapons, tactical nuclear doctrine was described in a separate, classified manual, FM 100–5-1.

19 Cited by Herbert, op cit., p. 93; emphasis in original. B. Lambeth, *The Transformation of American Air Power*, Ithaca, N.Y.: Cornell University Press, 2000, p. 83.

20 FM 100–5, 1976, pp. 3–4; emphasis in original.

21 Colonel Paul Herbert (2000) "Influence of Clausewitz on American Thought", e-mail (19 May 2000). Professor Peter Paret (2000) "Clausewitz and the US Military", e-mail (16 October 2000).

22 J. C. Studt, "Foreword", in W. Lind, *Maneuver Warfare Handbook*, Boulder, Colo.: Westview Press, 1985, pp. xi–xii.

23 W. Lind, "Some Doctrinal Questions for the United States Army", *Military Review*, Vol. 57, No. 3, March 1977.

24 W. Lind, L. D. Holder and R. M. Swain, "A Dialogue on the Evolution of Doctrine', *Military Review*, Vol. 69, No. 11, November 1989, p. 74.

25 Letter from Lind to Colonel Edward Bradford, editor of *Military Review*, 7 August 1978, Starry Papers, USAMHI, Carlisle Barracks, Pennsylvania. Clausewitz, of

course, had emphasised physical and psychological factors as being complementary to each other.

26 R. Leonhard, *The Art of Maneuver – Maneuver Warfare Theory and AirLand Battle*, Novato, Calif.: Presidio Press, 1991, pp. 87–8. G. T. Hammond, *The Mind of War – John Boyd and American Security*, Washington, DC, Smithsonian Institution Press, 2001.

27 Captain Timothy Keppler has shown that Clausewitz's explanation of the *Schwerpunkt* in Bk VI of *On War* has been distorted by being literally translated as "heavy point" when in fact the centre of gravity in this context does not necessarily refer to a geographical point. T. J. Keppler, "The Center of Gravity Concept: A Knowledge Engineering Approach to Improved Understanding and Application", School of Advanced Military Studies monograph, Fort Leavenworth, Kansas, June 1995.

28 Clausewitz, op cit., VII, 9, p. 535, cited by M. Wyly, "Lecture 1: Surfaces and Gaps", in Lind, *Maneuver Warfare Handbook*, p. 74; emphasis in original.

29 Lind, "Some Doctrinal Questions", p. 55.

30 TRADOC's reply of October 1976 to the draft of Lind's article cited by J. W. Romjue, *From Active Defense to AirLand Battle*, Fort Monroe, N.J.: TRADOC Historical Office, 1984, p. 15. Letter from General D. A. Starry to Major-General J. G. R. Allen, Director UK Royal Armoured Corps, 26 March 1975, Starry Papers.

31 Cited by Lind, "Some Doctrinal Questions", p. 58.

32 After 1979, a number of German officers who had fought against the Soviets in the Second World War participated in the Art of War Colloquium at the Army War College, including Generals Hermann Balck and F. W. von Mellenthin. They demonstrated the way in which outnumbered armies could fight and win through the use of superior command and control. Interview with Lieutenant-Colonel Antulio J. Echevarria II at the US Army War College, Carlisle Barracks, Penn., 19 September 2000.

33 FM 100–5, 1976, cited by Lind, "Some Doctrinal Questions", p. 64.

34 Clausewitz, op. cit., VI, 25, p. 471.

35 W. E. DePuy, transcript of oral history interview with R. L. Brownlee and W. J. Mullen, 1979, USAMHI, p. 192.

36 Lind, "Some Doctrinal Questions", p. 65.

37 Clausewitz, op. cit., VI, 22, p. 454. A. Jones, "The New FM 100–5: A View from the Ivory Tower", *Military Review*, Vol. 58, No. 2, February 1978, pp. 33–4.

38 J. Klinger, "The Social Science of Carl von Clausewitz", *Parameters*, Vol. 36, No. 1, Spring 2006, p. 83. J. Sumida, "On Defense as the Stronger Form of War". Online. Available ccw.politics.ox.ac.uk/events/archives/tt05_clausewitz_sumida.pdf (accessed 29 March 2005). S. Naveh, *In Pursuit of Military Excellence – The Evolution of Operational Theory*, London: Frank Cass, 1997. P. R. A. Doughty and L. D. Holder, "Images of the Future Battlefield", *Military Review*, Vol. 58, No. 1, January 1978, pp. 56–69. Jones, op. cit.

39 Correspondence between Haig and DePuy, 10 September 1976, cited by Herbert, *Deciding What Has to Be Done*, pp. 96–7.

40 Naveh, op cit., p. 255.

41 G. W. Smith, "Clausewitz in the 1970s: RX for Dilemma", *Military Review*, Vol. 52, No. 7, July 1972, p. 93.

42 Cited by L. Freedman, *The Evolution of Nuclear Strategy*, 2nd edn, London: Macmillan, 1989, p. 378.

43 Ibid., p. 369.

44 Cited by ibid., p. 369.

45 J. Richelson, "PD-59, NSDD13 and the Reagan Strategic Modernisation Program", *Journal of Strategic Studies*, Vol. 6, No. 2, June 1983, p. 143.

46 N. H. Fritz, "Clausewitz and US Nuclear Weapons Policy", *Air University Review*, Vol. 34, No. 1, November–December 1982, p. 23.

47 B. Brodie, "The Development of Nuclear Strategy", *International Security*, Vol. II, No. 4, Spring 1978, p. 80.
48 Cited by Freedman, op. cit., ibid., p. 388.
49 C. S. Gray, *The Future of Land-Based Missile Forces*, London: International Institute for Strategic Studies, 1978, p. 1.
50 Freedman, op cit., p. 392.
51 Cited by ibid., p. 393.
52 H. Brown, *Thinking About National Security: Defense and Foreign-Policy in a Dangerous World*, Boulder, Colo.: Westview Press, 1983, p. 82; emphasis in original.
53 Cited by C. Gray, *Modern Strategy*, Oxford: Oxford University Press, 1999, p. 309.
54 M. Howard, "The Forgotten Dimensions of Strategy", *Foreign Affairs*, Vol. 57, No. 5, Summer 1979, pp. 984 and 986.
55 H. Kissinger, *Diplomacy*, New York: Simon and Schuster, 1994, p. 76.
56 Brigadier-General (Retd.) Huba Wass de Czege (2000) "Clausewitz and FM 100–5", e-mail (22 June 2000).
57 Letter from Starry to Lieutenant-General Edward Meyer, 30 January 1979, Starry Papers, US Army Military History Institute, Carlisle Barracks, Pennsylvania. Citation by Naveh, op. cit., p. 313.
58 Professor Roger Spiller believes that Holder was the more influential of the two. Interview with Professor Roger Spiller, US Army Command and General Staff College, Fort Leavenworth, Kansas, 7 September 1999.
59 E. N. Luttwak, "The American Style in Warfare and the Military Balance", *Survival*, Vol. 21, No. 2, March–April 1979, pp. 57–60; emphasis in the original. Starry was so infuriated by Luttwak's criticisms of the military at the time that he reprimanded an officer who had invited Luttwak to speak at Leavenworth. Spiller interview.
60 E. N. Luttwak: "The Operational Level of War", *International Security*, Vol. 5, No. 3, Winter 1980–81, p. 61.
61 Naveh, op cit., p. 299; emphasis in original. J. J. Schneider and L. L. Izzo, "Clausewitz's Elusive Center of Gravity", *Parameters*, Vol. 27, No. 3, September 1987, p. 56; emphasis in original.
62 D. A. Starry, "Extending the Battlefield", *Military Review*, Vol. 61, No. 3, March 1981, p. 32. Meyer was a big influence on the new field manual. He had also sponsored the publication of Summers's *On Strategy*. C. Crane, *Avoiding Vietnam: The US Army's Response to Defeat in Southeast Asia*, Carlisle, Pa.: Strategic Studies Institute, 2002, p. 8.
63 Naveh, op cit., p. 295.
64 Ibid., p. 296.
65 Starry, "Extending the Battlefield", p. 32.
66 Ibid., p. 34.
67 Ibid.
68 Ibid., p. 39.
69 R. Lock-Pullan, "How to Rethink War: Conceptual Innovation and AirLand Battle Doctrine", *Journal of Strategic Studies*, Vol. 28, No. 4, August 2005, p. 681.
70 G. K. Otis, "The AirLand Battle" (letter for distribution), *Military Review*, Vol. 62, No. 5, May 1982.
71 Cited by Naveh, op. cit., p. 11.
72 Letter from Major-General Alexander M. Weyand to Starry, 29 April 1981, Starry Papers.
73 Department of the Army, FM 100–5: *Operations*, Washington, DC, August 1982, pp. 8–4. Clausewitz, op. cit., IV, 4, p. 231.
74 Wass de Czege, e-mail. J. Keegan, *The Face of Battle*, London: Penguin, 1976. C. J. J. Ardant du Picq, *Battle Studies: Ancient and Modern Battle*, New York: Military Service Publishing Co., 1921.
75 L. D. Holder and H. Wass de Czege, "The New FM 100–5", *Military Review*, Vol.

62, No. 7, July 1982, p. 70. Of course, one must not forget the impact of Soviet theories on the manual, as already discussed.

76 FM 100–5, 1982, pp. 2–3. Romjue, op. cit., p. 70.

77 G. Sude, "Defense in Clausewitz's *On War* and in FM 100–5 and in HDv 100/100", Master of Military Art and Science thesis, US Army Command and General Staff College, Fort Leavenworth, Kansas, 1985, p. 99.

78 Lock-Pullan, op. cit., p. 683.

79 Letter from Brigadier-General Crosbie E. Saint to Wass de Czege, 23 March 1981, Starry Papers.

80 S. Argersinger, "K. von Clausewitz: Analysis of FM 100–5", *Military Review*, Vol. 66, No. 2, February 1986, pp. 68–75. Clausewitz, op. cit., VI, 9, p. 391.

81 D. J. Alberts, "Deterrence in the 1980s – Part II. The Role of Conventional Air Power", London, International Institute for Strategic Studies, *Adelphi Paper* 193, Winter 1984, p. 36.

82 Clausewitz, op. cit., VI, 1, p. 357, and FM 100–5, 1982, p. 11–1.

83 Argersinger, op. cit., p. 68.

84 M. J. D'Amato, "Vigilant Warrior: General Donn A. Starry's AirLand Battle and How it Changed the Army", *Armor*, Vol. 109, No. 3, May–June 2000, p. 21. Winton, op. cit., p. 437. J. B. Rodgers, "Synchronizing the AirLand Battle", *Military Review*, Vol. 66, No. 4, April 1986, pp. 64–71. Leonhard, op. cit., pp. 132ff.

85 Romjue, op. cit., p. 5.

86 Wass de Czege, e-mail. D'Amato, op. cit., p. 22.

87 J. Tashjean, *The Transatlantic Clausewitz*, Carlisle, Pa.: Strategic Studies Institute, US Army War College, 1983, p. 18. Spiller interview. P. Paret, "Clausewitz", in H. S. Bausam (ed.), *Military Leadership and Command*, Lexington, Virginia Military Institute Foundation, 1987, p. 46.

5 American strategic thought under Reagan

1 C. Weinberger, *Fighting for Peace: Seven Critical Years at the Pentagon*, London: Michael Joseph, 1990, p. 25.

2 Cited by H. Kissinger, *Diplomacy*, New York: Simon and Schuster, 1994, p. 774.

3 C. S. Gray, "Nuclear Strategy: The Case for a Theory of Victory", *International Security*, Vol. 4, 1979, pp. 54–87. C. S. Gray and K. B. Payne, "Victory is Possible", *Foreign Policy*, Vol. 39, 1980, pp. 14–27.

4 Kissinger, op cit., pp. 764–5.

5 M. Handel, *Masters of War – Classical Strategic Thought*, 2nd edn, London: Frank Cass, 1996, p. 247.

6 Cited by A. F. Krepinevich, "Recovery from Defeat: The US Army and Vietnam", in G. J. Andreopoulos and H. E. Selesky, *The Aftermath of Defeat – Societies, Armed Forces and the Challenge of Recovery*, New Haven, Conn.: Yale University Press, 1994, p. 136.

7 Kissinger, op cit., p. 768.

8 N. Friedman, *The Fifty-Year War: Conflict and Strategy in the Cold War*, London: Chatham Publishing, 2003, p. 460.

9 Cited by L. Freedman, *Evolution of Nuclear Strategy*, 2nd edn, London: Macmillan, 1989, p. 406; my emphasis.

10 Cited by ibid., p. 406.

11 C. von Clausewitz, *On War*, Princeton, N.J.: Princeton University Press, 1984, trans. and ed. by M. Howard and P. Paret, Bk VIII, Ch. 6, p. 608. S. Cimbala, *Clausewitz and Escalation*, London: Frank Cass, 1991, p. 39.

12 N. H. Fritz, "Clausewitz and US Nuclear Weapons Policy", *Air University Review*, Vol. 34, No. 1, November–December 1982, p. 24.

13 L. Freedman, "The First Two Generations of Nuclear Strategists", in P. Paret *et al.*,

Makers of Modern Strategy from Machiavelli to the Nuclear Age, Princeton, N.J.: Princeton University Press, 1986, p. 776.

14 Cited by D. Kagan, "The End of Wars as the Basis for a Lasting Peace", *Naval War College Review*, Vol. 53, No. 4, Autumn 2000. Online. Available www.nwc.navy.mil/press/Review/2000/autumn/art1-a00.htm (accessed 18 October 2000).

15 Cited by Freedman, *Evolution*, p. 413.

16 Weinberger, op. cit., p. 216.

17 Freedman, *Evolution*, p. 413.

18 M. Bundy, G. Kennan and R. McNamara, "The President's Choice: Star Wars or Arms Control", *Foreign Affairs*, Vol. 63, No. 2, Winter 1984/5.

19 Weinberger, op. cit., p. 204.

20 Ibid., p. 224.

21 Cimbala, op. cit., p. 157.

22 Cited by C. Gray and K. Payne, "Nuclear Policy and the Defensive Transition", *Foreign Affairs*, Vol. 62, No. 4, Spring 1984, p. 855.

23 L. Freedman, "Strategic Defence in the Nuclear Age", Adelphi Paper 224, Autumn 1987, p. 42, International Institute for Strategic Studies.

24 Cimbala, op cit., p. 158.

25 Kissinger, op cit., p. 780.

26 The text of the speech is in Weinberger, op. cit., pp. 433–45.

27 R. Lock-Pullan, *US Intervention Policy and Army Innovation: From Vietnam to Iraq*, New York: Routledge, 2006, p. 119.

28 J. F. Otis, "Clausewitz: On Weinberger", *Marine Corps Gazette*, Vol. 72, No. 2, February 1988, p. 16. C. Crane, *Avoiding Vietnam: The US Army's Response to Defeat in Southeast Asia*, Carlisle, Pa.: Strategic Studies Institute, 2002, p. 14.

29 Weinberger, op. cit., p. 434.

30 Ibid., p. 444.

31 Clausewitz, op cit., VIII, 2, p. 579.

32 Ibid., I, 2, p. 91.

33 Handel, op cit., p. 197.

34 Clausewitz, op. cit., I, 1, p. 88.

35 D. Twining, "Vietnam and the Six Criteria for the Use of Military Force", *Parameters*, Vol. 15, No. 4, Winter 1985, p. 10.

36 Lock-Pullan, op. cit., p. 123.

37 B. Lambeth, *The Transformation of American Air Power*, Ithaca, N.Y.: Cornell University Press, 2000, p. 67.

38 J. Kitfield, *Prodigal Soldiers – How the Generation of Officers Born of Vietnam Revolutionized the American Style of War*, Washington, DC, Brassey's, 1997, p. 167.

39 Cited by H. Summers, *The New World Strategy*, New York: Touchstone, 1995, p. 107.

40 H. D. Belote, "Warden and the Air Corps Tactical School", *Airpower Journal*, Vol. 13, No. 3, Fall 1999, p. 41.

41 Cited by C. Bassford, *Clausewitz in English: The Reception of Clausewitz in Britain and America, 1815–1945*, New York: Oxford University Press, 1994, p. 204. H. R. Winton, "An Ambivalent Partnership: US Army and Air Force Perspectives on Air–Ground Operations, 1973–90", in P. S. Meilinger (ed.), *The Paths of Heaven – The Evolution of Airpower Theory*, Maxwell Air Force Base, Alabama: Air University Press, 1997, p. 415.

42 S. Fraser, *US Maritime Strategy: Issues and Implications*, Bailrigg Paper 25, Centre for Defence and International Security Studies, Lancaster University, 1997, p. 17.

43 J. Nathan, "The Future of the US Maritime Strategy", *Journal of Strategic Studies*, Vol. 11, No. 4, December 1988, p. 468.

44 C. A. Ford and D. A. Rosenberg, "The Naval Intelligence Underpinnings of Reagan's Maritime Strategy", *Journal of Strategic Studies*, Vol. 28, No. 2, April 2005, pp. 379–409. J. B. Hattendorf, *The Evolution of the US Navy's Maritime Strategy*, Newport Paper No. 19, Newport, R.I.: Naval War College Press, 2004. However, Vladimir Kuzin and Sergei Chernyavskii offer a contrary view, arguing that the Soviet Navy followed a "dual" strategy, incorporating offensive and defensive elements. V. Kuzin and S. Chernyavskii, "Russian Reactions to Reagan's 'Maritime Strategy'", *Journal of Strategic Studies*, Vol. 28, No. 2, April 2005, pp. 429–39.

45 Kitfield, op. cit., p. 285. Nathan, op. cit., p. 470.

46 J. Lehman, "Aircraft Carriers – The Real Choices", Washington Papers, Vol. VI, Center for Strategic and International Studies, Georgetown University, Washington, DC, 1978, pp. 15–16.

47 Ibid., p. 18.

48 Cited by Fraser, op cit., p. 9.

49 Cited by ibid., p. 21. Watkins, however, was of the opinion that Mahanian thinking remained vital, though it required updating. Hattendorf, op. cit., p. 75.

50 S. Turner and G. Thibault, "Preparing for the Unexpected: The Need for a New Military Strategy", *Foreign Affairs*, Vol. 61, No. 1, Fall 1982, p. 126.

51 Ibid.

52 R. S. Moore, "Blitzkrieg from the Sea: Maneuver Warfare and Amphibious Operations", *Naval War College Review*, Vol. 36, No. 6, November–December 1983, pp. 37–8 and 45.

53 Interview with Dr Steven Metz at the US Army War College, Carlisle Barracks, Pennsylvania, 19 September 2000.

54 Michael Evans has written of this distinction when discussing land power. M. Evans, *The Continental School of Strategy: The Past, Present and Future of Land Power*, Land Warfare Studies Centre, Study Paper No. 305, June 2004.

55 C. S. Gray, "Maritime Strategy", *US Naval Institute Proceedings*, Vol. 112, No. 2, February 1986, p. 36.

56 Nathan, op. cit., p. 474.

57 Gray, "Maritime Strategy", p. 38.

58 C. W. Weinberger, "US Defense Strategy", *Foreign Affairs*, Vol. 64, No. 4, Spring 1986, p. 696. Reagan's speech is cited in Kissinger, op. cit., p. 783.

59 Weinberger, "US Defense Strategy", p. 696.

60 Ibid., pp. 676–7.

61 R. M. Swain, "Clausewitz for the 20th Century: The Interpretation of Raymond Aron", *Military Review*, Vol. 66, No. 4, April 1986, p. 47.

62 D. Jablonsky, "Strategy and the Operational Level of War: Part II", *Parameters*, Vol. 17, No. 2, Summer 1987, p. 57.

63 Cited by ibid., p. 63.

64 C. D. McFetridge, "Foreign Policy and Military Strategy: The Civil–Military Equation", *Military Review*, Vol. 66, No. 4, April 1986, p. 30.

65 Cited by T. P. Reilly, "The National Security Strategy of the United States: Development of Grand Strategy", in W. Murray (ed.), *A Nation at War in an Era of Strategic Change*, Carlisle, Pa.: Strategic Studies Institute, 2004, p. 327.

66 Colonel Huba Wass de Czege, co-author of the manual, had already made this clear in a covering letter to a 1985 draft of the revised manual. H. Wass de Czege, cover letter to draft FM 100–5, 1 July 1985, "Subject: The Nature and Reasons for Changes in this Edition".

67 W. R. Richardson: "FM 100–5: The AirLand Battle in 1986", *Military Review*, Vol. 66, No. 3, March 1986, p. 8.

68 B. W. Rogers, "Follow-On Forces Attack: Myths and Realities", *NATO Review*, December 1984, pp. 5–6.

69 Jablonsky, op. cit., p. 64. Clausewitz, op. cit., VI, 5, p. 370.
70 Richardson, op. cit., p. 11. Clausewitz, op. cit., II, 2, p. 141. A. Galloway, "FM 100–5: Who Influenced Whom?", *Military Review*, Vol. 66, No. 3, March 1986, pp. 46–51. Brigadier-General (Retd.) Huba Wass de Czege (2000) "Clausewitz and FM 100–5", e-mail (22 June 2000).
71 Department of the Army, FM 100–5: *Operations*, Washington, DC, May 1986, p. 179.
72 Interview with Colonel Clinton J. Ancker III, director, Combined Arms Doctrine Directorate, Fort Leavenworth, at the Royal United Services Institute, London, 19 November 1999.
73 FM 100–5, 1986, pp. 17–18.
74 Ibid., p. 179. The manual also directly cited Clausewitz's passage from *On War*, which set out his definition of the centre of gravity. Clausewitz, op. cit., VIII, 3, pp. 595–6.
75 H. Wass de Czege, "Clausewitz: Historical Theories Remain Sound Compass References: The Catch Is Staying on Course", *ARMY*, Vol. 38, No. 9, September 1988, p. 42.
76 T. M. Kriwanek, "The Operational Center of Gravity", School of Advanced Military Studies monograph, US Army Command and General Staff College, Fort Leavenworth, Kansas, May 1986, pp. 20–1.
77 A. J. Echevarria, *Clausewitz's Center of Gravity: Changing our Warfighting Doctrine – Again!*, Carlisle, Pa.: Strategic Studies Institute, 2002, p. 12. Echevarria's interpretation of the centre of gravity is more sophisticated than that of FM 100–5, 1986. It is only in very recent years that the US military has adopted the notion of effects-based operations.
78 Warden is discussed in Chapter 6. J. J. Schneider and L. L. Izzo, "Clausewitz's Elusive Centre of Gravity", *Parameters*, Vol. 17, No. 3, September 1987, p. 49. S. Naveh, *In Pursuit of Military Excellence – The Evolution of Operational Theory*, London: Frank Cass, 1997, p. 48. Clausewitz, op. cit., VI, 27, p. 485. Interview with Lieutenant-Colonel Antulio J. Echevarria at the US Army War College, Carlisle Barracks, Pennsylvania, 19 September 2000.
79 Schneider and Izzo, op. cit., pp. 52 and 56. W. Lind, "The Operational Art", *Marine Corps Gazette*, Vol. 72, No. 4, April 1988, p. 45. Citations from Jomini by J. Shy, "Jomini" in P. Paret *et al.*, *Makers of Modern Strategy from Machiavelli to the Nuclear Age*, Princeton, N.J.: Princeton University Press, 1986, pp. 154 and 152. I am grateful to Antulio Echevarria for the insight concerning Jomini; Echevarria interview. Naveh, op. cit., p. 242.
80 Clausewitz, op. cit., VI, 28, p. 491; emphasis in original. Clausewitz understood the significance of the decisive point: "The best strategy is always to be very strong; first in general, and then at the decisive point" (ibid., III, 11, p. 204; emphasis in original).
81 Cited by J. T. Nelsen, "Auftragstaktik: A Case for Decentralized Battle", *Parameters*, Vol. 17, No. 3, September 1987, p. 28. Clausewitz, op. cit., II, 2, p. 136.
82 J. L. Silva, "Auftragstaktik: Its Origin and Development", *Infantry*, Vol. 79, No. 5, September–October 1989, p. 9.
83 FM 100–5, 1986, pp. 181–2. Clausewitz, op. cit., VII, 22, p. 570. Wass de Czege, "Clausewitz", p. 43.
84 Clausewitz, op. cit., VII, 22, p. 572. This citation is, in fact, from a chapter entitled "The Culminating Point of Victory", which complemented and expanded on the ideas expressed in an earlier chapter, "The Culminating Point of the Attack" (ibid., VII, 5, p. 528).
85 Cited by F. Kagan, "Army Doctrine and Modern War: Notes Toward a New Edition of FM 100–5", *Parameters*, Vol. 27, No. 1, Spring 1997. Online. Available carlisle-www.Army.mil/usawc/Parameters/97spring/kagan.htm (accessed 27 August 1999).

86 Wass de Czege, e-mail.
87 M. J. Redlinger, "Hans Delbrück and Clausewitz's Culminating Points", School of Advanced Military Studies monograph, US Army Command and General Staff College, Fort Leavenworth, Kansas, May 1988, p. 15.
88 Naveh, op. cit., p. 318.
89 J. B. Smith, "Some Thoughts on Clausewitz and Airplanes", *Air University Review*, Vol. 37, No. 3, March–April 1986, p. 57. Both General Michael Dugan and Lieutenant-Colonel Price Bingham of the Air Force criticised the Army's narrow, unilateral definition of synchronisation as presented by FM 100–5, 1986. M. J. Dugan, "Air Power: Concentration, Responsibilities and Operational Art", *Military Review*, Vol. 69, No. 7, July 1989, pp. 12–21, and P. T. Bingham, "Ground Maneuver and Air Interdiction in the Operational Art", *Parameters*, Vol. 19, No. 1, Spring 1989, pp. 16–31.
90 Wass de Czege, e-mail, and "Clausewitz", p. 43. Galloway, op. cit., p. 47. G. M. Harned, "Principles for Modern Doctrine from Two Venerated Theorists", *ARMY*, Vol. 36, No. 4, April 1986, p. 10. J. B. Saxman, "The Concept of Centers of Gravity: Does it have Utility in Joint Doctrine and Campaign Planning", School of Advanced Military Studies monograph, US Army Command and General Staff College, Fort Leavenworth, Kansas, May 1992, p. 1.
91 R. M. Swain, " 'The Hedgehog and the Fox': Jomini, Clausewitz, and History", *Naval War College Review*, Autumn 1990, p. 107.
92 T. B. Vaughn, "Clausewitz and Contemporary American Professionalism", *Military Review*, Vol. 62, No. 12, December 1982, p. 40.
93 *Command and General Staff College Catalogue, Academic Year 1989–90*, Fort Leavenworth, Kansas, p. 99.
94 Interview with Dr Earl Tilford, Strategic Studies Institute, US Army War College, 14 September 1999.
95 Aside from the monographs cited throughout this work, other works that specifically refer to Clausewitz include the following SAMS monographs: J. W. Karhohs, "The Economics of War Planning: An Addition to the Clausewitzian Trinity", May 1991; M. T. Inman, "The Tactical Center of Gravity: How Useful is the Concept?", January 1990; O. J. Moss, "Searching for the Stronger Form of War at the Operational Level in the 20th Century: The Defense or the Offense?", May 1988; D. J. Benjamin, Jun., "Prerequisite for Victory: The Discovery of the Culminating Point", May 1986; and G. S. Webb, "The Flashing Sword of Vengeance: The Force-Oriented Counterattack from a Historical Perspective with Implications for the AirLand Battle and Combat Aviation", December 1985. Also worthy of note is a Master of Military Art and Science thesis by L. W. Bentley, "Clausewitz and German Idealism: The Influence of G. W. F. Hegel on *On War*", June 1988.
96 Dr Earl Tilford, letter to the author, 24 June 1999.
97 Colonel James Holcomb, Department of National Security Studies, US Army War College (1999) "Clausewitz", e-mail to the author (8 July 1999).
98 L. J. Matthews, "On Clausewitz", *ARMY*, Vol. 38, No. 2, February 1988, p. 24.
99 E. Alterman, "The Uses and Abuses of Clausewitz", *Parameters*, Vol. 17, No. 2, Summer 1987, p. 30.
100 Matthews, op. cit., p. 23.
101 J. E. Shepherd, " 'On War': Is Clausewitz Still Relevant?", *Parameters*, Vol. 20, No. 3, September 1990, p. 98.
102 R. Swain, *Selected Papers of William E. DePuy*, Fort Leavenworth, Kans.: Combat Studies Institute, USACGSC, 1994, p. 413. DePuy quantified the difference in the complexity of war by showing that the 11 principal battle formations of Clausewitz's time had increased to 30 by the time of AirLand Battle.
103 J. C. Studt, "Foreword", in W. Lind, *Maneuver Warfare Handbook*, Boulder, Colo., Westview Press, 1985, p. xi.

104 Ibid., p. 50.
105 J. F. Schmitt, "The Great FMFM 1 Debate: Is There Anything New Here?", *Marine Corps Gazette*, Vol. 73, No. 11, November 1989, p. 26. A. M. Gray, "Foreword", in FMFM 1, *Warfighting*, as reproduced in H. T. Hayden (ed.), *Warfighting: Maneuver Warfare in the US Marine Corps*, London: Greenhill, 1995, p. 36; my emphasis (hereafter referred to as FMFM 1).
106 G. T. Hammond, *The Mind of War – John Boyd and American Security*, Washington, DC, Smithsonian Institution Press, 2001, p. 152.
107 FMFM 1, pp. 47 and 45; emphases in original.
108 W. Lind, "Misconceptions of Maneuver Warfare", *Marine Corps Gazette*, Vol. 72, No. 1, January 1988, p. 17.
109 J. J. Lloyd, "Our 'Warfighting' Philosophy", *Marine Corps Gazette*, Vol. 73, No. 11, November 1989, p. 25.
110 FMFM 1, p. 68.
111 E. J. Robeson, "Critique of 'FMFM 1, *Warfighting*'", *Marine Corps Gazette*, Vol. 73, No. 11, November 1989, pp. 27–9. C. A. Tucker, "False Prophet: The Myth of Maneuver Warfare and the Inadequacies of FMFM 1 *Warfighting*", School of Advanced Military Studies monograph, US Army Command and General Staff College, Fort Leavenworth, Kansas, 2nd Term, AY 1994–95.
112 Dr Christopher Bassford (2000), "The USMC and Clausewitz", e-mail (11 October 2000).
113 Tucker, op. cit., p. 46. P. M. Strain, "The Tactical Center of Gravity: Fact or Fallacy?", School of Advanced Military Studies monograph, US Army Command and General Staff College, Fort Leavenworth, Kansas, December 1992, p. 27.
114 FMFM 1, p. 74. "Focus of effort" was, in fact, Lind's translation of the German *Schwerpunkt* which, as we have seen, differs from Clausewitz's use of the term. Saxman, op. cit., p. 19.
115 Robeson, op. cit., p. 29; emphasis in original.
116 FMFM 1, p. 40.
117 Ibid., pp. 72–3. Lind, "Misconceptions", p. 17.
118 J. F. Schmitt, "Out of Sync with Maneuver Warfare", *Marine Corps Gazette*, Vol. 78, No. 8, August 1994, p. 19.
119 FMFM 1, p. 56.
120 Lock-Pullan, op. cit., p. 123.
121 W. Murray, "Operation Iraqi Freedom: Lessons for the Future", in Murray (ed.), op. cit., p. 11.

6 The Gulf War

1 J. J. Yeosock, "Army Operations in the Gulf Theater", *Military Review*, Vol. 71, No. 9, September 1991, p. 3. Among the general literature on the Gulf War are R. M. Swain, *"Lucky War": Third Army in Desert Storm*, 2nd edn, Fort Leavenworth, Kans,: US Army Command and General Staff College Press, 1997. M. R. Gordon and B. E. Trainor, *The Generals' War: The Inside Story of the Conflict in the Gulf*, Boston, Mass.: Little, Brown, 1995. R. H. Scales, *Certain Victory: The US Army in the Gulf War*, Fort Leavenworth, Kans.: US Army Command and General Staff College Press, 1994. R. P. Hallion, *Storm over Iraq – Air Power and the Gulf War*, Washington, DC, Smithsonian Institution Press, 1992. G. Bush and B. Scowcroft, *A World Transformed*, Alfred A. Knopf, 1998. H. N. Schwarzkopf, *It Doesn't Take a Hero*, New York: Bantam Books, 1992.
2 Cited by T. R. DuBois, "The Weinberger Doctrine and the Liberation of Kuwait", *Parameters*, Vol. 21, No. 4, Winter 1991–92, pp. 28–9.
3 Ibid., p. 28.
4 According to Colonel Richard Swain, the Americans took 88 days from 7 August to

generate a force of 184,000 men. In Vietnam, the same force had taken 365 days to generate. Swain, op. cit., p. 38.

5 Cited by S. Naveh, *In Pursuit of Military Excellence – The Evolution of Operational Theory*, London: Frank Cass, 1997, pp. 326–7.

6 J. Record, *The Creeping Irrelevance of US Force Planning*, Carlisle Barracks, Pa.: Strategic Studies Institute, US Army War College, 1998, p. 3.

7 C. von Clausewitz: *On War*, 2nd edn, Princeton, N.J.: Princeton University Press, 1984, Bk I, Ch. 6, p. 117, trans. and ed. M. Howard and P. Paret. The question as to whether Clausewitz meant this literally is discussed on pp. 148–9.

8 Cited by H. Summers, *The New World Strategy*, New York: Touchstone, 1995, p. 109.

9 Swain, op. cit., p. 206; emphasis in original.

10 Schwarzkopf, op. cit., p. 368.

11 C. E. Vuono, "Desert Storm and the Future of Conventional Forces", *Foreign Affairs*, Vol. 69, No. 4, Spring 1991, p. 66. After the Gulf War, sanctions against Iraq had little effect on Saddam's regime, as opposed to the Iraqi economy and people.

12 Clausewitz, op. cit., VI, 27, p. 486; emphasis in original.

13 Ibid., VIII, 4, p. 596.

14 Cited by E. Karsh, "Reflections on the 1990/91 Gulf Conflict", *Journal of Strategic Studies*, Vol. 19, No. 3, September 1996, p. 311.

15 This was the first case since 1945 of the US actually threatening to use nuclear weapons rather than just considering their use as they did during the Korean War. C. C. Crane, "To Avert Impending Disaster: American Plans to Use Atomic Weapons During the Korean War", *Journal of Strategic Studies*, Vol. 23, No. 2, June 2000, pp. 72–88.

16 Cited by DuBois, op. cit., pp. 29–30.

17 Cited by D. Jablonsky, "Strategic Vision and Presidential Authority in the post-Cold War Era", *Parameters*, Vol. 21, No. 4, Winter 1991–92, p. 2.

18 Cited by DuBois, op. cit., p. 34. One could argue that the failure officially to declare war, rather than approve of it, meant that Congress had a hand in the decision to end the war in February 1991. This would suggest that Congress approved of Bush's objective – the liberation of Kuwait – but not by employing the means needed to totally annihilate Saddam's military power.

19 Warden, cited by D. S. Fadok, "John Boyd and John Warden: Airpower's Quest for Strategic Paralysis", in P. S. Meilinger (ed.), *The Paths of Heaven – The Evolution of Airpower Theory*, Maxwell Air Force Base, Ala.: Air University Press, 1997, p. 374.

20 T. R. Reese, "Precision Firepower: 'Smart' Bombs, 'Dumb' Strategy", *Military Review*, Vol. 83, No. 4, July–August 2003, pp. 46–53.

21 Cited by Fadok, op. cit., p. 372.

22 C. A. Agee, "Peeling the Onion: The Iraqi Center of Gravity in Desert Storm", SAMS monograph, Fort Leavenworth, Kansas, US Army Command and General Staff College, April 1992, p. 10.

23 A. J. Echevarria, *Clausewitz's Center of Gravity: Changing our Warfighting Doctrine – Again!*, Carlisle, Pa.: Strategic Studies Institute, 2002, p. 15.

24 Cited by Fadok, op. cit., pp. 378–9.

25 H. D. Belote, "Warden and the Air Corps Tactical School", *Airpower Journal*, Vol. 13, No. 3, Fall 1999, p. 45.

26 Gordon and Trainor, op. cit., p. 268.

27 Clausewitz, op. cit., III, 8, p. 195.

28 E. Mann, "One Target, One Bomb: Is the Principle of Mass Dead?", *Military Review*, Vol. 73, No. 9, September 1993, p. 41. It should be noted, however, that only 8 per cent of munitions used in the campaign were precision. US General Accounting Office, *Operation Desert Storm: Evaluation of the Air Campaign*, Washington, DC, GAO/NSIAD-97-134, June 1997, p. 29.

29 Cited by M. Clodfelter, "Of Demons, Storms, and Thunder: A Preliminary Look at Vietnam's Impact on the Persian Gulf Air Campaign", *Airpower Journal*, Vol. 5, No. 4, Winter 1991. Online. Available www.airpower.maxwell.af.mil/airchronicles/ apj/clod.html (accessed 1 September 1999).
30 B. Lambeth, *The Transformation of American Air Power*, Ithaca, N.Y.: Cornell University Press, 2000, p. 104.
31 T. A. Keaney, "Surveying Gulf War Airpower", *Joint Force Quarterly*, No. 2, Autumn 1993, p. 36.
32 Cited by Swain, op. cit., p. 336.
33 A. D. Brown, "Defense Campaigns: Are They Still the Stronger Form of War?", School of Advanced Military Studies monograph, US Army Command and General Staff College, Fort Leavenworth, Kansas, May 1993, pp. 39–40. Brown defined Clausewitz's six criteria for a successful defence as surprise, benefit of terrain, counterattack (concentric attack), strength of theatre of operations, popular support and exploitation of moral factors.
34 Cited by P. S. Kindsvatter, "VII Corps in the Gulf War: Deployment and Preparation for Desert Storm", *Military Review*, Vol. 72, No. 1, January 1992, p. 15.
35 General Norman H. Schwarzkopf interviewed in "Hannibal and Desert Storm", *Timewatch*, BBC Television, 10 September 1996. R. Leonhard, *The Art of Maneuver – Maneuver Warfare Theory and AirLand Battle*, Novato, Calif.: Presidio Press, 1991, p. 268.
36 R. M. Citino, *Blitzkrieg to Desert Storm: The Evolution of Operational Warfare*, Lawrence: University Press of Kansas, 2004, p. 290.
37 H. T. Hayden (ed.), *Warfighting: Maneuver Warfare in the US Marine Corps*, London: Greenhill, 1995, p. 29.
38 Leonhard, op. cit., p. 263.
39 Schwarzkopf interview.
40 Clausewitz, op. cit., I, 6, p. 117.
41 V. M. Rosello, "Clausewitz's Contempt for Intelligence", *Parameters*, Vol. 21, No. 1, Spring 1991, p. 112.
42 A. M. Coroalles, "*On War* in the Information Age: A Conversation with Carl von Clausewitz", *ARMY*, Vol. 46, No. 5, May 1996, p. 34. It should be noted that the allies' use of intelligence and information assets allowed them to fulfil a Clausewitzian aim as David Lonsdale notes: "The coalition forces possessed information dominance, and were able to wage acts of political and psychological warfare, as well as acts of deception against the Iraqis." D. J. Lonsdale, "Information Power: Strategy, Geopolitics, and the Fifth Dimension", *Journal of Strategic Studies*, Vol. 22, Nos. 2/3, June/September 1999, p. 144.
43 Leonhard, op. cit., p. 294.
44 T. M. Huber, "Deceiving the Enemy in Operation Desert Storm", in R. J. Spiller (ed.), *Combined Arms in Battle Since 1939*, Fort Leavenworth, Kan.: US Army Command and General Staff College Press, 1992, p. 65.
45 A. R. Garrett, "Information Superiority and the Future of Mission Orders", *Military Review*, Vol. 79, No. 6, November–December 1999, p. 64.
46 Leonhard, op. cit., p. 270. P. S. Kindsvatter, "VII Corps in the Gulf War: Ground Offensive", *Military Review*, Vol. 72, No. 2, February 1992, p. 30.
47 Interview with Colonel Clinton J. Ancker III, Director, Combined Arms Doctrine Directorate, Fort Leavenworth at the Royal United Services Institute, London, 19 November 1999. Hayden, on the other hand, has written: "The speed and boldness of the Marine ground attack got inside the … 'OODA loop' of the Iraqis and created a total collapse of Iraqi command and control." Hayden, op. cit., p. 27.
48 Swain, op. cit., pp. 4–5, cites the 3rd Army's historian to this end.
49 B. D. Watts, *Clausewitzian Friction and Future War*, Washington, DC, Institute for National Strategic Studies, 2004. Clausewitz, op. cit., I, 7, pp. 119–21. Gordon and

Trainor, op. cit. B. D. Watts, "Friction in the Gulf War", *Naval War College Review*, Vol. 48, No. 4, Autumn 1995, pp. 93–109. Keaney is cited by Watts in *Clausewitzian Friction*. Both Watts and Keaney contributed to the Department of Defense's post-war air power survey on the conflict.

50 Watts, *Clausewitzian Friction*, pp. 31–2; emphasis in original.
51 P. S. Kindsvatter, "VII Corps in the Gulf War: Ground Offensive", *Military* Review, Vol. 72, No. 2, February 1992, p. 35.
52 Cited by Leonhard, op. cit., p. 281. Richard Swain has criticised Schwarzkopf for not leaving the decision to the VII Corps commander who was actually capable of seeing and "feeling" the forces that were at his mercy. Swain, op. cit., p. 341.
53 Schwarzkopf interview.
54 Schwarzkopf, *It Doesn't Take a Hero*, p. 465.
55 Cited by Summers, op. cit., p. 27.
56 M. Handel, *Masters of War – Classical Strategic Thought*, 2nd edn, London: Frank Cass, 1996, p. 15; Leonhard, op. cit., p. 281; Gordon and Trainor, op. cit., p. 470.
57 Clausewitz, op. cit., IV, 12, p. 267.
58 G. Bush and B. Scowcroft, "Why We Didn't Remove Saddam", *Time*, 2 March 1998.
59 F. S. Rudesheim, "Quick, Decisive Victory: Defining Maxim or Illusory Concept within Army Doctrine", School of Advanced Military Studies monograph, US Army Command and General Staff College, Fort Leavenworth, Kansas, May 1993, pp. 33–4.
60 Summers, op. cit., p. 45; Handel, op. cit., p. 202; DuBois, op. cit., p. 38.
61 Cited by Naveh, op. cit., p. 326.
62 Citino, op. cit., p. 364.
63 C. Bassford, "Clausewitz and His Works". Online. Available www.clausewitz.com/CWZHOME/CWZSUMM/CWORKHOL.htm (accessed 19 April 2000).
64 Scales, op. cit., pp. 106–7.
65 The Iraqi armed forces were modelled to some extent on those of the Warsaw Pact. Interview with Dr Stephen Blank at the US Army War College, Carlisle Barracks, Pennsylvania, 19 September 2000. Brigadier-General (Retd) Huba Wass de Czege (2000), "Clausewitz and FM 100–5", e-mail to the author, 22 June 2000.
66 Cited by M. Horowitz and S. Rosen, "Evolution or Revolution?", *Journal of Strategic Studies*, Vol. 28, No. 3, June 2005, p. 440.
67 D. A. Starry, "Reflections", in G. F. Hofmann and D. A. Starry, *Camp Colt to Desert Storm: The History of US Armored Forces*, Lexington, University Press of Kentucky, 1999, p. 557.
68 Cited by C. Bassford, *Clausewitz in English – The Reception of Clausewitz in Britain and America, 1815–1945*, New York: Oxford University Press, 1994, p. 200; emphasis in the original.
69 A. Beyerchen, "Clausewitz and the Nonlinear Nature of Warfare", paper presented at Oxford Leverhulme Programme Conference on Clausewitz and the 21st Century, Oxford, March 2005.
70 Clausewitz, op. cit., VIII, 6, p. 607.

7 The problem of low-intensity conflict from Vietnam to Panama

1 W. Hahlweg, "Clausewitz and Guerrilla Warfare", in M. I. Handel (ed.), *Clausewitz and Modern Strategy*, London: Frank Cass, 1986, p. 128. P. Paret, *Clausewitz and the State – The Man, His Theories, and His Times*, Princeton, N.J.: Princeton University Press, 1985, p. 190.
2 C. von Clausewitz, *On War*, 2nd edn, Princeton, N.J.: Princeton University Press, 1984, Bk VI, Ch. 6, p. 479, trans. and ed. M. Howard and P. Paret.

3 Ibid.
4 Interview with Dr Steven Metz at the US Army War College, Carlisle Barracks, Pennsylvania, 19 September 2000.
5 D. P. Junior and E. E. Duarté, "The Concept of Logistics Derived from Clausewitz: All that is Required so that the Fighting Force Can be Taken as a Given", *Journal of Strategic Studies*, Vol. 28, No. 4, August 2005, p. 651.
6 F. G. Hoffmann, "Small Wars Revisited: The United States and Nontraditional Wars", *Journal of Strategic Studies*, Vol. 28, No. 6, December 2005, pp. 915–16.
7 Cited by *CALL 90–4: Low-Intensity Conflict*, Center for Army Lessons Learned, Fort Leavenworth, Kansas, 1990. Online. Available call.army.mil/call/ctc_bull/90–4/90–4note.htm (accessed 21 March 2000).
8 R. Paschall, "Low-Intensity Conflict Doctrine: Who Needs It?", *Parameters*, Vol. 15, No. 3, Autumn 1985, p. 41. R. F. Weigley, *History of the United States Army*, New York: Macmillan, 1967, p. 161. However, these authors overlook the wider significance of Clausewitz.
9 Cited by H. G. Summers, "Principles of War and Low-Intensity Conflict", *Military Review*, Vol. 65, No. 3, March 1985, p. 44.
10 Paschall, op. cit., p. 43.
11 R. Leonhard, *The Art of Maneuver – Maneuver Warfare Theory and AirLand Battle*, Novato, Calif.: Presidio Press, 1991, pp. 228–9.
12 M. L. R. Smith, "Guerrillas in the Mist: Reassessing Strategy and Low Intensity Warfare", *Review of International Studies*, 1, 2003, p. 31.
13 A. Kober, "Low-intensity conflicts: Why the Gap Between Theory and Practice?", *Defense and Security Analysis*, Vol. 18, No. 1, 2002, p. 19. J. Tashjean, *The Transatlantic Clausewitz*, Carlisle, Pa.: US Army Military History Institute, 1982.
14 J. R. Johnson, "People's War and Conventional Armies", *Military Review*, Vol. 54, No. 1, January 1974, p. 27. S. C. Sarkesian, "Low-Intensity Conflict: Concepts, Principles, and Policy Guidelines", *Air University Review*, Vol. 36, No. 2, January–February 1985. Online. Available www.airpower.maxwell.af.mil/airchronicles/aureview/1985/jan-feb/sarkesian.html (accessed 18 January 2000). J. C. Buckley II, "A Model of Insurgency: Reflections of Clausewitz's 'Paradoxical Trinity' – Lessons for Operational Planners Considering Conventional Forces in Unconventional Operations", School of Advanced Military Studies monograph, US Army Command and General Staff College, Fort Leavenworth, Kansas, May 1995, pp. 10–11.
15 E. Luttwak, "Notes on Low-Intensity Warfare", *Parameters*, Vol. 13, No. 4, December 1983, p. 11.
16 D. B. Vought, "Preparing for the Wrong War?", *Military Review*, Vol. 57, No. 5, May 1977, p. 19.
17 Cited by ibid., p. 32.
18 R. G. Irani, "US Strategic Interests in Iran and Saudi Arabia", *Parameters*, Vol. 7, No. 4, December 1977, p. 33.
19 J. Kitfield, *Prodigal Soldiers – How the Generation of Officers Born of Vietnam Revolutionized the American Style of War*, Washington, DC, Brassey's, 1997, p. 224. Anon., "Recent Soviet Commentary Favorable to US Army Special-operations Forces", *Special Warfare*, the Professional Bulletin of the John F. Kennedy Special Warfare Centre and School, Vol. 5, No. 1, March 1992, Online. Available call.army.mil/call/fmso/sof/issues/mar92.htm (accessed 15 May 2000).
20 Cited by H. G. Summers, "Delta Force – America's Counterterrorist Unit and the Mission to Rescue the Hostages in Iran", *Military Review*, Vol. 63, No. 11, November 1983, p. 25. Clausewitz, op. cit., I, 3, pp. 104–5.
21 J. Lehman: "Aircraft Carriers – The Real Choices", *The Washington Papers*, Vol. VI, Georgetown University, Washington, DC, Center for Strategic and International Studies, 1978, p. 12. J. J. A. Wallace, "Manoeuvre Theory in Operations Other Than War", *Journal of Strategic Studies*, Vol. 19, No. 4, December 1996, pp. 207–26.

22 Cited by J. D. Waghelstein, "Post-Vietnam Counterinsurgency Doctrine", *Military Review*, Vol. 65, No. 5, May 1985, p. 42 .
23 Paschall, op. cit., p. 44.
24 Department of the Army, FM 100–5: *Operations*, Washington, DC, August 1982, Ch. 3.
25 D. R. Morelli and M. M. Ferguson, "Low-Intensity Conflict: An Operational Perspective", *Military Review*, Vol. 64, No. 11, November 1984, p. 9.
26 Cited by S. Metz, *Counterinsurgency: Strategy and the Phoenix of American Capability*, Carlisle Barracks, Pa.: Strategic Studies Institute, 1995. A good general account of the events alluded to is P. J. Schraeder (ed.), *Intervention in the 1980s – US Foreign Policy in the Third World*, London: Lynne Rienner, 1989. More specifically, see S. S. Harrison, "Afghanistan: Soviet Intervention, Afghan Resistance, and the American Role", in M. T. Klare and P. Kornbluh (eds), *Low-Intensity Warfare: Counterinsurgency, Proinsurgency, and Antiterrorism in the Eighties*, New York: Pantheon, 1988, and K. J. Dougherty, "Indirect Application of Military Power – US Policy Toward Nicaragua", *Military Review*, Vol. 74, No. 10, October 1994, pp. 52–63.
27 Clausewitz, op. cit., I, 2, p. 92; emphasis in the original.
28 C. Weinberger, *Fighting for Peace: Seven Critical Years at the Pentagon*, London: Michael Joseph, 1990, p. 102.
29 Eric Hammel, serving with the Marines at the time, cites two examples of the restrictive rules of engagement under which the Marines operated: "Call local forces (the Lebanese Armed Forces) to assist in self-defense efforts. Notify headquarters." And: "Use only the minimum degree of force to accomplish any mission." E. Hammel, *The Root – The Marines in Beirut, August 1982 – February 1984*, Pacifico, Calif.: Pacifico Press, 1993, p. 427.
30 D. J. Schuster, "Achieving Victory in Peace Operations: An Application for Clausewitz's Theory on Culmination", School of Advanced Military Studies monograph, US Army Command and General Staff College, Fort Leavenworth, Kansas, December 1994, p. 9.
31 Clausewitz, op. cit., Vol. VII, 22, p. 570.
32 Schuster, op. cit.
33 Hammel, op. cit., p. 422. R. M. Swain, "Removing Square Pegs from Round Holes. Low-Intensity Conflict in Army Doctrine", *Military Review*, Vol. 67, No. 12, December 1987, p. 10.
34 Schuster, op. cit., p. 26. R. M. Swain, *Selected Papers of William E. DePuy*, Fort Leavenworth, Kans.: Combat Studies Institute, US Army Command and General Staff College, 1994, p. 447.
35 Cited by FMFM 1–3, *Tactics*, as reproduced in H. T. Hayden (ed.), *Warfighting: Maneuver Warfare in the US Marine Corps*, London: Greenhill, 1995, p. 165. D. P. Bolger, "Special Operations and the Grenada Campaign", *Parameters*, Vol. 18, No. 4, December 1988, p. 55.
36 Bolger, op. cit., p. 56.
37 L. J. Barranto, "Grenada Post-Mortem: A 'Report' That Wasn't", *ARMY*, Vol. 34, No. 6, June 1984, p. 12. Barranto praised the use of deception on Grenada, remarking that "the after-action report is sure to be studied in military classrooms for years to come".
38 Swain, *Selected Papers*, p. 447.
39 Weinberger, op. cit., p. 87.
40 Dougherty, op. cit., p. 55.
41 J. S. Fulton, "The Debate About Low-Intensity Conflict", *Military Review*, Vol. 66, No. 2, February 1986, p. 61. Gorman cited on p. 62.
42 S. Metz, "AirLand Battle and Counterinsurgency", *Military Review*, Vol. 70, No. 1, January 1990, pp. 32–41. FM 100–5, 1986, cited by A. Krepinevich, "Recovery from Defeat – The US Army and Vietnam", in G. J. Andreopoulos and H. E. Selesky, *The*

Aftermath of Defeat – Societies, Armed Forces and the Challenge of Recovery, New Haven, Conn.: Yale University Press, 1994, p. 137.

43 M. E. Kosnik, "The Military Response to Terrorism", *Naval War College Review*, Vol. 53, No. 2, Spring 2000. Online. Available www.nwc.navy.mil/press/Review/2000/spring/art1-sp0.htm (accessed 12 June 2000).

44 Weinberger, op. cit., pp. 140–1.

45 Cited by Metz, *Counterinsurgency*, p. 12.

46 Metz, "AirLand Battle and Counterinsurgency", p. 39. S. Sloan, "US Strategy for LIC: An Enduring Legacy or Passing Fad?", *Military Review*, Vol. 70, No. 1, January 1990, pp. 42–9.

47 P. J. Schraeder, "Paramilitary Intervention", in Schraeder (ed.), op. cit., p. 121.

48 Cited by Metz, *Counterinsurgency*, p. 15.

49 Krepinevich, op. cit., pp. 139–40.

50 Dougherty, op cit., p. 61.

51 J. J. Montano and D. H. Long, "Clausewitz's Advice to the New US President", *Parameters*, Vol. 18, No. 4, December 1988, p. 33.

52 Hayden, op. cit., pp. 186–7.

53 L. A. Yates, "The US–Panama Crisis, 1987–1990", in R. J. Spiller (ed.), *Combined Arms in Battle Since 1939*, Fort Leavenworth, Kans.: US Army Command and General Staff College Press, 1992, p. 205.

54 Leonhard, op. cit., pp. 214–15.

55 S. N. Collins, "*Just Cause* Up Close: A Light Infantryman's View of LIC", *Parameters*, Vol. 22, No. 2, Summer 1992, p. 64.

56 J. Fishel, *The Fog of Peace: Planning and Executing the Restoration of Panama*, Carlisle Barracks, Pa.: Strategic Studies Institute, 1992.

57 Cited by Anon., op. cit., p. 1.

58 M. De Mayo, letter to *Parameters*, Vol. 20, No. 3, September 1990, p. 109. T. Donnelly, "Don't Underestimate the US Army", *Parameters*, Vol. 20, No. 1, March 1990, p. 102. E. N. Luttwak, "Just Cause – A Military Score Sheet", *Parameters*, Vol. 20, No. 1, March 1990, pp. 100–1. This was a reprint of Luttwak's *Washington Post* article.

59 Departments of the Army and Air Force: FM 100–20/AFP 3–20, *Military Operations in Low Intensity Conflict*, Washington, DC, 5 December 1990, Introduction.

60 The manual also took on board the related lesson from Vietnam that an understanding of host nation culture was crucial and that the task of the United States was to support, not lead, the host nation's effort.

61 Clausewitz, op. cit., I, 1, p. 88. Cited by FM 100–20/AFP 3–20, Introduction.

62 J. E. Shepherd, "'*On War*': Is Clausewitz Still Relevant?", *Parameters*, Vol. 20, No. 3, September 1990, p. 86.

63 S. Metz, "US Strategy and the Changing LIC Threat", *Military Review*, Vol. 71, No. 6, June 1991, p. 26.

8 Strategy and policy during the 1990s

1 Cited by S. Metz, *American Strategy: Issues and Alternatives for the Quadrennial Defense Review*, Carlisle, Pa.: Strategic Studies Institute, 2000, p. 9.

2 Cited by R. M. Cassidy, "Prophets or Praetorians? The Uptonian Paradox and the Powell Corollary", *Parameters*, Vol. 33, No. 3, Autumn 2003, p. 140. C. Powell, "US Forces: Challenges Ahead", *Foreign Affairs*, Vol. 72, No. 5, Winter 1992–93. Online. Available www.foreignaffairs.org/19921201faessay5851/colin-l-powell/u-s-forces-challenges-ahead.html (accessed 29 November 2005). Powell, who has been described as "a disciple of Clausewitz" by Richard Lock-Pullan, describes the way in which his thought on the doctrine developed in C. Powell, *My American Journey*, New York: Random House, 1995. R. Lock-Pullan, *US Intervention Policy and Army Innovation: From Vietnam to Iraq*, New York: Routledge, 2006, p. 119.

3 Cassidy, op cit., p. 141. Cassidy, a major in the US Army, traces the beginning of this trend back to the first translation of Clausewitz to appear in the United States in 1873 and its subsequent continuation through the world wars, Vietnam, the Howard and Paret translation of *On War*, and Summers's *On Strategy*. Powell, "US Forces".

4 Powell, "US Forces".

5 Ibid. Powell referred to humanitarian relief operations in Iraq, Somalia, Bangladesh, Russia, and Bosnia as well as interventions in Panama and the Philippines.

6 J. Record, "Weinberger–Powell Doctrine Doesn't Cut It", US Naval Institute *Proceedings*, Vol. 126/10/1, No. 172, October 2000, Online. Available www.navalinstitute.org/Proceedings/Articles00/Prorecord.htm (accessed 10 February 2006). See also J. Record, "Operation Allied Force: Yet Another Wake-Up Call for the Army?", *Parameters*, Vol. 29, No. 4, Winter 1999–2000. Online. Available carlisle-www.army.mil/usawc/Parameters/99winter/Record.htm (accessed 25 November 1999).

7 P. E. Herrly, "The Plight of Joint Doctrine after Kosovo", *Joint Force Quarterly*, No. 19, Summer 1999, p. 100. Joint Chiefs-of-Staff, Joint Publication 1, *Joint Warfare of the US Armed Forces*, Washington, DC, 1991.

8 Colonel Paul Herbert (2000) "Influence of Clausewitz on American Thought", e-mail (19 May 2000).

9 Department of the Army, FM 100–5, *Operations*, Washington, DC, June 1993, pp. 1–4.

10 Ibid., pp. 2–9.

11 Ibid., pp. 2–0.

12 Joint Chiefs-of-Staff, Joint Publication 3–0, *Doctrine for Joint Operations*, Washington, DC, 1993.

13 R. M. Citino: *Blitzkrieg to Desert Storm: The Evolution of Operational Warfare*, Lawrence: University Press of Kansas, 2004, p. 294. Frank Hoffman has dismissed OOTW as "probably one of the most bizarre terms of military terminology". F. G. Hoffman, "Small Wars Revisited: The United States and Nontraditional Wars", *Journal of Strategic Studies*, Vol. 28, No. 6, December 2005, p. 916.

14 FM 100–5, 1993, pp. 1–5 and 2–6. Department of the Army, FM 7–92, *Operations in Low Intensity Conflict*, Washington, DC, 1992.

15 R. J. Bunker, "Rethinking OOTW", *Military Review*, Vol. 75, No. 6, November–December 1995, pp. 34–41. Bunker cited Martin van Creveld and Steven Metz in his article. M. van Creveld: *On Future War*, London: Brassey's, 1991; in the United States, this was published as the *Transformation of War*. S. Metz, "A Wake for Clausewitz: Toward a Philosophy of 21st Century Warfare", *Parameters*, Vol. 24, No. 4, Winter 1994–95, pp. 124–32.

16 Bunker, "Rethinking OOTW".

17 FM 100–5, 1993, pp. 2–4.

18 Ibid., pp. 2–7.

19 Ibid., pp. 6–8.

20 Ibid.

21 C. von Clausewitz, *On War*, 2nd edn, Princeton, N.J.: Princeton University Press, 1984, Bk VIII, Ch. 3b, p. 593, trans. and ed. M. Howard and P. Paret.

22 W. Murray and R. H. Scales, jun., *The Iraq War: A Military History*, Cambridge, Mass.: Harvard University Press, 2003, p. 35.

23 Cited by D. Jablonsky, "Army Transformation: A Tale of Two Doctrines", *Parameters*, Vol. 31, No. 3, Autumn 2001. Online. Available carlisle-www.army.mil/usawc/Parameters/01autumn/Jablonsk.htm (accessed 22 August 2001). A scathing critique of the administration's approach is T. L. Friedman, "Clinton's 'Mother Teresa' School of Foreign Policy", *International Herald Tribune*, 7 December 1995.

24 Cited by D. E. Delaney, "Cutting, Running or Otherwise? The US Decision to withdraw from Somalia", *Journal of Small Wars and Insurgencies*, Vol. 15, No. 3, Winter 2004, p. 33.
25 Cited by ibid., p. 34. Among those who expressed concern about the new mandate was Major-General Thomas Montgomery, US Army, the deputy commander of the UN operation.
26 M. Berdal, "Fateful Encounter: The United States and UN Peacekeeping", *Survival*, Vol. 36, No. 1, Spring 1994, p. 40.
27 Delaney, op. cit., p. 34. The rest of the US contingent were logistics troops.
28 W. Clarke and J. Herbst, "Somalia and the Future of Humanitarian Intervention", *Foreign Affairs*, Vol. 75, No. 2, March–April 1996, p. 72.
29 The Americans had initially been hesitant about deploying this force mainly because of concerns raised by Powell. Powell, *My American Journey*, pp. 583–84.
30 Delaney, op. cit., pp. 36–7. T. Farrell, "US Marine Corps Operations in Somalia: A Model for the Future", in G. Till (ed.), *Amphibious Warfare*, Occasional Paper No. 31, Camberley: Strategic and Combat Studies Institute, 1997, pp. 43–56. M. Bowden, *Black Hawk Down: A Story of Modern War*, New York: Signet, 1999. This was the book that inspired the eponymous movie.
31 Record, "Weinberger–Powell".
32 Lock-Pullan, op. cit., p. 158.
33 Powell, "US Forces".
34 M. Evans, *The Continental School of Strategy: The Past, Present and Future of Land Power*, Canberra: Land Warfare Studies Centre, Study Paper No. 305, June 2004, p. 141.
35 Department of Defense, *Report of the Quadrennial Defense Review*, Washington, DC, 1997. Citation from NSS 1994 by T. P. Reilly, "The National Security Strategy of the United States: Development of Grand Strategy". in W. Murray (ed.), *A Nation at War in an Era of Strategic Change*, Carlisle, Pa.: Strategic Studies Institute monograph, 2004, p. 331.
36 Cited by A. W. Dowd, "Thirteen Years: The Causes and Consequences of the War in Iraq", *Parameters*, Vol. 33, No. 3, Autumn 2003, p. 49.
37 An excellent analysis of the Bosnian conflict is in P. Bobbitt, *The Shield of Achilles – War, Peace and the Course of History*, London: Penguin, 2003, pp. 416–67.
38 B. Lambeth, *The Transformation of American Air Power*, Ithaca, N.Y.: Cornell University Press, 2000, p. 177.
39 Cited by M. Hastings, "Ordeal of Bosnia 'has cast UN and NATO into crisis'", *Daily Telegraph*, 30 June 1995.
40 Cited by Reilly, op. cit., p. 332.
41 Lambeth, op. cit., p. 217. Citation from M. Weller, "The United States, Iraq, and the Use of Force in a Bipolar World", *Survival*, Vol. 41, No. 4, Winter 1999–2000, p. 87.
42 M. Kelly, "War on Bush's Watch", *Washington Post*, 6 February 2002.
43 Metz, *American Strategy*, p. 22. Joint Chiefs-of-Staff, *Joint Vision 2010*, Washington, DC, 1995.
44 Cited by Farrell, op. cit., p. 54. C. C. Krulak, "Operational Maneuver from the Sea", *Joint Force Quarterly*, No. 21, Spring 1999, pp. 78–86.
45 Department of the Navy, Marine Corps Doctrinal Publication 1, *Warfighting*, Washington, DC, 1997, p. 23. Bassford describes the context in which the Marines' manuals were written in C. Bassford, "Doctrinal Complexity", Online. Available www.clausewitz.com/CLWHOME/Complex/DOCTNEW.htm (accessed 20 February 2006).
46 MCDP 1, p. 3. It is important to note that, in this context, manoeuvre warfare is more of a thought process about war in general rather than a narrow construct based on exploiting rapid movement in battle.
47 Department of the Navy, Marine Corps Doctrinal Publication 1–1, *Strategy*, Washington, DC, 1997, p. 13.

48 MCDP 1, p. 100.
49 Ibid., p. 4.
50 Ibid., pp. 24–5 and 100. In fairness to Delbrück, he also wrote of a strategy of erosion, though *ermattungsstrategie* tends to be translated as "strategy of attrition". MCDP 1 emphasised that both terms are interchangeable. H. Delbrück, *History of the Art of War within the Framework of Political History*, trans. W. J. Renfroe, jun., Westport, Conn.: Greenwood Press, 1975.
51 MCDP 1–1, p. 15. Major Adam Strickland would later imply that MCDP 1 would teach the military all it needed to know about counterinsurgency. A. T. Strickland, "MCDP 1, Warfighting Revisited", *Marine Corps Gazette*, Vol. 89, No. 7, July 2005, p. 52.
52 Strickland, op. cit., pp. 32 and 56.
53 MCDP 1, p. 47.
54 A. J. Echevarria, *Clausewitz's Center of Gravity: Changing our Warfighting Doctrine – Again!*, Carlisle, Pa.: Strategic Studies Institute, 2002, p. 5.
55 MCDP 1–1, p. 88.
56 Ibid., pp. 5–6.
57 J. F. Schmitt, "Command and (Out of) Control: The Military Implications of Complexity Theory", in D. S. Alberts and T. J. Czerwinski, *Complexity, Global Politics, and National Security*, Washington, DC, National Defense University, 1997, p. 221. Barry Watts provides an overview of Newton's impact on military thought in his analysis of friction. B. D. Watts, *Clausewitzian Friction and Future War*, McNair Paper 68, Washington, DC, Institute for National Strategic Studies, 2004.
58 MCDP 1, p. 12, MCDP 1–1, p. 17, and Bassford, "Doctrinal Complexity".
59 Bassford, "Doctrinal Complexity".
60 Cited by G. T. Hammond, "Myths of the Air War over Serbia – Some 'Lessons' Not to Learn", *Aerospace Power Journal*, Vol. 14, No. 4, Winter 2000, p. 81.
61 Lambeth, op. cit., p. 226.
62 E.H. Tilford, jun., "Operation Allied Force and the Role of Air Power", *Parameters*, Vol. 29, No. 4, Winter 1999–2000. Online. Available carlisle-www.army.mil/usawc/Parameters/99winter/tilford.htm (accessed 2 December 1999).
63 Naumann speaking on 9 May 1999; cited in C. C. Hodge, "Woodrow Wilson in Our Time: NATO's Goals in Kosovo", *Parameters*, Vol. 31, No. 1, Spring 2001, Online. Available www.carlisle.army.mil/usawc/parameters/01spring/hodge.htm (accessed 2 March 2006).
64 Lambeth, op. cit., p. 210. Record, "Operation Allied Force".
65 Of course, such an approach would have called the whole campaign into question among the populations of the NATO Alliance. S. Biddle, "The New Way of War? Debating the Kosovo Model", *Foreign Affairs*, Vol. 81, No. 3, May–June 2002. Online. Available www.foreignaffairs.org/20020501faessay8063/stephen-biddle/the-new-way-of-war.htm (accessed 28 November 2005).
66 Lambeth, op. cit., p. 191.
67 W. Clark, *Waging Modern War: Bosnia, Kosovo and the Future of Combat*, Oxford: Perseus, 2001. M. N. Vego, "Operational Command and Control in the Information Age", *Joint Force Quarterly*, 35, 2004, p. 104.
68 Tilford, op. cit. A. J. Bacevich and E. A. Cohen, (eds), *War over Kosovo: Politics and Strategy in a Global Age*, New York: Columbia University Press, 2001.
69 Hammond, op. cit.
70 Cited by Herrly, op. cit., p. 101. Lock-Pullan, op. cit., p. 175.
71 Clark, op. cit., p. 427. H. Strachan, "The Lost Meaning of Strategy", *Survival*, Vol. 47, No. 3, Autumn 2005, p. 50. T. L. Thomas, "Kosovo and the Current Myth of Information Superiority", *Parameters*, Vol. 30, No. 1, Spring 2000. Online. Available www.carlisle.army.mil/usawc/Parameters/00spring/thomas.htm (accessed 10 August 2000). M. Evans, "From Kadesh to Kandahar – Military Theory and the Future of War", *Naval War College Review*, Vol. 56, No. 3, Summer 2003, p. 136.

72 Clark, op. cit., p. 427.
73 D. Johnson, "First, Read Clausewitz", *Daily Telegraph*, 17 April 1999. Clausewitz, op. cit., I, 2.
74 Lock-Pullan, op. cit., p. 157.
75 Citino, op. cit., p. 296.
76 Watts, op. cit.

9 American strategy and policy in the age of terror

1 T. F. Friedman, *The Lexus and the Olive Tree*, New York: Anchor, 2000. T. F. Friedman, *The World is Flat – A Brief History of the Twenty-First Century*, New York: Allen Lane, 2005. J. H. Mittelman, *The Globalization Syndrome: Transformation and Resistance*, Princeton, N.J.: Princeton University Press, 2000. See also the essays on globalisation and warfare in *The European Legacy*, Vol. 8, No. 3, June 2003, pp. 277–352.
2 C. S. Gray, "How Has War Changed Since the End of the Cold War?", *Parameters*, Vol. 35, No. 1, Spring 2005, p. 20.
3 A. F. Krepinevich, "Cavalry to Computer: The Pattern of Military Revolutions", *The National Interest*, Fall 1994, pp. 30–42. D. Jablonsky: *The Owl of Minerva Flies at Twilight: Doctrinal Change and Continuity and the Revolution in Military Affairs*, Carlisle, Pa.: Strategic Studies Institute, May 1994. W. Murray, "Thinking about Revolutions in Military Affairs", *Joint Force Quarterly*, No. 16, Summer 1997, pp. 69–76. M. Knox and W. Murray (eds), *The Dynamics of Military Revolution 1300–2050*, Cambridge: Cambridge University Press, 2001. See also the essays in "Perspectives on the Revolution in Military Affairs", *Parameters*, Vol. 25, No. 2, Summer 1995, pp. 7–54; and in the Special Issue on Information and Revolutions in Military Affairs, *Journal of Strategic Studies*, Vol. 27, No. 2, June 2004. For a Clausewitzian perspective, see A. J. Echevarria, "War, Politics, and RMAs: The Legacy of Clausewitz", *Joint Force Quarterly*, No. 10, Winter 1995–96, pp. 76–80; and B. D. Watts, Clausewitzian *Friction and Future War*, McNair Paper 68, Washington, DC, Institute for National Strategic Studies, 2004.
4 Cited by D. Jablonsky, "Army Transformation: A Tale of Two Doctrines", *Parameters*, Vol. 31, No. 3, Autumn 2001. Online. Available carlisle-www.army.mil/usawc/Parameters/01autumn/Jablonsk.htm (accessed 22 August 2001).
5 W. A. Owens, *Lifting the Fog of War*, London: Johns Hopkins University Press, 2000.
6 W. A. Owens, "The American Revolution in Military Affairs", *Joint Force Quarterly*, No. 10, Winter 1995–96, pp. 37–8.
7 Major-General Robert Scales alluded to the trend in non-Western military thought to counter the type of warfare championed by Owens. Scales wrote that "US analysts have missed much of [this] discourse and experimentation". R. H. Scales, jun., "Adaptive Enemies: Achieving Victory by Avoiding Defeat", *Joint Force Quarterly*, Autumn–Winter 1999–2000, pp. 7–14.
8 Dr Antulio Echevarria of the US Army War College has observed that human intelligence was overlooked during the beginnings of the transformation effort. A. J. Echevarria, "Clausewitz and the War on Terror", paper presented at Oxford Leverhulme Programme Conference on Clausewitz and the 21st Century, Oxford, March 2005.
9 K. F. McKenzie, "An Ecstasy of Fumbling: Doctrine and Innovation", *Joint Force Quarterly*, No. 10, Winter 1995–96, p. 62.
10 D. S. Alberts, J. J. Gartska and F. P. Stein, *Network Centric Warfare: Developing and Leveraging Information Superiority*, Washington, DC, C4ISR Cooperative Research Program, 1999, p. 2. A. K. Cebrowski and J. J. Gartska, "Network-Centric Warfare:

Its Origins and Future", US Naval Institute *Proceedings*, Vol. 124/1/1, No. 139, January 1998.

11 J. F. Schmitt, "Command and (Out of) Control: The Military Implications of Complexity Theory", in D. S. Alberts and T. J. Czerwinski, *Complexity, Global Politics, and National Security*, Washington, DC, National Defense University, 1997. Gray, op. cit. J. M. Dubik, "Has Warfare Changed? Sorting Apples from Oranges", *Landpower Essay*, No. 2–03, Institute of Land Warfare, July 2002.

12 M. Boot, "The New American Way of War", *Foreign Affairs*, Vol. 82, No. 4, July–August 2003. Online. Available www.foreignaffairs.org/20030701/faessay 15404/max-boot/the-new-american-way-of-war.html (accessed 28 November 2005).

13 C. von Clausewitz, *On War*, 2nd edn, ed. and trans. M. Howard and P. Paret, Princeton, N.J.: Princeton University Press, 1984, Bk I, Ch. 3, pp. 100–12.

14 R. L. DiNardo and D. J. Hughes, "Some Cautionary Thoughts on Information Warfare", *Airpower Journal*, Vol. 9, No. 4, Winter 1995.

15 O. E. Jensen, "Information Warfare: Principles of Third-Wave War", *Airpower Journal*, Vol. 8, No. 4, Winter 1994, pp. 35–6. R. J. Bunker, "Generations, Waves and Epochs: Modes of Warfare and the RPMA", *Airpower Journal*, Vol. 10, No. 1, Spring 1996, pp. 1–10. The "P" stands for Political. A. Toffler and H. Toffler, *War and Anti-War: Survival at the Dawn of the 21st Century*, New York: Little, Brown and Co., 1993. DiNardo and Hughes, op. cit.

16 Bunker, op. cit., p. 7.

17 Ibid., pp. 3–4. For a masterly comparison of Sun Tzu and Clausewitz, see M. Handel, *Masters of War – Classical Strategic Thought*, 2nd edn, London: Frank Cass, 1996.

18 I. Kass, "An Instructor's Guide to Teaching Clausewitz". Online. Available www.Clausewitz.com/CWZHOME/KassNWC/KassNotes3.html (accessed 11 February 2006).

19 C. Rice, "Promoting the National Interest", *Foreign Affairs*, Vol. 79, No. 1, January–February 2000. Online. Available www.foreignaffairs.org/20000101faessay/ condoleeza-rice/campaign-2000-promoting-the-national-interest.htm (accessed 26 November 2005).

20 "Statement of Principles", Project for the New American Century. Online. Available www.newamericancentury.org/Statementofprinciples.htm (accessed 28 November 2005).

21 Cited by Jablonsky, "Army Transformation".

22 Cited by D. W. Pendall, "Effects-Based Operations and the Exercise of National Power", *Military Review*, Vol. 84, No. 1, January–February 2004, p. 30.

23 Cited by A. Newman, "Arms Control, Proliferation and Terrorism: The Bush Administration's Post-September 11 Security Strategy", *Journal of Strategic Studies*, Vol. 27, No. 1, March 2004, p. 60. G. J. Ikenberry, "American Grand Strategy in the Age of Terror", *Survival*, Vol. 43, No. 4, Winter 2001, pp. 19–34. Anon., "Cannon to the right of him, cannon to the left", *The Economist*, 30 June 2001.

24 Jablonsky, "Army Transformation". A. J. Echevarria, "Interdependent Maneuver for the 21st Century", *Joint Force Quarterly*, No. 23, Autumn/Winter 2000, pp. 11–19.

25 Joint Chiefs-of-Staff, Joint Publication 3–0, *Doctrine for Joint Operations*, Washington, DC, 2001.

26 Clausewitz, op. cit., I, 1, p. 75. JP 3–0, 2001, pp. I–3; emphasis in original. JP 3–0 also described six principles for OOTW: objective, unity of effort, security, restraint, perseverance and legitimacy. Ibid., pp. V-2 to V-6.

27 JP 3–0, pp. III-10 to III-14.

28 Ibid., p. III-16. Clausewitz, op. cit., I, 1, p. 75.

29 JP 3–0, 2001, p. III-22; emphasis in original.

30 A. J. Echevarria, *Clausewitz's Center of Gravity: Changing our Warfighting Doctrine – Again!*, Carlisle, Pa.: Strategic Studies Institute, 2002, p. 16.

31 D. L. Johnson, "Center of Gravity: The Source of Operational Ambiguity and Linear

Thinking in the Age of Complexity", School of Advanced Military Studies mono-graph, US Army Command and General Staff College, Fort Leavenworth, Kansas, December 1998, p. 14.

32 Echevarria, *Clausewitz's Center of Gravity*, pp. 11 and 24. Echevarria's translation equates to the passage that appears in Clausewitz, op. cit., VIII, 3, pp. 595–6. Johnson, op. cit.

33 JP 3–0, 2001, p. III-23.

34 G. R. Sullivan, "A Vision for the Future", *Military Review*, Vol. 75, No. 4, May–June 1995, p. 8. US Army Training and Doctrine Command, *Force XXI Operations: A Concept for the Evolution of Full-Dimensional Operations for the Strategic Army of the Early Twenty-First Century*, Pamphlet 525–5, Fort Monroe, Va.: TRADOC, August 1994.

35 Department of the Army, FM 3–0, *Operations*, Washington, DC, June 2001, pp. 1–14.

36 Ibid., pp. 1–8 to 1–15.

37 Ibid., pp. 4–11 to 4–12 and 4–15 to 4–17.

38 Ibid., pp. 4–31.

39 L. Freedman, "The Third World War?", *Survival*, Vol. 43, No. 4, Winter 2001, p. 70.

40 FM 3–0, 2001, pp. 4–31.

41 B. Heuser, *Reading Clausewitz*, London: Pimlico, 2002, p. 137.

42 C. S. Gray, "Thinking Asymmetrically in Times of Terror", *Parameters*, Vol. 32, No. 1, Spring 2002, pp. 5–14.

43 W. M. Steele, "The Army Launches an Attack-Focused Doctrine for the Joint Fight", *ARMY*, August 2001. Online. Available www.ausa.org/webpub/DeptArmy-Magazine.nsf/byid/CCRN-6CCRYM (accessed 25 August 2004).

44 C. Crane, *Avoiding Vietnam: The US Army's Response to Defeat in Southeast Asia*, Carlisle, Pa.: Strategic Studies Institute, 2002, p. 13.

45 FM 3–0, 2001, pp. 1–17 and 4–12.

46 W. Murray, "Operation Iraqi Freedom: Lessons for the Future", in W. Murray, *A Nation at War*, Carlisle, Pa., Strategic Studies Institute, p. 12.

47 R. Godson, "Clancy is a Better Guide than von Clausewitz", *Daily Telegraph*, 13 September 2001.

48 J. Keegan, *A History of Warfare*, London: Hutchinson, 1993. M. van Creveld, *On Future War*, London: Brassey's, 1991.

49 M. Kaldor, *New and Old Wars: Organized Violence in a Global Era*, Stanford, Calif.: Stanford University Press, 1999.

50 C. von Clausewitz, "Agitation", in C. von Clausewitz, *Historical and Political Writings*, trans. and ed. D. Moran and P. Paret, Princeton, N.J.: Princeton University Press, 1992, p. 346.

51 Freedman, "The Third World War?", p. 74.

52 W. Lind, "Fourth-Generation Warfare's First Blow: A Quick Look", *Marine Corps Gazette*, Vol. 85, No. 11, November 2001, p. 72. S. Metz, "A Wake for Clausewitz: Toward a Philosophy of 21st Century Warfare", *Parameters*, Vol. 24, No. 4, pp. 124–32. Bunker, op. cit. W. Lind, K. M. Nightengale, J. Schmitt, J. W. Sutton and G. I. Wilson, "The Changing Face of War – Into the Fourth Generation", *Military Review*, Vol. 69, No. 10, October 1989, pp. 2–11. The first "three generations" had begun in 1648, 1815 and 1918, respectively, and were based on the development of new technology and/or ideas. Lind has recently described the use of the word "generation" as meaning a "dialectically qualitative shift". W. Lind, "Understanding Fourth Generation Warfare", *Military Review*, Vol. 84, No. 5, September–October 2004, pp. 12–16.

53 Office for the Secretary of Defense, *Quadrennial Defense Review*, Washington, DC, 30 September 2001. C. S. Gray, *Transformation and Strategic Surprise*, Carlisle, Pa.:

Strategic Studies Institute, 2005, p. 9. J. L. Gaddis, *Surprise, Security and the American Experience*, Cambridge, Mass.: Harvard University Press, 2004, p. 37.

54 F. Sobchak, "Clausewitz: 'On Afghanistan'", *Military Review*, Vol. 85, No. 4, July–August 2005, pp. 89–91.

55 Stephen Biddle's numerous commentaries are a sound guide to the progress of the Afghan campaign even though some of his assumptions and analyses are open to question. S. Biddle, "Afghanistan and the Future of Warfare", *Foreign Affairs*, Vol. 82, No. 2, March–April 2003, pp. 31–46; also, *Afghanistan and the Future of Warfare: Implications for Army and Defense Policy*, Carlisle, Pa.: Strategic Studies Institute, 2002; and "The New Way of War? Debating the Kosovo Model", *Foreign Affairs*, Vol. 81, No. 3, May–June 2002 (online, available www.foreignaffairs.org/20020501faessay8063/stephen-biddle/the-new-way-of-war.htm[accessed 28 November 2005]).

56 D. H. Rumsfeld, "Transforming the Military", *Foreign Affairs*, Vol. 81, No. 3, May–June 2002. Online. Available www.foreignaffairs.org/20020501faessay8140/donald-h-rumsfeld/transforming-the-military.htm> (accessed 28 November 2005).

57 Boot, "The New American Way of War". C. S. Gray, *Defining and Achieving Decisive Victory*, Carlisle, Pa.: Strategic Studies Institute, 2002, p. 32. S. Biddle, "The New Way of War?"

58 Cited by A. Geibel, "Operation Anaconda, Shah-i-Kot Valley, Afghanistan, 2–10 March 2002", *Military Review*, Vol. 82, No. 3, May–June 2002, p. 75. S. Biddle, "Afghanistan and the Future of Warfare".

59 Cited by M. Kelly, "War on Bush's Watch", *Washington Post*, 6 February 2002.

60 Cited by C. Coughlin, "Tell me – what do you *really* think of Tony Blair, Mr President?", *Daily Telegraph*, 22 April 2006.

61 Cited by C. Moore, "Colin Powell: 'I'm very sore'", *Daily Telegraph*, 26 February 2005.

62 Cited by T. P. Reilly, "The National Security Strategy of the United States", in W. Murray (ed.), *A Nation at War in an Era of Strategic Change*, Carlisle, Pa.: Strategic Studies Institute, 2004, p. 334.

63 Cited by J. Record, "The Bush Doctrine and War with Iraq", *Parameters*, Vol. 33, No. 1, Spring 2003, p. 7. Anon, "Unprecedented power, colliding ambitions", *The Economist*, 28 September 2002.

64 The invasion of Afghanistan in 2001 provides a good example of collective self-defence given that the other NATO member states supported the Americans through invoking Article 5 of the North Atlantic Treaty (1949), which stipulated that an attack on one member of the Alliance constituted an attack on all the others as well.

65 L. Freedman, *The Evolution of Nuclear Strategy*, 2nd edn, London: Macmillan, 1989, p. 126.

66 Cited by Record, "The Bush Doctrine", p. 8.

67 Reilly, op. cit., p. 336. Gaddis argues that the United States practised pre-emption during its interventions in the Caribbean and Central America during the early twentieth century. Gaddis, op. cit., p. 22.

68 Clausewitz, op. cit., VI, 8, p. 380. J. Sumida, "On Defense as the Stronger Form of War", paper presented at Oxford Leverhulme Programme Conference on Clausewitz and the 21st Century, Oxford, March 2005.

69 H. Strachan, "The Lost Meaning of Strategy", *Survival*, Vo. 47, No. 3, Autumn 2005, p. 50.

70 M. F. Morris, "Al Qaeda as Insurgency", *Joint Force Quarterly*, No. 39, 2005, pp. 41–50.

71 Comment made by C. Daase, "Clausewitz and Small Wars", paper presented at Oxford Leverhulme Programme Conference on Clausewitz and the 21st Century, Oxford, March 2005.

72 M. Evans, "From Kadesh to Kandahar – Military Theory and the Future of War", *Naval War College Review*, Vol. 56, No. 3, Summer 2003, p. 142.
73 N. Ferguson, *Colossus – The Rise and Fall of the American Empire*, Penguin edn, London: Penguin, 2005, p. 151.
74 Echevarria, *Clausewitz's Center of Gravity*, p. 18. Clausewitz did advocate that, where feasible, the weight of the enemy's force should be reduced to as few centres of gravity as possible – ideally one.
75 Clausewitz, op. cit., VIII, 3a, p. 596. This citation is as perfect a summation of the contemporary notion of effects-based warfare as one could hope for.
76 Ibid., I, 1, p. 89.
77 Echevarria, *Clausewitz's Center of Gravity*, p. 3.
78 Cited by Watts, op. cit., p. v. Boot, "The New American Way of War".
79 Cited by A. S. Hashim, "The World According to Usama bin Laden", *Naval War College Review*, Vol. 54, No. 4, Autumn 2001, p. 26.

10 Iraq – invasion and insurgency

 1 N. Ferguson, *Colossus – The Rise and Fall of the American Empire*, London: Penguin, 2005, p. xiii. Seventeen resolutions on Iraq were passed by the Security Council between 1999 and 2002. Ibid., p. 154. D. Rennie, "Bush 'planned to topple Saddam before Sept 11'", *Daily Telegraph*, 12 January 2004.
 2 Woodward, cited by A. Finlan, "Trapped in the Dead Ground: US Counter-insurgency Strategy in Iraq", *Small Wars and Insurgencies*, Vol. 16, No. 1, March 2005, p. 17.
 3 C. Moore, "Colin Powell: 'I'm very sore'", *Daily Telegraph*, 26 February 2005.
 4 R. Jervis, "Reports, Politics, and Intelligence Failures: The Case of Iraq", *Journal of Strategic Studies*, Vol. 29, No. 1, February 2006, p. 13. C. von Clausewitz, *On War*, 2nd edn, ed. and trans. M. Howard and P. Paret, Princeton, N.J.: Princeton University Press, 1984, Bk I, Ch. 6, p. 117. Jervis says that the only flaw in Clausewitz's analysis is that he restricts it to wartime (Jervis, op. cit., p. 11).
 5 Cited by W. Murray and R. H. Scales, jun., *The Iraq War: A Military History*, Cambridge, Mass.: Harvard University Press, 2003, p. 42; emphasis in original.
 6 M. R. Laird, "Iraq: Learning the Lessons of Vietnam", *Foreign Affairs*, Vol. 84, No. 6, November–December 2005. Online. Available www.foreignaffairs.org/20051101faessay84604/melvin-r-laird/iraq-learning-the-lessons-of-Vietnam.htm (accessed 26 November 2005).
 7 Cited by Finlan, op. cit., p. 6.
 8 A. F. Sidoti, "The Relevance of Carl von Clausewitz to Operation Iraqi Freedom", *Air and Space Power Chronicles Online Journal*, 21 January 2004. Online. Available nss.csusb.edu/nsspubs/nssstpub04sidoti.htm (accessed 24 November 2005).
 9 Cited by J. Achenbach, "Military Theory and the Force of Ideas – From Sparta to Baghdad, Paradigms Have Shifted. Human Nature Has Not", *Washington Post*, 23 March 2003.
10 H. Ullman and J. Wade jun., *Shock and Awe: Achieving Rapid Dominance*, Washington, DC, National Defense University Press, 1996.
11 Cited by H. D. Belote, "Paralyzed or Pulverized? The Fall of the Republican Guard", *Joint Force Quarterly*, No. 37, 2005, p. 41. Lieutenant-Colonel David Fadok has described strategic paralysis as being "a strategy neither of annihilation nor attrition but a third type of warfare … it seeks rapid decision via enemy incapacitation by fusing battle and maneuver". D. S. Fadok, "John Boyd and John Warden: Airpower's Quest for Strategic Paralysis", in P. S. Meilinger (ed.), *The Paths of Heaven – The Evolution of Airpower Theory*, Maxwell Air Force Base, Ala.: Air University Press, 1997, p. 360.
12 Murray and Scales, op. cit., p. 197.
13 Cited by Belote, op. cit., p. 41.

14 J. L. Strange and R. Iron, "Center of Gravity – What Clausewitz Really Meant", *Joint Force Quarterly*, No. 35, 2004, pp. 20–7.

15 F. Harris, "Baghdad Bridges Mystery Resolved", *Daily Telegraph*, 14 March 2006.

16 Murray and Scales, op. cit., p. 199.

17 Ibid., p. 227. Harris, op. cit.

18 R. M. Citino, *Blitzkrieg to Desert Storm: The Evolution of Operational Warfare*, Lawrence: University Press of Kansas, 2004, p. 297.

19 Cited by A. Roberts, "The 'War on Terror' in Historical Perspective", *Survival*, Vol. 47, No. 2, Summer 2005, p. 113.

20 Although this does not appear to have been a problem in Iraqi Freedom, the presence of lawyers in various commands allowed them to have a say in targeting decisions.

21 Belote, op. cit., p. 45.

22 W. Murray, "Operation Iraqi Freedom: Lessons for the Future", in W. Murray (ed.), *A Nation at War in an Era of Strategic Change*, Carlisle, Pa.: Strategic Studies Institute, 2004, p. 6. M. Boot, "The New American Way of War", *Foreign Affairs*, Vol. 82, No. 4, July–August 2003. Online. Available www.foreignaffairs.org/20030701/faessay 15404/max-boot/the-new-american-way-of-war.html (accessed 28 November 2005). Technology did, of course, play a crucial role. To give one example, whereas in the Gulf War 1,500 precision-guided munitions were used, in Iraqi Freedom over 16,000 were used. Sidoti, op. cit. R. Peters, "In Praise of Attrition", *Parameters*, Vol. 34, No. 2, Summer 2004, p. 26.

23 Cited by Moore, op. cit.

24 H. Strachan, "The Lost Meaning of Strategy", *Survival*, Vol. 47, No. 3, Autumn 2005, p. 51. S. Metz and R. Millen, "Intervention, Stabilization, and Transformation Operations: The Role of Landpower in the New Strategic Environment", *Parameters*, Vol. 35, No. 1, Spring 2005, pp. 41–52. A. J. Echevarria, *Toward an American Way of War*, Carlisle, Pa.: Strategic Studies Institute, 2004, p. 14. Joint Chiefs-of-Staff, Joint Publication 3–0, *Doctrine for Joint Operations*, Washington, DC, 2001, pp. I–11.

25 D. R. Drechsler, "Reconstructing the Interagency Process after Iraq", *Journal of Strategic Studies*, Vol. 28, No. 1, February 2005, p. 18.

26 Shinseki, cited by Finlan, op. cit., p. 8. F. G. Hoffmann, "Small Wars Revisited: The United States and Nontraditional Wars", *Journal of Strategic Studies*, Vol. 28, No. 6, December 2005, pp. 913–40. C. C. Crane, "Phase IV Operations: Where Wars are Really Won", *Military Review*, Vol. 85, No. 3, May–June 2005, pp. 27–36.

27 Cited by Moore, op. cit. D. C. Hendrickson and R. W. Tucker, "Revisions in Need of Revising: What Went Wrong in the Iraq War", *Survival*, Vol. 47, No. 2, Summer 2005, pp. 13 and 16.

28 Hendrickson and Tucker, op. cit., p. 13.

29 Cited by Finlan, op. cit., p. 9. Hendrickson and Tucker, op. cit., pp. 21–2.

30 R. H. Scales, "Urban Warfare: A Soldier's View", *Military Review*, Vol. 85, No. 1, January–February 2005, pp. 9–18. R. A. Bunker and J. P. Sullivan, "Suicide Bombings in Operation Iraqi Freedom", *Military Review*, Vol. 85, No. 1, January–February 2005, pp. 69–79.

31 Cited by J. Record, "The Bush Doctrine and War with Iraq", *Parameters*, Vol. 33, No. 1, Spring 2003, pp. 11–12.

32 Cited by D. H. Allin and S. Simon, "America's Predicament", *Survival*, Vol. 46, No. 4, Winter 2004–05, p. 30.

33 Laird, op. cit. J. R. S. Batiste and P. R. Daniels, "The Fight for Samarra: Full Spectrum Operations in Modern Warfare", *Military Review*, Vol. 85, No. 3, May–June 2005, pp. 13–21.

34 Hendrickson and Tucker, op. cit., p. 21. T. H. Hayden, "Counterinsurgency in Iraq started with Fallujah", *Marine Corps Gazette*, Vol. 89, No. 7, July 2005, p. 28. Metz and Millen, op. cit., p. 45.

35 As early as September 2003 Bush had approached the UN in the hope of troop

contributions, but was rebuffed. D. Rennie, "Bush Seeks Fresh Allies in UN climb-down", *Daily Telegraph*, 4 September 2003.

36 O. Poole, "Casualty-hit US Marines Use Dummies to Fool Rebels", *Daily Telegraph*, 26 April 2005.

37 Letter from S. J. Gras printed in *Military Review*, Vol. 86, No. 2, March–April 2006, p. 119.

38 F. J. West, "The Fall of Fallujah", *Marine Corps Gazette*, Vol. 89, No. 7, July 2005, p. 55.

39 R. Gedye, "Battered Fallujah Takes First Steps to Normality", *Daily Telegraph*, 24 December 2004. T. Harnden, "Fighters' Leaders Flee as Fallujah Falls to US troops", *Daily Telegraph*, 15 November 2004. West, op. cit., p. 55.

40 J. A. Nagl, *Counterinsurgency Lessons from Malaya and Vietnam: Learning to Eat Soup with a Knife*, Westport, Conn.: Praeger, 2002. The subtitle is taken from a phrase attributed to Lawrence of Arabia.

41 T. Harnden, "Iraqis Using 'New Hizbollah Bombs' to Kill British troops", *Sunday Telegraph*, 30 April 2006. Finlan, op. cit., p. 13.

42 For example, General William Wallace, now the commandant of TRADOC, wrote to *Military Review* crediting the article for contributing to intellectual discourse within his organisation. Letter from W. S. Wallace printed in *Military Review*, Vol. 86, No. 2, March–April 2006, pp. 117–18. N. Aylwin-Foster, "Changing the Army for Counterinsurgency operations", *Military Review*, Vol. 85, No. 6, November–December 2005, pp. 2–15. Aylwin-Foster served as the deputy commander of the Office of Security Transition in the Coalition Office for Training and Organizing Iraq's Armed Forces. His comments are based on observations of US Army operations between December 2003 and November 2004.

43 Department of the Army, Field Manual-Interim 3–07.22, *Counterinsurgency Operations*, Washington, DC, October 2004. Aylwin-Foster, op. cit., pp. 3 and 5.

44 Cited by S. Rayment, " 'Heavy-handed' US to Adopt British Softly-softly Line", *Sunday Telegraph*, 26 March 2006.

45 Hendrickson and Tucker, op. cit., p. 11.

46 W. M. Darley, "Clausewitz's Theory of War and Information Operations", *Joint Force Quarterly*, No. 40, Spring 2006, p. 76. D. Moran, "Aims and Objectives in War", paper presented at Oxford Leverhulme Programme Conference on Clausewitz and the 21st Century, Oxford, March 2005. Clausewitz wrote "[p]olitical considerations do not determine the posting of guards or the employment of patrols". Clausewitz, op. cit., VIII, 6b, p. 606.

47 B. D. Watts, *Clausewitzian Friction and Future War*, McNair Paper 68, Washington, DC, Institute for National Strategic Studies, 2004, pp. vi–vii; emphasis in original.

48 J. White and A. Scott Tyson, "Rumsfeld Offers Strategies for Current War – Pentagon to Release 20-Year Plan Today", *Washington Post*, 3 February 2006. A. Russell, "Pentagon Promises 'Long War' Strategy as Violence Threatens Withdrawal", *Daily Telegraph*, 25 February 2006.

49 S. G. Jones, "Averting Failure in Afghanistan", *Survival*, Vol. 48, No. 1, Spring 2006, pp. 111–28.

Conclusion

1 C. von Clausewitz, *On War*, 2nd edn, Princeton, N.J.: Princeton University Press, 1984, Bk VI, Ch. 8, p. 386, and IV, 3, p. 228, trans. and ed. M. Howard and P. Paret. Although Clausewitz's understanding of strategy in this context relates to our contemporary understanding of the operational level of war, the point is that strategy as we know it is dependent on operational and tactical success.

2 A. J. Echevarria, "Neo-Clausewitzianism: Freytag-Loringhoven and the Militarization of Clausewitz in German Military Literature before the First World War", Ph.D. Dissertation, Princeton University, 1994, p. 60.

3   Cited by J. S. Robbins, "Contemporary Operational-Level War Fighting", *Naval War College Review*, Vol. 59, No. 2, Spring 2006, p. 158.

4   H. Strachan, "The Lost Meaning of Strategy", *Survival*, Vol. 47, No. 3, Autumn 2005, p. 47.

5   Captain Matthew Collins, USMC, makes a similar point. M. Collins, "Clausewitz and Summers on Vietnam: A Contemporary Analysis of *On Strategy*", *Small Wars Journal*, Vol. 3, October 2005, p. 20.

6   J. Stone, "Politics, Technology and the Revolution in Military Affairs", *Journal of Strategic Studies*, Vol. 27, No. 3, September 2004, p. 418.

7   A. J. Echevarria, *Toward an American Way of War*, Carlisle, Pa.: Strategic Studies Institute, 2004.

8   R. D. Hooker, jun., "Beyond *Vom Kriege*: The Character and Conduct of War", *Parameters*, Vol. 35, No. 2, Summer 2005, p. 4.

9   Cited by C. Gray, *Defining and Achieving Decisive Victory*, Carlisle, Pa.: Strategic Studies Institute, 2002, p. 15.

10 R. F. Baumann, "Historical Perspectives on Future War", *Military Review*, Vol. 77, No. 2, March–April 1997. Online. Available www.cgsc.army.mil/milrev/English/marapr97/baumann.htm (accessed 14 February 2002).

11 J. A. Nagl, *Counterinsurgency Lessons from Malaya and Vietnam: Learning to Eat Soup with a Knife*, Westport, Conn.: Praeger, 2002.

12 W. Murray, "Operation Iraqi Freedom: Lessons for the Future", in W. Murray (ed.), *A Nation at War in an Era of Strategic Change*, Carlisle, Pa.: Strategic Studies Institute, 2004, p. 12.

13 Cited by L. J. Matthews, "The Uniformed Intellectual and his Place in American Arms", *ARMY*, Vol. 52, No. 8, August 2002. Online. Available www.ausa.org/webpub/DeptArmyMagazine.nsf/byid/CCRN-6CCS56 (accessed 8 September 2005).

14 A. J. Echevarria, "Clausewitz and the War on Terror", paper presented at Oxford Leverhulme Programme Conference on Clausewitz and the 21st Century, Oxford, March 2005. R. Lock-Pullan, "How to Rethink War: Conceptual Innovation and AirLand Battle Doctrine", *Journal of Strategic Studies*, Vol. 28, No. 4, August 2005, p. 680.

15 H. Wass de Czege, "How to Change an Army", *Military Review*, Vol. 77, No. 1, January–February 1997. Online. Available www-cgsc.army.mil/milrev/English/janfeb97/czege.htm (accessed 10 November 1999). This was a reprint of an article first published in the same journal in November 1984.

16 Department of the Navy, Marine Corps Doctrinal Publication 1, *Warfighting*, Washington, DC, 1997, p. 26.

17 N. Aylwin-Foster, "Changing the Army for Counterinsurgency Operations", *Military Review*, Vol. 85, No. 6, November–December 2005, p. 9.

18 S. J. Newland, *Victories are Not Enough – Limitations of the German Way of War*, Letort Paper, Carlisle, Pa.: Strategic Studies Institute, 2005.

Bibliography

Primary sources

Documents

US Army Military History Institute

Major-General Cushman, Commandant of Combined Arms Center, Fort Leavenworth, Kansas, note to generals Creighton Abrams and William E. DePuy, 4 May 1974, DePuy Papers.

General W. E. DePuy, transcript of oral history interview with R. L. Brownlee and W. J. Mullen, 1979, DePuy Papers.

W. Lind, letter to Colonel Edward Bradford, editor of *Military Review*, 7 August 1978, Starry Papers.

Colonel R. Paschall, letter to General William E. DePuy, 25 April 1985, DePuy Papers.

Brigadier-General Crosbie E. Saint, letter to Lieutenant-Colonel Huba Wass de Czege, 23 March 1981, Starry Papers.

General D. A. Starry, letter to Major-General J. G. R. Allen, director UK Royal Armoured Corps, 26 March 1975, Starry Papers.

General D. A. Starry, letter to Lieutenant-General Edward Meyer, 30 January 1979, Starry Papers.

Colonel Huba Wass de Czege, "Subject: The Nature and Reasons for Changes in this Edition", cover letter to draft FM 100–5, 1 July 1985.

Major-General A. M. Weyand, letter to General D. A. Starry, 29 April 1981, Starry Papers.

US Army Command and General Staff College

Pearlman, M., Interview with General William E. DePuy, 15 January 1987, file CTAC-027.

Official documents

Department of Defense, *Report of the Quadrennial Defense Review*, Washington, DC, 1997.

Joint Chiefs-of-Staff, *Joint Vision 2010*, Washington, DC, 1995.

Office for the Secretary of Defense, *Quadrennial Defense Review*, Washington, DC, 30 September 2001.
US Army Training and Doctrine Command, *Force XXI Operations: A Concept for the Evolution of Full-Dimensional Operations for the Strategic Army of the Early Twenty-First Century*, TRADOC Pamphlet 525–5, Fort Monroe, Va., August 1994.

Military manuals

Joint Chiefs-of-Staff, Joint Publication 1, *Joint Warfare of the US Armed Forces*, Washington, DC, 1991.
Joint Chiefs-of-Staff, Joint Publication 3–0, *Doctrine for Joint Operations*, Washington, DC, 1993.
Joint Chiefs-of-Staff, Joint Publication 3–0, *Doctrine for Joint Operations*, Washington, DC, 2001.
Department of the Army, FM 100–5: *Operations*, Washington, DC, 1976.
Department of the Army, FM 100–5: *Operations*, Washington, DC, 1982.
Department of the Army, FM 100–5: *Operations*, Washington, DC, 1986.
Department of the Army, FM 7–92, *Operations in Low Intensity Conflict*, Washington, DC, 1992.
Department of the Army, FM 100–5: *Operations*, Washington, DC, 1993.
Department of the Army, FM 3–0, *Operations*, Washington, DC, 2001.
Department of the Army, Field Manual-Interim 3–07.22, *Counterinsurgency Operations*, Washington, DC, 2004.
Departments of the Army and Air Force, FM 100–20/AFP 3–20, *Military Operations in Low Intensity Conflict*, Washington, DC, 1990.
Department of the Navy, Headquarters Marine Corps, FMFM 1: *Warfighting*, Washington, DC, 1989.
Department of the Navy, Headquarters Marine Corps, FMFM 1–3: *Tactics*, Washington, DC, 1990.
Department of the Navy, Marine Corps Doctrinal Publication 1, *Warfighting*, Washington, DC, 1997.
Department of the Navy, Marine Corps Doctrinal Publication 1–1, *Strategy*, Washington, DC, 1997.

Interviews by the author

Colonel Clinton J. Ancker III, Royal United Services Institute, London, 19 November 1999.
Dr Stephen Blank, Strategic Studies Institute, US Army War College, Carlisle Barracks, Pennsylvania, 19 September 2000.
Lieutenant-Colonel Antulio J. Echevarria II, Strategic Studies Institute, US Army War College, Carlisle Barracks, Pennsylvania, 19 September 2000.
Dr Steven Metz, Strategic Studies Institute, US Army War College, Carlisle Barracks, Pennsylvania, 19 September 2000.
Professor Roger Spiller, US Army Command and General Staff College, Fort Leavenworth, Kansas, 7 September 1999.
Dr. Earl Tilford, Strategic Studies Institute, US Army War College, Carlisle Barracks, Pennsylvania, 14 September 1999.

Correspondence with the author

Dr Christopher Bassford, e-mail, 11 October 2000.
Dr Antulio Echevarria, e-mail, 7 August 2002.
Colonel Paul Herbert, e-mail, 19 May 2000.
Colonel James Holcomb, e-mail, 8 July 1999.
Professor Peter Paret, e-mail, 16 October 2000.
Dr Earl Tilford, letter, 24 June 1999.
Brigadier-General Huba Wass de Czege, e-mail, 22 June 2000.

Secondary sources

Books and essays therein

Alberts, D. J., "Deterrence in the 1980s – Part II. The Role of Conventional Air Power", *Adelphi Paper* 193, London: International Institute for Strategic Studies, Winter 1984.

Alberts, D. S., Gartska J. J. and Stein, F. P., *Network Centric Warfare: Developing and Leveraging Information Superiority*, Washington, DC, C4ISR Cooperative Research Program, 1999.

Ardant du Picq, C. J. J, *Battle Studies: Ancient and Modern Battle*, trans. by J. N. Greely and R. C. Cotton, New York: Macmillan, 1921.

Bacevich, A. J. and Cohen, E. A. (eds), *War over Kosovo: Politics and Strategy in a Global Age*, New York: Columbia University Press, 2001.

Ball, D., "The Development of the SIOP, 1960–1983", in D. Ball and J. Richelson (eds), *Strategic and Nuclear Targeting*, Ithaca, N.Y.: Cornell University Press, 1986.

Bassford, C., *Clausewitz in English – The Reception of Clausewitz in Britain and America, 1815–1945*, New York: Oxford University Press, 1994.

Berlin, I., *Against the Current: Essays in the History of Ideas*, London: Pimlico, 1997.

Biddle, S., *Afghanistan and the Future of Warfare: Implications for Army and Defense Policy*, Carlisle, Pa.: Strategic Studies Institute, 2002.

Bobbitt, P., *The Shield of Achilles – War, Peace and the Course of History*, London: Penguin, 2003.

Boot, M., *Savage Wars of Peace: Small Wars and the Rise of American Power*, New York: Perseus Books, 2002.

Bowden, M., *Black Hawk Down: A Story of Modern War*, New York: Signet, 1999.

Brodie, B. *Strategy in the Missile Age*, Princeton, N.J.: Princeton University Press, 1959.

Brodie, B., (ed.), *The Absolute Weapon: Atomic Power and World Order*, New York: Harcourt Brace, 1946.

Brown, H., *Thinking About National Security: Defense and Foreign-Policy in a Dangerous World*, Boulder, Colo.: Westview Press, 1983.

Bush, G. and Scowcroft, B., *A World Transformed*, New York: Alfred A. Knopf, 1998.

Buzzanco, R., *Masters of War: Military Dissent and Politics in the Vietnam Era*, Cambridge: Cambridge University Press, 1996.

Cimbala, S., *Clausewitz and Escalation*, London: Frank Cass, 1991.

Citino, R. M., *Blitzkrieg to Desert Storm: The Evolution of Operational Warfare*, Lawrence: University Press of Kansas, 2004.

Clark, W., *Waging Modern War: Bosnia, Kosovo and the Future of Combat*, Oxford: Perseus, 2001.

Clausewitz, C. von, *On War*, trans. by J. J. Matthijs Jolles, New York: Random House, 1943.

Clausewitz, C. von, *On War*, ed. A. Rapoport, Harmondsworth: Penguin, 1968.

Clausewitz, C. von, *On War*, 2nd edn, trans. and ed. by M. Howard and P. Paret, Princeton, N.J.: Princeton University Press, 1984.

Clausewitz, C. von, *Historical and Political Writings*, trans. and ed. P. Paret and D. Moran, Princeton, N.J.: Princeton University Press, 1992.

Clodfelter, M., "Molding Airpower Convictions: Development and Legacy of William Mitchell's Strategic Thought", in P. S. Meilinger, (ed.), *The Paths of Heaven – The Evolution of Airpower Theory*, Maxwell Air Force Base, Ala.: Air University Press, 1997.

Corbett, J. S., *Some Principles of Maritime Strategy*, ed. E. J. Grove, Annapolis, Md: Naval Institute Press, 1988.

Craig, G. A. and Gilbert, F., "Reflections on Strategy in the Present and Future", in P. Paret *et al.*, *Makers of Modern Strategy from Machiavelli to the Nuclear Age*, Princeton, N.J.: Princeton University Press, 1986.

Crane, C., *American Airpower Strategy in Korea*, Lawrence: University of Kansas Press, 2002.

Crane, C. C., *Avoiding Vietnam: The US Army's Response to Defeat in Southeast Asia*, Carlisle, Pa.: Strategic Studies Institute, 2002.

Creveld, M. van, "The Eternal Clausewitz", in M. Handel (ed.), *Clausewitz and Modern Strategy*, London: Frank Cass, 1986.

Creveld, M. van, *On Future War*, London: Brassey's, 1991.

Crowl, P. A., "Alfred Thayer Mahan: The Naval Historian", in P. Paret *et al.*, *Makers of Modern Strategy from Machiavelli to the Nuclear Age*, Princeton, N.J.: Princeton University Press, 1986.

Delbrück, H., *History of the Art of War within the Framework of Political History*, trans. W. J. Renfroe, jun., Westport, Conn.: Greenwood Press, 1975.

D'Este, C., *A Genius for War – A Life of General George S. Patton*, London: HarperCollins, 1995.

Doughty, R. A., *The Evolution of US Army Tactical Doctrine, 1946–76*, Leavenworth Paper No. 1, Fort Leavenworth, Kans.: Combat Studies Institute, 1979.

Echevarria, A. J., *After Clausewitz – German Military Thinkers before the Great War*, Lawrence: University Press of Kansas, 2000.

Echevarria, A. J., *Clausewitz's Center of Gravity: Changing our Warfighting Doctrine – Again!*, Carlisle, Pa.: Strategic Studies Institute, 2002.

Echevarria, A. J., *Globalization and the Nature of War*, Carlisle, Pa.: Strategic Studies Institute, 2003.

Echevarria, A. J., *Toward an American Way of War*, Carlisle, Pa.: Strategic Studies Institute, 2004.

Enthoven, A. C. and Wayne Smith, K., *How Much is Enough? Shaping the Defense Program, 1961–1969*, New York: Harper and Row, 1971.

Epstein, R. M., *Napoleon's Last Victory and the Emergence of Modern War*, Lawrence: Kansas University Press, 1994.

Evans, M., *The Continental School of Strategy: The Past, Present and Future of Land Power*, Land Warfare Studies Centre, Study Paper No. 305, June 2004.

Fadok, D. S., "John Boyd and John Warden: Airpower's Quest for Strategic Paralysis", in P. S. Meilinger (ed.), *The Paths of Heaven – The Evolution of Airpower Theory*, Maxwell Air Force Base, Ala.: Air University Press, 1997.

Farrell, T., "US Marine Corps Operations in Somalia: A Model for the Future", in G. Till (ed.), *Amphibious Warfare*, Occasional Paper No. 31, Camberley: Strategic and Combat Studies Institute, 1997.

Ferguson, N., *Colossus – The Rise and Fall of the American Empire*, London: Penguin, 2005.

Fishel, J., *The Fog of Peace: Planning and Executing the Restoration of Panama*, Carlisle Barracks, Pa.: Strategic Studies Institute, 1992.

Foley, R. T. (trans. and ed.), *Alfred von Schlieffen's Military Writings*, London: Frank Cass, 2003.

Ford, R. E., *Tet 1968 – Understanding the Surprise*, London: Frank Cass, 1995.

Fraser, S., *US Maritime Strategy – Issues and Implications*, Bailrigg Paper 25, Centre for Defence and International Security Studies, Lancaster University, 1997.

Freedman, L., *The Evolution of Nuclear Strategy*, 2nd edn, London: Macmillan, 1989.

Freedman, L., "The First Two Generations of Nuclear Strategists" in P. Paret *et al.*, *Makers of Modern Strategy from Machiavelli to the Nuclear Age*, Princeton, N.J.: Princeton University Press, 1986.

Freedman, L., "Strategic Defence in the Nuclear Age", *Adelphi Paper* 224, London: International Institute for Strategic Studies, Autumn 1987.

Friedman, N., *The Fifty-Year War: Conflict and Strategy in the Cold War*, London: Chatham Publishing, 2003.

Friedman, T. F., *The Lexus and the Olive Tree*, New York: Anchor, 2000.

Friedman, T. F., *The World is Flat – A Brief History of the Twenty-First Century*, New York: Allen Lane, 2005.

Fukuyama, F., *The End of History and the Last Man*, New York: Free Press, 1992.

Gat, A., *A History of Military Thought from the Enlightenment to the Cold War*, Oxford: Oxford University Press, 2001.

Gordon, M. R. and Trainor, B. E., *The Generals' War: The Inside Story of the Conflict in the Gulf*, Boston, Mass.: Little Brown, 1995.

Gray, C. S., *The Future of Land-Based Missile Forces*, London: International Institute for Strategic Studies, 1978.

Gray, C. S., "Strategy in the Nuclear Age", in M. Knox, A. Bernstein and W. Murray, *The Making of Strategy – Rulers, States and War*, Cambridge: Cambridge University Press, 1993.

Gray, C. S., *Modern Strategy*, Oxford: Oxford University Press, 1999.

Gray, C. S., *Defining and Achieving Decisive Victory*, Carlisle, Pa.: Strategic Studies Institute, 2002.

Gray, C. S., *Transformation and Strategic Surprise*, Carlisle, Pa.: Strategic Studies Institute, 2005.

Hahlweg, W., "Clausewitz and Guerrilla Warfare", in M. Handel (ed.), *Clausewitz and Modern Strategy*, London: Frank Cass, 1986.

Hallion, R. P., *Storm over Iraq: Air Power and the Gulf War*, Washington, DC, Smithsonian Institution Press, 1992.

Hammel, E., *The Root – The Marines in Beirut, August 1982 – February 1984*, Pacifico, Calif.: Pacifico Press, 1993.

Hammond, G. T., *The Mind of War – John Boyd and American Security*, Washington, DC: Smithsonian Institution Press, 2001.

Handel, M., *Masters of War – Classical Strategic Thought*, 2nd edn, London: Frank Cass, 1996.

Harrison, R. W., *The Russian Way of War: Operational Art, 1904–1940*, Lawrence: Kansas University Press, 2001.

Harrison, S. S., "Afghanistan: Soviet Intervention, Afghan Resistance, and the American Role", in M. T. Klare and P. Kornbluh (eds), *Low-Intensity Warfare: Counterinsurgency, Proinsurgency, and Antiterrorism in the Eighties*, New York: Pantheon, 1988.

Hattendorf, J. B., *The Evolution of the US Navy's Maritime Strategy*, Newport Paper No. 19, Newport, R.I.: Naval War College Press, 2004.

Hayden, H. T. (ed.), *Warfighting – Maneuver Warfare in the US Marine Corps*, London: Greenhill, 1995.

Henderson, H. J., "Brown-Water Navies and Counterinsurgency Operations", in A. D. English (ed.), *The Changing Face of War – Learning from History*, Montreal: McGill-Queens University Press, 1998.

Herbert, P. H., *Deciding What Has to Be Done – General William E. DePuy and the 1976 Edition of FM 100–5, Operations*, Leavenworth Paper No. 16, Fort Leavenworth, Kans.: Combat Studies Institute, US Army Command and General Staff College, 1988.

Heuser, B., *Reading Clausewitz*, London: Pimlico, 2002.

Higginbotham, D. A., *The War of American Independence*, New York: Macmillan, 1971.

Huber, T. M., "Deceiving the Enemy in Operation Desert Storm", in R. J. Spiller (ed.), *Combined Arms in Battle Since 1939*, Fort Leavenworth, Kans.: US Army Command and General Staff College Press, 1992.

Hughes, D. J. (ed.), *Moltke on the Art of War – Selected Writings*, New York: Presidio Press, 1993.

Jablonsky, D., *The Owl of Minerva Flies at Twilight: Doctrinal Change and Continuity and the Revolution in Military Affairs*, Carlisle, Pa.: Strategic Studies Institute, May 1994.

Johnson, C., *Autopsy on People's War*, Berkeley, Calif.: California University Press, 1973.

Kahn, H., *On Thermonuclear War*, Princeton, N.J.: Princeton University Press, 1961.

Kaldor, M., *New and Old Wars: Organized Violence in a Global Era*, Stanford, Calif.: Stanford University Press, 1999.

Keegan, J., *The Face of Battle*, London: Cape, 1976.

Keegan, J., *The Mask of Command*, Harmondsworth: Penguin, 1987.

Keegan, J., *A History of Warfare*, London: Hutchinson, 1993.

Kissinger, H., *Nuclear Weapons and Foreign-Policy*, New York: Harper, 1957.

Kissinger, H., *White House Years*, Boston: Little Brown and Co., 1979.

Kissinger, H., *Diplomacy*, New York: Simon and Schuster, 1994.

Kitfield, J., *Prodigal Soldiers – How the Generation of Officers Born of Vietnam Revolutionized the American Style of War*, Washington, DC, Brassey's, 1997.

Knorr, K. and Read, T. (eds), *Limited Strategic War*, London: Praeger, 1962.

Knox, M., "Continuity and Revolution in the Making of Strategy", in M. Knox A. Bernstein and W. Murray, *The Making of Strategy – Rulers, States and War*, Cambridge: Cambridge University Press, 1993.

Knox, M., "The Prussian Idea of Freedom and the 'Career Open to Talent': Battlefield Initiative and Social Ascent from Prussian Reform to Nazi Revolution, 1807 to 1944", in M. Knox, *Common Destiny – Dictatorship, Foreign-Policy, and War in Fascist Italy and Nazi Germany*, Cambridge: Cambridge University Press, 2000.

Knox, M. and Murray, W. (eds), *The Dynamics of Military Revolution 1300–2050*, Cambridge: Cambridge University Press, 2001.

Krepinevich, A., *The Army and Vietnam*, Baltimore, Md.: Johns Hopkins University Press, 1986.

Krepinevich, A., "Recovery from Defeat – The US Army and Vietnam", in G. J.

Andreopoulos and H. E. Selesky, *The Aftermath of Defeat – Societies, Armed Forces, and the Challenge of Recovery*, New Haven, Conn.: Yale University Press, 1994.

Lambeth, B., *The Transformation of American Air Power*, Ithaca, N.Y.: Cornell University Press, 2000.

Lehman, J., *Aircraft Carriers – The Real Choices*, The Washington Papers, Vol. VI, Center for Strategic and International Studies, Georgetown University, Washington, DC, 1978.

Leonhard, R. R., *The Art of Maneuver – Maneuver Warfare Theory and AirLand Battle*, Novato, Calif.: Presidio Press, 1991.

Leonhard, R. R., *The Principles of War for the Information Age*, Novato, Calif.: Presidio Press, 1998.

Lind, W., *Maneuver Warfare Handbook*, Boulder, Colo.: Westview Press, 1985.

Lock-Pullan, R., *US Intervention Policy and Army Innovation: From Vietnam to Iraq*, New York: Routledge, 2006.

McMaster, H. R., *Dereliction of Duty – Lyndon Johnson, Robert McNamara, the JCS, and the Lies that Led to Vietnam*, New York: HarperCollins.

McNamara, R. S., *In Retrospect: The Tragedy and Lessons of Vietnam*, New York: Random House, 1995.

Mahan, A. T., *Naval Strategy Compared and Contrasted with the Principles and Practice of Military Operations on Land*, Westport, Conn.: Greenwood Press, 1975 (reprint).

Matloff, M., "Allied Strategy in Europe", in P. Paret *et al.*, *Makers of Modern Strategy from Machiavelli to the Nuclear Age*, Princeton, N.J.: Princeton University Press, 1986.

Metz, S., *Counterinsurgency – Strategy and the Phoenix of American Capability*, Carlisle Barracks, Pa.: Strategic Studies Institute, 1995.

Metz, S., *American Strategy: Issues and Alternatives for the Quadrennial Defense Review*, Carlisle, Pa.: Strategic Studies Institute, 2000.

Mittelman, J. H., *The Globalization Syndrome: Transformation and Resistance*, Princeton, N.J.: Princeton University Press, 2000.

Murray, W., "Operation Iraqi Freedom: Lessons for the Future", in W. Murray (ed.), *A Nation at War in an Era of Strategic Change*, Carlisle, Pa.: Strategic Studies Institute, 2004.

Murray, W. and Scales, jun., R. H., *The Iraq War: A Military History*, Cambridge, Mass.: Harvard University Press, 2003.

Nagl, J. A., *Counterinsurgency Lessons from Malaya and Vietnam: Learning to Eat Soup with a Knife*, Westport, Conn.: Praeger, 2002.

Naveh, S., *In Pursuit of Military Excellence – The Evolution of Operational Theory*, London: Frank Cass, 1997.

Newland, S. J., *Victories are Not Enough – Limitations of the German Way of War*, Letort Paper, Carlisle, Pa.: Strategic Studies Institute, 2005.

Osgood, R. E., *Limited War – The Challenge to American Strategy*, Chicago, Ill.: University of Chicago Press, 1957.

Owens, W. A., *Lifting the Fog of War*, London: Johns Hopkins University Press, 2000.

Palmer, B., *The 25-Year War – America's Military Role in Vietnam*, Lexington: University Press of Kentucky, 1984.

Paret, P., *Clausewitz and the State – The Man, His Theories, and His Times*, 2nd edn, Princeton, N.J.: Princeton University Press, 1985.

Paret, P., "Clausewitz", in H. S. Bauman (ed.), *Military Leadership and Command*, Lexington: Virginia Military Institute Foundation, 1987.

Paret, P., "Clausewitz: Life and Thought", in P. Paret, *Understanding War – Essays on Clausewitz and the History of Military Power*, Princeton, N.J.: Princeton University Press, 1992.

Paret, P., "The Relationship between the American Revolutionary War and European Military Thought and Practice", in P. Paret, *Understanding War – Essays on Clausewitz and the History of Military Power*, Princeton, N.J.: Princeton University Press, 1992.

Powell, C., *My American Journey*, New York: Random House, 1995.

Record, J., *The Creeping Irrelevance of US Force Planning*, Carlisle Barracks, Pa.: Strategic Studies Institute, US Army War College, 1998.

Reid, B. H., *Studies in British Military Thought – Debates with Fuller and Liddell Hart*, Lincoln: University of Nebraska Press, 1998.

Reilly, T. P., "The National Security Strategy of the United States: Development of Grand Strategy", in W. Murray (ed.), *A Nation at War in an Era of Strategic Change*, Carlisle, Pa.: Strategic Studies Institute, 2004.

Romjue, J. W., *From Active Defense to AirLand Battle*, Fort Monroe, N.J.: TRADOC Historical Office, 1984.

Romjue, J. W., "Evolution of American Army Doctrine", in J. Gooch (ed.), *The Origins of Contemporary Doctrine*, Occasional Paper No. 30, Camberley: Strategic and Combat Studies Institute, 1997.

Rosenberg, D. A., "Nuclear War Planning", in M. Howard, G. J. Andreopoulos and M. R. Shulman, *The Laws of War: Constraints on Warfare in the Western World*, New Haven, Conn.: Yale University Press, 1994.

Rothenburg, G. E., "Moltke, Schlieffen, and the Doctrine of Strategic Envelopment", in P. Paret *et al.*, *Makers of Modern Strategy from Machiavelli to the Nuclear Age*, Princeton, N.J.: Princeton University Press, 1986.

Rothfels, H., "Clausewitz", in E. M. Earle (ed.), *Makers of Modern Strategy from Machiavelli to Hitler*, Princeton, N.J.: Princeton University Press, 1943.

Russett, B. M., *Grasping the Democratic Peace – Principles for a Post-Cold War World*, Princeton, N.J.: Princeton University Press, 1993.

Scales, R. H., *Certain Victory – The US Army in the Gulf War*, Fort Leavenworth, Kans.: US Army Command and General Staff College Press, 1994.

Schmitt, J. F., "Command and (Out of) Control: The Military Implications of Complexity Theory", in D. S. Alberts and T. J. Czerwinski, *Complexity, Global Politics, and National Security*, Washington, DC, National Defense University, 1997.

Schraeder, P. J., "Paramilitary Intervention", in P. J. Schraeder (ed.), *Intervention in the 1980s – US Foreign Policy in the Third World*, London: Lynne Rienner, 1989.

Schwarzkopf, H. N., *It Doesn't Take a Hero*, New York: Bantam Books, 1992.

Shy, J., "Jomini", in P. Paret *et al.*, *Makers of Modern Strategy from Machiavelli to the Nuclear Age*, Princeton, N.J.: Princeton University Press, 1986.

Shy, J. and Collier, T., "Revolutionary War", in P. Paret *et al.*, *Makers of Modern Strategy from Machiavelli to the Nuclear Age*, Princeton, N.J.: Princeton University Press, 1986.

Simpkin, R., *Race to the Swift – Thoughts on 21st Century Warfare*, London: Brassey's, 1985.

Simpkin, R., *Deep Battle – The Brainchild of Marshal Tukhachevskii*, London: Brassey's, 1987.

Sorley, L., *A Better War*, New York: Harcourt Brace, 1999.

Starry, D. A., "Reflections", in G. F. Hofmann and D. A. Starry, *Camp Colt to Desert*

Storm – The History of US Armored Forces, Lexington: University Press of Kentucky, 1999.

Summers, H. S., *On Strategy – A Critical Analysis of the Vietnam War*, Novato, Calif.: Presidio Press, 1982.

Summers, H. S., *The New World Strategy*, New York: Touchstone, 1995.

Swain, R. M., *Selected Papers of William E. DePuy*, Fort Leavenworth, Kans.: Combat Studies Institute, US Army Command and General Staff College Press, 1994.

Swain, R. M., *"Lucky War" – Third Army in Desert Storm*, 2nd edn, Fort Leavenworth, Kans.: US Army Command and General Staff College Press, 1997.

Tashjean, J., *The Transatlantic Clausewitz*, Carlisle, Pa.: US Army Military History Institute, 1982.

Thompson, W. S. and Frizzell, D. D. (eds), *The Lessons of Vietnam*, New York: Crane, Rusack and Co., 1977.

Toffler, A. and Toffler, H., *War and Anti-War – Survival at the Dawn of the 21st Century*, Boston, Mass.: Little, Brown, 1993.

Ullman, H. and Wade jun., J., *Shock and Awe: Achieving Rapid Dominance*, Washington, DC, National Defense University Press, 1996.

US General Accounting Office, *Operation Desert Storm – Evaluation of the Air Campaign*, June 1997, GAO/NSIAD-97–134.

Watts, B., *Clausewitzian Friction and Future War*, McNair Paper 68, Washington, DC, Institute for National Strategic Studies, 2004.

Weigley, R. F., "American Strategy from its Beginnings through the First World War", in P. Paret *et al.*, *Makers of Modern Strategy from Machiavelli to the Nuclear Age*, Princeton, N.J.: Princeton University Press, 1986.

Weigley, R. F., *History of the United States Army*, New York: Macmillan, 1967.

Weigley, R. F., *The American Way of War – A History of United States Military Strategy and Policy*, 2nd edn, Bloomington: Indiana University Press, 1977.

Weigley, R. F., *The Age of Battles – The Quest for Decisive Warfare from Breitenfeld to Waterloo*, Bloomington: Indiana University Press, 1991.

Weinberger, C., *Fighting for Peace – Seven Critical Years at the Pentagon*, London: Michael Joseph, 1990.

Westmoreland, W. C., *A Soldier Reports*, Garden City, N.Y.: Doubleday, 1976.

Winton, H. R., "An Ambivalent Partnership: US Army and Air Force Perspectives on Air–Ground Operations, 1973–90", in P. S. Meilinger (ed.), *The Paths of Heaven – The Evolution of Airpower Theory*, Maxwell Air Force Base, Ala.: Air University Press, 1997.

Wynnyk, P. F., "Vo Nguyen Giap: A Strategy for Protracted Revolutionary War", in A. D. English (ed.), *The Changing Face of War – Learning from History*, Montreal: McGill-Queens University Press, 1998.

Yates, L. A., "The US–Panama Crisis, 1987–1990", in R. J. Spiller (ed.), *Combined Arms in Battle Since 1939*, Fort Leavenworth, Kans.: US Army Command and General Staff College Press, 1992.

Articles

Allin, D. H. and Simon, S., "America's Predicament", *Survival*, Vol. 46, No. 4, Winter 2004–05.

Alterman, E., "The Uses and Abuses of Clausewitz", *Parameters*, Vol. 17, No. 2, Summer 1987.

Anon., "Recent Soviet Commentary favourable to US Army Special-operations Forces", *Special Warfare*, The Professional Bulletin of the John F. Kennedy Special Warfare Centre and School, Vol. 5, No. 1, March 1992.

Argersinger, S., "K. von Clausewitz: Analysis of FM 100–5", *Military Review*, Vol. 66, No. 2, February 1986.

Aylwin-Foster, N., "Changing the Army for Counterinsurgency operations", *Military Review*, Vol. 85, No. 6, November–December 2005.

Barranto, L. J., "Grenada Post-Mortem: A 'Report' That Wasn't", *ARMY*, Vol. 34, No. 6, June 1984.

Batiste, J. R. S. and Daniels, P. R., "The Fight for Samarra: Full Spectrum Operations in Modern Warfare", *Military Review*, Vol. 85, No. 3, May–June 2005.

Baumann, R. F., "Historical Perspectives on Future War", *Military Review*, Vol. 77, No. 2, March–April 1997.

Belote, H. D., "Warden and the Air Corps Tactical School", *Airpower Journal*, Vol. 13, No. 3, Fall 1999.

Belote, H. D., "Paralyzed or Pulverized? The Fall of the Republican Guard", *Joint Force Quarterly*, No. 37, 2005.

Berdal, M., "Fateful Encounter: The United States and UN Peacekeeping", *Survival*, Vol. 36, No. 1, Spring 1994.

Biddle, S., "The New Way of War? Debating the Kosovo Model", *Foreign Affairs*, Vol. 81, No. 3, May–June 2002.

Biddle, S., "Afghanistan and the Future of Warfare", *Foreign Affairs*, Vol. 82, No. 2, March–April 2003.

Bingham, P. T., "Ground Maneuver and Air Interdiction in the Operational Art", *Parameters*, Vol. 19, No. 1, Spring 1989.

Bolger, D. P., "Special Operations and the Grenada Campaign", *Parameters*, Vol. 18, No. 4, December 1988.

Boot, M., "The New American Way of War", *Foreign Affairs*, Vol. 82, No. 3, July–August 2003.

Brodie, B., "The Development of Nuclear Strategy", *International Security*, Vol. 2, No. 4, Spring 1978.

Brodie, B., "Strategy as an Art and a Science", *Naval War College Review*, Vol. 51, No. 1, Winter 1998.

Brown, M. L., "Vietnam: Learning from the Debacle", *Military Review*, Vol. 67, No. 2, February 1987.

Bundy, M., Kennan, G. and McNamara, R., "The President's Choice: Star Wars or Arms Control", *Foreign Affairs*, Vol. 63, No. 2, Winter 1984–85.

Bunker, R. A. and Sullivan, J. P., "Suicide Bombings in Operation Iraqi Freedom", *Military Review*, Vol. 85, No. 1, January–February 2005.

Bunker, R. J., "Rethinking OOTW", *Military Review*, Vol. 75, No. 6, November–December 1995.

Bunker, R. J., "Generations, Waves and Epochs: Modes of Warfare and the RPMA", *Airpower Journal*, Vol. 10, No. 1, Spring 1996.

Cassidy, R. M., "Prophets or Praetorians? The Uptonian Paradox and the Powell Corollary", *Parameters*, Vol. 33, No. 3, Autumn 2003.

Cebrowski, A. K. and Gartska, J. J., "Network-Centric Warfare: Its Origins and Future", *US Naval Institute Proceedings*, Vol. 124/1, 1998.

Cillessen, B. J., "Embracing the Bomb: Ethics, Morality and Nuclear Deterrence in the US Air Force, 1945–1955", *Journal of Strategic Studies*, Vol. 21, No. 1, March 1998.

Clarke, W. and Herbst, J., "Somalia and the Future of Humanitarian Intervention", *Foreign Affairs*, Vol. 75, No. 2, March–April 1996.

Clodfelter, M., "Of Demons, Storms, and Thunder: A Preliminary Look at Vietnam's Impact on the Persian Gulf Air Campaign", *Airpower Journal*, Vol. 5, No. 4, Winter 1991.

Collins, M., "Clausewitz and Summers on Vietnam: A Contemporary Analysis of *On Strategy*", *Small Wars Journal*, Vol. 3, October 2005.

Collins, S. N., "*Just Cause* Up Close: A Light Infantryman's View of LIC", *Parameters*, Vol. 22, No. 2, Summer 1992.

Coroalles, A. M., "*On War* in the Information Age: A Conversation with Carl von Clausewitz", *ARMY*, Vol. 46, No. 5, May 1996.

Crane, C., "To Avert Impending Disaster: American Plans to Use Atomic Weapons During the Korean War", *Journal of Strategic Studies*, Vol. 23, No. 2, June 2000.

Crane, C. C., "Phase IV Operations: Where Wars are Really Won", *Military Review*, Vol. 85, No. 3, May–June 2005.

D'Amato, M. J., "Vigilant Warrior: General Donn A. Starry's AirLand Battle and How it Changed the Army", *Armor*, Vol. 109, No. 3, May–June 2000.

Delaney, D. E., "Cutting, Running or Otherwise? The US Decision to Withdraw from Somalia", *Journal of Small Wars and Insurgencies*, Vol. 15, No. 3, Winter 2004.

DiNardo, R. L. and Hughes, D. J., "Some Cautionary Thoughts on Information Warfare", *Airpower Journal*, Vol. 9, No. 4, Winter 1995.

Donnelly, T., "Don't Underestimate the US Army", *Parameters*, Vol. 20, No. 1, March 1990.

Dougherty, K. J., "Indirect Application of Military Power – US Policy Toward Nicaragua", *Military Review*, Vol. 74, No. 10, October 1994.

Doughty, R. A. and Holder, L. D., "Images of the Future Battlefield", *Military Review*, Vol. 58, No. 1, January 1978.

Dowd, A. W., "Thirteen Years: The Causes and Consequences of the War in Iraq", *Parameters*, Vol. 33, No. 3, Autumn 2003.

Doyle, M., "Kant: Liberalism and World Politics", *American Political Science Review*, Vol. 80, No. 4, December 1986.

Drechsler, D. R., "Reconstructing the Interagency Process after Iraq", *Journal of Strategic Studies*, Vol. 28, No. 1, February 2005.

Dubik, J. M., "Has Warfare Changed? Sorting Apples from Oranges", *Landpower Essay*, No. 2–03, Institute of Land Warfare, July 2002.

DuBois, T. R., "The Weinberger Doctrine and the Liberation of Kuwait", *Parameters*, Vol. 21, No. 4, Winter 1991–92.

Dugan, M. J., "Air Power: Concentration, Responsibilities and Operational Art", *Military Review*, Vol. 69, No. 7, July 1989.

Echevarria, A. J., "Clausewitz: Toward a Theory of Applied Strategy", *Defense Analysis*, Vol. 11, No. 3, 1995.

Echevarria, A. J., "War, Politics, and RMAs: The Legacy of Clausewitz", *Joint Force Quarterly*, No. 10, Winter 1995–96.

Echevarria, A. J., "Borrowing from the Master: Uses of Clausewitz in German Military Literature before the Great War", *War in History*, Vol. 3, No. 3, July 1996.

Echevarria, A. J., "Interdependent Maneuver for the 21st Century", *Joint Force Quarterly*, No. 23, Autumn/Winter 2000.

Evans, M., "From Kadesh to Kandahar – Military Theory and the Future of War", *Naval War College Review*, Vol. 56, No. 3, Summer 2003.

Finlan, A., "Trapped in the Dead Ground: US Counter-insurgency Strategy in Iraq", *Small Wars and Insurgencies*, Vol. 16, No. 1, March 2005.

Fleming, B., "Can Reading Clausewitz Save Us from Future Mistakes?", *Parameters*, Vol. 34, No. 1, Spring 2004.

Ford, C. A. and Rosenberg, D. A., "The Naval Intelligence Underpinnings of Reagan's Maritime Strategy", *Journal of Strategic Studies*, Vol. 28, No. 2, April 2005.

Freedman, L., "The Third World War?", *Survival*, Vol. 43, No. 4, Winter 2001.

Freudenberg, G. F., "A Conversation with General Clausewitz", *Military Review*, Vol. 57, No. 10, October 1977.

Fritz, N. H., "Clausewitz and US Nuclear Weapons Policy", *Air University Review*, Vol. 34, No. 1, November–December 1982.

Fulton, J. S., "The Debate About Low-Intensity Conflict", *Military Review*, Vol. 66, No. 2, February 1986.

Galloway, A., "FM 100–5: Who Influenced Whom?", *Military Review*, Vol. 66, No. 3, March 1986.

Garrett, A. R., "Information Superiority and the Future of Mission Orders", *Military Review*, Vol. 79, No. 6, November–December 1999.

Geibel, A., "Operation Anaconda, Shah-i-Kot Valley, Afghanistan, 2–10 March 2002", *Military Review*, Vol. 82, No. 3, May–June 2002.

Gibbs, N. H., "Clausewitz on the Moral Forces in War", *Naval War College Review*, Vol. 27, No. 4, January–February 1975.

Goldman, E. O., "The US Military in Uncertain Times: Organisations, Ambiguity and Strategic Alignments", *Journal of Strategic Studies*, Vol. 20, No. 2, June 1997.

Gray, C. S., "Nuclear Strategy: The Case for a Theory of Victory", *International Security*, Vol. 4, No. 1, Summer 1979.

Gray, C. S., "Maritime Strategy", US Naval Institute *Proceedings*, Vol. 112, No. 2, February 1986.

Gray, C. S., "Thinking Asymmetrically in Times of Terror", *Parameters*, Vol. 32, No. 1, Spring 2002.

Gray, C. S., "How Has War Changed Since the End of the Cold War?", *Parameters*, Vol. 35, No. 1, Spring 2005.

Gray, C. S. and Payne, K. B., "Victory is Possible", *Foreign Policy*, Vol. 39, No. 1, Summer 1980.

Gray, C. S. and Payne, K. B., "Nuclear Policy and the Defensive Transition", *Foreign Affairs*, Vol. 62, No. 4, Spring 1984.

Hammond, G. T., "Myths of the Air War over Serbia – Some 'Lessons' Not to Learn", *Aerospace Power Journal*, Vol. 14, No. 4, Winter 2000.

Handel, M. I., "Corbett, Clausewitz, and Sun Tzu", *Naval War College Review*, Vol. 53, No. 4, Autumn 2000.

Harned, G. M., "Principles for Modern War from Two Venerated Theorists", *ARMY*, Vol. 36, No. 4, April 1986.

Hashim, A. S., "The World According to Usama bin Laden", *Naval War College Review*, Vol. 54, No. 4, Autumn 2001.

Hayden, T. H., "Counterinsurgency in Iraq Started with Fallujah", *Marine Corps Gazette*, Vol. 89, No. 7, July 2005.

Hendrickson, D. C. and Tucker, R. W., "Revisions in Need of Revising: What Went Wrong in the Iraq War", *Survival*, Vol. 47, No. 2, Summer 2005.

Herrera, G. L., "Inventing the Railroad and Rifle Revolution: Information, Military Innovation and the Rise of Germany", *Journal of Strategic Studies*, Vol. 27, No. 2, June 2004.

Herrly, P. E., "The Plight of Joint Doctrine after Kosovo", *Joint Force Quarterly*, No. 19, Summer 1999.

Herwig, H. H., "The Prussian Model and Military Planning Today", *Joint Force Quarterly*, No. 18, Spring 1998.

Hodge, C. C., "Woodrow Wilson in Our Time: NATO's Goals in Kosovo", *Parameters*, Vol. 31, No. 1, Spring 2001.

Hoffmann, F. G., "Small Wars Revisited: The United States and Nontraditional Wars", *Journal of Strategic Studies*, Vol. 28, No. 6, December 2005.

Holder, L. D. and Wass de Czege, H., "The New FM 100–5", *Military Review*, Vol. 62, No. 7, July 1982.

Hooker, jun., R. D., "Beyond *Vom Kriege*: The Character and Conduct of War", *Parameters*, Vol. 35, No. 2, Summer 2005.

Horowitz, M. and Rosen, S., "Evolution or Revolution?", *Journal of Strategic Studies*, Vol. 28, No. 3, June 2005.

Howard, M., "The Forgotten Dimensions of Strategy", *Foreign Affairs*, Vol. 57, No. 5, Summer 1979.

Ikenberry, G. J., "American Grand Strategy in the Age of Terror", *Survival*, Vol. 43, No. 4, Winter 2001.

Irani, R. G., "US Strategic Interests in Iran and Saudi Arabia", *Parameters*, Vol. 7, No. 4, December 1977.

Jablonsky, D., "Strategy and the Operational Level of War: Part II", *Parameters*, Vol. 17, No. 2, Summer 1987.

Jablonsky, D., "Strategic Vision and Presidential Authority in the post-Cold War Era", *Parameters*, Vol. 21, No. 4, Winter 1991–92.

Jablonsky, D., "Army Transformation: A Tale of Two Doctrines", *Parameters*, Vol. 31, No. 3, Autumn 2001.

Jensen, O. E., "Information Warfare: Principles of Third-Wave War", *Airpower Journal*, Vol. 8, No. 4, Winter 1994.

Jervis, R., "Reports, Politics, and Intelligence Failures: The Case of Iraq", *Journal of Strategic Studies*, Vol. 29, No. 1, February 2006.

Johnson, J. R., "People's War and Conventional Armies", *Military Review*, Vol. 54, No. 1, January 1974.

Jones, A., "The New FM 100–5: A View from the Ivory Tower", *Military Review*, Vol. 58, No. 2, February 1978.

Jones, S. G., "Averting Failure in Afghanistan", *Survival*, Vol. 48, No. 1, Spring 2006.

Junior, D. P. and Duarté, E. E., "The Concept of Logistics Derived from Clausewitz: All That is Required so That the Fighting Force Can be Taken as a Given", *Journal of Strategic Studies*, Vol. 28, No. 4, August 2005.

Kagan, D., "The End of Wars as the Basis for a Lasting Peace", *Naval War College Review*, Vol. 53, No. 4, Autumn 2000.

Kagan, F., "Army Doctrine and Modern War: Notes Toward a New Edition of FM 100–5", *Parameters*, Vol. 27, No. 1, Spring 1997.

Karsh, E., "Reflections on the 1990–91 Gulf Conflict", *Journal of Strategic Studies*, Vol. 19, No. 3, September 1996.

Keaney, T. A., "Surveying Gulf War Airpower", *Joint Force Quarterly*, No. 2, Autumn 1993.

Kelly, J. D., "War as a Whole: Operational Shock and Operational Art", *Australian Defence Force Journal*, No. 162, September/October 2003.

Kiesling, E. C., "'On War' Without the Fog", *Military Review*, Vol. 81, No. 5, September–October 2001.

Kindsvatter, P. S., "VII Corps in the Gulf War: Deployment and Preparation for Desert Storm", *Military Review*, Vol. 72, No. 1, January 1992.

Kindsvatter, P. S., "VII Corps in the Gulf War: Ground Offensive", *Military Review*, Vol. 72, No. 2, February 1992.

King, J. E., "On Clausewitz: Master Theorist of War", *Naval War College Review*, Vol. 30, No. 2, Fall 1977.

Kinross, S., "Clausewitz and Low Intensity Conflict", *Journal of Strategic Studies*, Vol. 27, No. 1, March 2004.

Kiszely, J., "The British Army and Approaches to Warfare since 1945", *Journal of Strategic Studies*, Vol. 19, No. 4, December 1996.

Klinger, J., "The Social Science of Carl von Clausewitz", *Parameters*, Vol. 36, No. 1, Spring 2006.

Kober, A., "Low-intensity Conflicts: Why the Gap Between Theory and Practice?", *Defense and Security Analysis*, Vol. 18, No. 1, 2002.

Kosnik, M. E., "The Military Response to Terrorism", *Naval War College Review*, Vol. 53, No. 2, Spring 2000.

Krepinevich, A. F., "Cavalry to Computer: The Pattern of Military Revolutions", *The National Interest*, Fall 1994.

Kuzin, V. and Chernyavskii, S., "Russian Reactions to Reagan's 'Maritime Strategy'", *Journal of Strategic Studies*, Vol. 28, No. 2, April 2005.

Laird, M. R., "Iraq: Learning the Lessons of Vietnam", *Foreign Affairs*, Vol. 84, No. 6, November–December 2005.

Layne, C., "Kant or Cant: The Myth of the Democratic Peace", *International Security*, Vol. 19, No. 2, Fall 1994.

Lee, M. J., "Clausewitz on Friction", *Marine Corps Gazette*, Vol. 83, No. 2, February 1999.

Lepper, S. J., "On (The Law of) War: What Clausewitz 'Meant' to Say", *Airpower Journal*, Vol. 13, No. 2, Summer 1999.

Lind, W., "Some Doctrinal Questions for the US Army", *Military Review*, Vol. 57, No. 3, March 1977.

Lind, W., "Misconceptions of Maneuver Warfare", *Marine Corps Gazette*, Vol. 72, No. 1, January 1988.

Lind, W., "The Operational Art", *Marine Corps Gazette*, Vol. 72, No. 4, April 1988.

Lind, W., "Fourth-Generation Warfare's First Blow: A Quick Look", *Marine Corps Gazette*, Vol. 85, No. 11, November 2001.

Lind, W., "4th Generation Warfare and the Dangers of Being the Only Superpower: A Warning from Clausewitz", *CounterPunch*, 8 March 2003.

Lind, W., "Understanding Fourth Generation Warfare", *Military Review*, Vol. 84, No. 5, September–October 2004.

Lind, W., Holder, L. D. and Swain, R. M., "A Dialogue on the Evolution of Doctrine", *Military Review*, Vol. 69, No. 11, November 1989.

Lind, W., Nightengale, K. M., Schmitt, J., Sutton, J. W. and Wilson, G. I., "The Changing Face of War: Into the Fourth Generation", *Military Review*, Vol. 69, No. 10, October 1989.

Linn, B. M., "*The American Way of War* Revisited", *Journal of Military History*, Vol. 66, No. 2, April 2002.

Lloyd, J. J., "Our 'Warfighting' Philosophy", *Marine Corps Gazette*, Vol. 73, No. 11, November 1989.

Lock-Pullan, R., "How to Rethink War: Conceptual Innovation and AirLand Battle Doctrine", *Journal of Strategic Studies*, Vol. 28, No. 4, August 2005.

Lossow, W. von, "Mission Type Orders versus Order Type Tactics", *Military Review*, Vol. 57, No. 6, June 1977.

Lonsdale, D. J., "Information Power: Strategy, Geopolitics, and the Fifth Dimension", *Journal of Strategic Studies*, Vol. 22, Nos. 2–3, June–September 1999.

Luttwak, E. N., "The American Style in Warfare and the Military Balance", *Survival*, Vol. 21, No. 2, March–April 1979.

Luttwak, E. N., "The Operational Level of War", *International Security*, Vol. 5, No. 3, Winter 1980–81.

Luttwak, E. N., "Notes on Low-Intensity Warfare", *Parameters*, Vol. 13, No. 4, December 1983.

Luttwak, E. N., "Just Cause – A Military Score Sheet", *Parameters*, Vol. 20, No. 1, March 1990.

Lynn, J. A., "War of Annihilation, War of Attrition, and War of Legitimacy: A Neo-Clausewitzian Approach to Twentieth-Century Conflicts", *Marine Corps Gazette*, Vol. 80, No. 10, October 1996.

McFetridge, C. D., "Foreign Policy and Military Strategy: The Civil–Military Equation", *Military Review*, Vol. 66, No. 4, April 1986.

McKenzie, K. F., "An Ecstasy of Fumbling: Doctrine and Innovation", *Joint Force Quarterly*, No. 10, Winter 1995–96.

Mann, E., "One Target, One Bomb: Is the Principle of Mass Dead?", *Military Review*, Vol. 73, No. 9, September 1993.

Matthews, L. J., "On Clausewitz", *ARMY*, Vol. 38, No. 2, February 1988.

Matthews, L. J., "The Uniformed Intellectual and his Place in American Arms", *ARMY*, Vol. 52, No. 8, August 2002.

Menning, B. W., "Operational Art's Origins", *Military Review*, Vol. 77, No. 5, September–October 1997.

Metz, S., "AirLand Battle and Counterinsurgency", *Military Review*, Vol. 70, No. 1, January 1990.

Metz, S., "US Strategy and the Changing LIC Threat", *Military Review*, Vol. 71, No. 6, June 1991.

Metz, S., "A Wake for Clausewitz: Toward a Philosophy of 21st Century Warfare", *Parameters*, Vol. 24, No. 4, Winter 1994–95.

Metz, S. and Millen, R., "Intervention, Stabilization, and Transformation Operations: The Role of Landpower in the New Strategic Environment", *Parameters*, Vol. 35, No. 1, Spring 2005.

Montano, J. J. and Long, D. H., "Clausewitz's Advice to the New US President", *Parameters*, Vol. 18, No. 4, December 1988.

Moore, S., "Blitzkrieg from the Sea: Maneuver Warfare and Amphibious Operations", *Naval War College Review*, Vol. 36, No. 6, November–December 1983.

Morelli, D. R. and Ferguson, M. M., "Low-Intensity Conflict: An Operational Perspective", *Military Review*, Vol. 64, No. 11, November 1984.

Morris, M. F., "Al Qaeda as Insurgency", *Joint Force Quarterly*, No. 39, 2005.

Murray, W., "Thinking about Revolutions in Military Affairs", *Joint Force Quarterly*, No. 16, Summer 1997.

Nathan, J., "The Future of the US Maritime Strategy", *Journal of Strategic Studies*, Vol. 11, No. 4, December 1988.

Nelsen, J. T., "'Aufragstaktik': A Case for Decentralised Battle", *Parameters*, Vol. 17, No. 3, September 1987.

Newman, A., "Arms Control, Proliferation and Terrorism: The Bush Administration's

Post-September 11 Security Strategy", *Journal of Strategic Studies*, Vol. 27, No. 1, March 2004.

Otis, G., "The AirLand Battle" (letter for distribution), *Military Review*, Vol. 62, No. 5, May 1982.

Otis, J. F., "Clausewitz: On Weinberger", *Marine Corps Gazette*, Vol. 72, No. 2, February 1988.

Owens, W. A., "The American Revolution in Military Affairs", *Joint Force Quarterly*, No. 10, Winter 1995–96.

Paschall, R., "Low-Intensity Conflict Doctrine: Who Needs It?", *Parameters*, Vol. 15, No. 3, Autumn 1985.

Pendall, D. W., "Effects-Based Operations and the Exercise of National Power", *Military Review*, Vol. 84, No. 1, January–February 2004.

Peters, R., "In Praise of Attrition", *Parameters*, Vol. 34, No. 2, Summer 2004.

Pickett, W., "Eisenhower as a Student of Clausewitz", *Military Review*, Vol. 65, No. 7, July 1985.

Powell, C., "US Forces: Challenges Ahead", *Foreign Affairs*, Vol. 72, No. 5, Winter 1992–93.

Record, J., "Vietnam in Retrospect: Could We Have Won?", *Parameters*, Vol. 26, No. 4, Winter 1996–97.

Record, J., "Weinberger–Powell Doctrine Doesn't Cut It", US Naval Institute *Proceedings*, Vol. 126/10/1, No. 172, October 2000.

Record, J., "Operation Allied Force: Yet Another Wake-Up Call for the Army?", *Parameters*, Vol. 29, No. 4, Winter 1999–2000.

Record, J., "The Bush Doctrine and War with Iraq", *Parameters*, Vol. 33, No. 1, Spring 2003.

Reese, T. R., "Precision Firepower: 'Smart' Bombs, 'Dumb' Strategy", *Military Review*, Vol. 83, No. 4, July–August 2003.

Rice, C., "Promoting the National Interest", *Foreign Affairs*, Vol. 79, No. 1, January–February 2000.

Richardson, W. R., "FM 100–5: The AirLand Battle in 1986", *Military Review*, Vol. 66, No. 3, March 1986.

Richelson, J., "PD-59, NSDD13 and the Reagan Strategic Modernisation Programme", *Journal of Strategic Studies*, Vol. 6, No. 2, June 1983.

Robbins, J. S., "Contemporary Operational-Level War Fighting", *Naval War College Review*, Vol. 59, No. 2, Spring 2006.

Roberts, A., "The 'War on Terror' in Historical Perspective", *Survival*, Vol. 47, No. 2, Summer 2005.

Robeson, E. J., "Critique of 'FMFM 1, Warfighting'", *Marine Corps Gazette*, Vol. 73, No. 11, November 1989.

Rodgers, J. B., "Synchronizing the AirLand Battle", *Military Review*, Vol. 66, No. 4, April 1986.

Rogers, B. W., "Follow-On Forces Attack: Myths and Realities", *NATO Review*, December 1984.

Rosello, V. M., "Clausewitz's Contempt for Intelligence", *Parameters*, Vol. 21, No. 1, Spring 1991.

Rosinski, H., "Scharnhorst to Schlieffen: The Rise and Decline of German Military Thought", *Naval War College Review*, Vol. 29, No. 1, Summer 1976.

Sarkesian, S. C., "Low-Intensity Conflict: Concepts, Principles, and Policy Guidelines", *Air University Review*, Vol. 36, No. 2, January–February 1985.

Scales, jun., R. H., "Adaptive Enemies: Achieving Victory by Avoiding Defeat", *Joint Force Quarterly*, Autumn–Winter 1999–2000.

Scales, jun., R. H., "Urban Warfare: A Soldier's View", *Military Review*, Vol. 85, No. 1, January–February 2005.

Schmitt, J. F., "The Great FMFM 1 Debate: Is There Anything New Here?", *Marine Corps Gazette*, Vol. 73, No. 11, November 1989.

Schmitt, J. F., "Out of Sync with Maneuver Warfare", *Marine Corps Gazette*, Vol. 78, No. 8, August 1994.

Schneider, J. J., "Theoretical Implications of Operational Art", *Military Review*, Vol. 70, No. 9, September 1990.

Schneider, J. J., "Black Lights – Chaos, Complexity, and the Promise of Information Warfare", *Joint Force Quarterly*, No. 15, Spring 1997.

Schneider, J. J. and Izzo, L. L., "Clausewitz's Elusive Center of Gravity", *Parameters*, Vol. 17, No. 3, September 1987.

Shepherd, J. E., "'On War': Is Clausewitz Still Relevant?", *Parameters*, Vol. 20, No. 3, September 1990.

Shultz, R. H., "The Great Divide – Strategy and Covert Action in Vietnam", *Joint Force Quarterly*, No. 23, Autumn/Winter 1999–2000.

Silva, J. L., "'Aufragstaktik': Its Origin and Development", *Infantry*, Vol. 79, No. 5, September–October 1989.

Sloan, S., "US Strategy for LIC: An Enduring Legacy or Passing Fad?", *Military Review*, Vol. 70, No. 1, January 1990.

Smith, G. W., "Clausewitz in the 1970s: RX for Dilemma", *Military Review*, Vol. 52, No. 7, July 1972.

Smith, J. B., "Some Thoughts on Clausewitz and Airplanes", *Air University Review*, Vol. 37, No. 3, March–April 1986.

Smith, M. L. R., "Guerrillas in the Mist: Reassessing Strategy and Low Intensity Warfare", *Review of International Studies*, 1, 2003.

Sobchak, F., "Clausewitz: 'On Afghanistan'", *Military Review*, Vol. 85, No. 4, July–August 2005.

Sorley, L., "Courage and Blood: South Vietnam's Repulse of the 1972 Easter Invasion", *Parameters*, Vol. 29, No. 2, Summer 1999.

Spiller, R. J., "In the Shadow of the Dragon: Doctrine and the US Army after Vietnam", *RUSI Journal*, Vol. 142, No. 6, December 1997.

Starry, D. A., "Extending the Battlefield", *Military Review*, Vol. 61, No. 3, March 1981.

Starry, D. A., "A Perspective on American Military Thought", *Military Review*, Vol. 69, No. 7, July 1989.

Staudenmaier, W. O., "Vietnam, Mao, and Clausewitz", *Parameters*, Vol. 7, No. 1, Spring 1977.

Steele, W. M., "The Army Launches an Attack-Focused Doctrine for the Joint Fight", *ARMY*, Vol. 51, No. 8, August 2001.

Stone, J., "Politics, Technology and the Revolution in Military Affairs", *Journal of Strategic Studies*, Vol. 27, No. 3, September 2004.

Strachan, H., "The Lost Meaning of Strategy", *Survival*, Vol. 47, No. 3, Autumn 2005.

Strange, J. L. and Iron, R., "Center of Gravity – What Clausewitz Really Meant", *Joint Force Quarterly*, No. 35, 2004.

Strickland, A. T., "MCDP 1, Warfighting Revisited", *Marine Corps Gazette*, Vol. 89, No. 7, July 2005.

Sullivan, G. R., "A Vision for the Future", *Military Review*, Vol. 75, No. 4, May–June 1995.

Summers, H. G., "Delta Force – America's Counterterrorist Unit and the Mission to Rescue the Hostages in Iran", *Military Review*, Vol. 63, No. 11, November 1983.

Swain, R. M., "Clausewitz for the 20th Century: The Interpretation of Raymond Aron", *Military Review*, Vol. 66, No. 4, April 1986.

Swain, R. M., "Removing Square Pegs from Round Holes. Low-Intensity Conflict in Army Doctrine", *Military Review*, Vol. 67, No. 12, December 1987.

Swain, R. M., "'The Hedgehog and the Fox': Jomini, Clausewitz, and History", *Naval War College Review*, Autumn 1990.

Swain, R. M., Review of H. S. Summers, *On Strategy II*, *Military Review*, Vol. 72, No. 6, June 1992.

Thomas, T. L., "Kosovo and the Current Myth of Information Superiority", *Parameters*, Vol. 30, No. 1, Spring 2000.

Tilford, jun., E. H., "Operation Allied Force and the Role of Air Power", *Parameters*, Vol. 29, No. 4, Winter 1999–2000.

Townsend, P. L., "Clausewitz Would Have Wondered at the Way We Fought in Vietnam", *Marine Corps Gazette*, Vol. 62, No. 6, June 1978.

Tsybulskiy, I. V., "Carl von Clausewitz and the Present", *Voennaya Mysl (Military Thought)*, No. 8, August 1991.

Turner, S., "Convocation Address", *Naval War College Review*, Vol. 51, No. 1, Winter 1997–98.

Turner, S. and Thibault, G., "Preparing for the Unexpected: The Need for a New Military Strategy", *Foreign Affairs*, Vol. 61, No. 1, Fall 1982.

Twining, D., "Vietnam and the Six Criteria for the Use of Military Force", *Parameters*, Vol. 15, No. 4, Winter 1985.

Vaughn, T. B., "Clausewitz and Contemporary American Professionalism", *Military Review*, Vol. 62, No. 12, December 1982.

Vego, M. N., "Operational Command and Control in the Information Age", *Joint Force Quarterly*, 35, 2004.

Villacres, E. and Bassford, C., "Reclaiming the Clausewitzian Trinity", *Parameters*, Vol. 25, No. 3, Autumn 1995.

Vought, D. B., "Preparing for the Wrong War?", *Military Review*, Vol. 57, No. 5, May 1977.

Vuono, C. E., "Desert Storm and the Future of Conventional Forces", *Foreign Affairs*, Vol. 69, No. 4, Spring 1991.

Waghelstein, J. D., "Post-Vietnam Counterinsurgency Doctrine", *Military Review*, Vol. 65, No. 5, May 1985.

Wallace, J. J. A., "Manoeuvre Theory in Operations Other Than War", *Journal of Strategic Studies*, Vol. 19, No. 4, December 1996.

Wallach, J. L., "Misperceptions of Clausewitz's On War by the German Military", *Journal of Strategic Studies*, Vol. 9, Nos. 2–3, June–September 1986.

Waltz, K. N., "Structural Realism after the Cold War", *International Security*, Vol. 25, No. 1, Summer 2000.

Wass de Czege, H., "Clausewitz: Historical Theories Remain Sound Compass References; The Catch is Staying on Course", *ARMY*, Vol. 38, No. 9, September 1988.

Wass de Czege, H., "How to Change an Army", *Military Review*, Vol. 77, No. 1, January–February 1997.

Watts, B. D., "Friction in the Gulf War", *Naval War College Review*, Vol. 48, No. 4, Autumn 1995.

Weigley, R. F., "Response to Brian McAllister Linn", *Journal of Military History*, Vol. 66, No. 2, April 2002.

Weinberger, C., "US Defense Strategy", *Foreign Affairs*, Vol. 64, No. 4, Spring 1986.

Weller, M., "The United States, Iraq, and the Use of Force in a Bipolar World", *Survival*, Vol. 41, No. 4, Winter 1999–2000.

West, F. J., "The Fall of Fallujah", *Marine Corps Gazette*, Vol. 89, No. 7, July 2005.

Williams, G. K., " 'The Shank of the Drill': Americans and Strategic Aviation in the Great War", *Journal of Strategic Studies*, Vol. 19, No. 3, September 1996.

Yeosock, J. J., "Army Operations in the Gulf Theater", *Military Review*, Vol. 71, No. 9, September 1991.

Internet

Bassford, C., "Clausewitz and His Works", www.clausewitz.com/CWZHOME/CWZSUMM/CWORKHOL.htm.

Bassford, C., "Doctrinal Complexity", www.clausewitz.com/CLWHOME/Complex/DOCTNEW.htm.

CALL 90–4: Low-Intensity Conflict, Center for Army Lessons Learned, Fort Leavenworth, Kansas, 1990, call.army.mil/call/ctc_bull/90–4/90–4note.htm.

Matheny, M. R., "The Roots of Modern American Operational Art", www.carlisle.army.mil/usawc/dmspo/Staff%20Publications/modern_operations.pdf.

Moran, D., "Strategic Theory and the History of War", www.clausewitz.com/CWZHOME/Bibl/Moran-StrategicTheory.pdf.

Sidoti, A. F., "The Relevance of Carl von Clausewitz to Operation Iraqi Freedom", *Air and Space Power Chronicles Online Journal*, 21 January 2004, //nss.csusb.edu/nsspubs/nssstpub04sidoti.htm.

Sumida, J., "On Defense as the Stronger Form of War", ccw.politics.ox.ac.uk/events/archives/tt05_clausewitz_sumida.pdf.

"Statement of Principles", Project for the New American Century, www.newamericancentury.org/Statementofprinciples.htm.

Television

BBC TV, "Hannibal and Desert Storm", *Timewatch*, 10 September 1996.

Unpublished material

Agee, C. A., "Peeling the Onion: The Iraqi Center of Gravity in Desert Storm", School of Advanced Military Studies (SAMS) Monograph, US Army Command and General Staff College (USACGSC), Fort Leavenworth, Kansas, April 1992.

Benjamin, jun., D. J., "Prerequisite for Victory: The Discovery of the Culminating Point", SAMS Monograph, USACGSC, Fort Leavenworth, Kansas, May 1986.

Bentley, L. W., "Clausewitz and German Idealism: The Influence of G. W. F. Hegel on On War", Master of Military Art and Science (MMAS) thesis, USACGSC, Fort Leavenworth, Kansas, June 1988.

Brady, M. T., "The Army and the Strategic Military Legacy of Vietnam", MMAS thesis, Fort Leavenworth, Kansas: USACGSC, 1990.

Brown, A. D., "Defense Campaigns: Are they Still the Stronger Form of War?", SAMS Monograph, USACGSC, Fort Leavenworth, Kansas, May 1993.

Buckley II, J. C., "A Model of Insurgency: Reflections of Clausewitz's 'Paradoxical

Trinity' – Lessons for Operational Planners Considering Conventional Forces in Unconventional Operations", SAMS Monograph, USACGSC, Fort Leavenworth, Kansas, May 1995.

Cranz, D., "Understanding Change: Sigismund von Schlichting and the Operational Level of War", SAMS Monograph, USACGSC, Fort Leavenworth, Kansas, May 1989.

Echevarria, A. J., "Neo-Clausewitzianism: Freytag-Loringhoven and the Militarization of Clausewitz in German Military Literature before the First World War", Ph.D. Dissertation, Princeton University, 1994.

Harrop, D. J., "Clausewitz for Modern Readers: A Revision", Military Studies Programme Paper, US Army War College (USAWC), Carlisle Barracks, Pa.: 1992.

Inman, M. T., "The Tactical Center of Gravity: How Useful is the Concept?", SAMS Monograph, USACGSC, Fort Leavenworth, Kansas, January 1990.

Johnson, D. L., "Center of Gravity: The Source of Operational Ambiguity and Linear Thinking in the Age of Complexity", SAMS Monograph, USACGSC, Fort Leavenworth, Kansas, December 1998.

Karhohs, J. W., "The Economics of War Planning: An Addition to the Clausewitzian Trinity", SAMS Monograph, USACGSC, Fort Leavenworth, Kansas, May 1991.

Keppler, T. J., "The Center of Gravity Concept: A Knowledge Engineering Approach to Improved Understanding and Application", SAMS Monograph, USACGSC, Fort Leavenworth, Kansas, June 1995.

Kriwanek, T. M., "The Operational Center of Gravity", SAMS Monograph, USACGSC, Fort Leavenworth, Kansas, May 1986.

Mock, D. C., "A Look at Deep Operations: The Option of Deep Maneuver", SAMS Monograph, USACGSC, Fort Leavenworth, Kansas, December 1987.

Moss, O. J., "Searching for the Stronger Form of War at the Operational Level in the 20th Century: The Defense or the Offense?", SAMS Monograph, USACGSC, Fort Leavenworth, Kansas, May 1988.

Perry, H. S., "Clausewitz and Torgau", USAWC Monograph, USAWC, Carlisle Barracks, Pa., 1992.

Redlinger, M. J., "Hans Delbrück and Clausewitz's Culminating Points", SAMS Monograph, USACGSC, Fort Leavenworth, Kansas, May 1988.

Rundesheim, F. S., "Quick, Decisive Victory: Defining Maxim or Illusory Concept within Army Doctrine", SAMS Monograph, USACGSC, Fort Leavenworth, Kansas, May 1993.

Saxman, J. B., "The Concept of Centers of Gravity: Does it have Utility in Joint Doctrine and Campaign Planning", SAMS Monograph, USACGSC, Fort Leavenworth, Kansas, May 1992.

Schuster, D. J., "Achieving Victory in Peace Operations: An Application for Clausewitz's Theory on Culmination", SAMS Monograph, USACGSC, Fort Leavenworth, Kansas, December 1994.

Strain, P. M., "The Tactical Center of Gravity: Fact or Fallacy?", SAMS Monograph, USACGSC, Fort Leavenworth, Kansas, December 1992.

Sude, G., "Defense in Clausewitz's On War and in FM 100–5 and Hdv 100–100", MMAS Thesis, USACGSC, Fort Leavenworth, Kansas, 1985.

Tucker, C. A., "False Prophet: The Myth of Maneuver Warfare and the Inadequacies of FMFM 1 Warfighting", SAMS Monograph, USACGSC, Fort Leavenworth, Kansas, AY 1994–95.

Webb, G. S., "The Flashing Sword of Vengeance: The Force-Oriented Counterattack from a Historical Perspective with Implications for the AirLand Battle and Combat Aviation", SAMS Monograph, USACGSC, Fort Leavenworth, Kansas, December 1985.

Index

Lightning Source UK Ltd.
Milton Keynes UK
27 February 2010

150737UK00003B/27/P

9 780415 569637